JACK

The Amityville

FROST

JINHO KO

4

The Amityville

JACK FROST

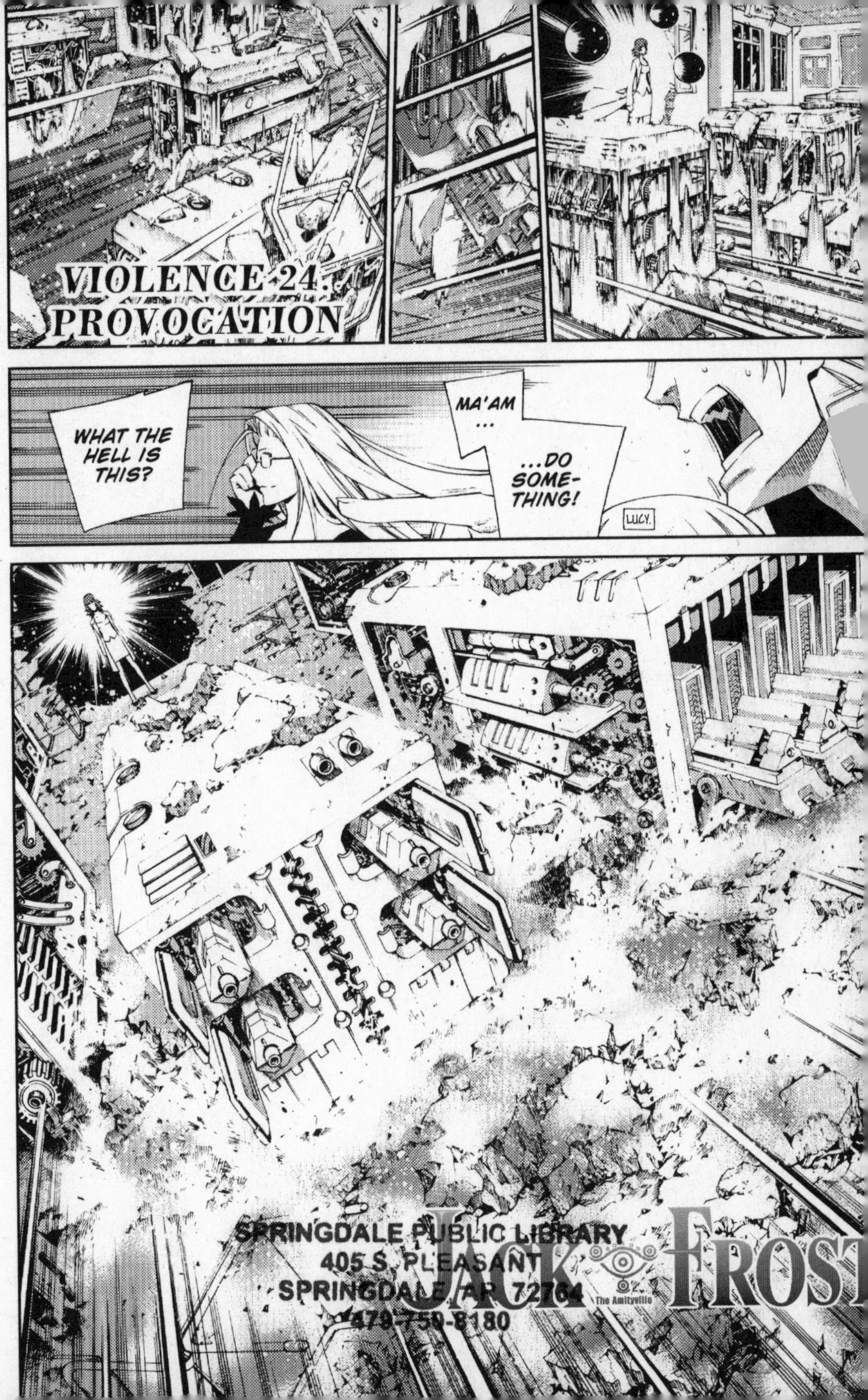
VIOLENCE 24. PROVOCATION
WHAT THE HELL IS THIS?
MA'AM ...
...DO SOME-THING!
LUCY.
JACK FROST
The Amityville

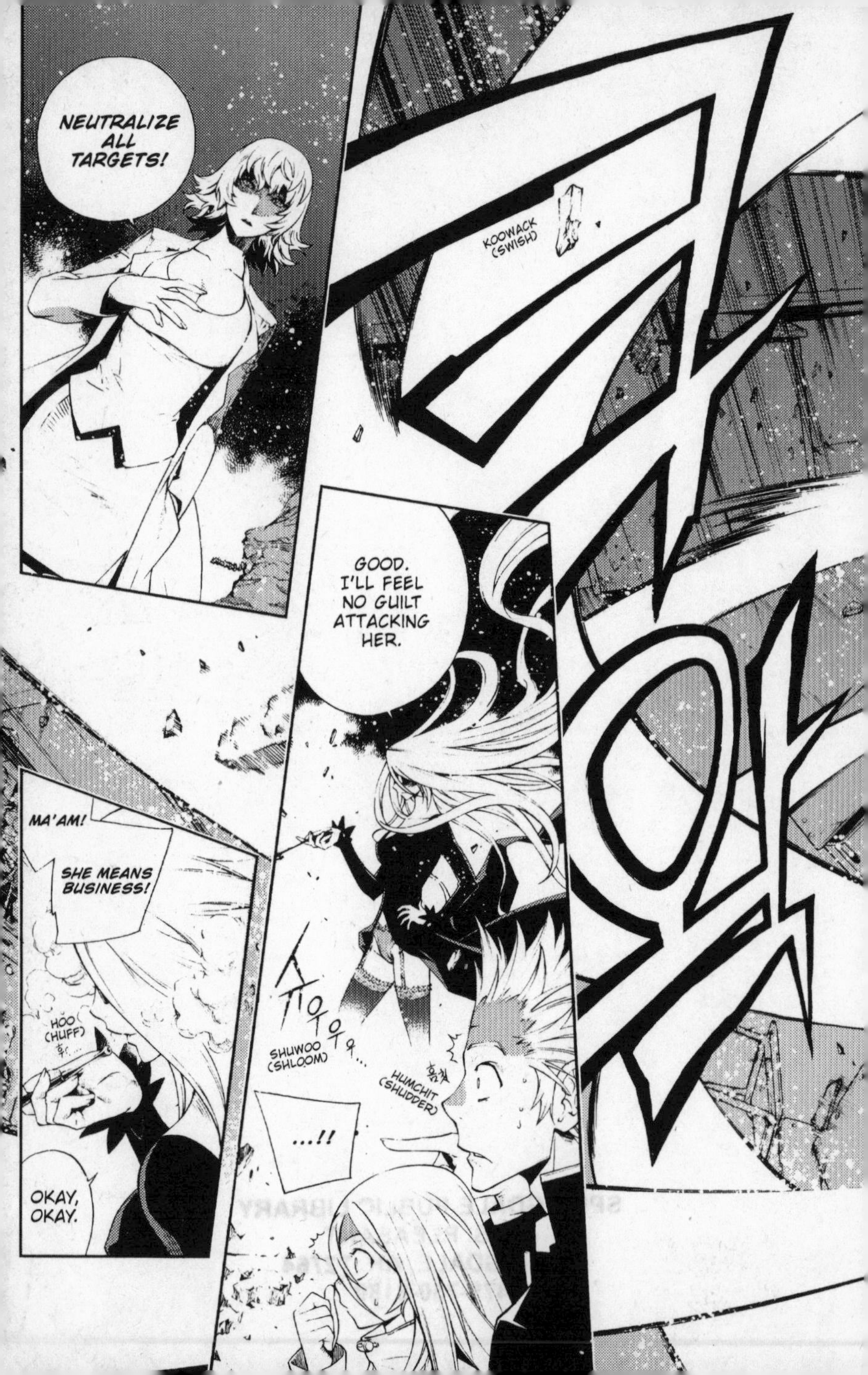
NEUTRALIZE ALL TARGETS!
MA'AM!
SHE MEANS BUSINESS!
HOO (HUFF)
OKAY, OKAY.
GOOD. I'LL FEEL NO GUILT ATTACKING HER.
SHUWOO (SHLOOM)
HUMCHIT (SHUDDER)
...!!
KOOWACK (SWISH)

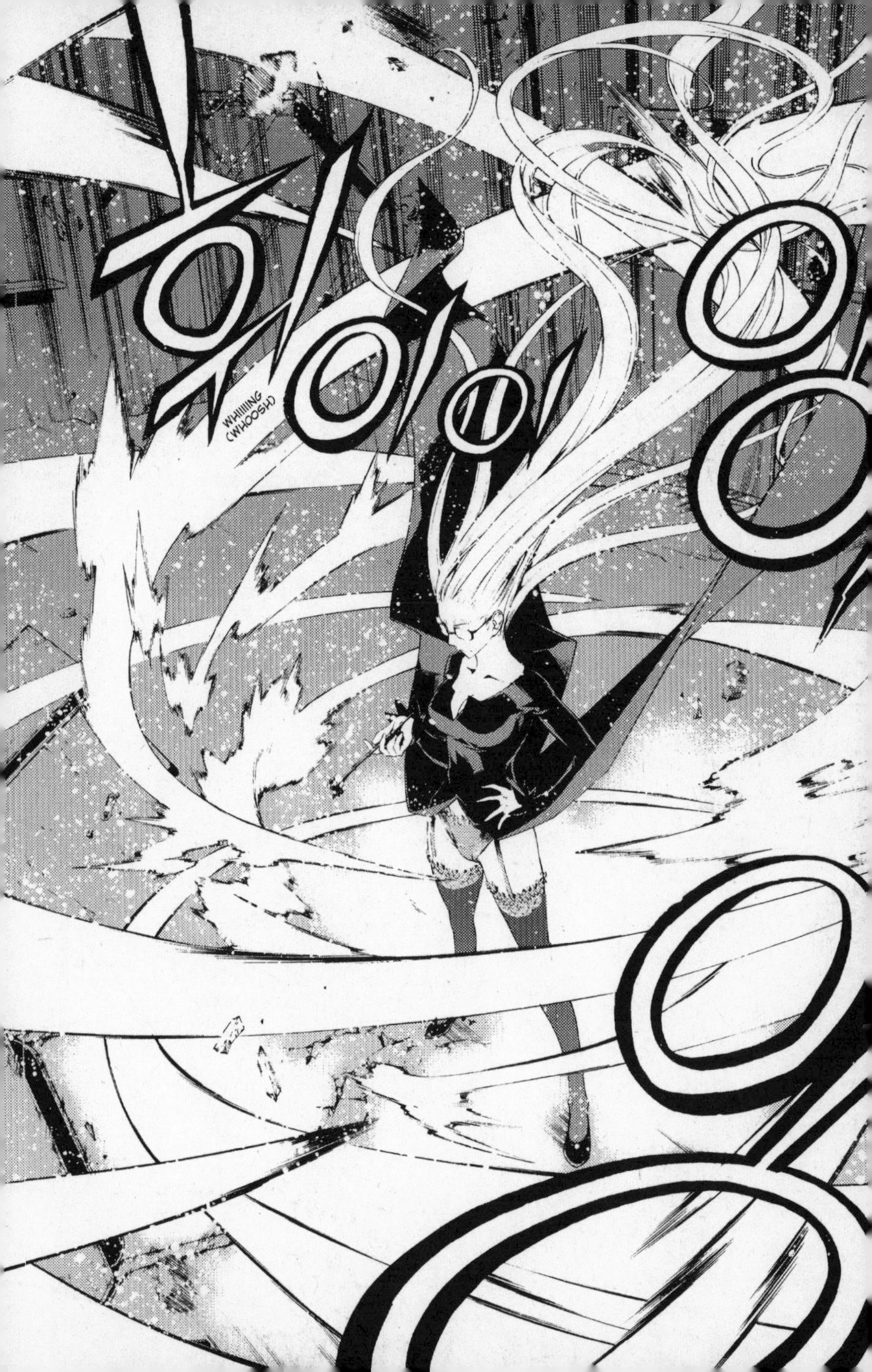
WHIIIIING
(WHOOSH)

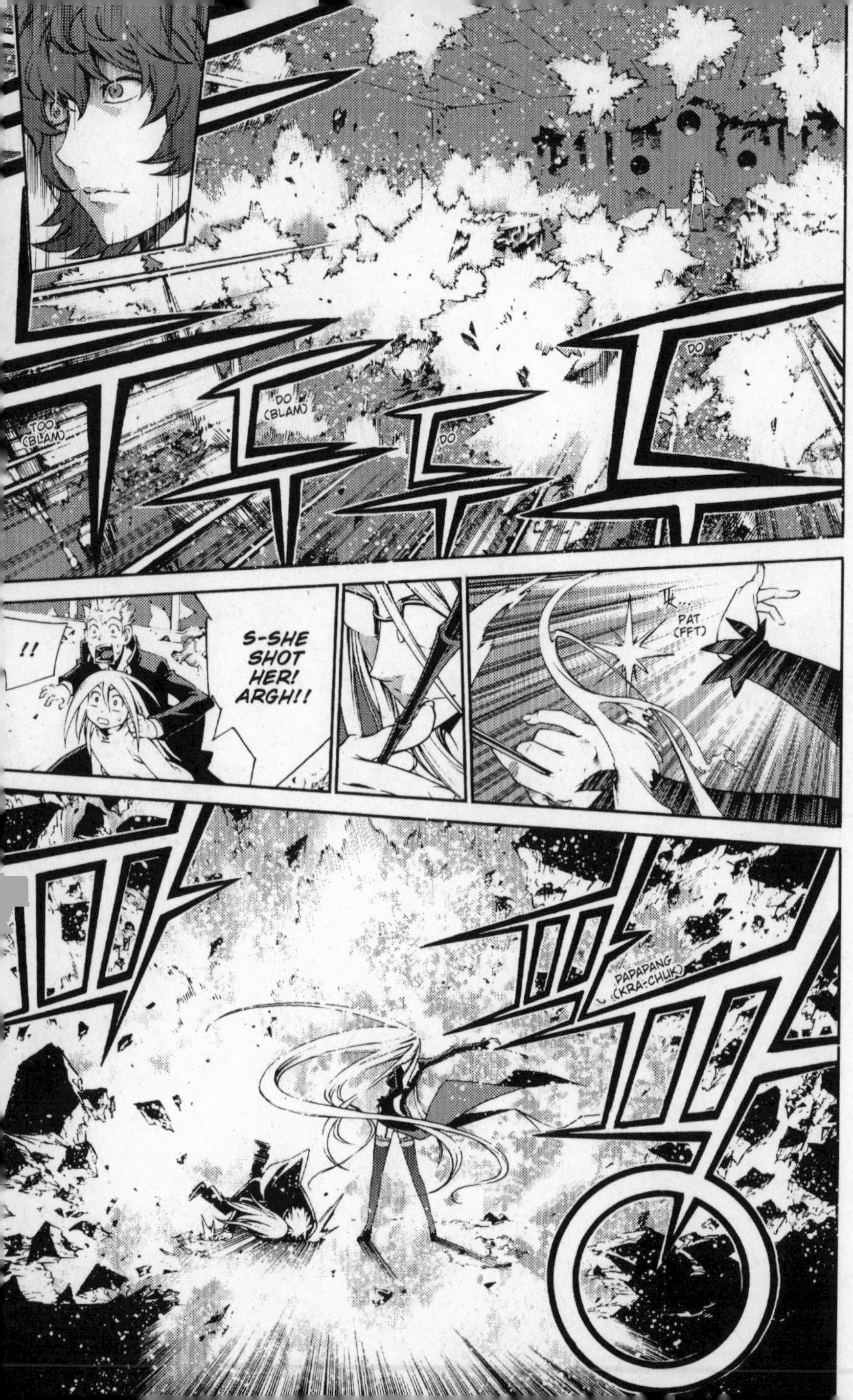
TOO
(BLAM)
DO
(BLAM)
DO
DO
!!
S-SHE SHOT HER! ARGH!!
PAT
(FFT)
PAPAPANG
(KRA-CHUK)

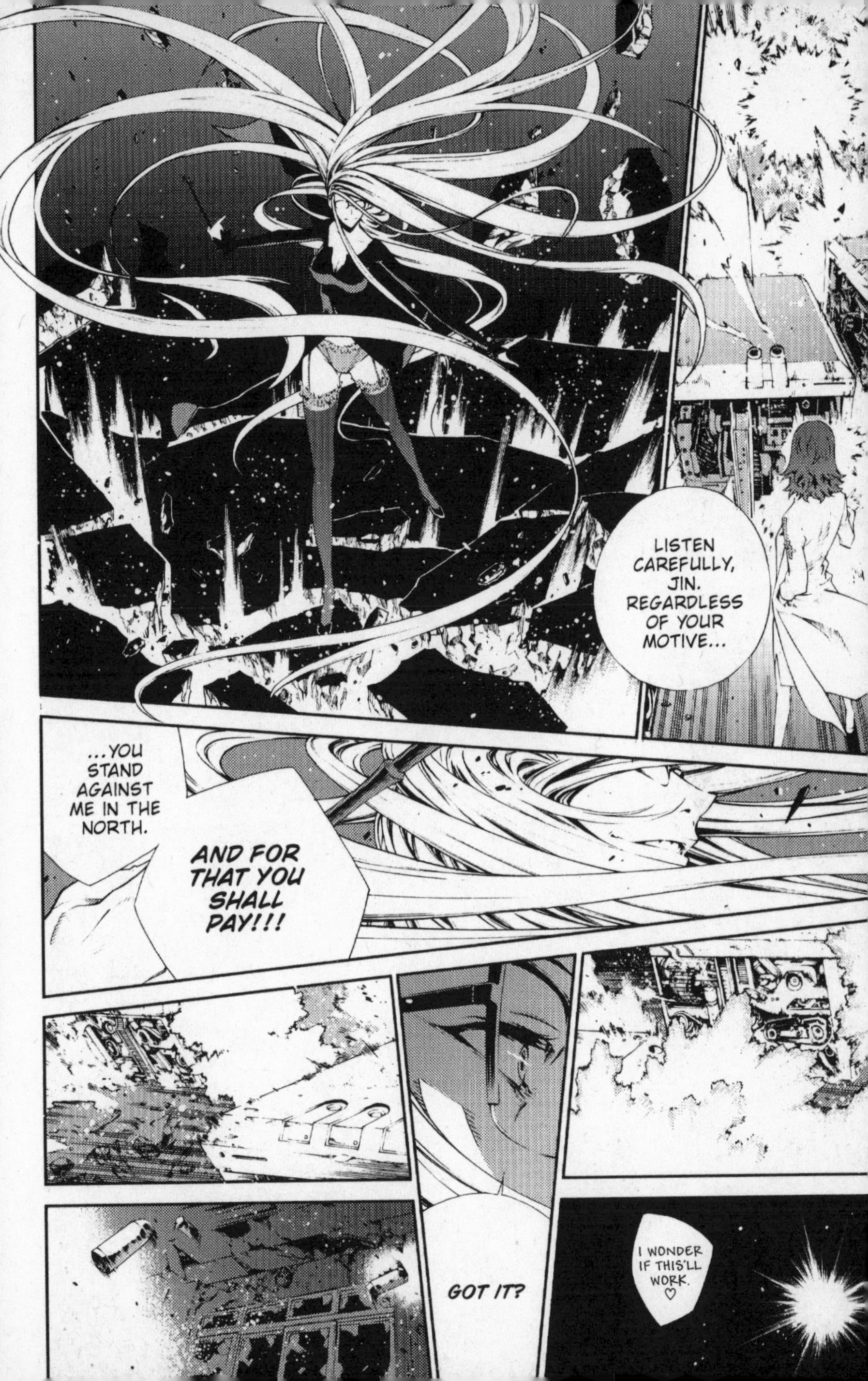
LISTEN CAREFULLY, JIN. REGARDLESS OF YOUR MOTIVE...
...YOU STAND AGAINST ME IN THE NORTH.
AND FOR THAT YOU SHALL PAY!!!
GOT IT?
I WONDER IF THIS'LL WORK. ♡

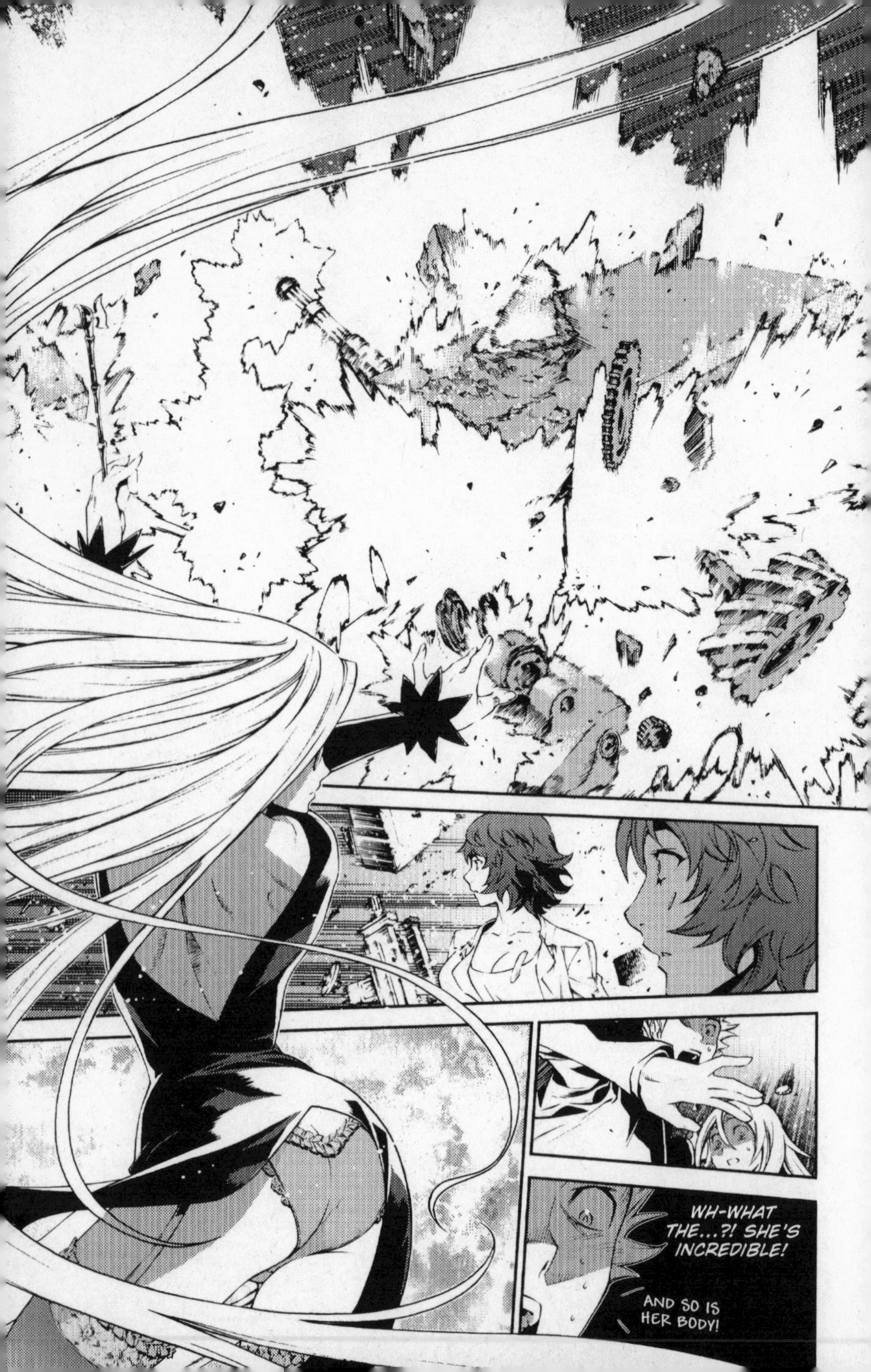
WH-WHAT THE...?! SHE'S INCREDIBLE!
AND SO IS HER BODY!

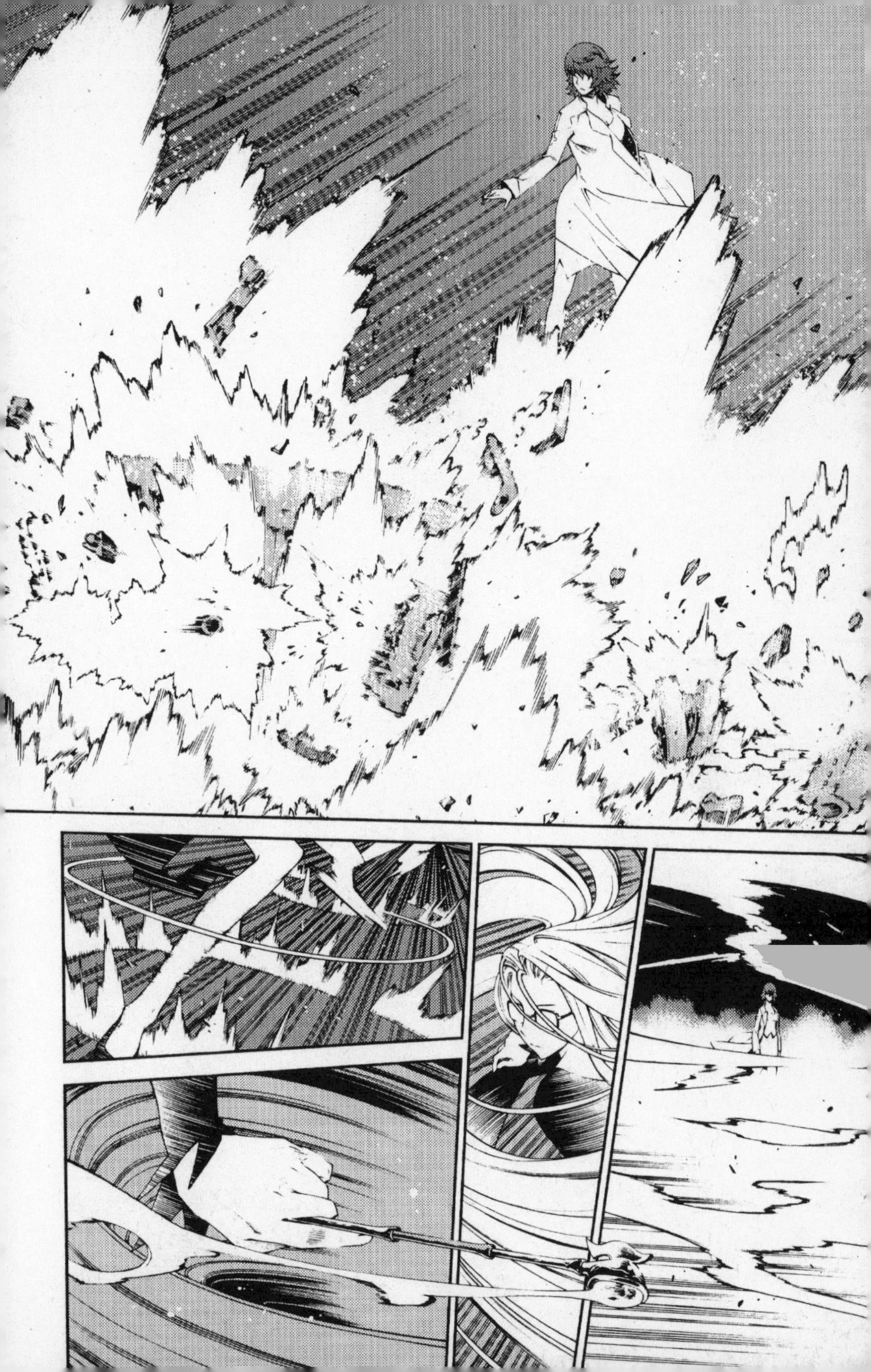

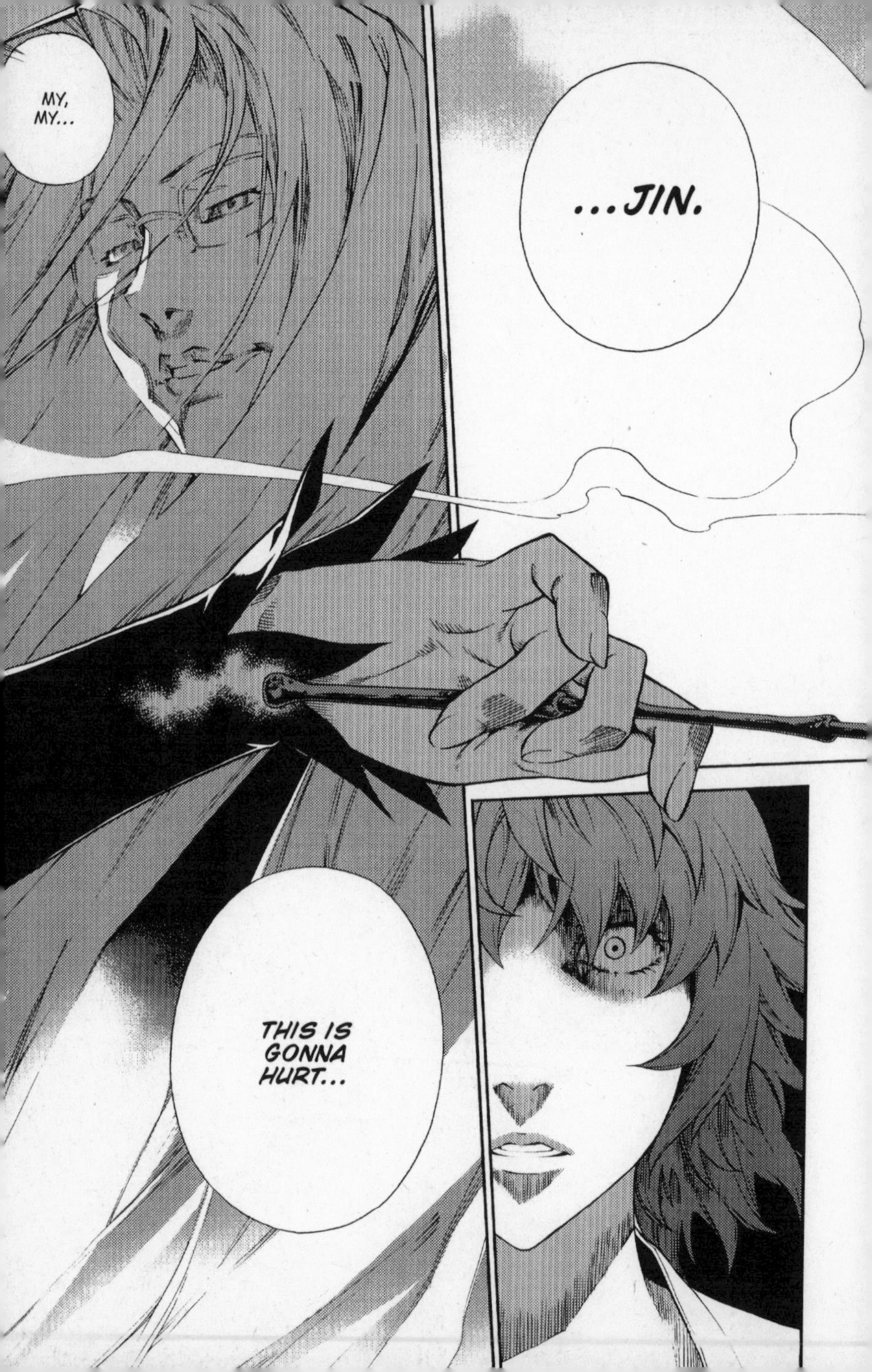
MY, MY...
...JIN.
THIS IS GONNA HURT...

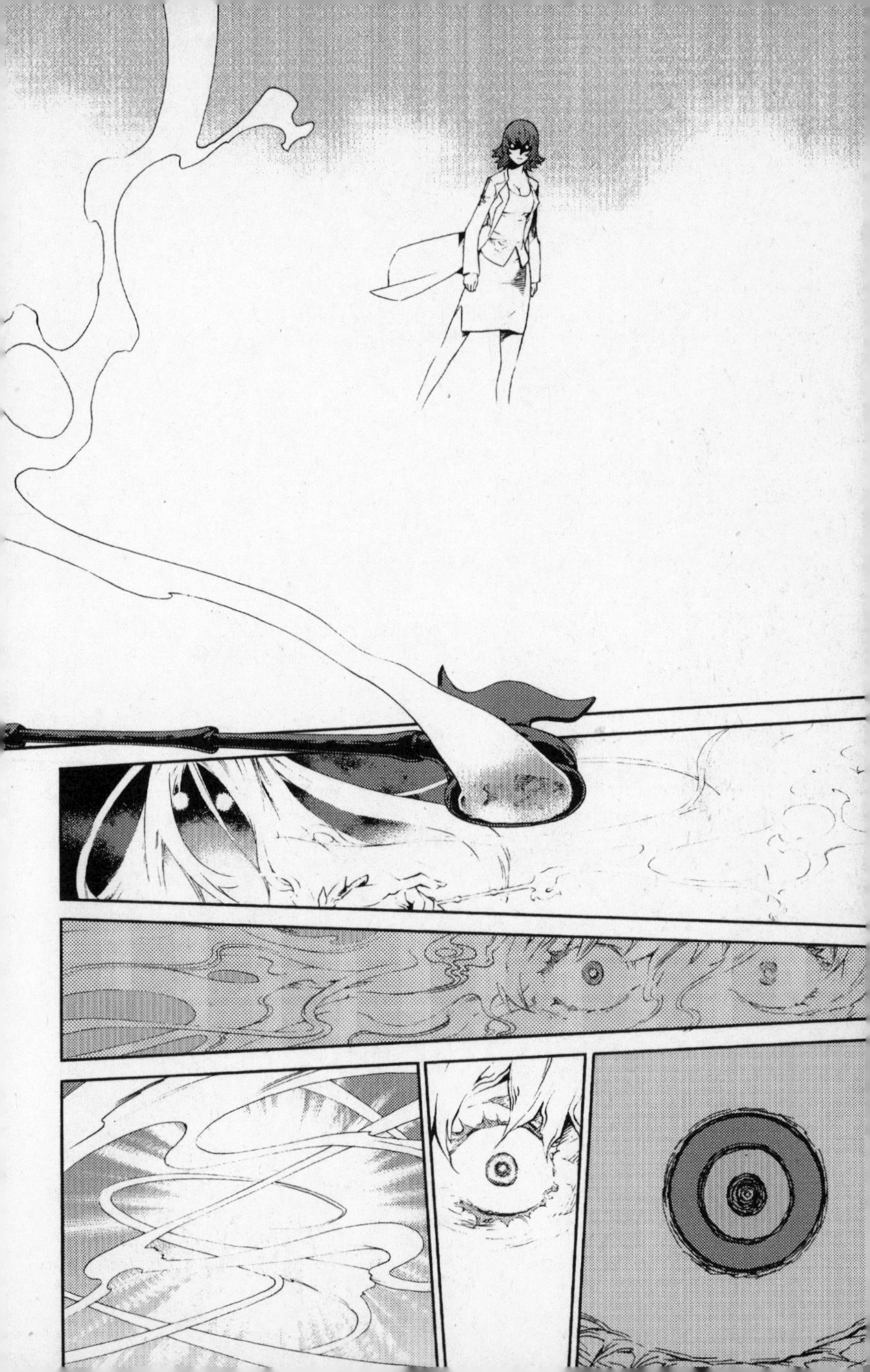

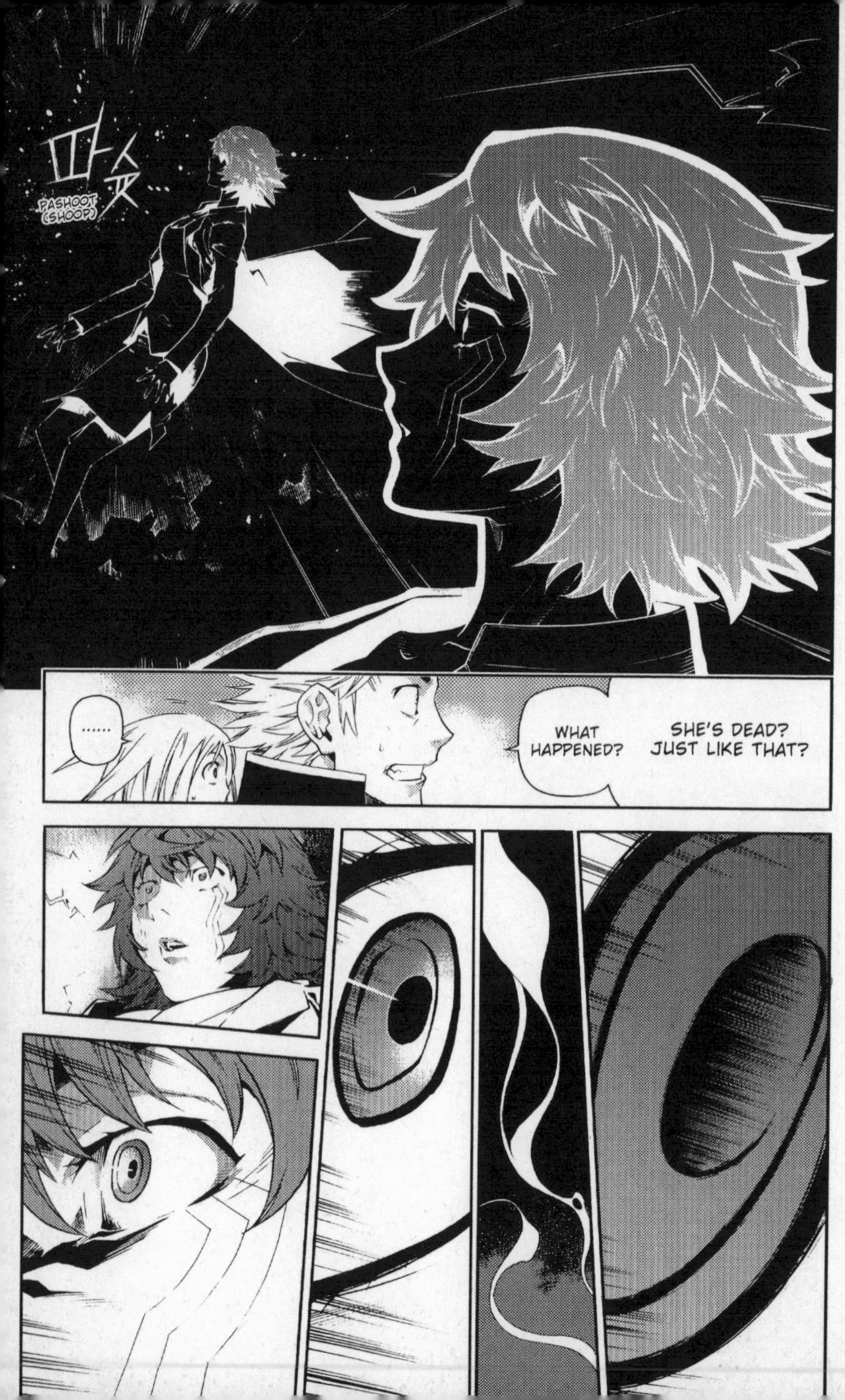
PASHOOT (SHOOP)
......
WHAT HAPPENED?
SHE'S DEAD? JUST LIKE THAT?

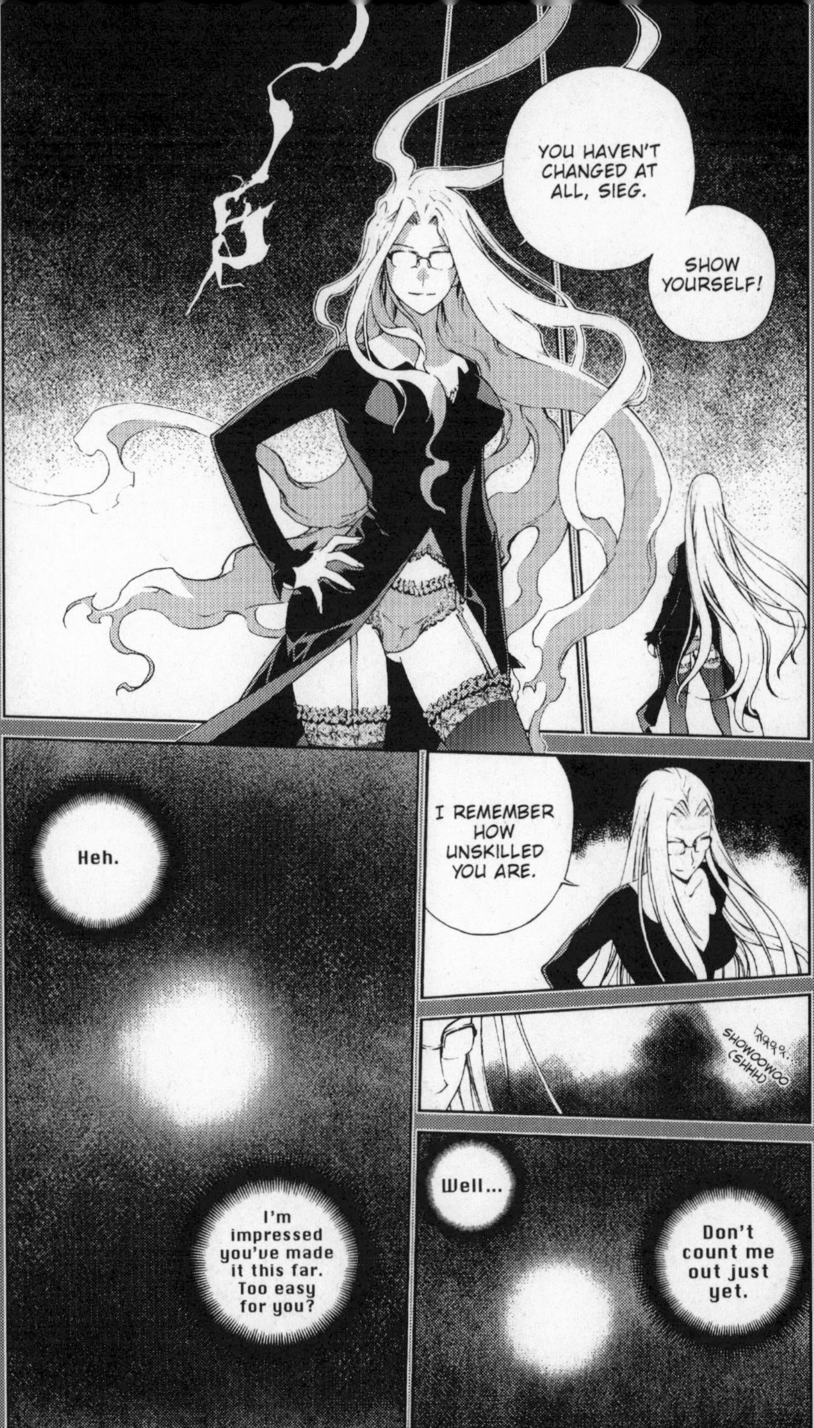
YOU HAVEN'T CHANGED AT ALL, SIEG.
SHOW YOURSELF!
Heh.
I'm impressed you've made it this far. Too easy for you?
I REMEMBER HOW UNSKILLED YOU ARE.
SHOWOOWOO (SHHH)
Well...
Don't count me out just yet.

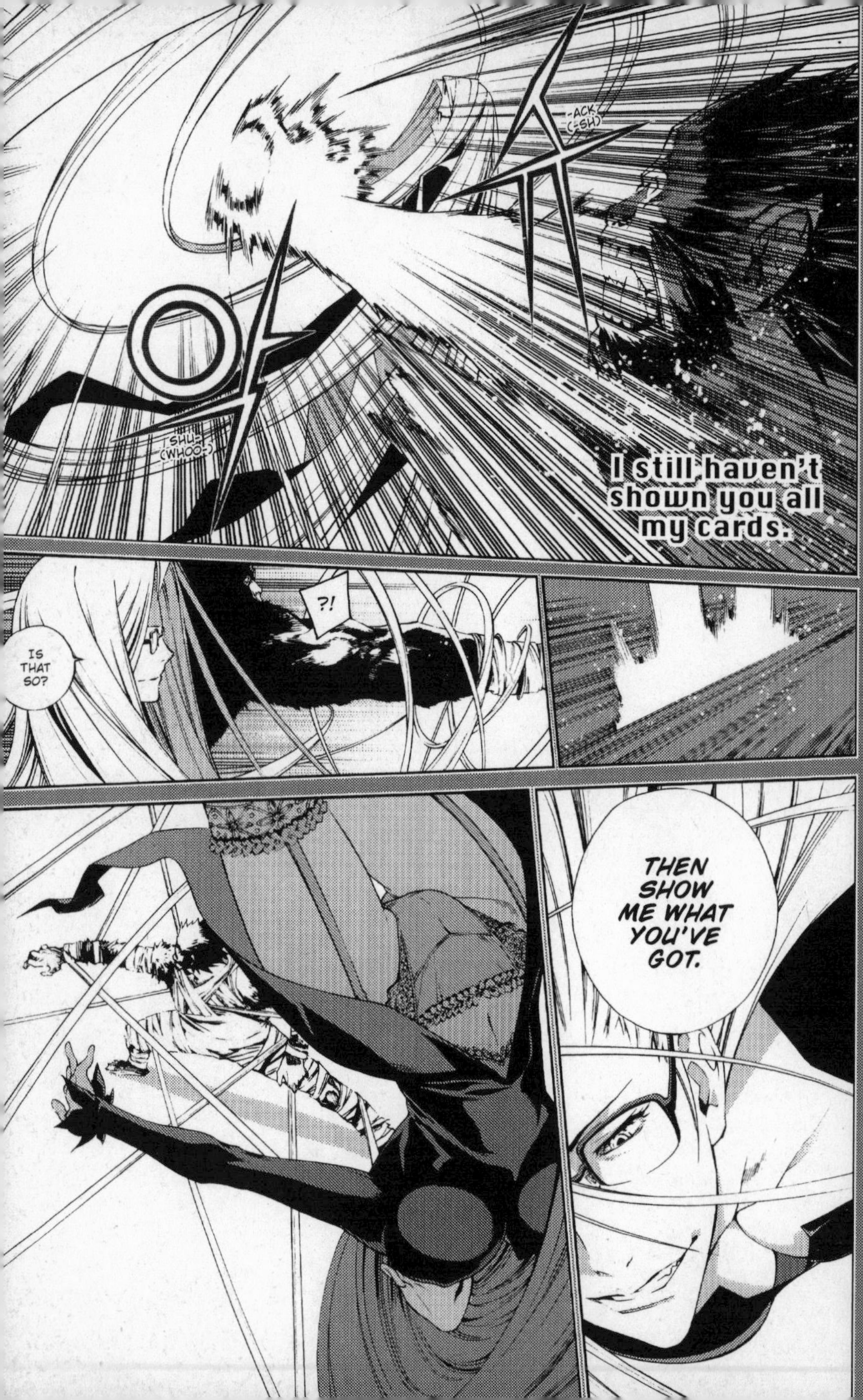
-ACK (-SH)
SHU- (WHOO-)
I still haven't shown you all my cards.
IS THAT SO?
?!
THEN SHOW ME WHAT YOU'VE GOT.

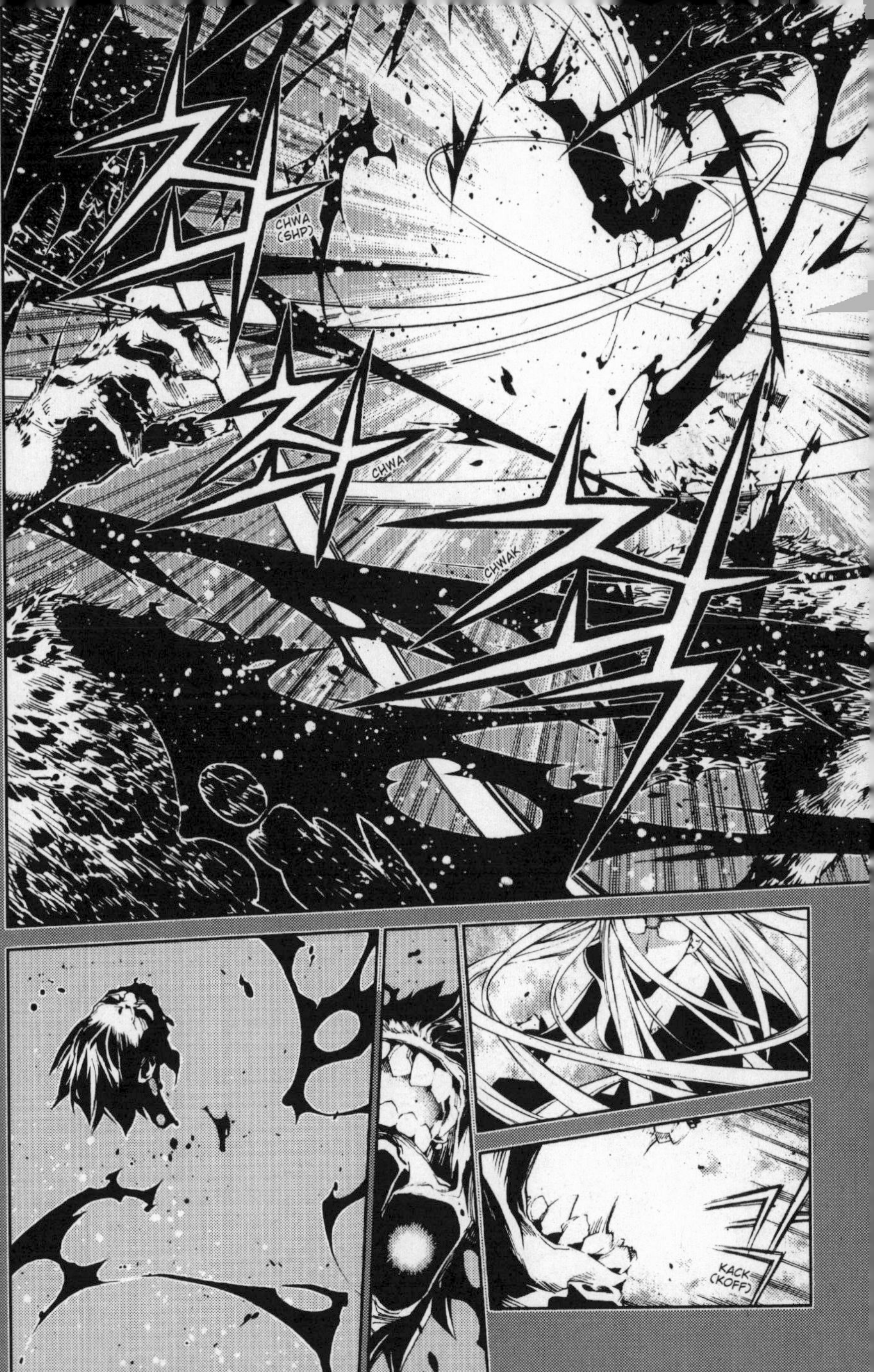
CHWA (SHP)
CHWA
CHWAK
KACK (KOFF)

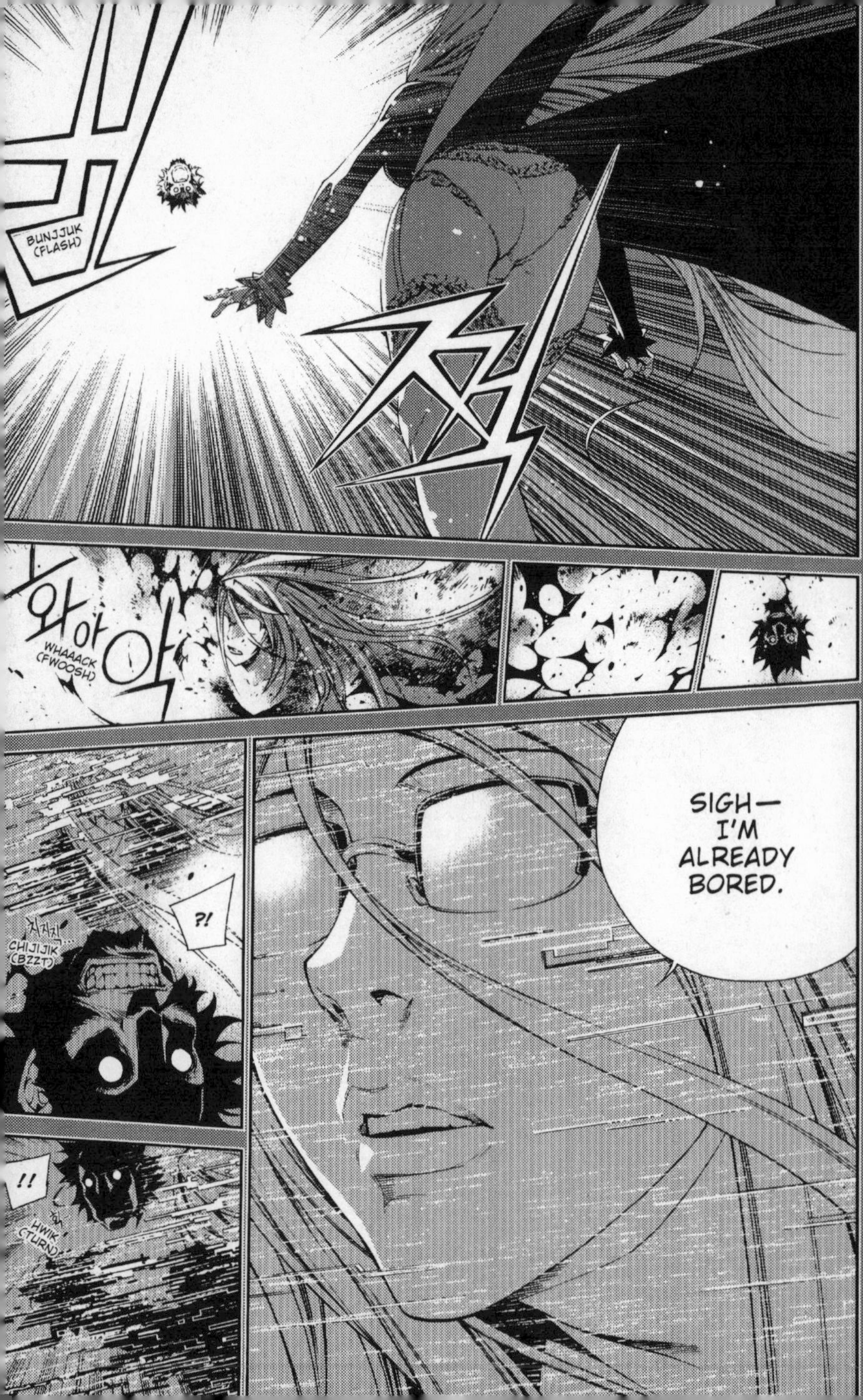
BUNJJUK (FLASH)
WHAAACK (FWOOSH)
?!
CHIJIJIK (BZZT)
!!
HWIK (TURN)
SIGH— I'M ALREADY BORED.

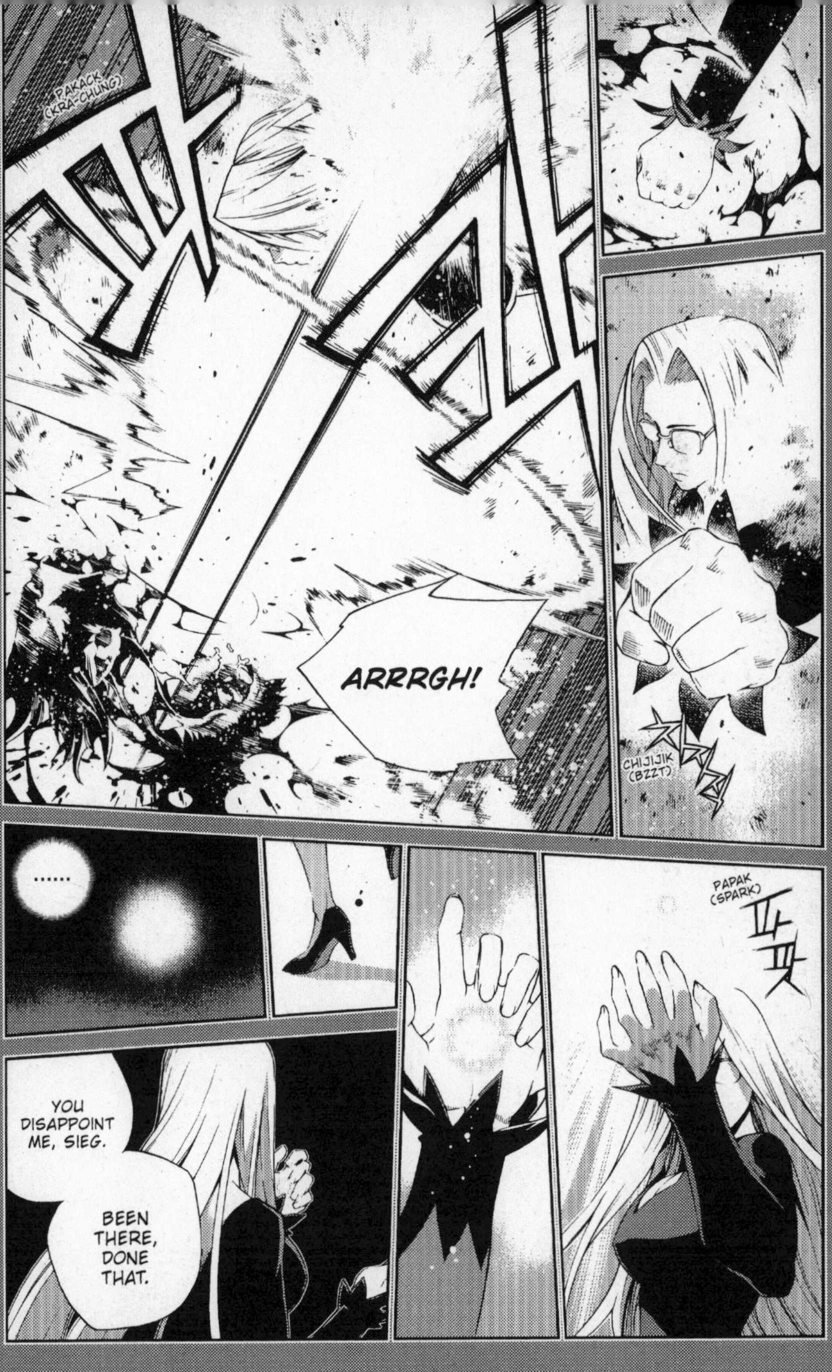
PAKACK (KRA-CHUNG)
ARRRGH!
CHIJIJIK (BZZT)
......
YOU DISAPPOINT ME, SIEG.
BEEN THERE, DONE THAT.
PAPAK (SPARK)

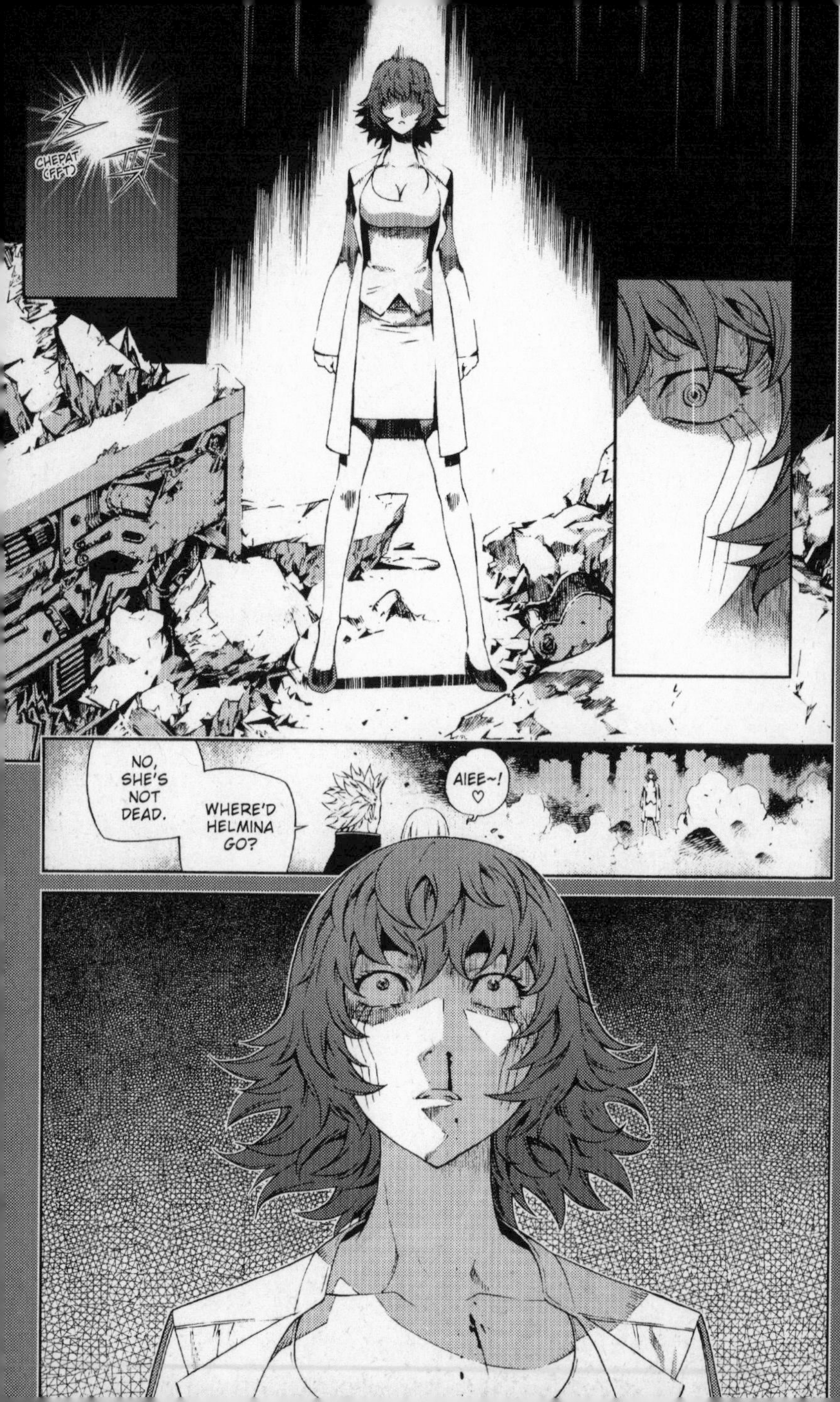
CHEPAT (FFT)
NO, SHE'S NOT DEAD.
WHERE'D HELMINA GO?
AIEE~! ♡

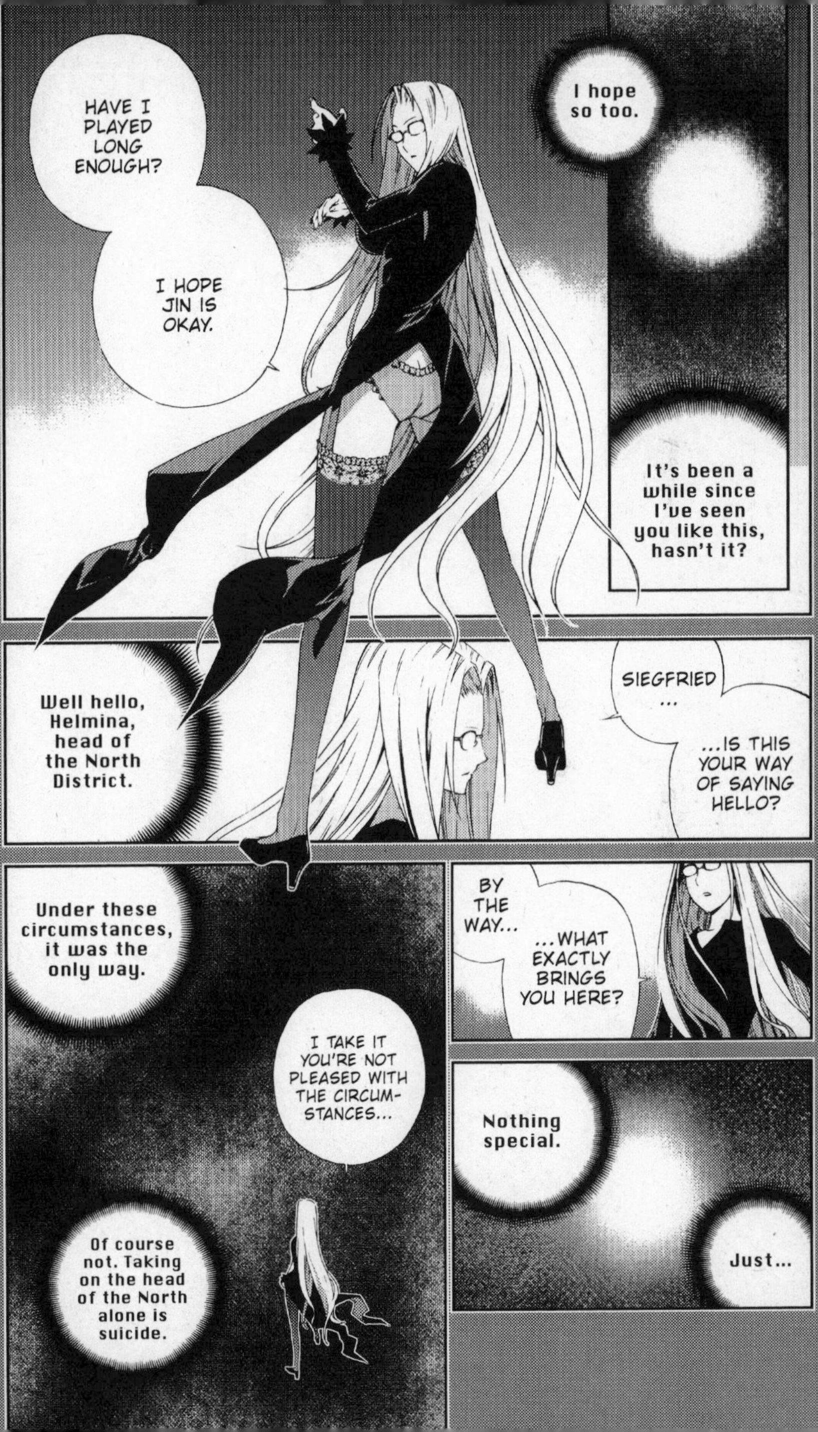
HAVE I PLAYED LONG ENOUGH?
I HOPE JIN IS OKAY.
I hope so too.
It's been a while since I've seen you like this, hasn't it?
Well hello, Helmina, head of the North District.
SIEGFRIED ...
...IS THIS YOUR WAY OF SAYING HELLO?
Under these circumstances, it was the only way.
I TAKE IT YOU'RE NOT PLEASED WITH THE CIRCUM-STANCES...
Of course not. Taking on the head of the North alone is suicide.
BY THE WAY...
...WHAT EXACTLY BRINGS YOU HERE?
Nothing special.
Just...

...seemed like the best response to your declaration of war.

SINCE WHEN DO YOU CARE?

We've always admired you. Besides, we're a bit desperate.

OF COURSE YOU ARE.

YOU'RE DEALING WITH THE NORTH, WHERE JACK AND I LIVE!

Ah...You misunder-stand me.

MIS...

...UNDER-STAND?

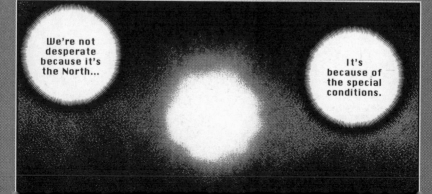

We're not desperate because it's the North...

It's because of the special conditions.

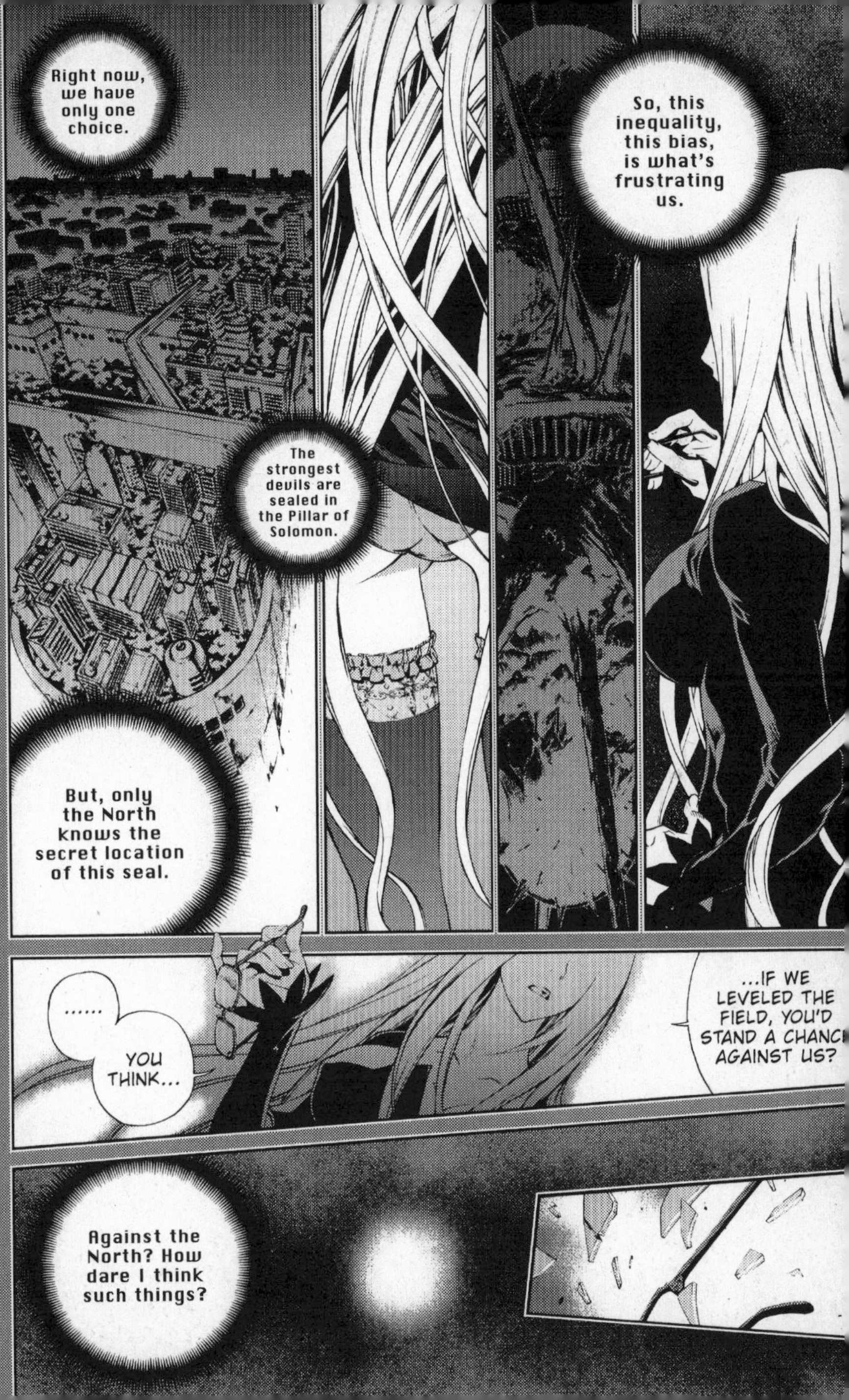
Right now, we have only one choice.
The strongest devils are sealed in the Pillar of Solomon.
But, only the North knows the secret location of this seal.
So, this inequality, this bias, is what's frustrating us.
......
YOU THINK...
...IF WE LEVELED THE FIELD, YOU'D STAND A CHANC AGAINST US?
Against the North? How dare I think such things?

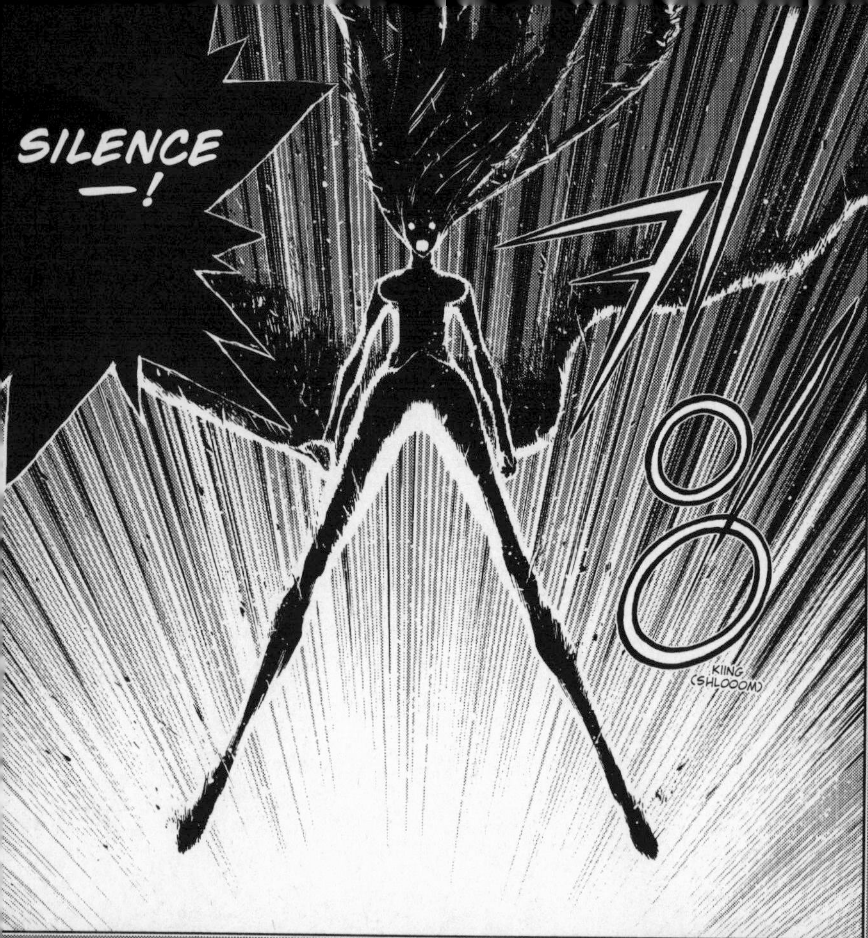
SILENCE
—!
KIING
(SHLOOOM)
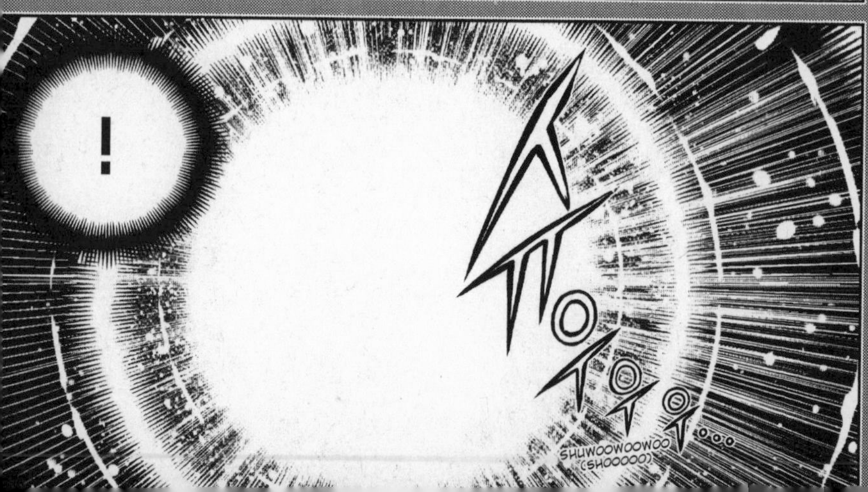
!
SHUWOOWOOWOO
(SHOOOOO)

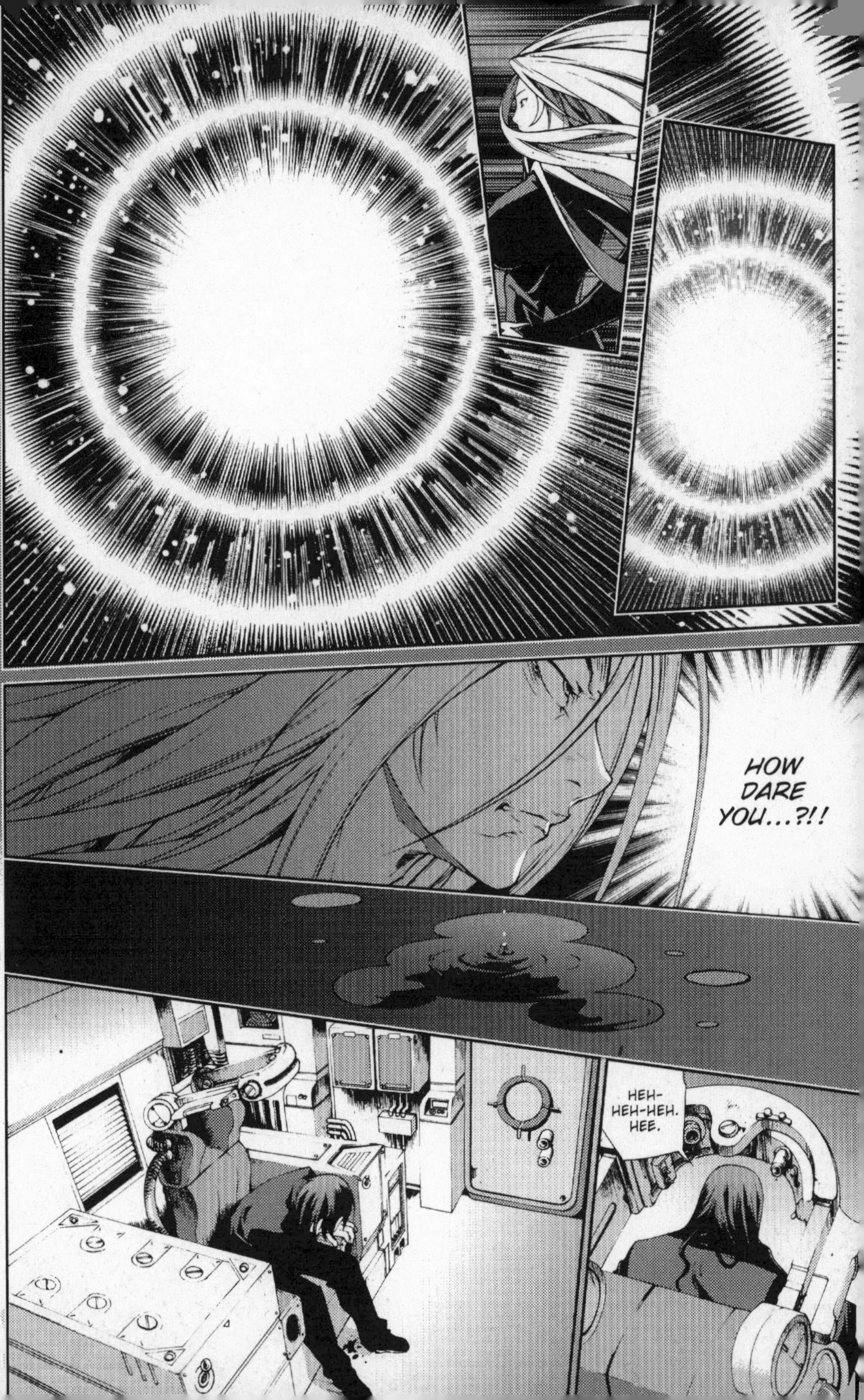
HOW DARE YOU...?!!
HEH-HEH-HEH. HEE.

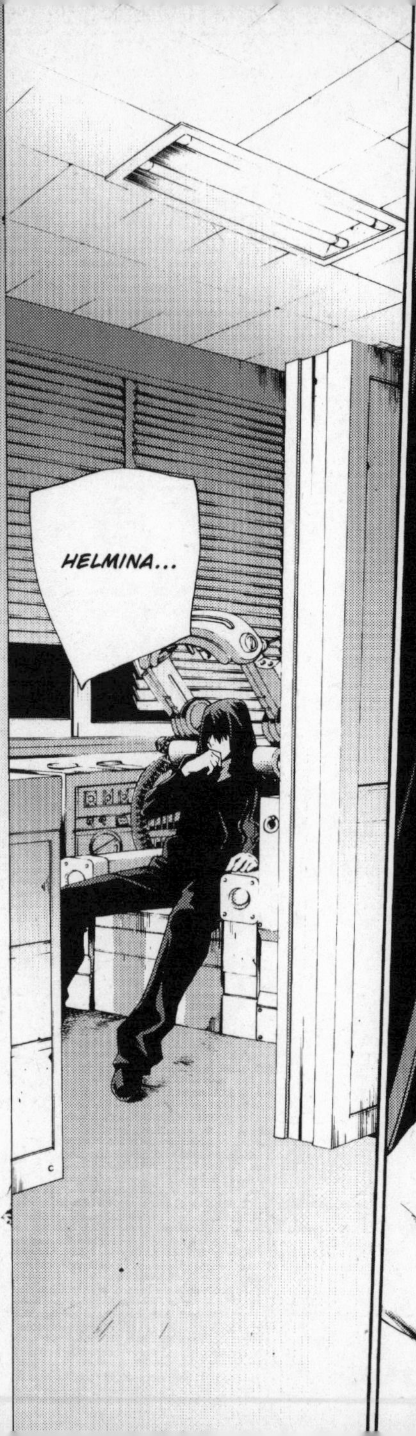
HELMINA...
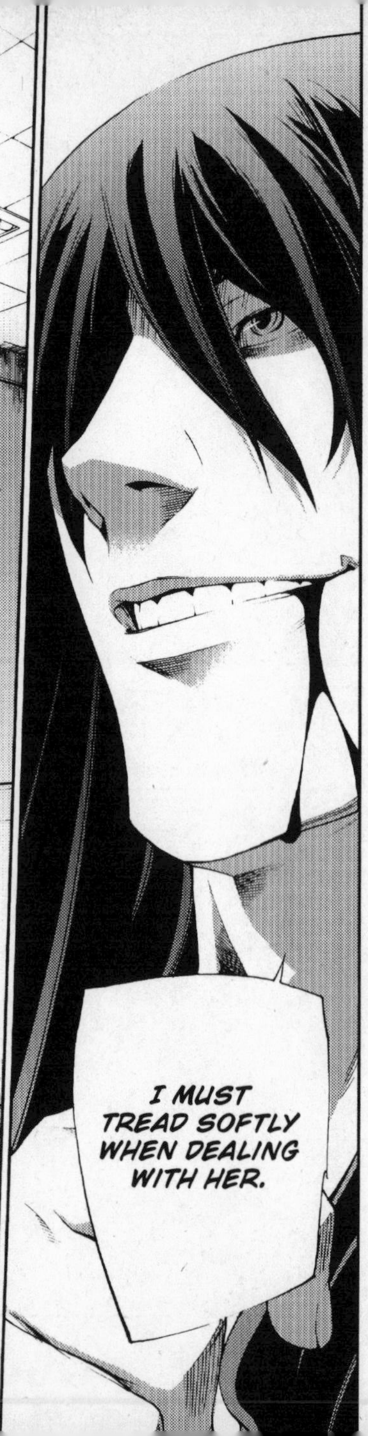
I MUST TREAD SOFTLY WHEN DEALING WITH HER.

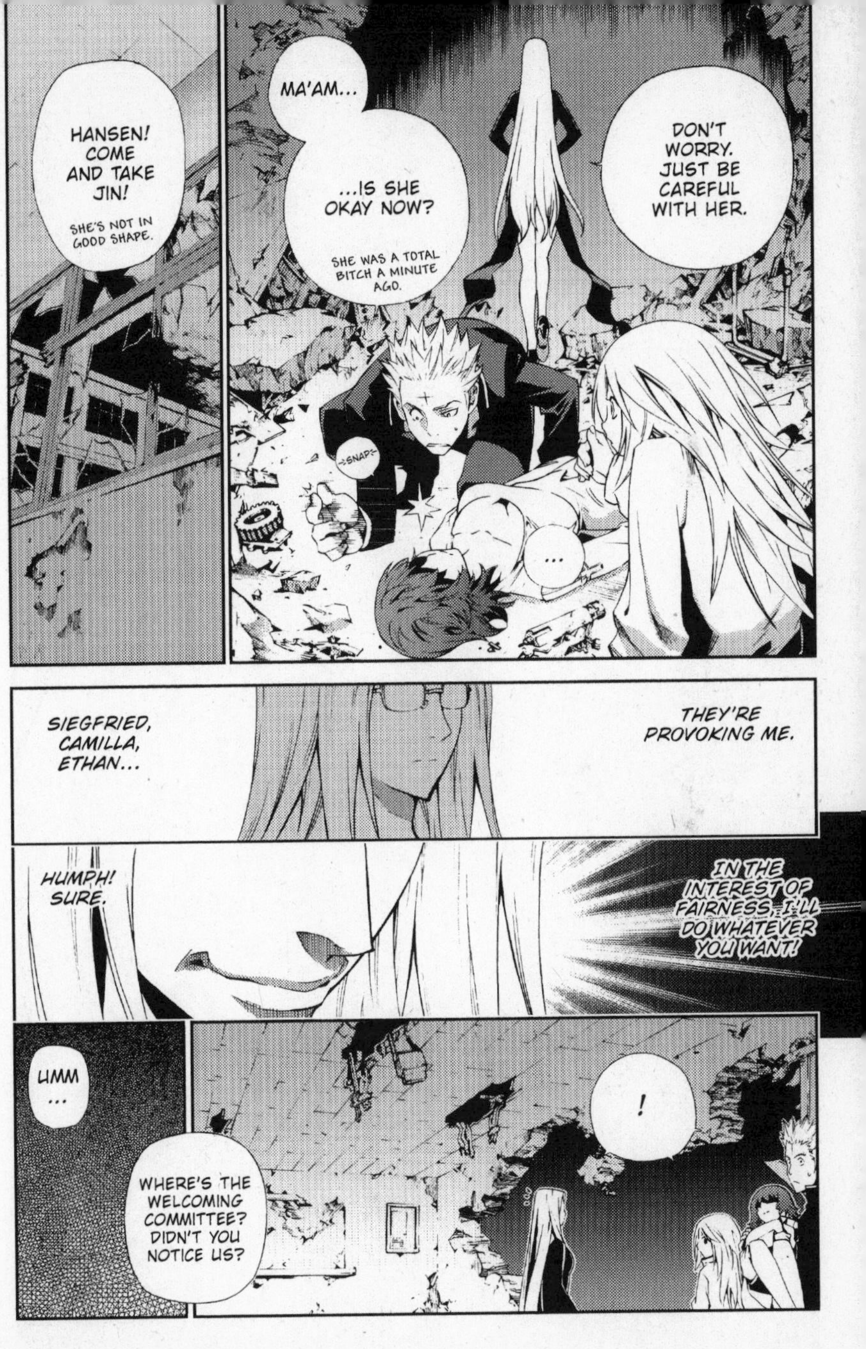
HANSEN! COME AND TAKE JIN!
SHE'S NOT IN GOOD SHAPE.
MA'AM...
...IS SHE OKAY NOW?
SHE WAS A TOTAL BITCH A MINUTE AGO.
DON'T WORRY. JUST BE CAREFUL WITH HER.
SNAP
...
SIEGFRIED, CAMILLA, ETHAN...
THEY'RE PROVOKING ME.
HUMPH! SURE.
IN THE INTEREST OF FAIRNESS, I'LL DO WHATEVER YOU WANT!
UMM ...
WHERE'S THE WELCOMING COMMITTEE? DIDN'T YOU NOTICE US?
!

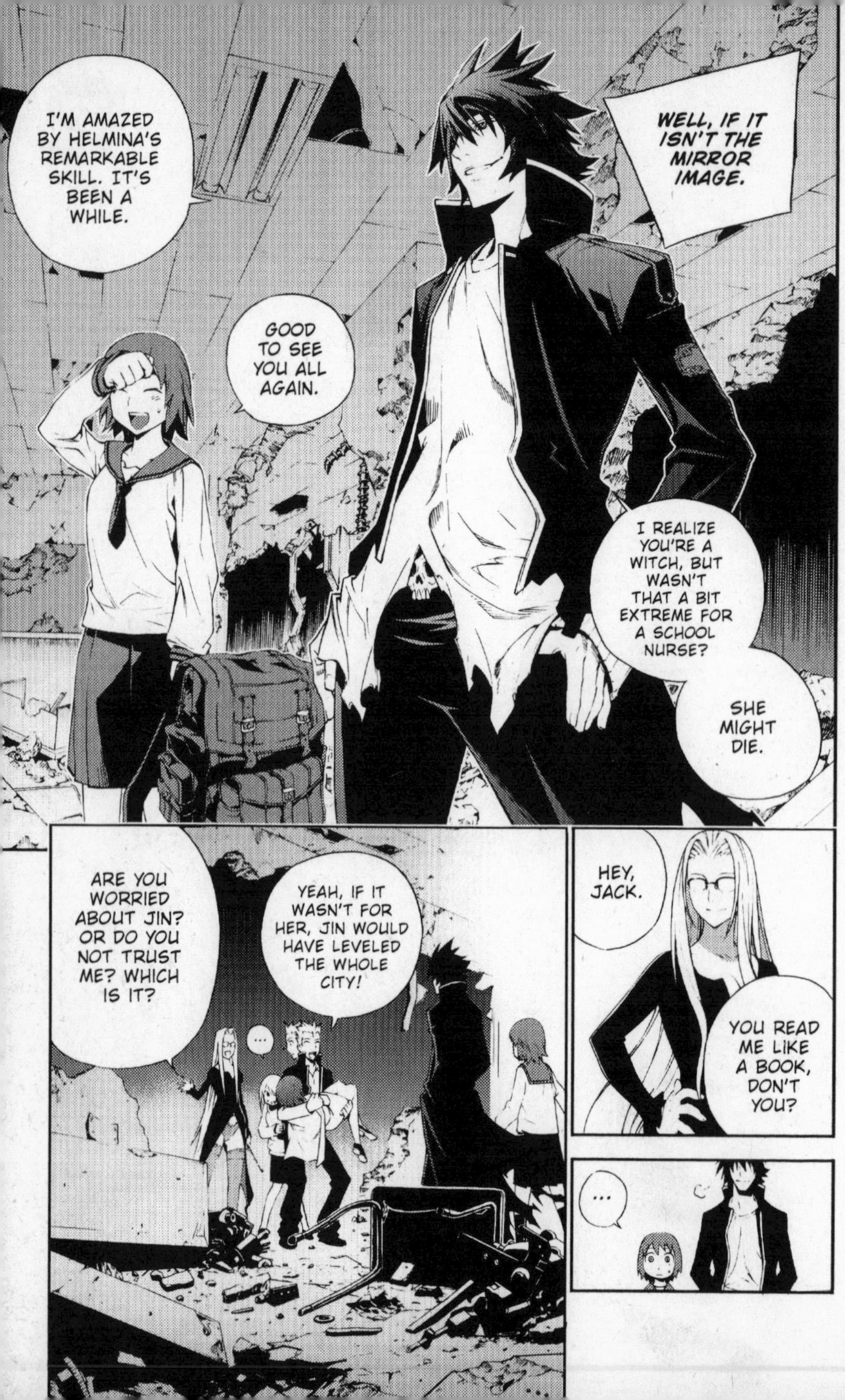
I'M AMAZED BY HELMINA'S REMARKABLE SKILL. IT'S BEEN A WHILE.
WELL, IF IT ISN'T THE MIRROR IMAGE.
GOOD TO SEE YOU ALL AGAIN.
I REALIZE YOU'RE A WITCH, BUT WASN'T THAT A BIT EXTREME FOR A SCHOOL NURSE?
SHE MIGHT DIE.
ARE YOU WORRIED ABOUT JIN? OR DO YOU NOT TRUST ME? WHICH IS IT?
YEAH, IF IT WASN'T FOR HER, JIN WOULD HAVE LEVELED THE WHOLE CITY!
...
HEY, JACK.
YOU READ ME LIKE A BOOK, DON'T YOU?
...

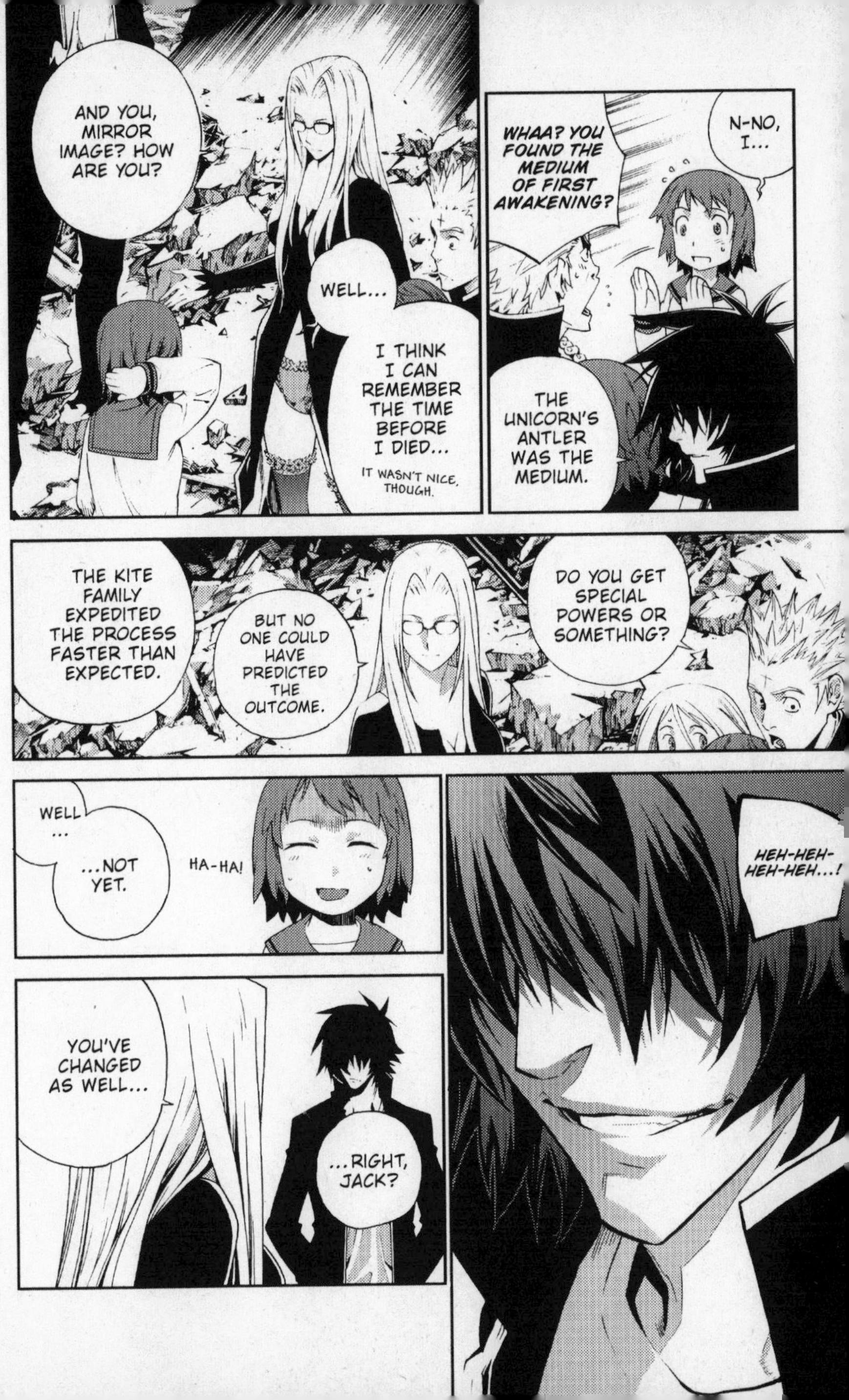
AND YOU, MIRROR IMAGE? HOW ARE YOU?
WELL...
I THINK I CAN REMEMBER THE TIME BEFORE I DIED...
IT WASN'T NICE, THOUGH.
WHAA? YOU FOUND THE MEDIUM OF FIRST AWAKENING?
N-NO, I...
THE UNICORN'S ANTLER WAS THE MEDIUM.
THE KITE FAMILY EXPEDITED THE PROCESS FASTER THAN EXPECTED.
BUT NO ONE COULD HAVE PREDICTED THE OUTCOME.
DO YOU GET SPECIAL POWERS OR SOMETHING?
WELL ...
...NOT YET.
HA-HA!
YOU'VE CHANGED AS WELL...
...RIGHT, JACK?
HEH-HEH-HEH-HEH...!

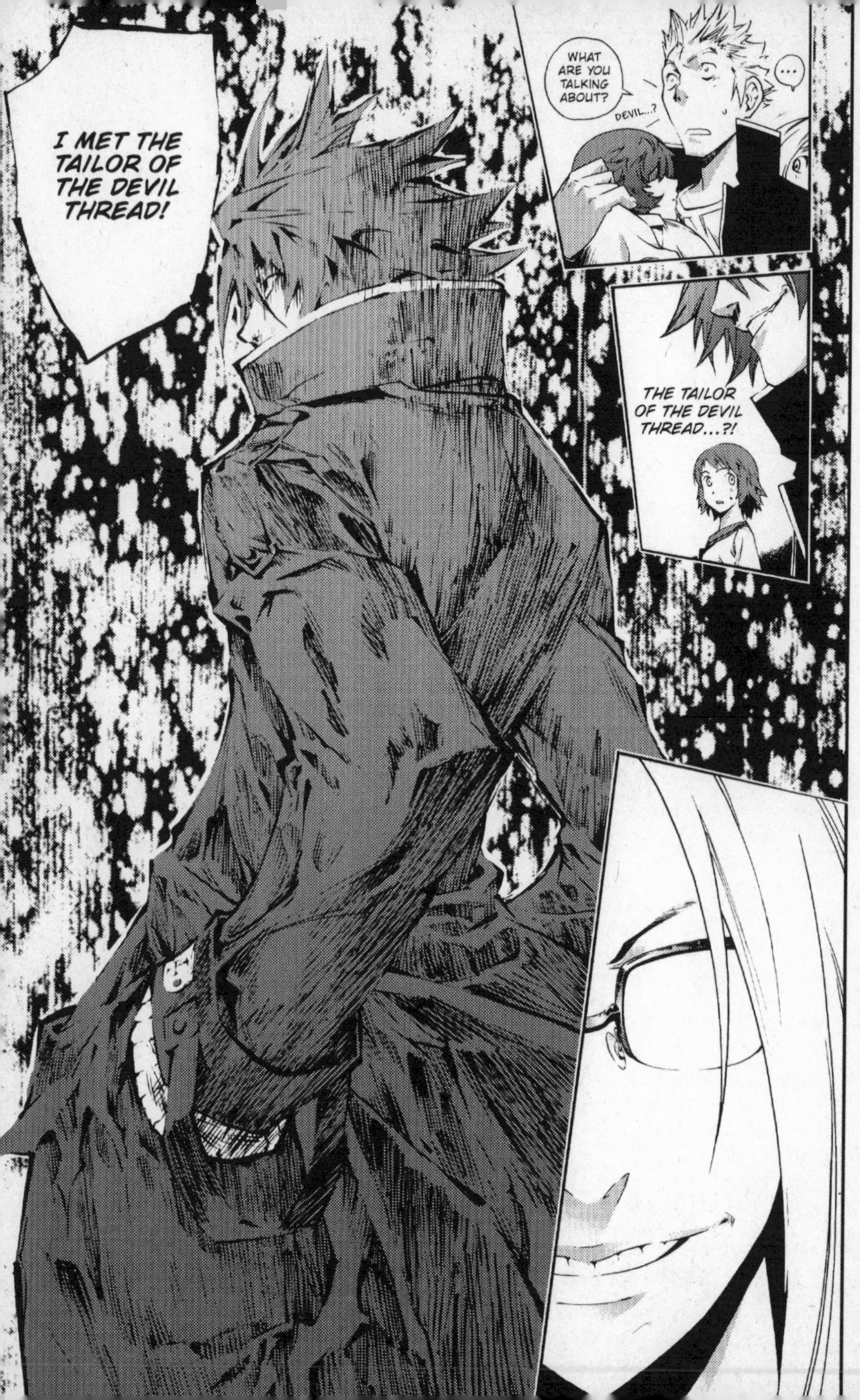
I MET THE TAILOR OF THE DEVIL THREAD!
WHAT ARE YOU TALKING ABOUT?
DEVIL...?
...
THE TAILOR OF THE DEVIL THREAD...?!

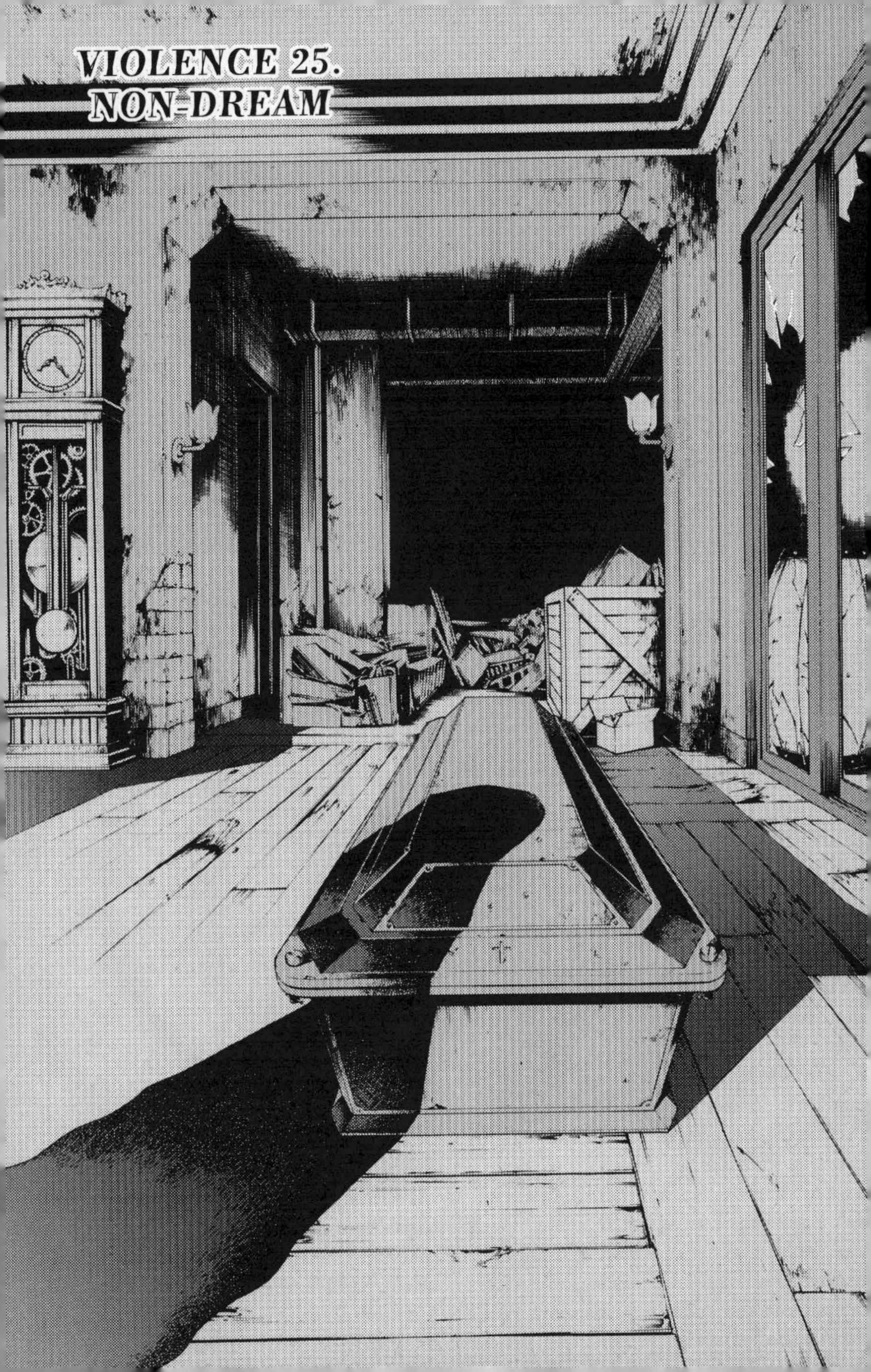
VIOLENCE 25.
NON-DREAM

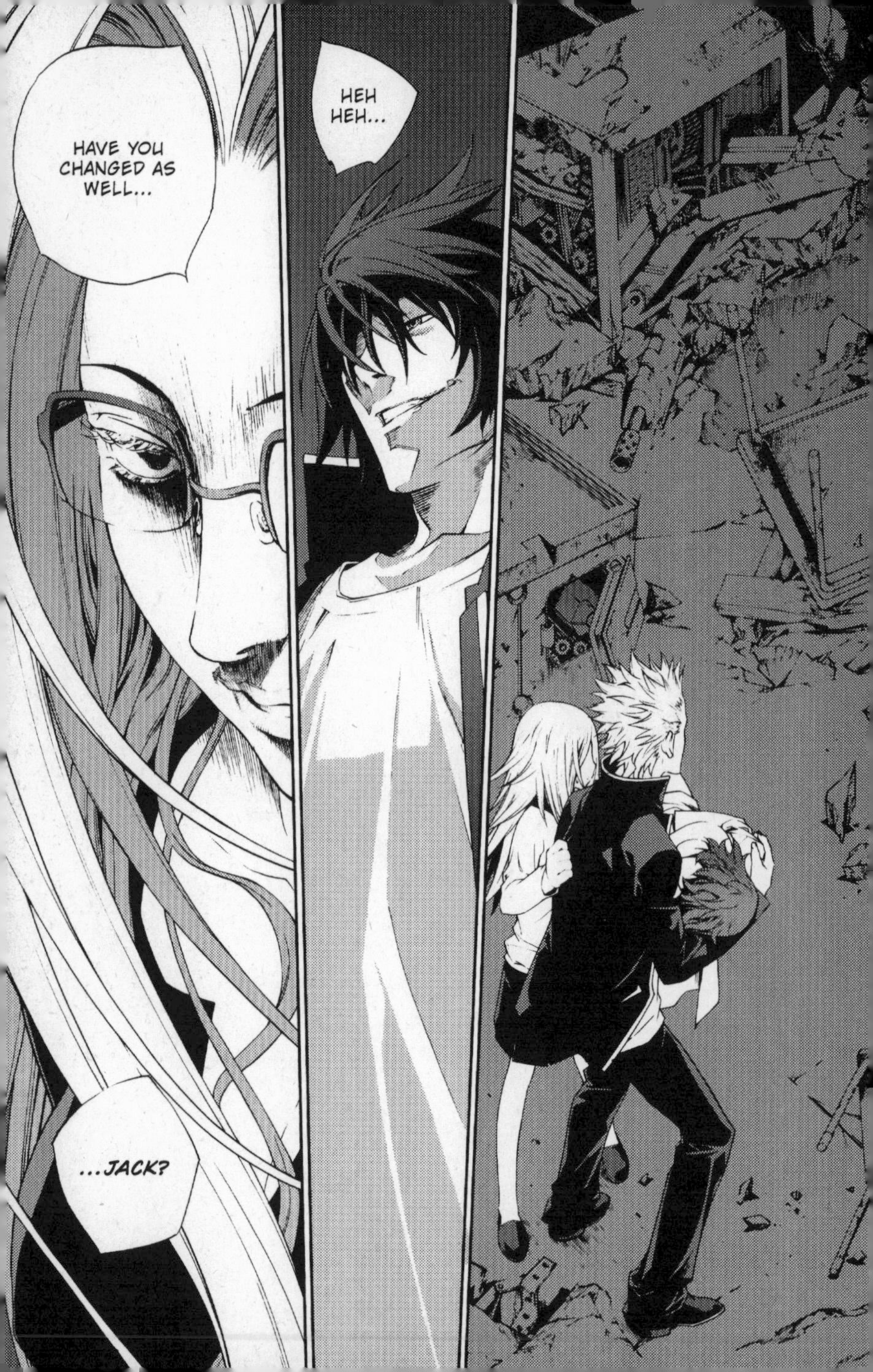
HAVE YOU CHANGED AS WELL...
...JACK?
HEH HEH...

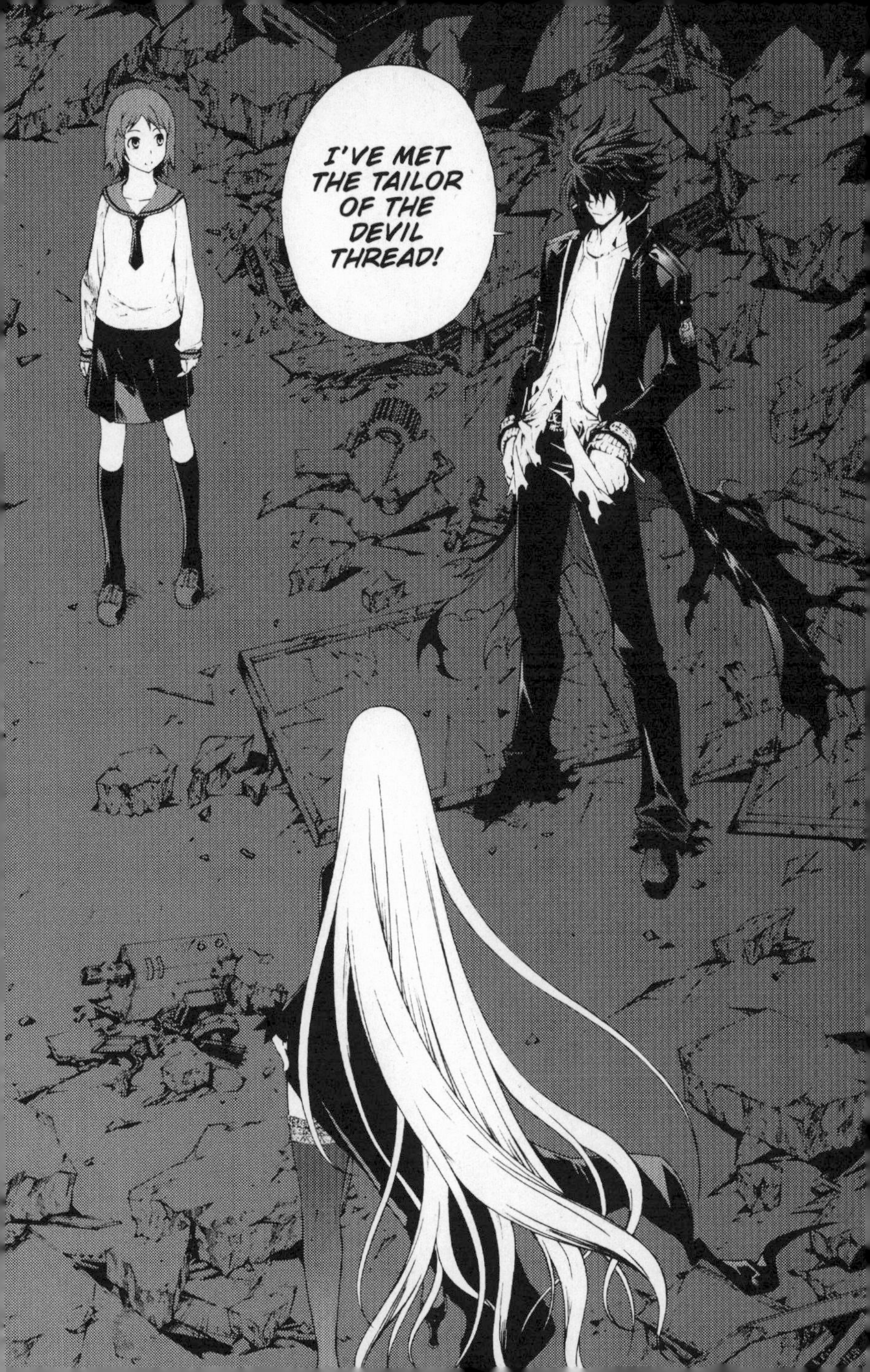
I'VE MET THE TAILOR OF THE DEVIL THREAD!

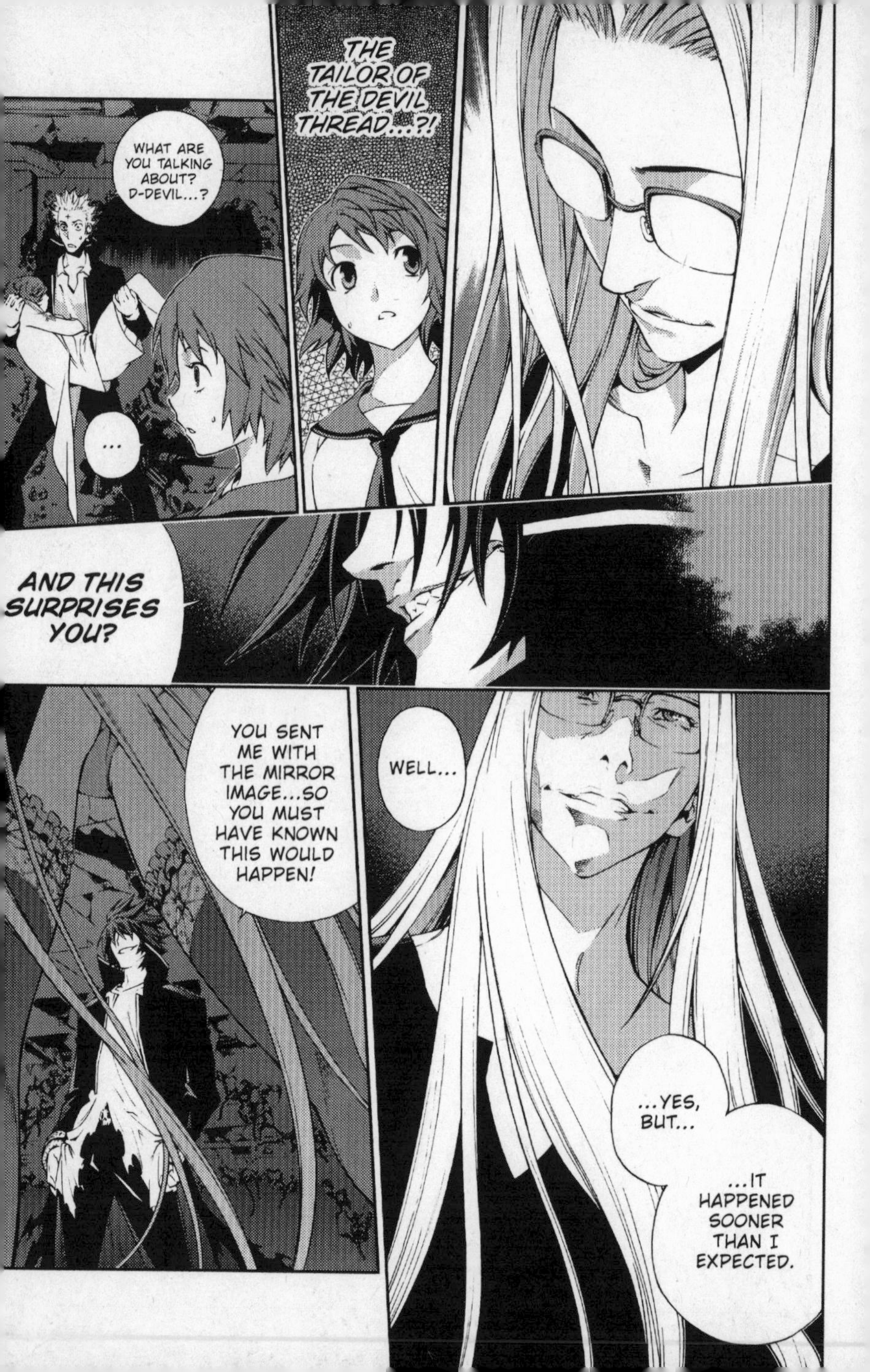
WHAT ARE YOU TALKING ABOUT? D-DEVIL...?
...
THE TAILOR OF THE DEVIL THREAD...?!
AND THIS SURPRISES YOU?
YOU SENT ME WITH THE MIRROR IMAGE...SO YOU MUST HAVE KNOWN THIS WOULD HAPPEN!
WELL...
...YES, BUT...
...IT HAPPENED SOONER THAN I EXPECTED.

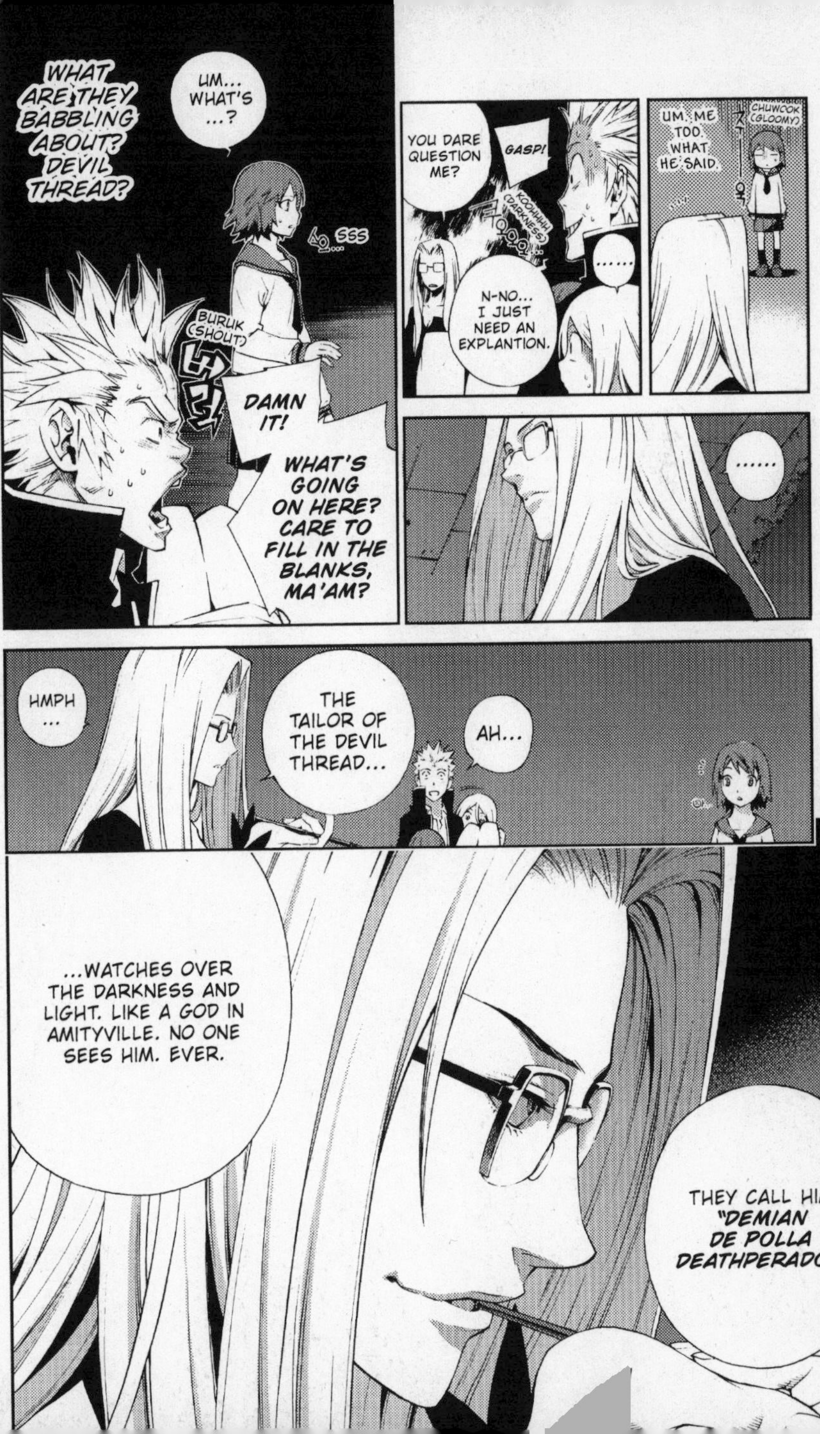
WHAT ARE THEY BABBLING ABOUT? DEVIL THREAD?
UM... WHAT'S ...?
SSS
BURUK (SHOUT)
DAMN IT!
WHAT'S GOING ON HERE? CARE TO FILL IN THE BLANKS, MA'AM?
YOU DARE QUESTION ME?
GASP!
KOOHHHH (DARKNESS)
......
N-NO... I JUST NEED AN EXPLANTION.
UM, ME TOO. WHAT HE SAID.
CHUWCOK (GLOOMY)
......
HMPH ...
THE TAILOR OF THE DEVIL THREAD...
AH...
...WATCHES OVER THE DARKNESS AND LIGHT. LIKE A GOD IN AMITYVILLE. NO ONE SEES HIM. EVER.
THEY CALL HIM "DEMIAN DE POLLA DEATHPERADO."

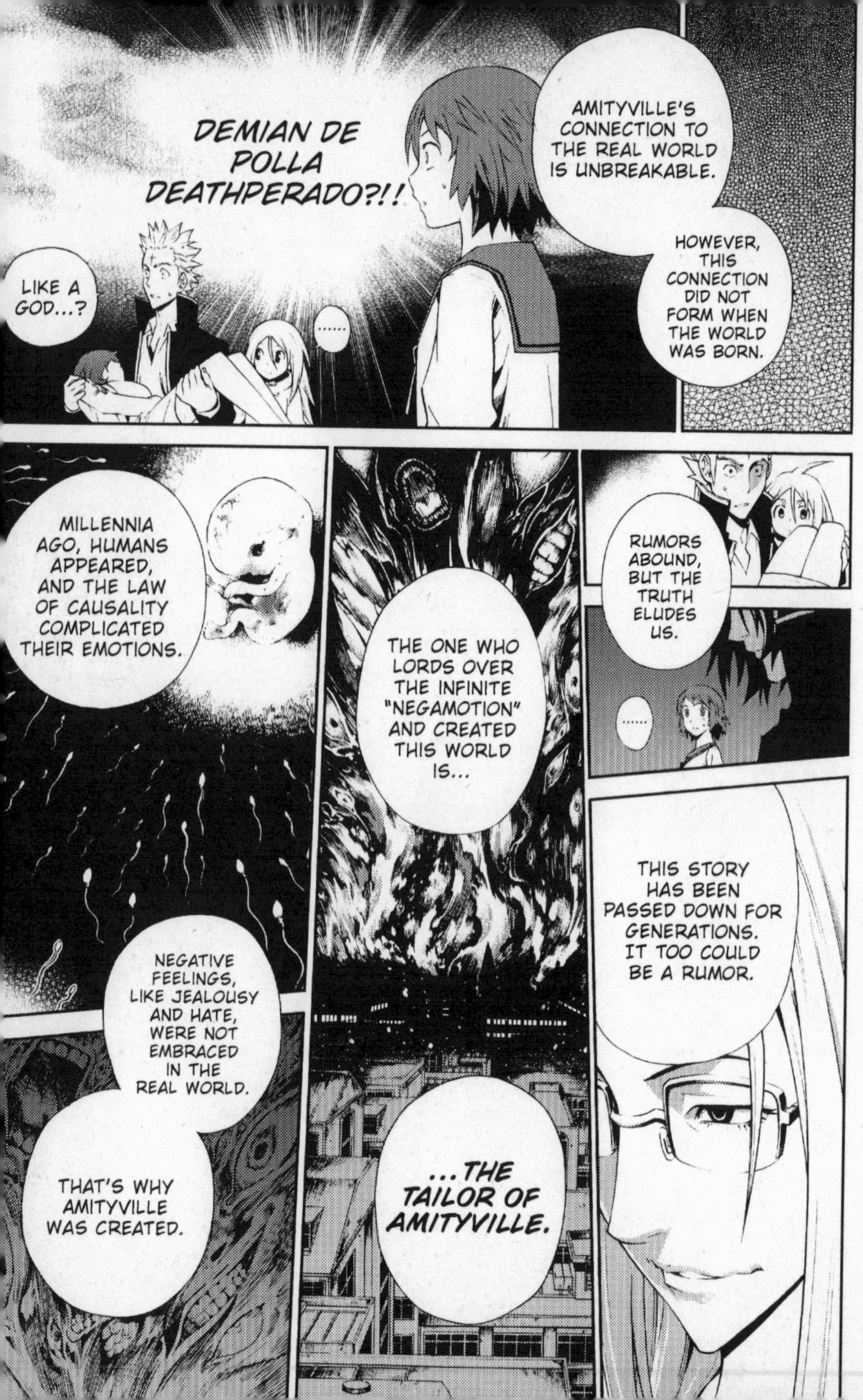
DEMIAN DE POLLA DEATHPERADO?!!
LIKE A GOD...?
......
AMITYVILLE'S CONNECTION TO THE REAL WORLD IS UNBREAKABLE.
HOWEVER, THIS CONNECTION DID NOT FORM WHEN THE WORLD WAS BORN.
MILLENNIA AGO, HUMANS APPEARED, AND THE LAW OF CAUSALITY COMPLICATED THEIR EMOTIONS.
NEGATIVE FEELINGS, LIKE JEALOUSY AND HATE, WERE NOT EMBRACED IN THE REAL WORLD.
THAT'S WHY AMITYVILLE WAS CREATED.
THE ONE WHO LORDS OVER THE INFINITE "NEGAMOTION" AND CREATED THIS WORLD IS...
...THE TAILOR OF AMITYVILLE.
RUMORS ABOUND, BUT THE TRUTH ELUDES US.
......
THIS STORY HAS BEEN PASSED DOWN FOR GENERATIONS. IT TOO COULD BE A RUMOR.

I KNEW THAT COAT WAS SPECIAL. IT SEEMS ALIVE!

I GUESS IT'S SAFE TO SAY, THOUGH, THAT THE DEVIL THREAD IS HIS "BRAND."

I THOUGHT IT WAS A MONSTER...

JACK MEETING THE TAILOR IS A MONUMENTAL OCCASION.

IT'S BEEN TOO QUIET SINCE THE LAST WAR, SO, LIKE KARMA, IT'S TIME TO STIR THINGS UP.

THE GOD OF DARK-NESS...

I GUESS HE GOT BORED OF AMITYVILLE AS IS, RIGHT?

....

HEH HEH...

HEH HEH...

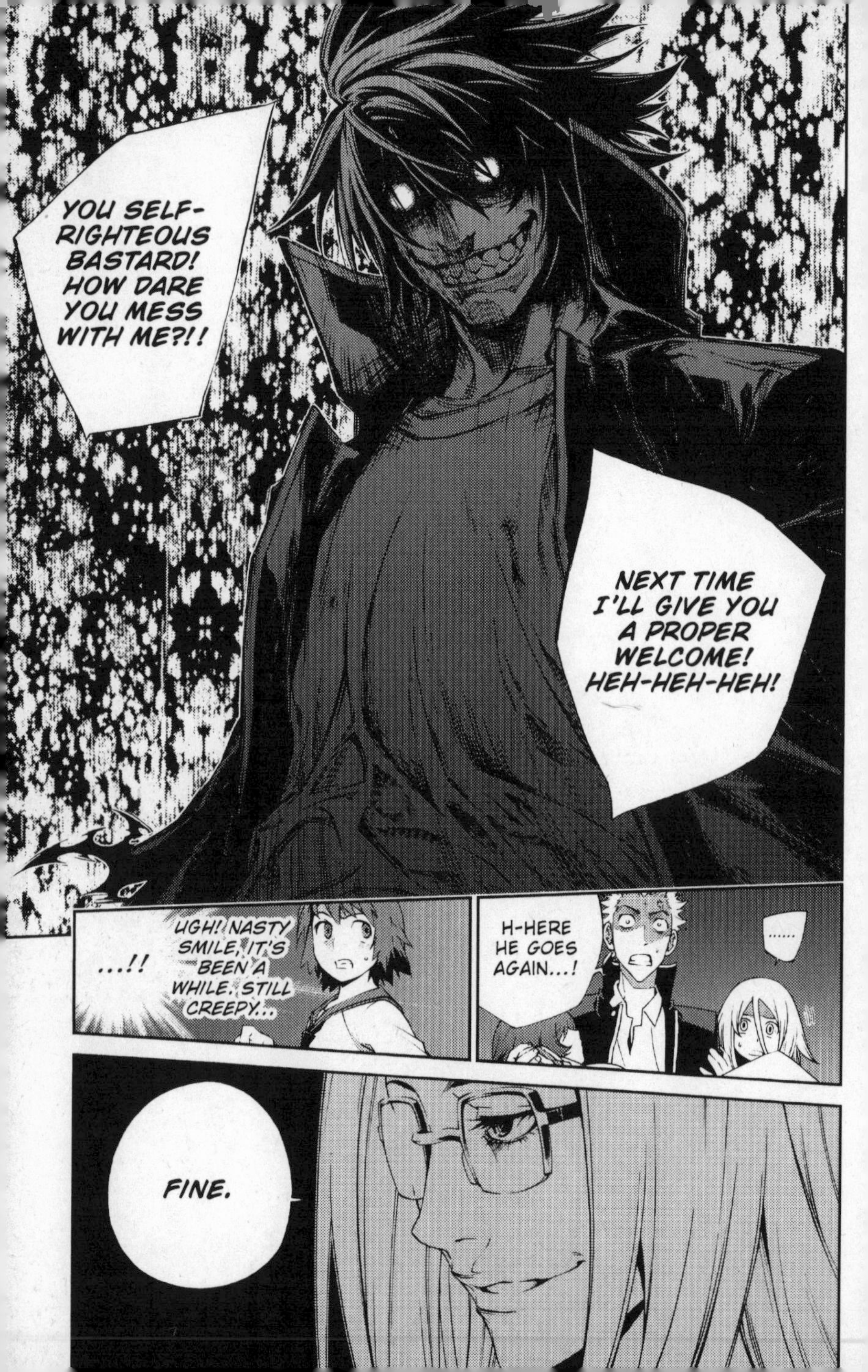
YOU SELF-RIGHTEOUS BASTARD! HOW DARE YOU MESS WITH ME?!!
NEXT TIME I'LL GIVE YOU A PROPER WELCOME! HEH-HEH-HEH!
...!!
UGH! NASTY SMILE, IT'S BEEN A WHILE. STILL CREEPY...
H-HERE HE GOES AGAIN...!
......
FINE.

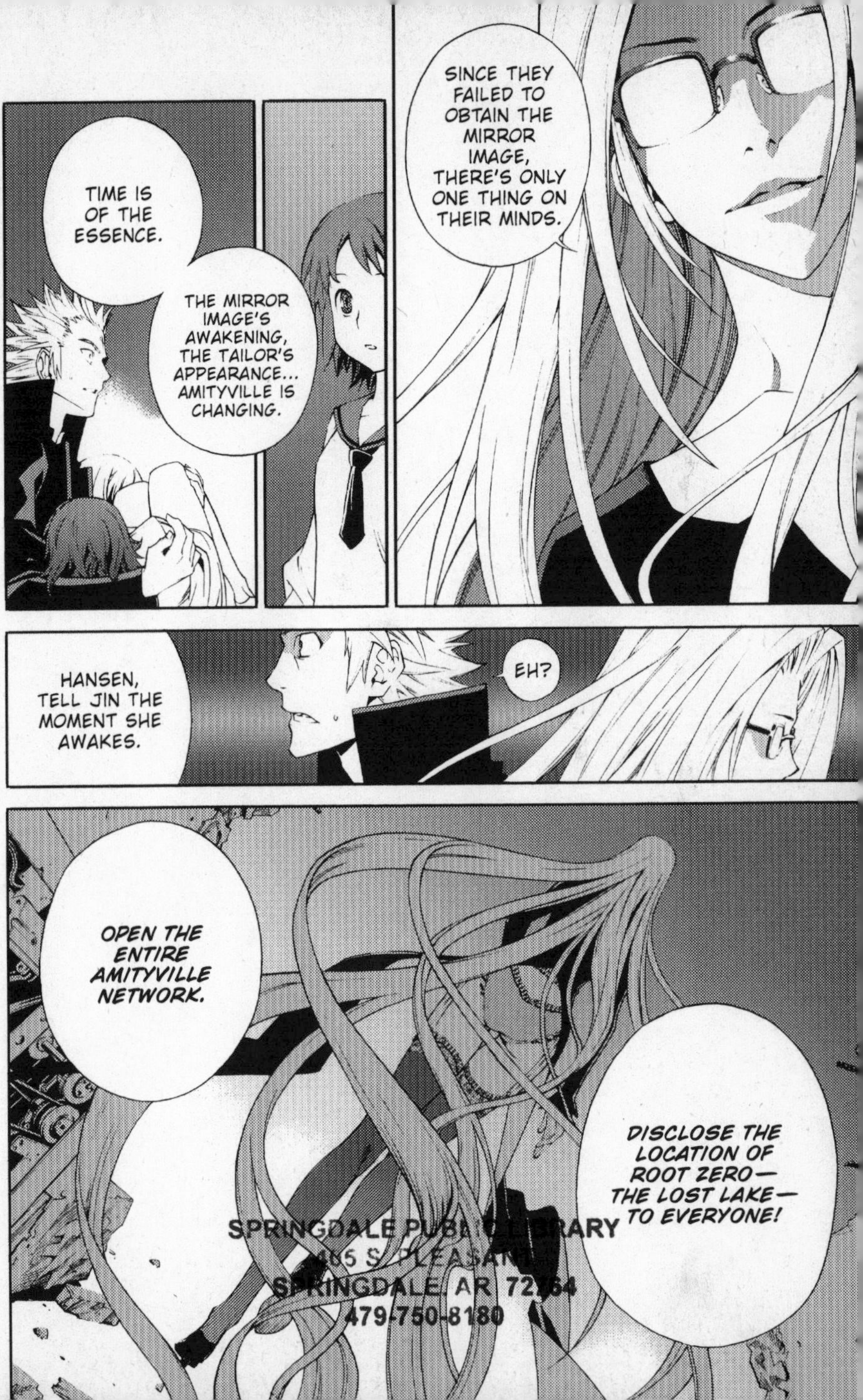
TIME IS OF THE ESSENCE.
THE MIRROR IMAGE'S AWAKENING, THE TAILOR'S APPEARANCE... AMITYVILLE IS CHANGING.
SINCE THEY FAILED TO OBTAIN THE MIRROR IMAGE, THERE'S ONLY ONE THING ON THEIR MINDS.
HANSEN, TELL JIN THE MOMENT SHE AWAKES.
EH?
OPEN THE ENTIRE AMITYVILLE NETWORK.
DISCLOSE THE LOCATION OF ROOT ZERO— THE LOST LAKE— TO EVERYONE!

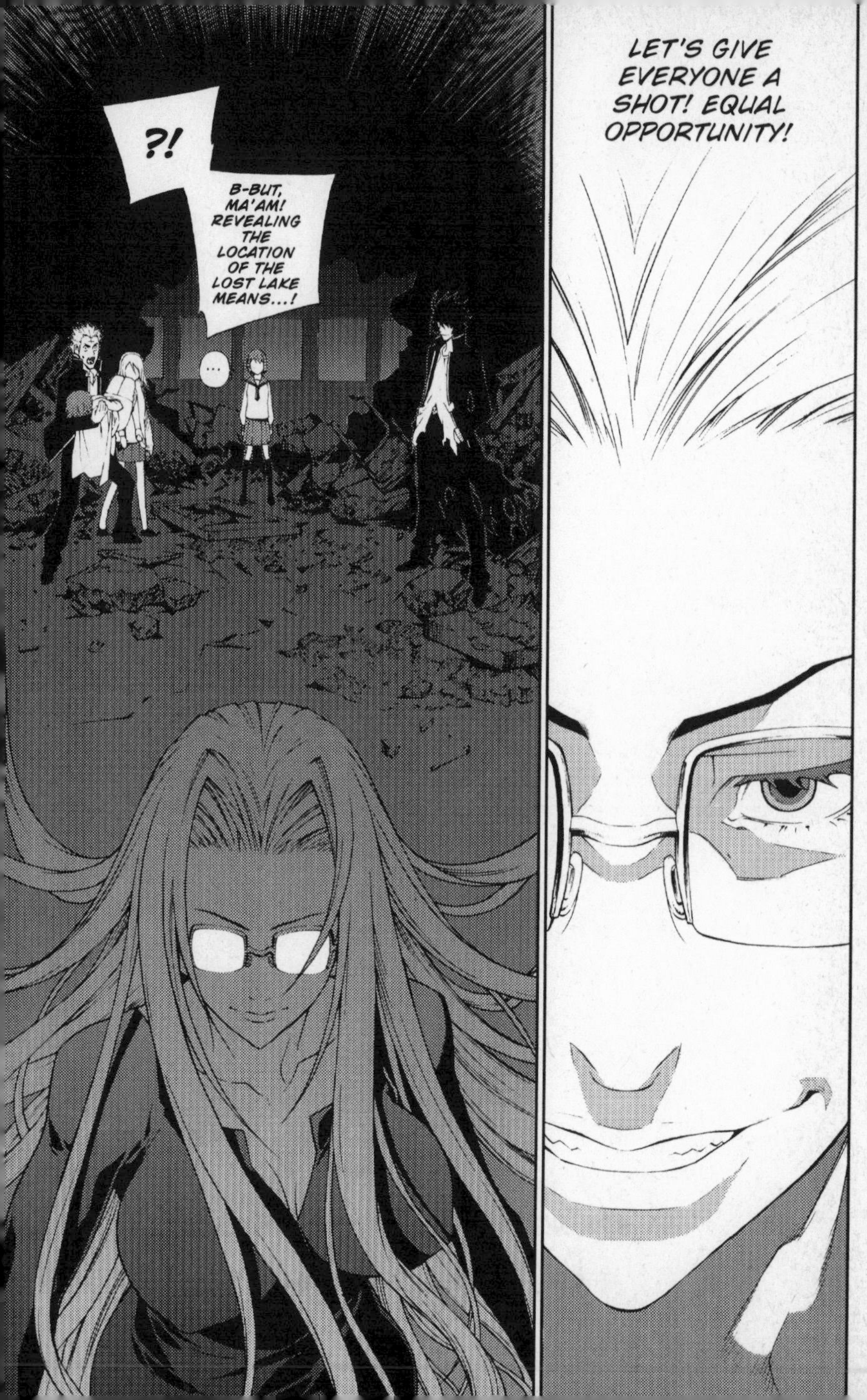
?!
B-BUT, MA'AM! REVEALING THE LOCATION OF THE LOST LAKE MEANS...!
...
LET'S GIVE EVERYONE A SHOT! EQUAL OPPORTUNITY!

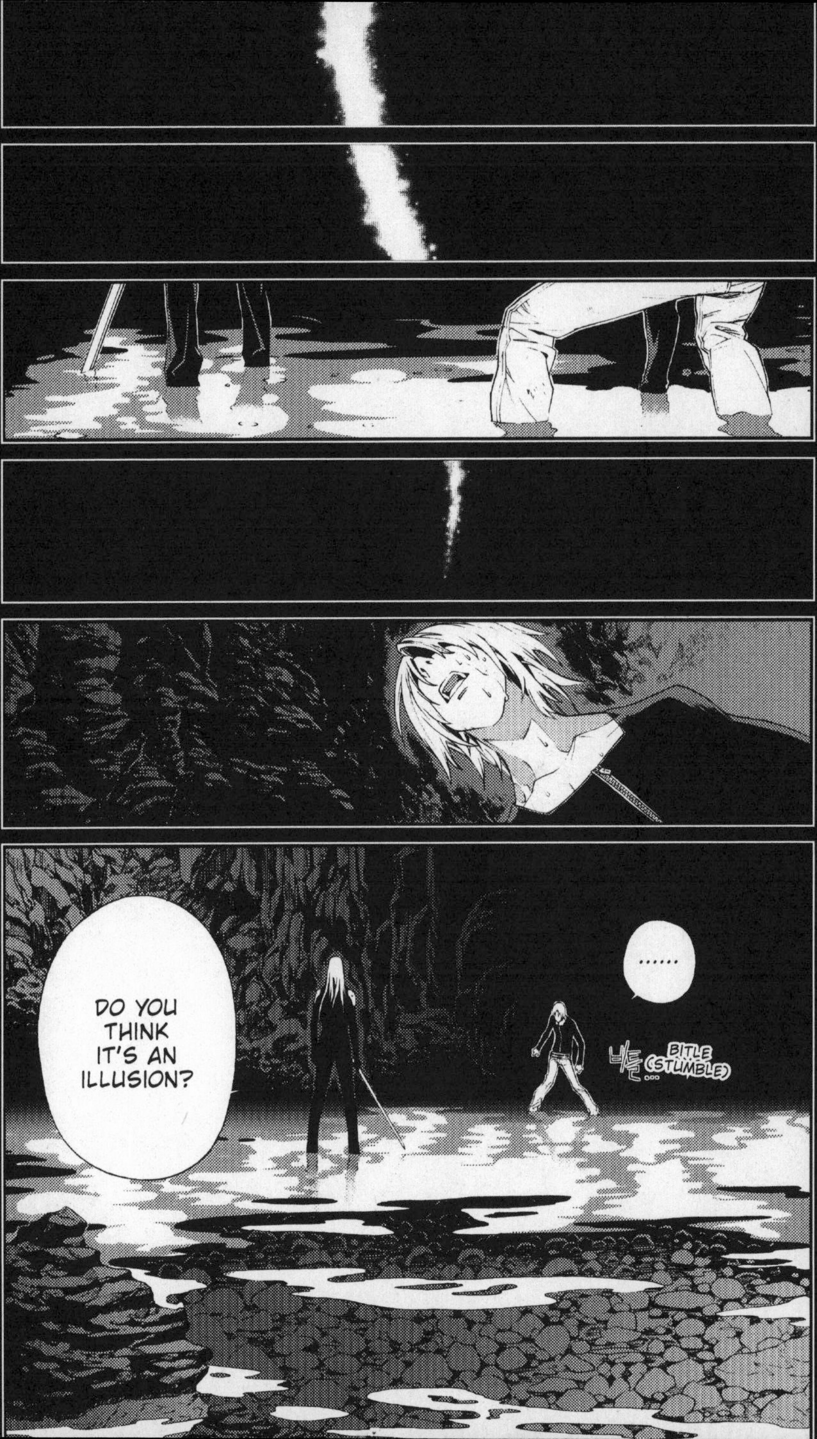
DO YOU THINK IT'S AN ILLUSION?
......
비틀...
BITLE (STUMBLE)

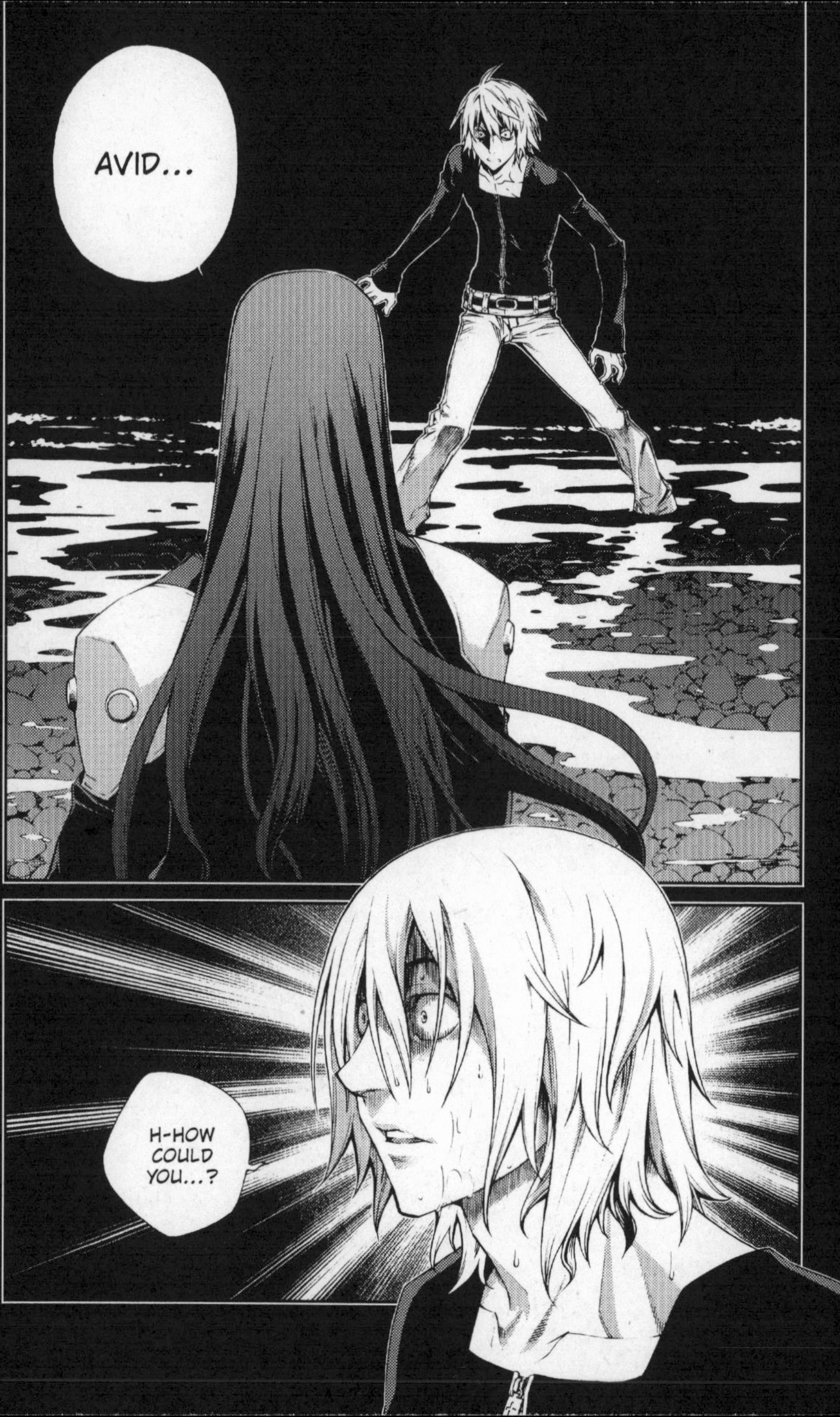
AVID...
H-HOW COULD YOU...?

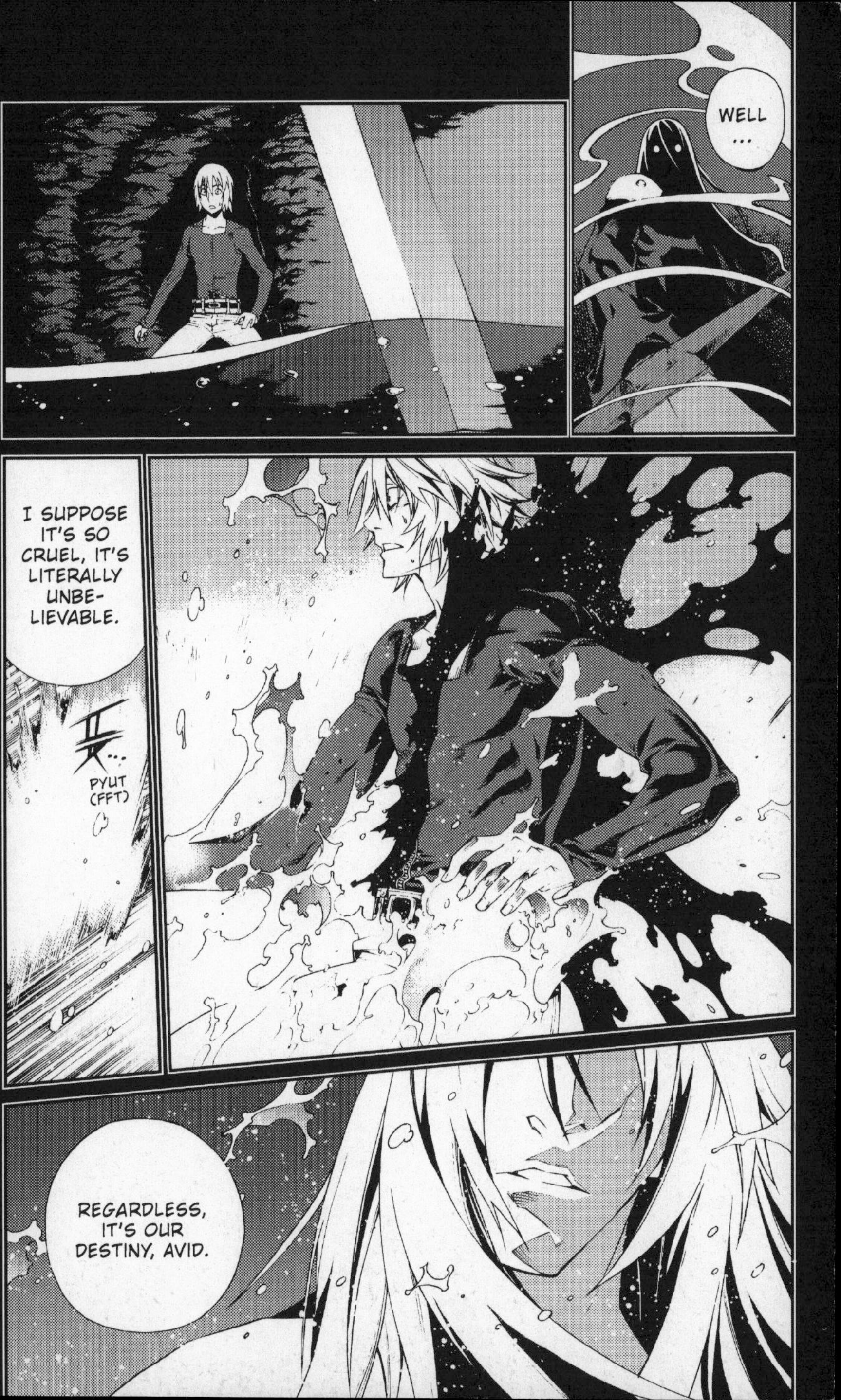
WELL ...
I SUPPOSE IT'S SO CRUEL, IT'S LITERALLY UNBE-LIEVABLE.
PYUT (FFT)
REGARDLESS, IT'S OUR DESTINY, AVID.

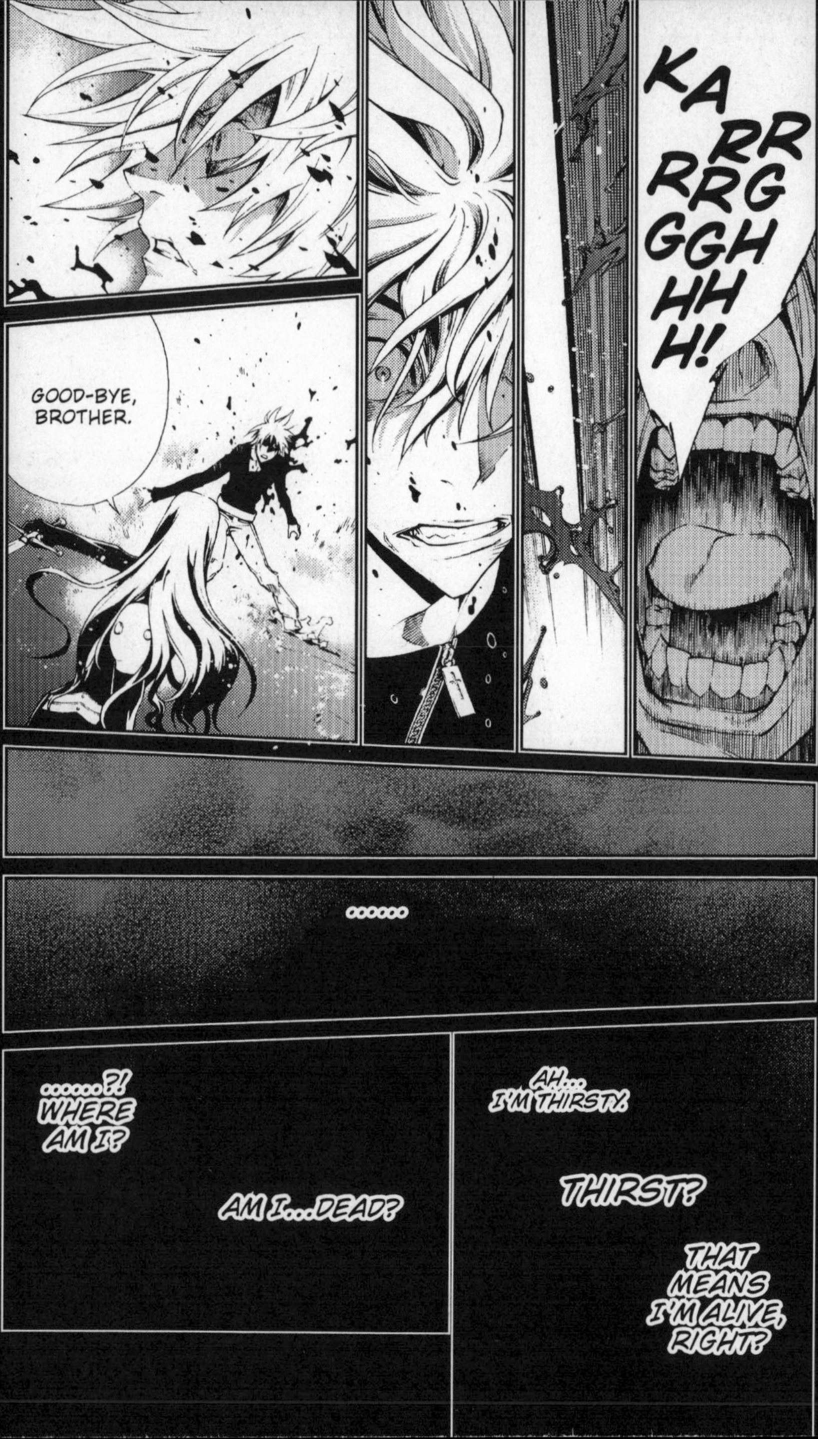
GOOD-BYE, BROTHER.
KARRRRGGGHHHH!
......
......?! WHERE AM I?
AM I...DEAD?
AH... I'M THIRSTY.
THIRST?
THAT MEANS I'M ALIVE, RIGHT?

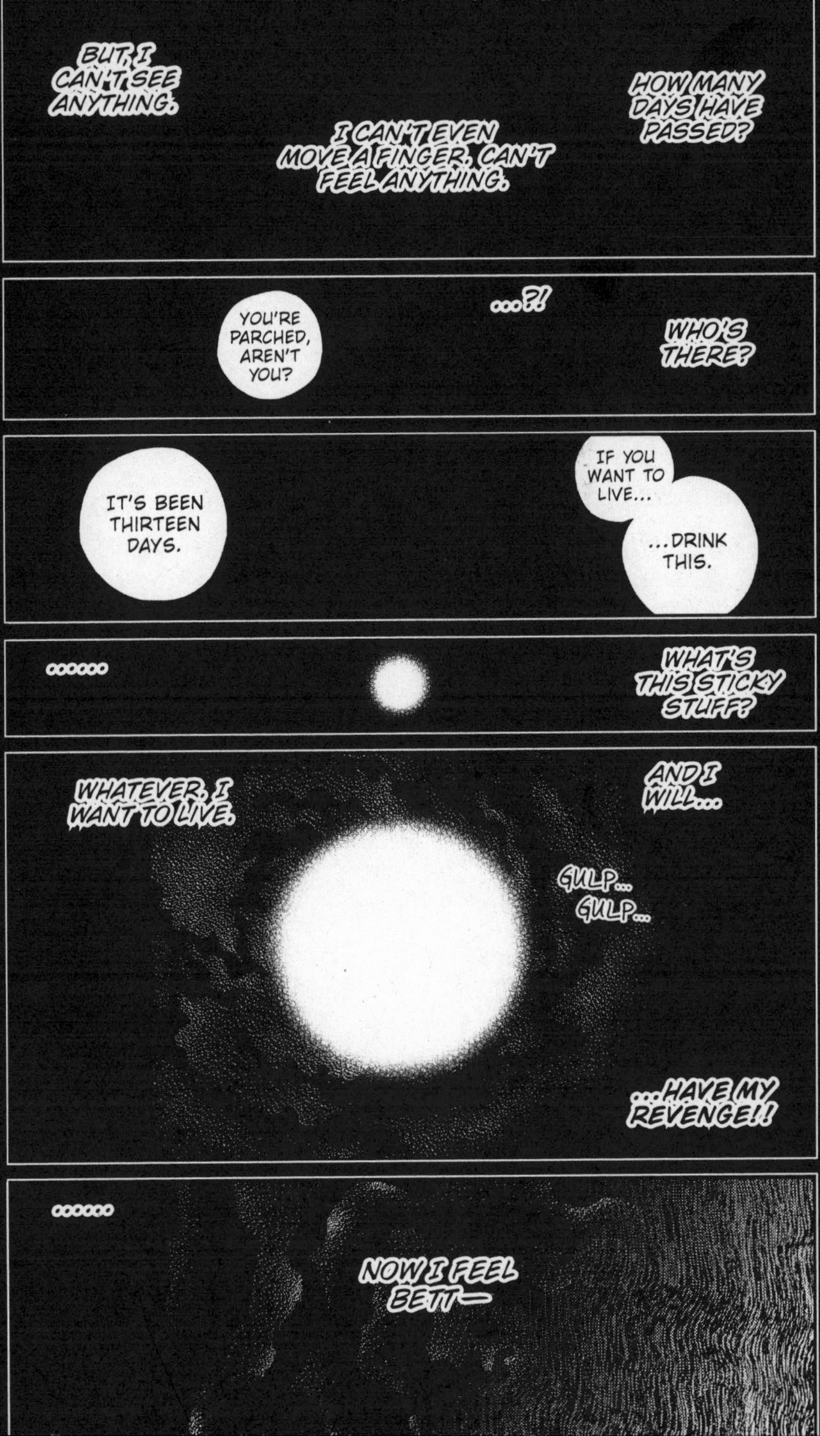
BUT, I CAN'T SEE ANYTHING.
I CAN'T EVEN MOVE A FINGER, CAN'T FEEL ANYTHING.
HOW MANY DAYS HAVE PASSED?
YOU'RE PARCHED, AREN'T YOU?
...?!
WHO'S THERE?
IT'S BEEN THIRTEEN DAYS.
IF YOU WANT TO LIVE...
...DRINK THIS.
......
WHAT'S THIS STICKY STUFF?
WHATEVER, I WANT TO LIVE.
AND I WILL...
GULP... GULP...
...HAVE MY REVENGE!!
......
NOW I FEEL BETT—

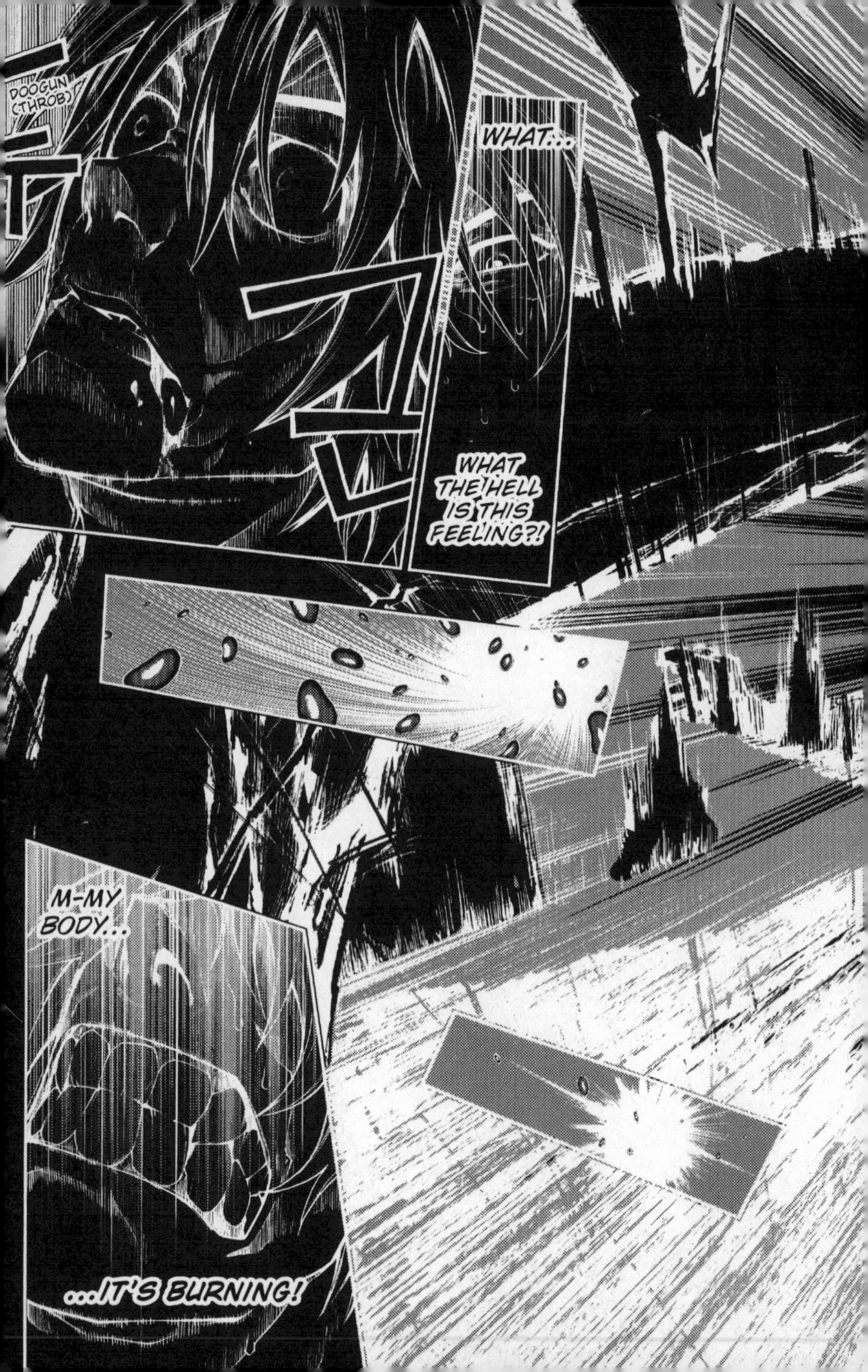
DOOGUN (THROB)
WHAT...
WHAT THE HELL IS THIS FEELING?!
M-MY BODY...
...IT'S BURNING!

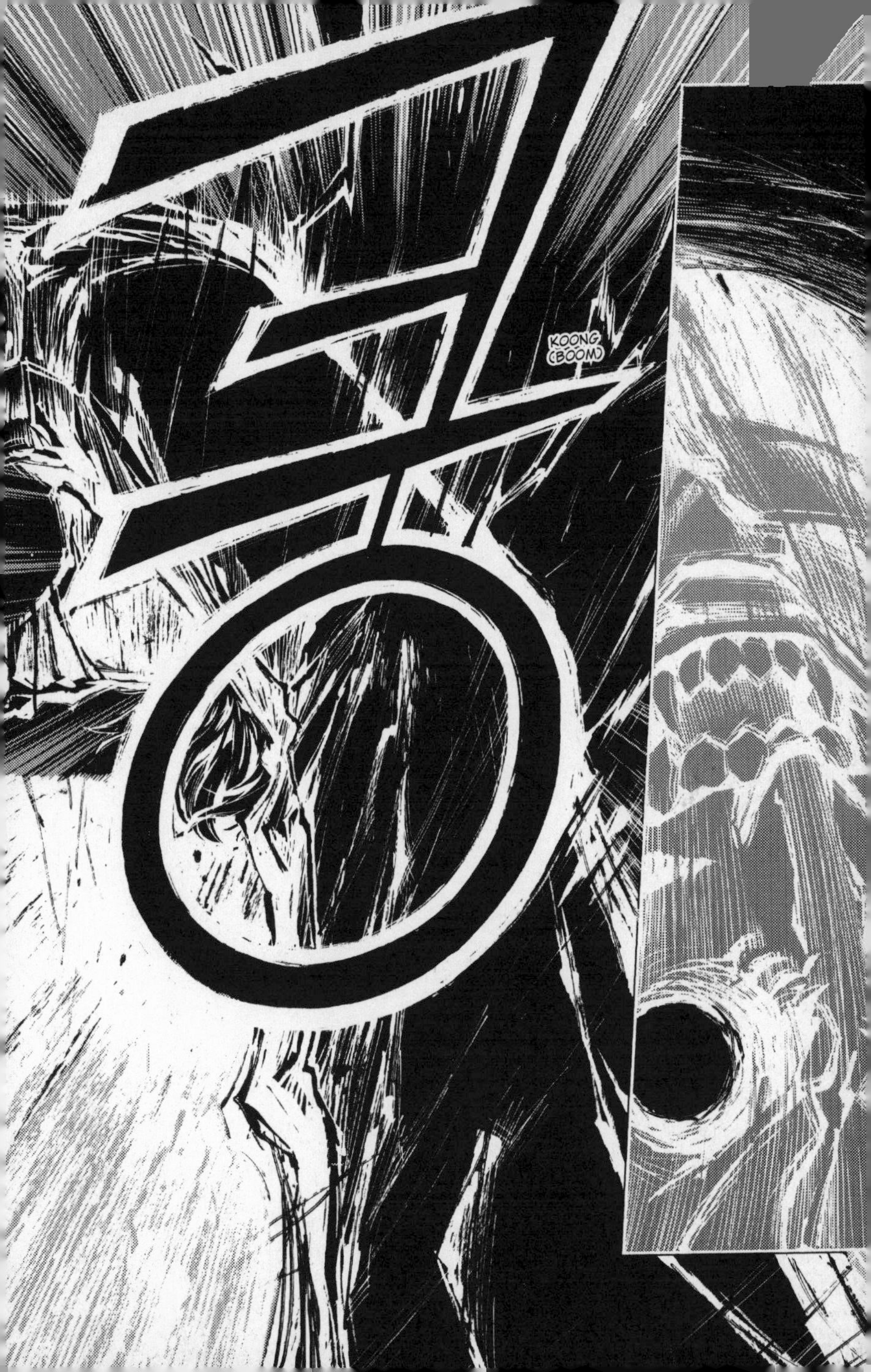
KOONG
(BOOM)

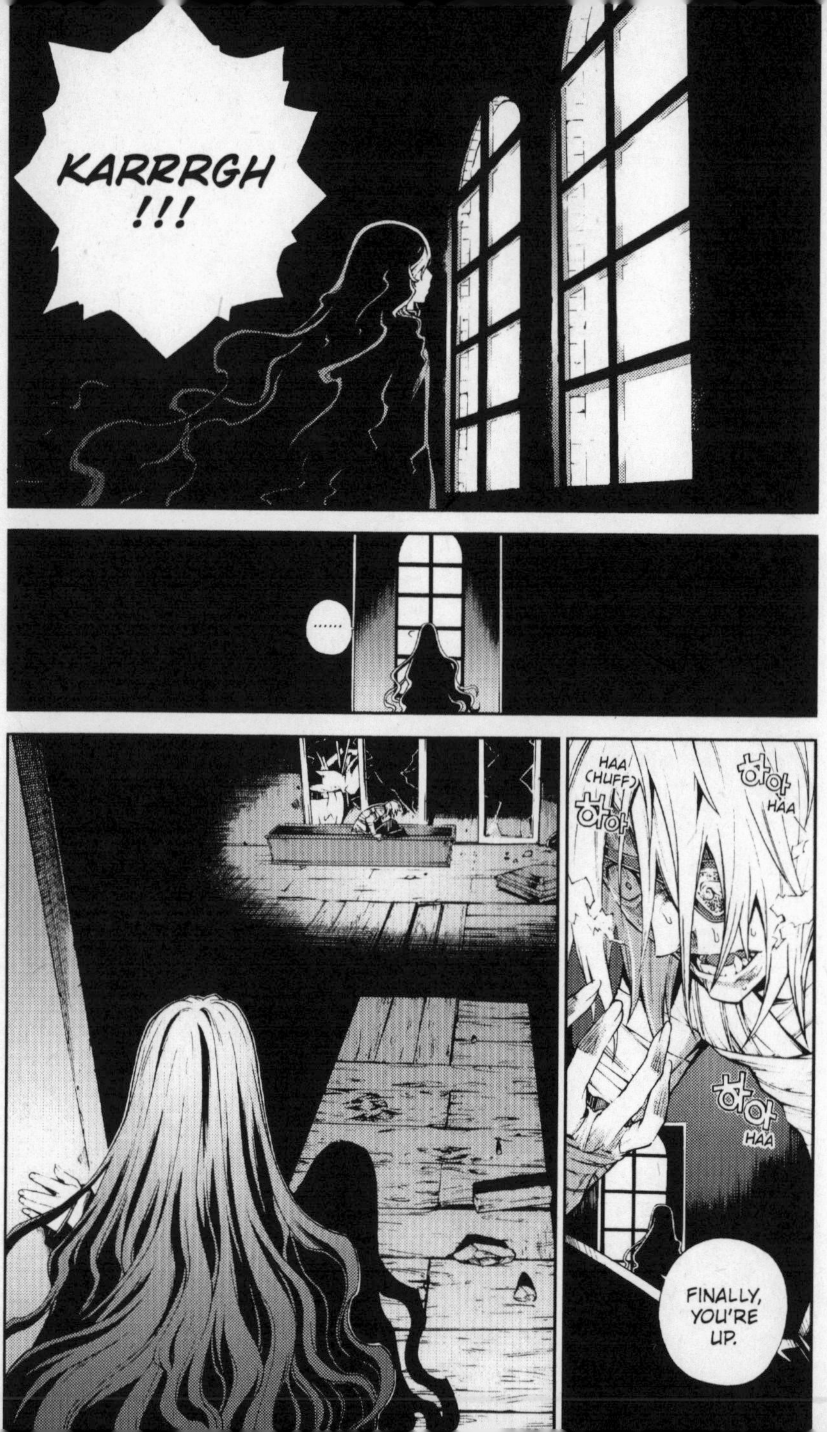
KARRRGH !!!
......
HAA (HUFF)
하아
하아
HAA
하아
HAA
FINALLY, YOU'RE UP.

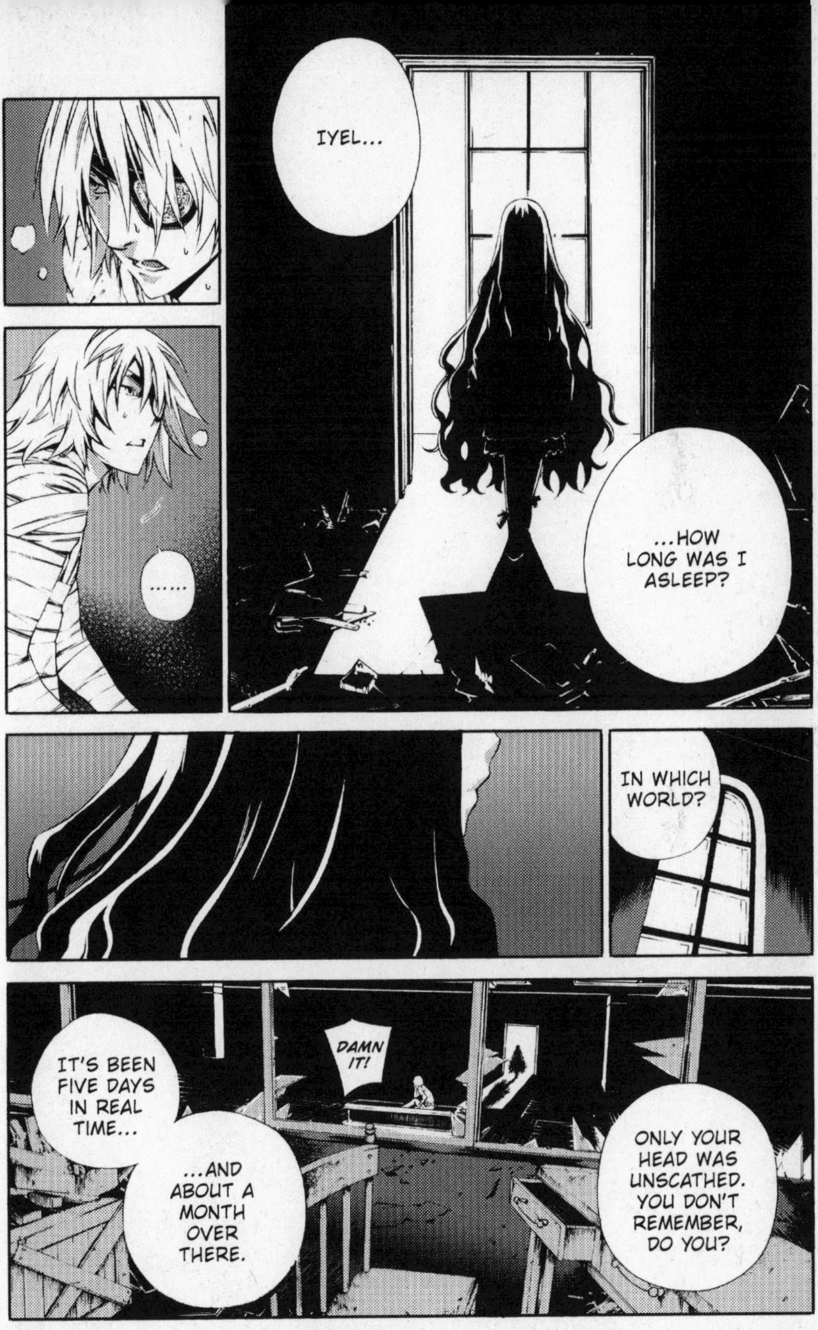
IYEL...
......
...HOW LONG WAS I ASLEEP?
IN WHICH WORLD?
IT'S BEEN FIVE DAYS IN REAL TIME...
...AND ABOUT A MONTH OVER THERE.
DAMN IT!
ONLY YOUR HEAD WAS UNSCATHED. YOU DON'T REMEMBER, DO YOU?

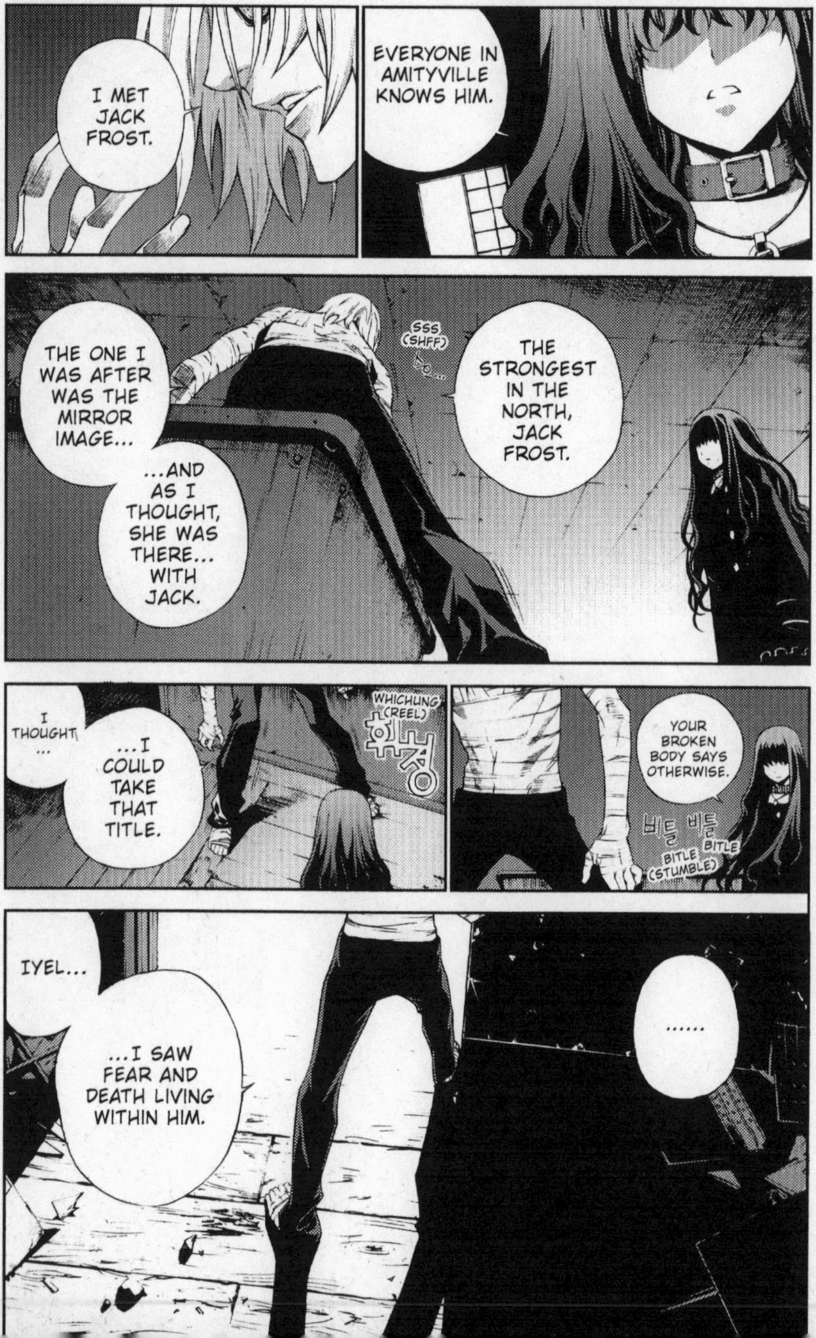
I MET JACK FROST.
EVERYONE IN AMITYVILLE KNOWS HIM.
THE ONE I WAS AFTER WAS THE MIRROR IMAGE...
...AND AS I THOUGHT, SHE WAS THERE... WITH JACK.
SSS (SHFF)
THE STRONGEST IN THE NORTH, JACK FROST.
I THOUGHT...
...I COULD TAKE THAT TITLE.
WHICHUNG (REEL)
휘청
YOUR BROKEN BODY SAYS OTHERWISE.
비틀 비틀
BITLE BITLE (STUMBLE)
IYEL...
...I SAW FEAR AND DEATH LIVING WITHIN HIM.
......

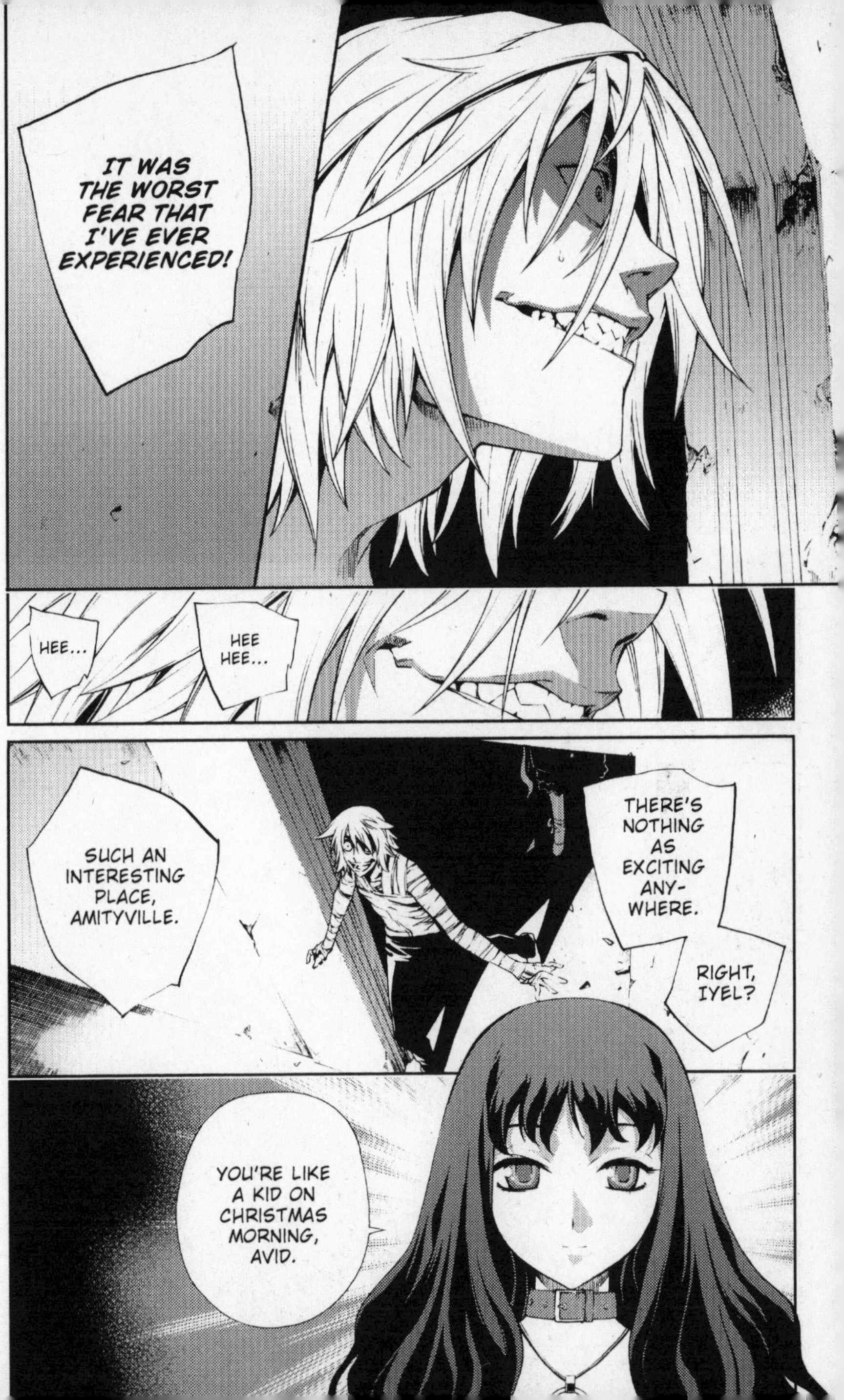
IT WAS THE WORST FEAR THAT I'VE EVER EXPERIENCED!
HEE...
HEE HEE...
SUCH AN INTERESTING PLACE, AMITYVILLE.
THERE'S NOTHING AS EXCITING ANY-WHERE.
RIGHT, IYEL?
YOU'RE LIKE A KID ON CHRISTMAS MORNING, AVID.

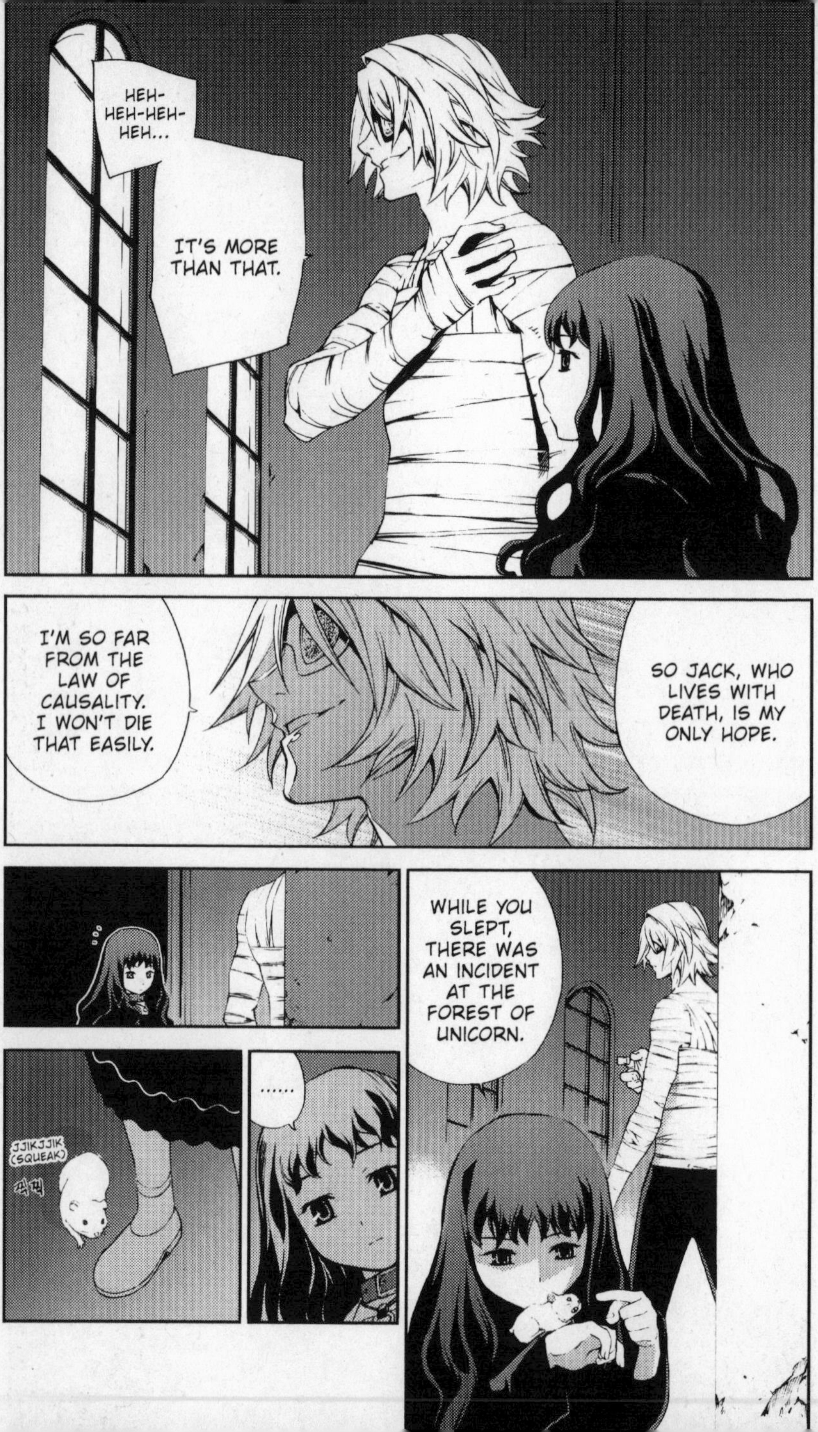
HEH-HEH-HEH-HEH...
IT'S MORE THAN THAT.
I'M SO FAR FROM THE LAW OF CAUSALITY. I WON'T DIE THAT EASILY.
SO JACK, WHO LIVES WITH DEATH, IS MY ONLY HOPE.
JJIKJJIK (SQUEAK)
......
WHILE YOU SLEPT, THERE WAS AN INCIDENT AT THE FOREST OF UNICORN.

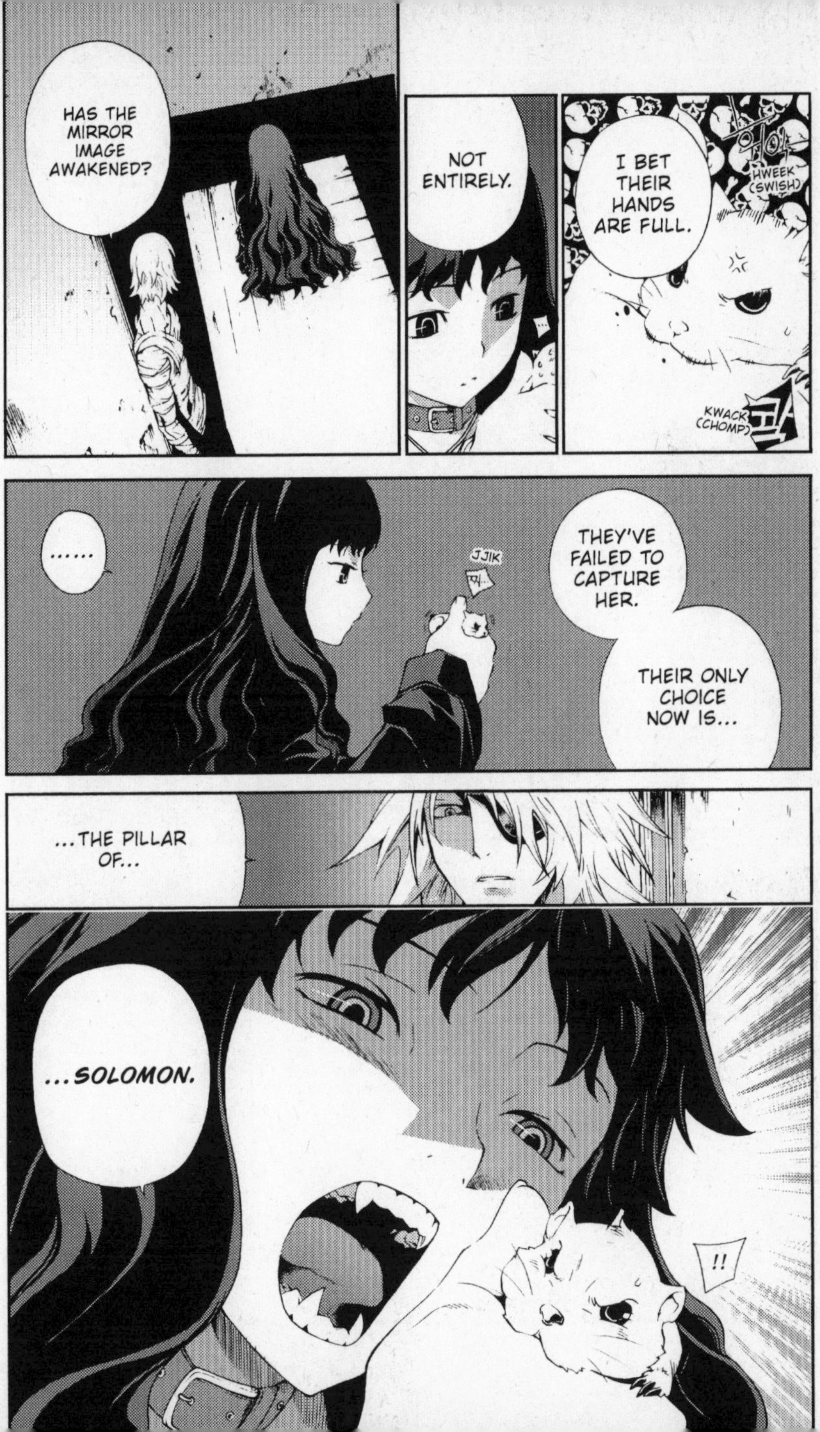
HAS THE MIRROR IMAGE AWAKENED?
NOT ENTIRELY.
...
I BET THEIR HANDS ARE FULL.
HWEEK (SWISH)
KWACK (CHOMP)
......
JJIK
THEY'VE FAILED TO CAPTURE HER.
THEIR ONLY CHOICE NOW IS...
...THE PILLAR OF...
...SOLOMON.
!!

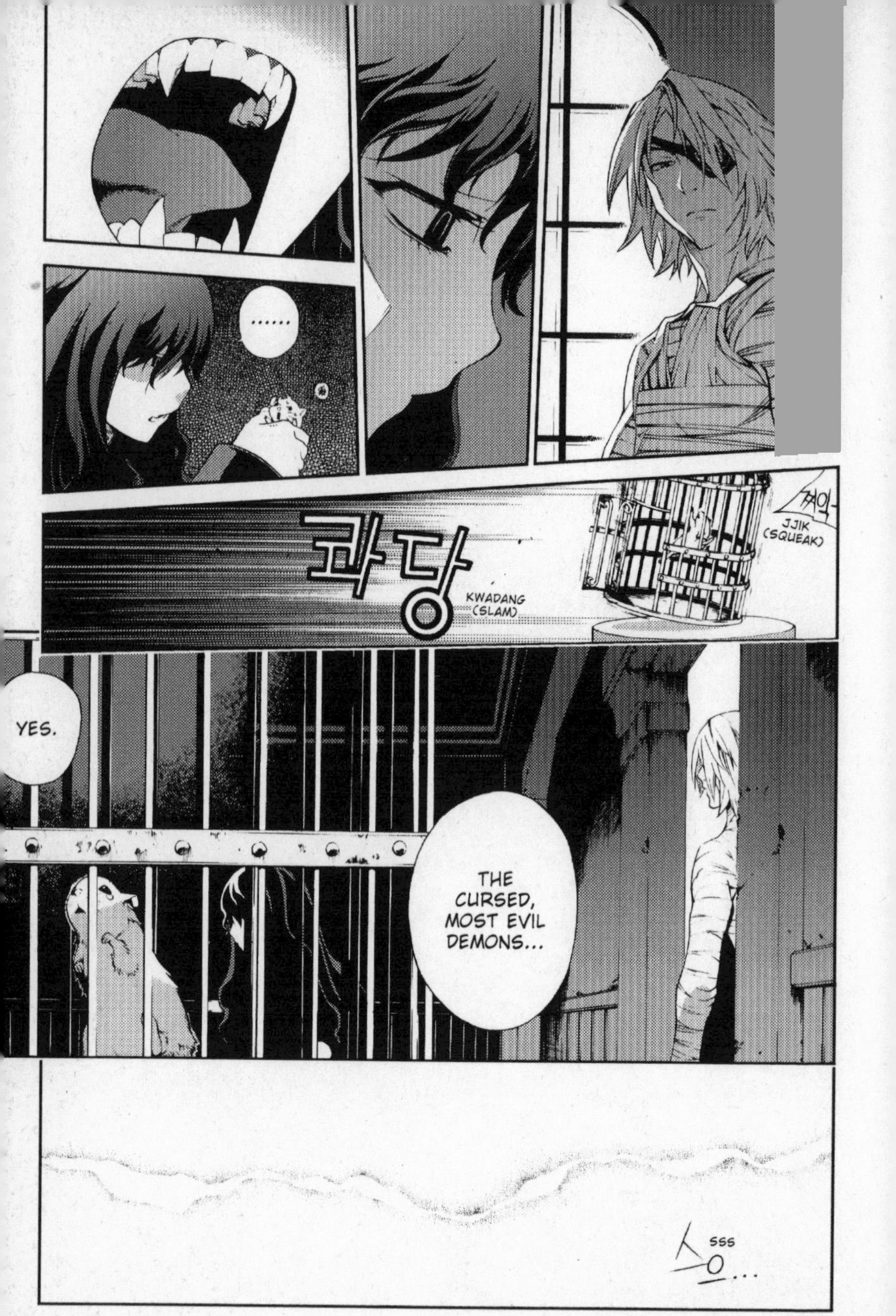
......
콰당
KWADANG (SLAM)
JJIK (SQUEAK)
YES.
THE CURSED, MOST EVIL DEMONS...
스으...
SSS

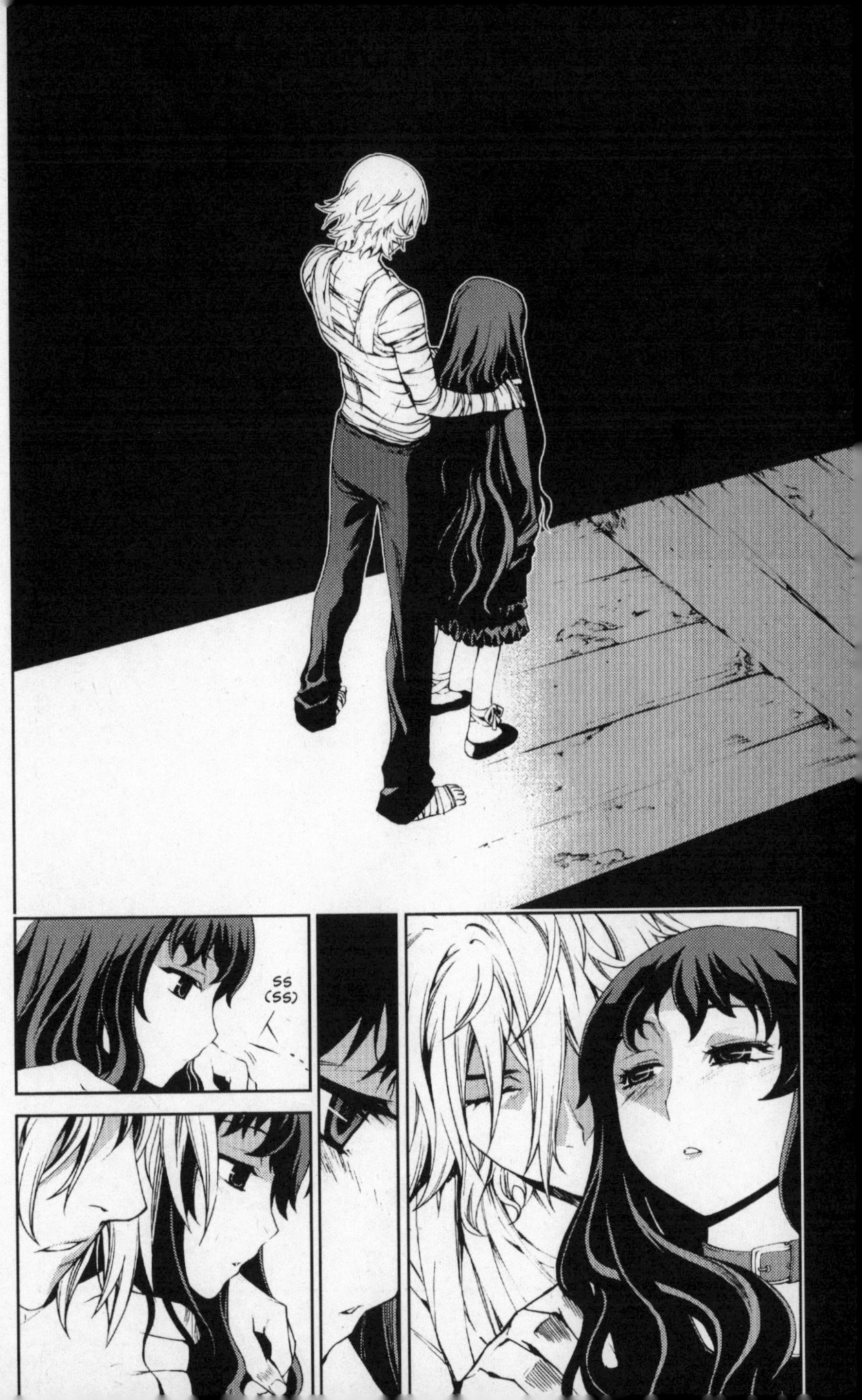
SS
(SS)

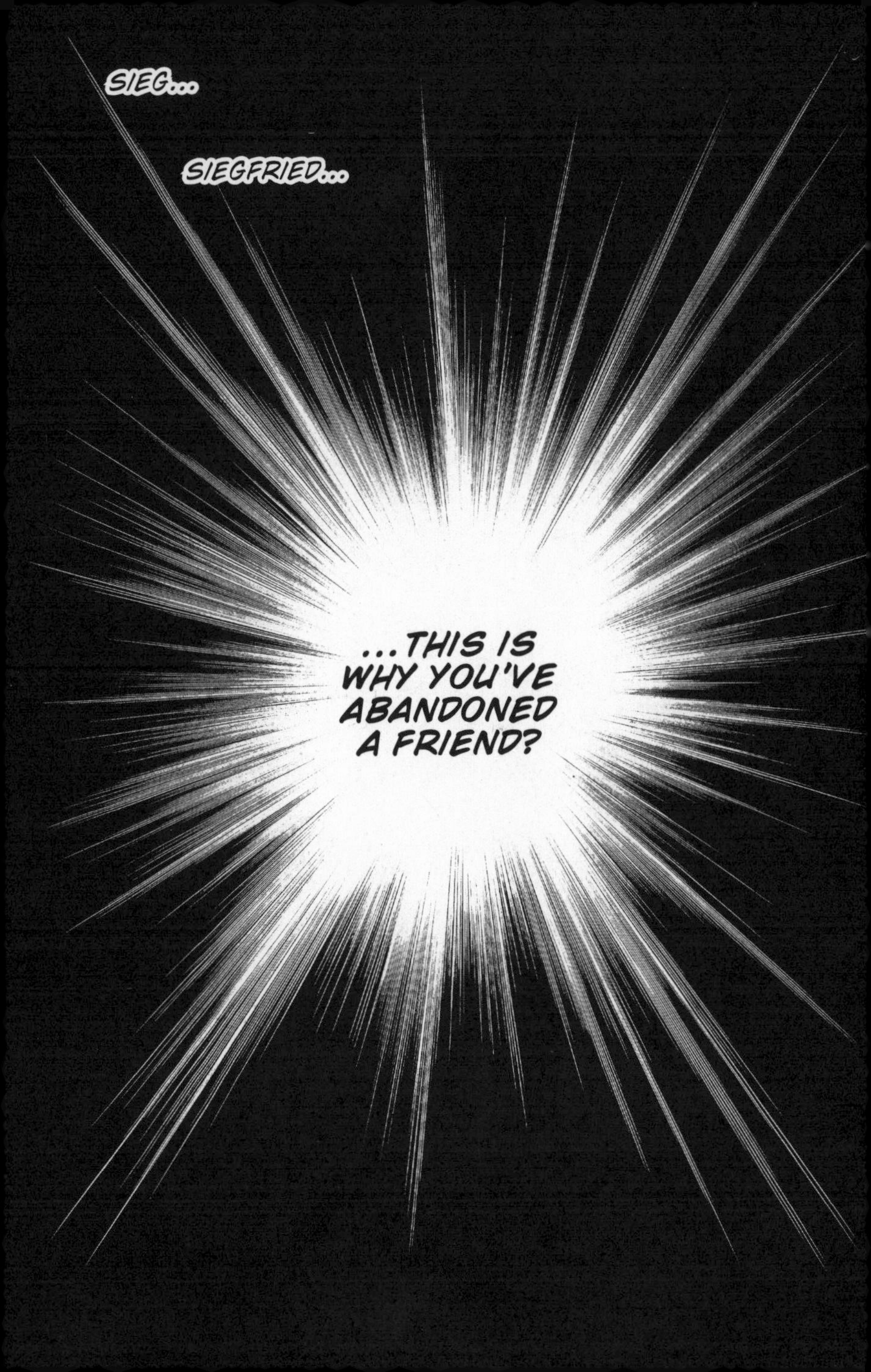
SIEG...
SIEGFRIED...
...THIS IS WHY YOU'VE ABANDONED A FRIEND?

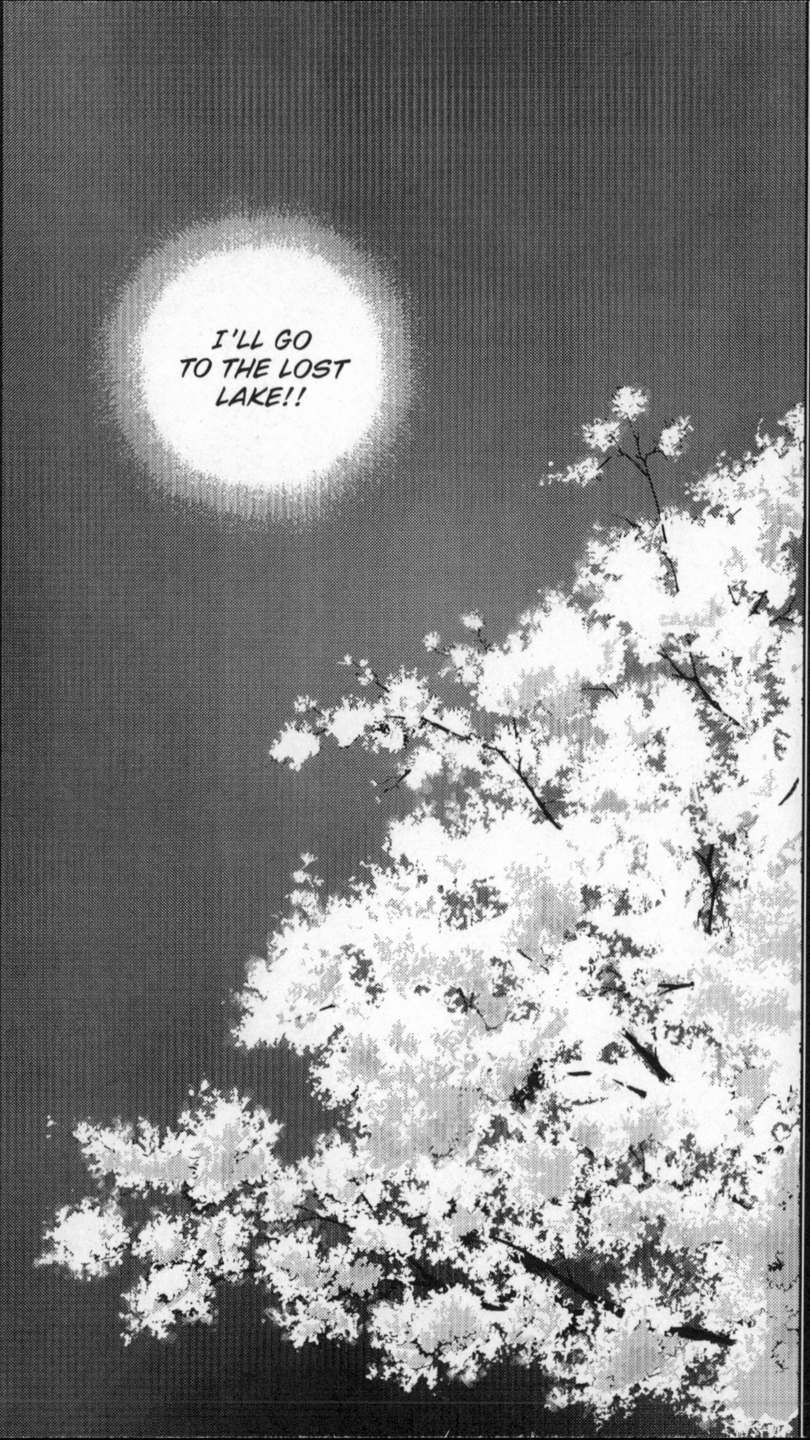
I'LL GO TO THE LOST LAKE!!

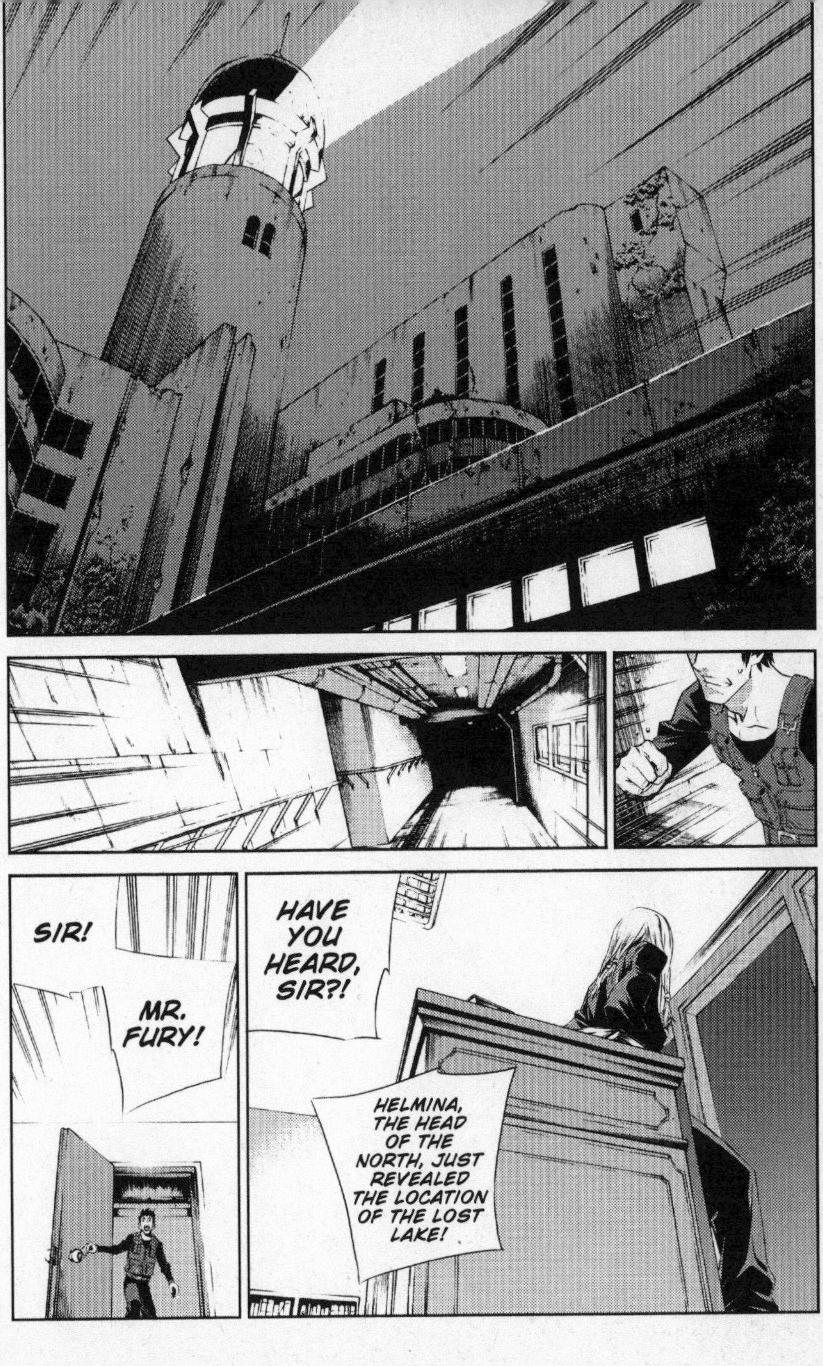
SIR!
MR. FURY!
HAVE YOU HEARD, SIR?!
HELMINA, THE HEAD OF THE NORTH, JUST REVEALED THE LOCATION OF THE LOST LAKE!

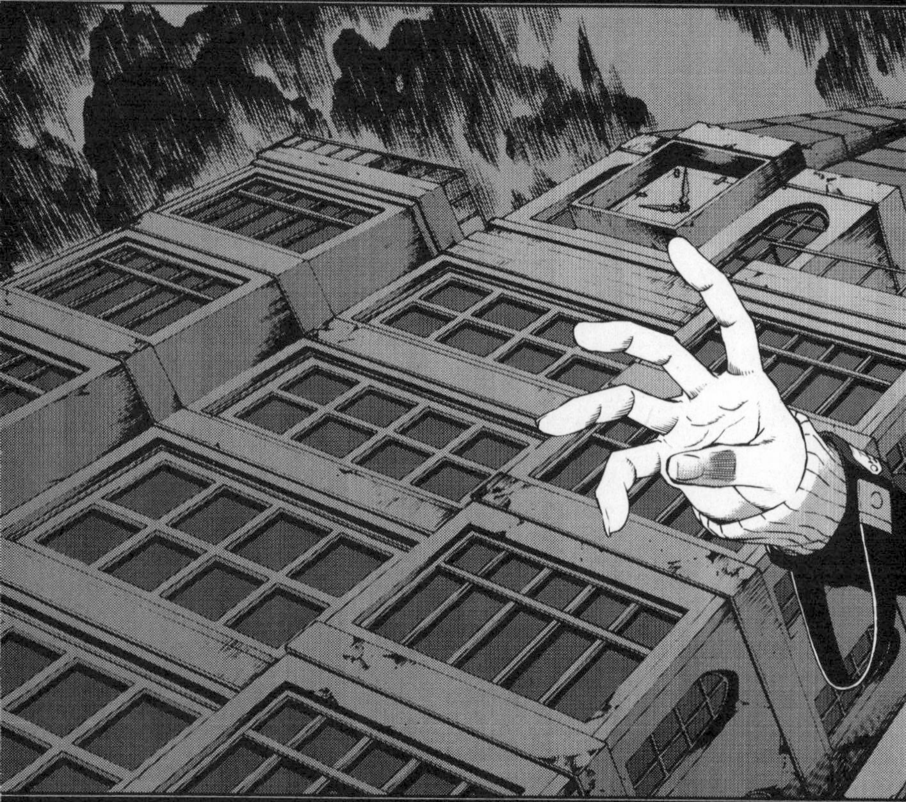

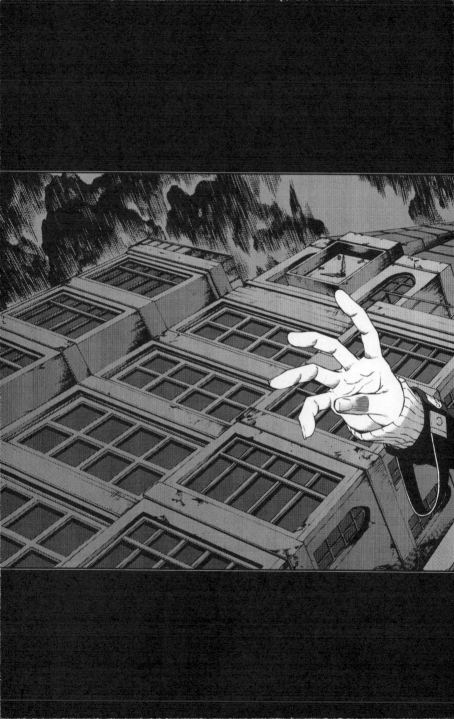

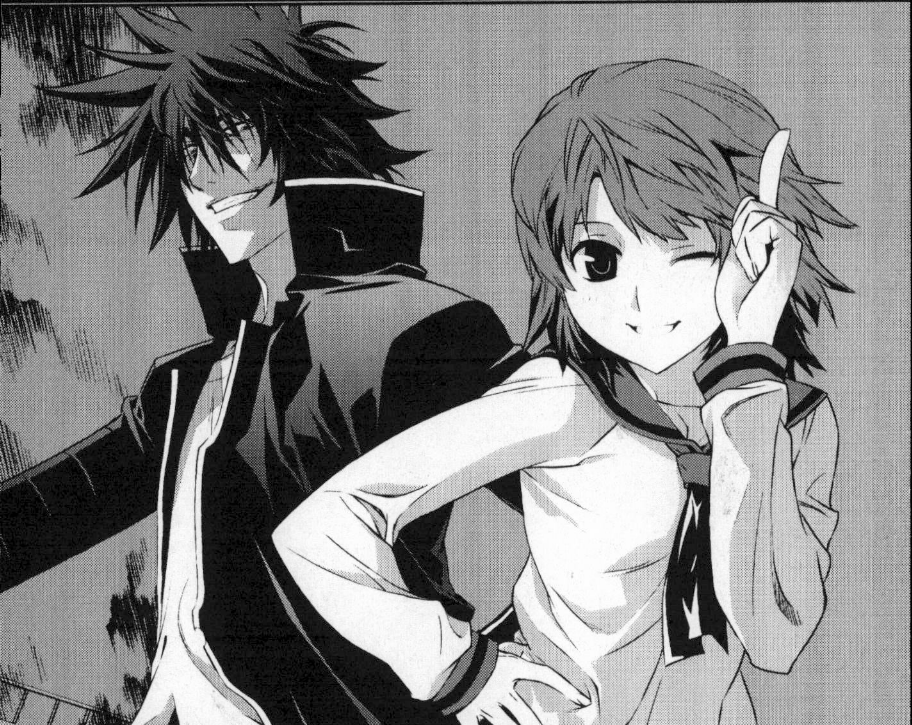

VIOLENCE 26.
DER FREISCHÜTZ - PART I

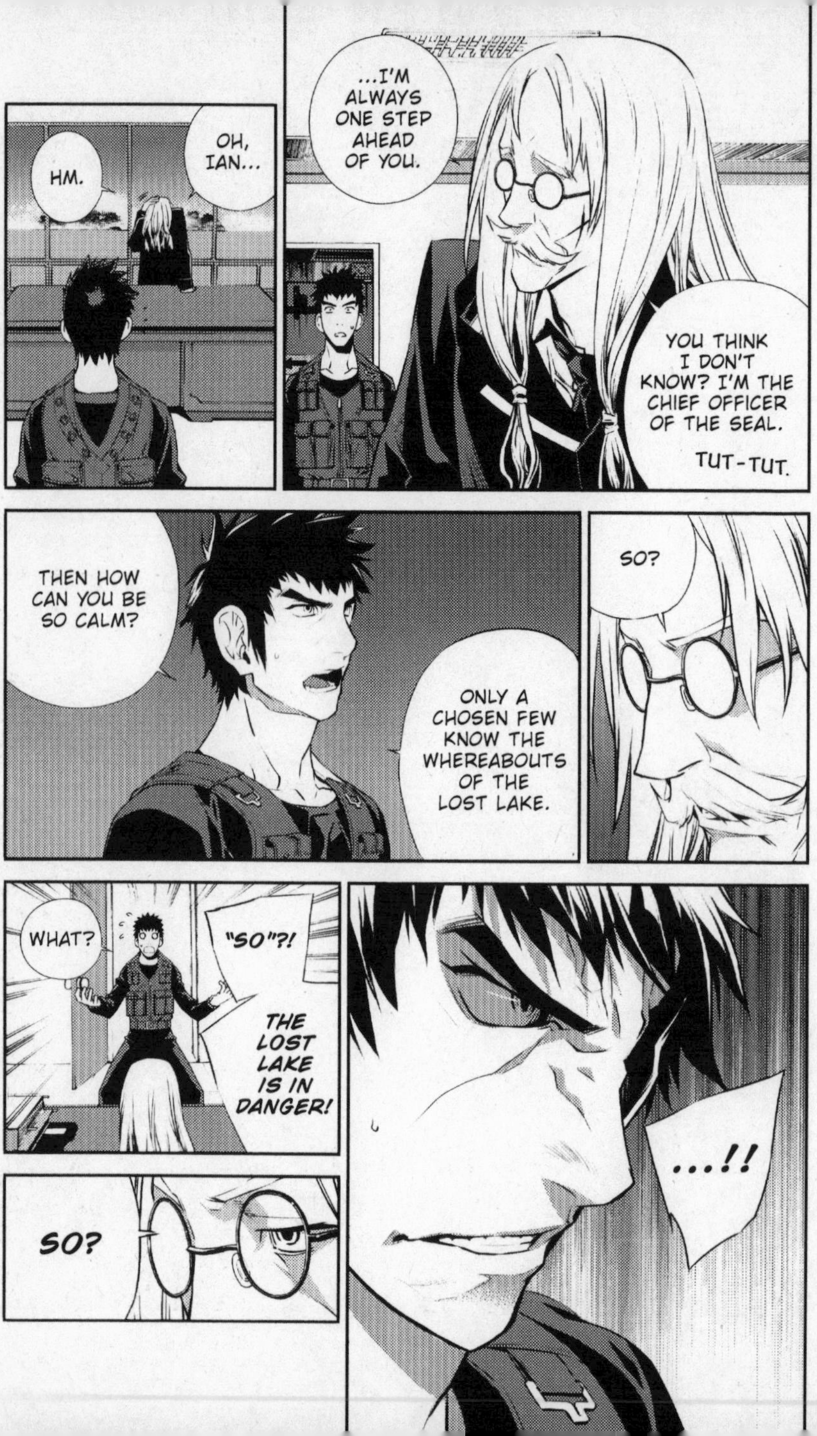
HM.
OH, IAN...
...I'M ALWAYS ONE STEP AHEAD OF YOU.
YOU THINK I DON'T KNOW? I'M THE CHIEF OFFICER OF THE SEAL.
TUT-TUT.
THEN HOW CAN YOU BE SO CALM?
ONLY A CHOSEN FEW KNOW THE WHEREABOUTS OF THE LOST LAKE.
SO?
WHAT?
"SO"?!
THE LOST LAKE IS IN DANGER!
SO?
...!!

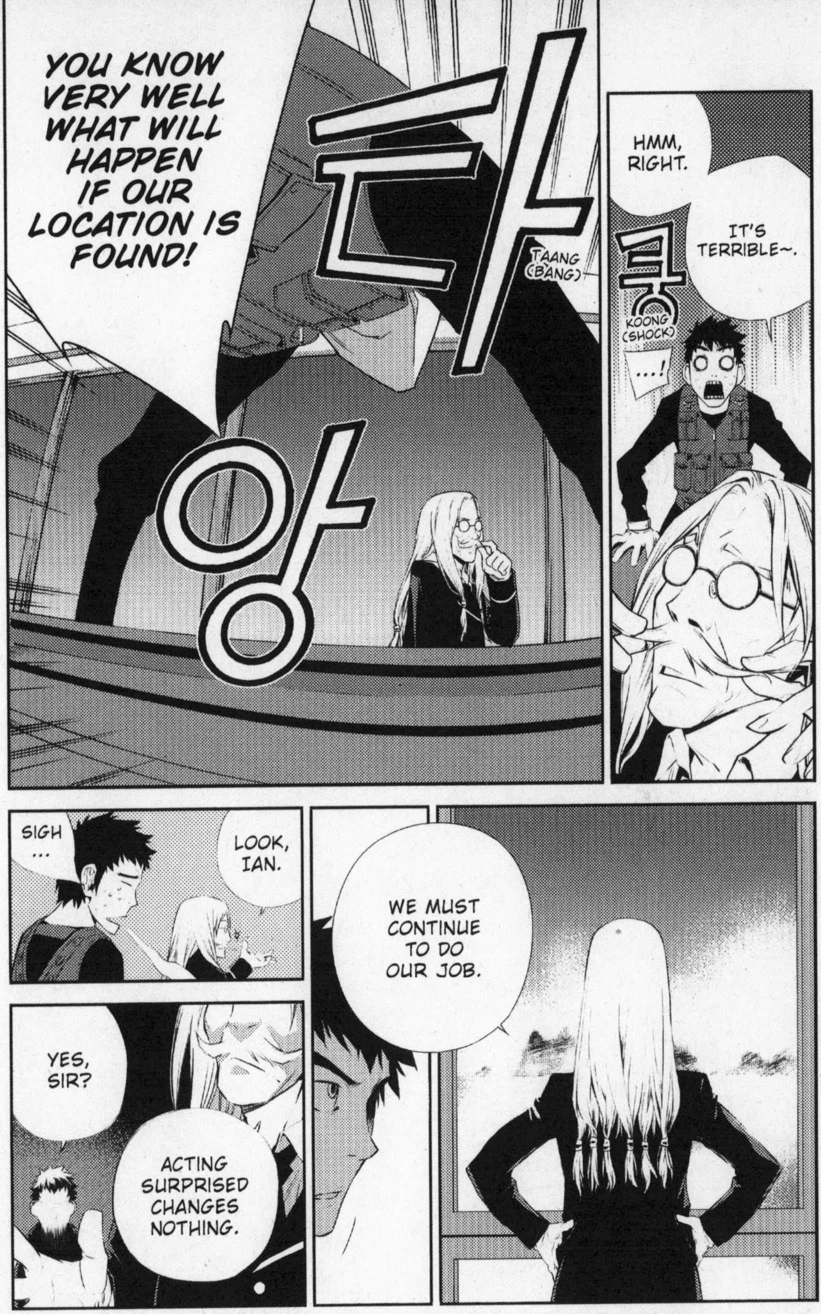
YOU KNOW VERY WELL WHAT WILL HAPPEN IF OUR LOCATION IS FOUND!
타앙
TAANG (BANG)
HMM, RIGHT.
IT'S TERRIBLE~.
쿵
KOONG (SHOCK)
...!
SIGH ...
LOOK, IAN.
YES, SIR?
ACTING SURPRISED CHANGES NOTHING.
WE MUST CONTINUE TO DO OUR JOB.

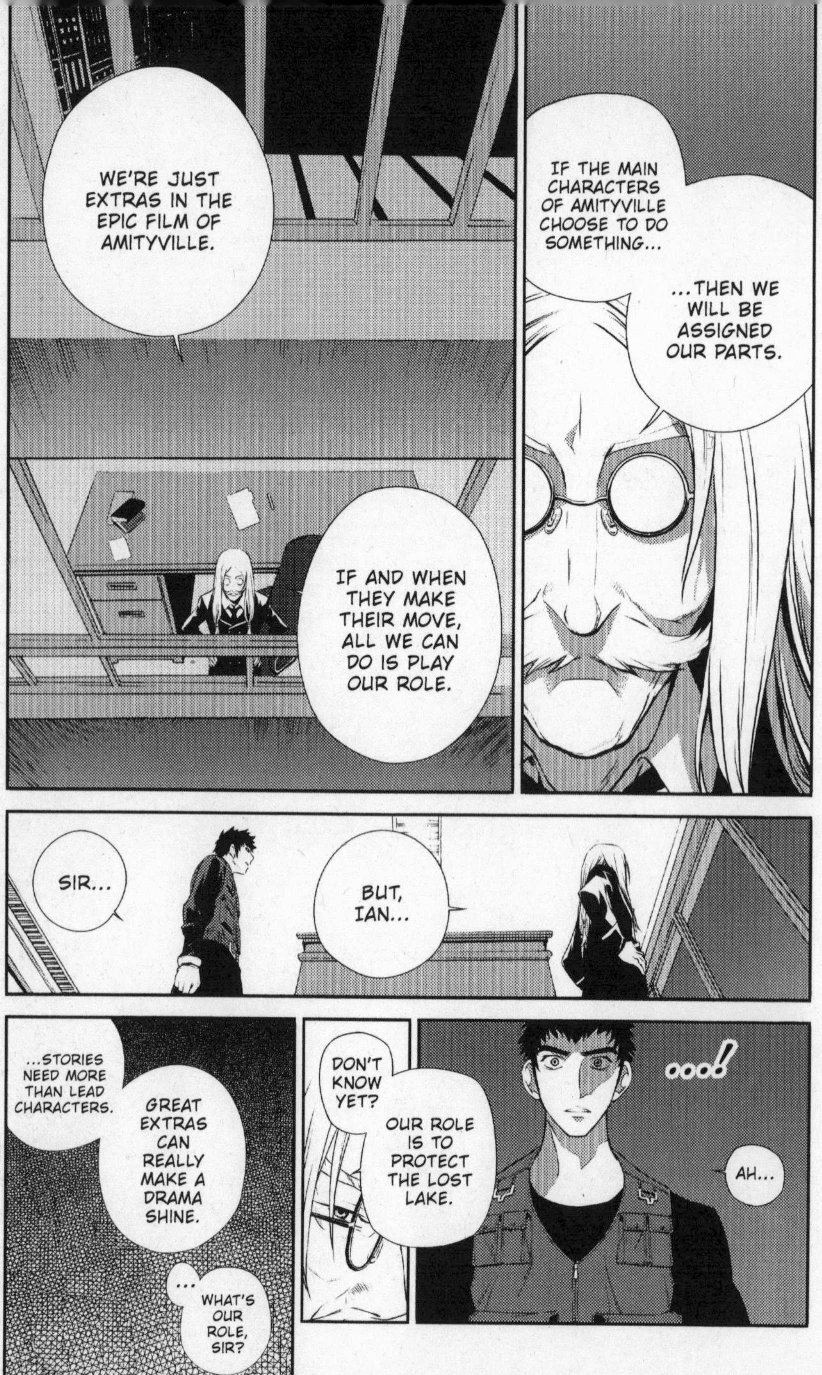
WE'RE JUST EXTRAS IN THE EPIC FILM OF AMITYVILLE.
IF AND WHEN THEY MAKE THEIR MOVE, ALL WE CAN DO IS PLAY OUR ROLE.
IF THE MAIN CHARACTERS OF AMITYVILLE CHOOSE TO DO SOMETHING...
...THEN WE WILL BE ASSIGNED OUR PARTS.
SIR...
BUT, IAN...
...STORIES NEED MORE THAN LEAD CHARACTERS.
GREAT EXTRAS CAN REALLY MAKE A DRAMA SHINE.
...
WHAT'S OUR ROLE, SIR?
DON'T KNOW YET?
OUR ROLE IS TO PROTECT THE LOST LAKE.
ooo!
AH...

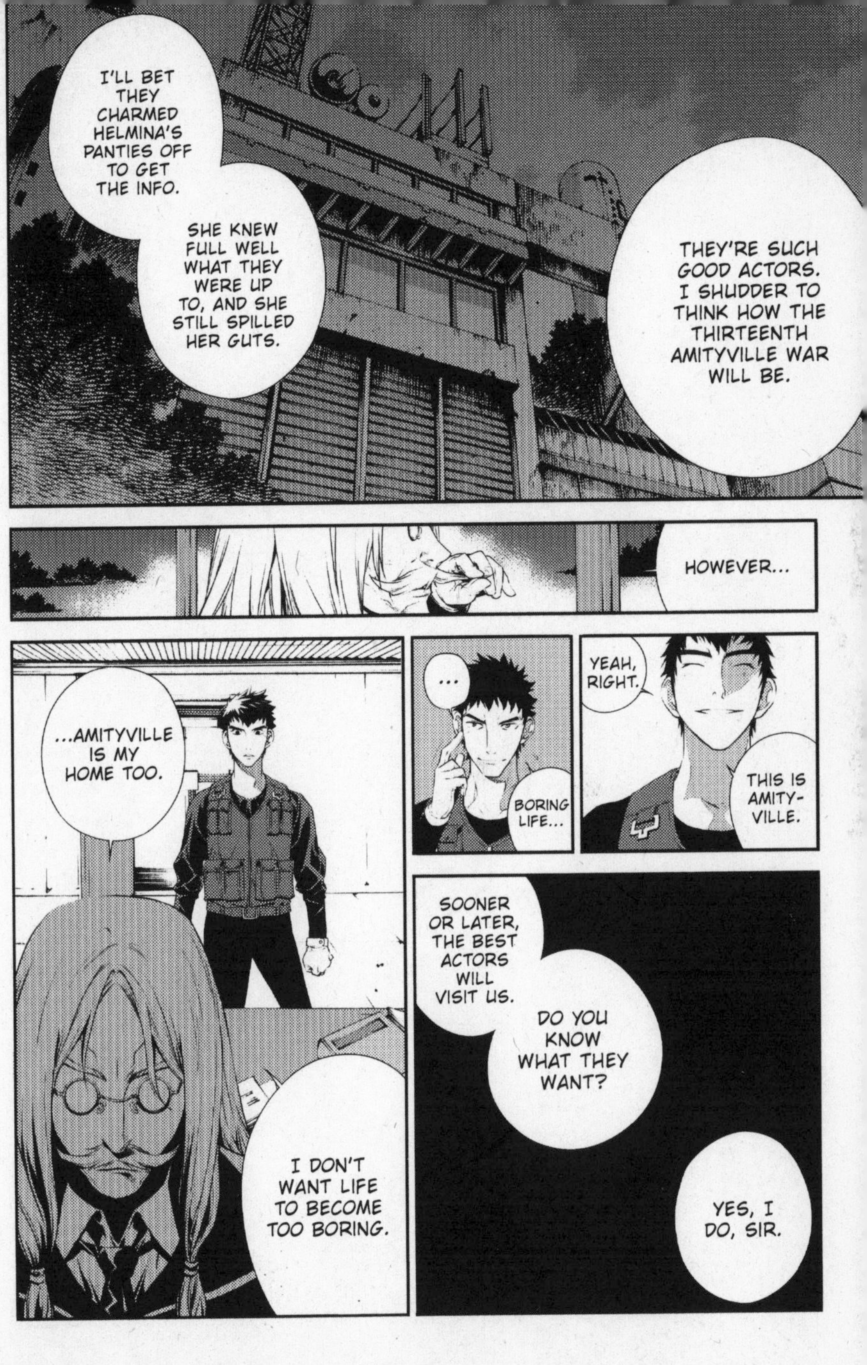
I'LL BET THEY CHARMED HELMINA'S PANTIES OFF TO GET THE INFO.
SHE KNEW FULL WELL WHAT THEY WERE UP TO, AND SHE STILL SPILLED HER GUTS.
THEY'RE SUCH GOOD ACTORS. I SHUDDER TO THINK HOW THE THIRTEENTH AMITYVILLE WAR WILL BE.
HOWEVER...
...AMITYVILLE IS MY HOME TOO.
I DON'T WANT LIFE TO BECOME TOO BORING.
...
BORING LIFE...
YEAH, RIGHT.
THIS IS AMITY-VILLE.
SOONER OR LATER, THE BEST ACTORS WILL VISIT US.
DO YOU KNOW WHAT THEY WANT?
YES, I DO, SIR.

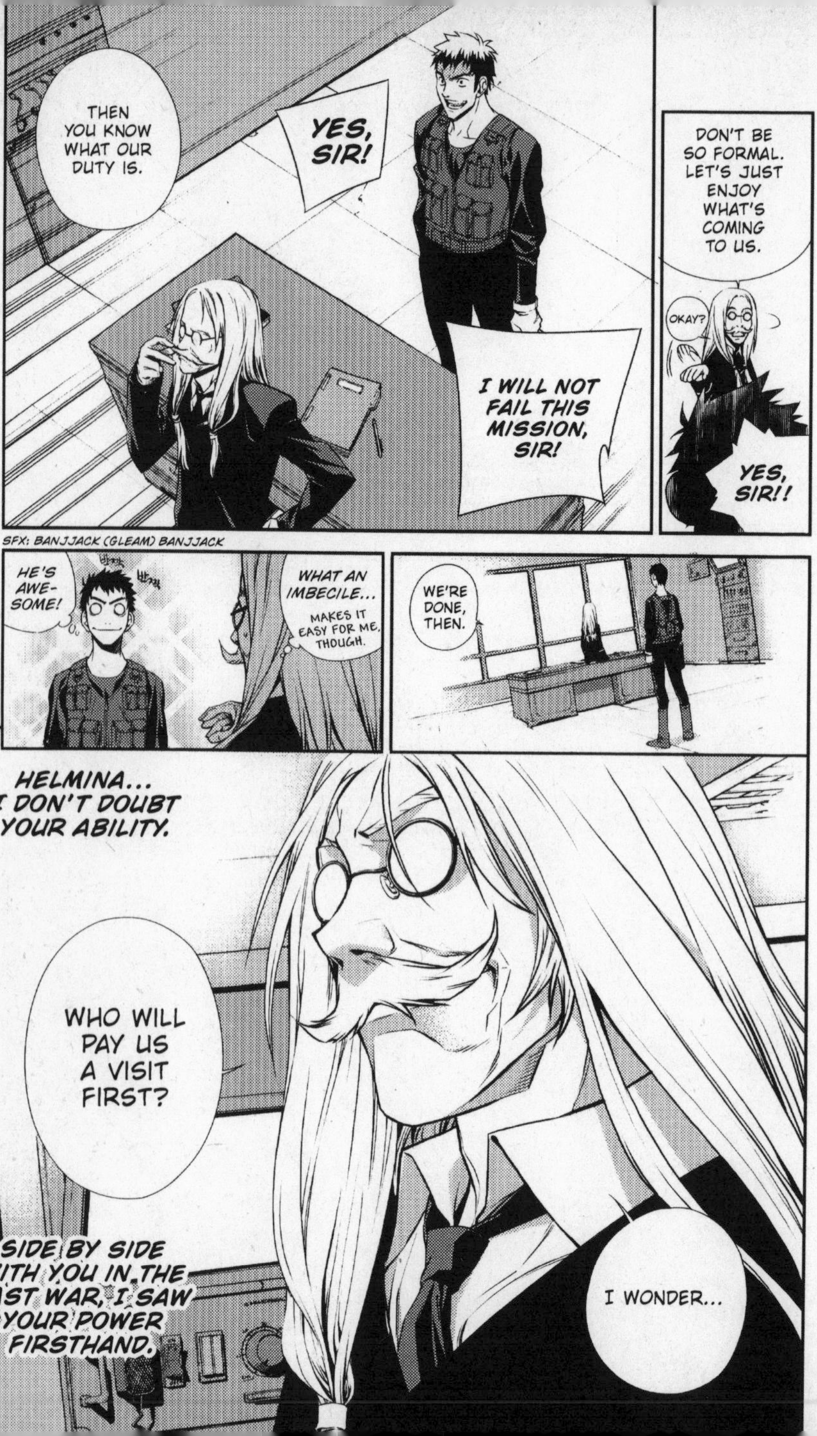
THEN YOU KNOW WHAT OUR DUTY IS.
YES, SIR!
I WILL NOT FAIL THIS MISSION, SIR!
DON'T BE SO FORMAL. LET'S JUST ENJOY WHAT'S COMING TO US.
OKAY?
YES, SIR!!
SFX: BANJJACK (GLEAM) BANJJACK
HE'S AWE-SOME!
WHAT AN IMBECILE...
MAKES IT EASY FOR ME, THOUGH.
WE'RE DONE, THEN.
HELMINA... I DON'T DOUBT YOUR ABILITY.
WHO WILL PAY US A VISIT FIRST?
SIDE BY SIDE WITH YOU IN THE LAST WAR, I SAW YOUR POWER FIRSTHAND.
I WONDER...

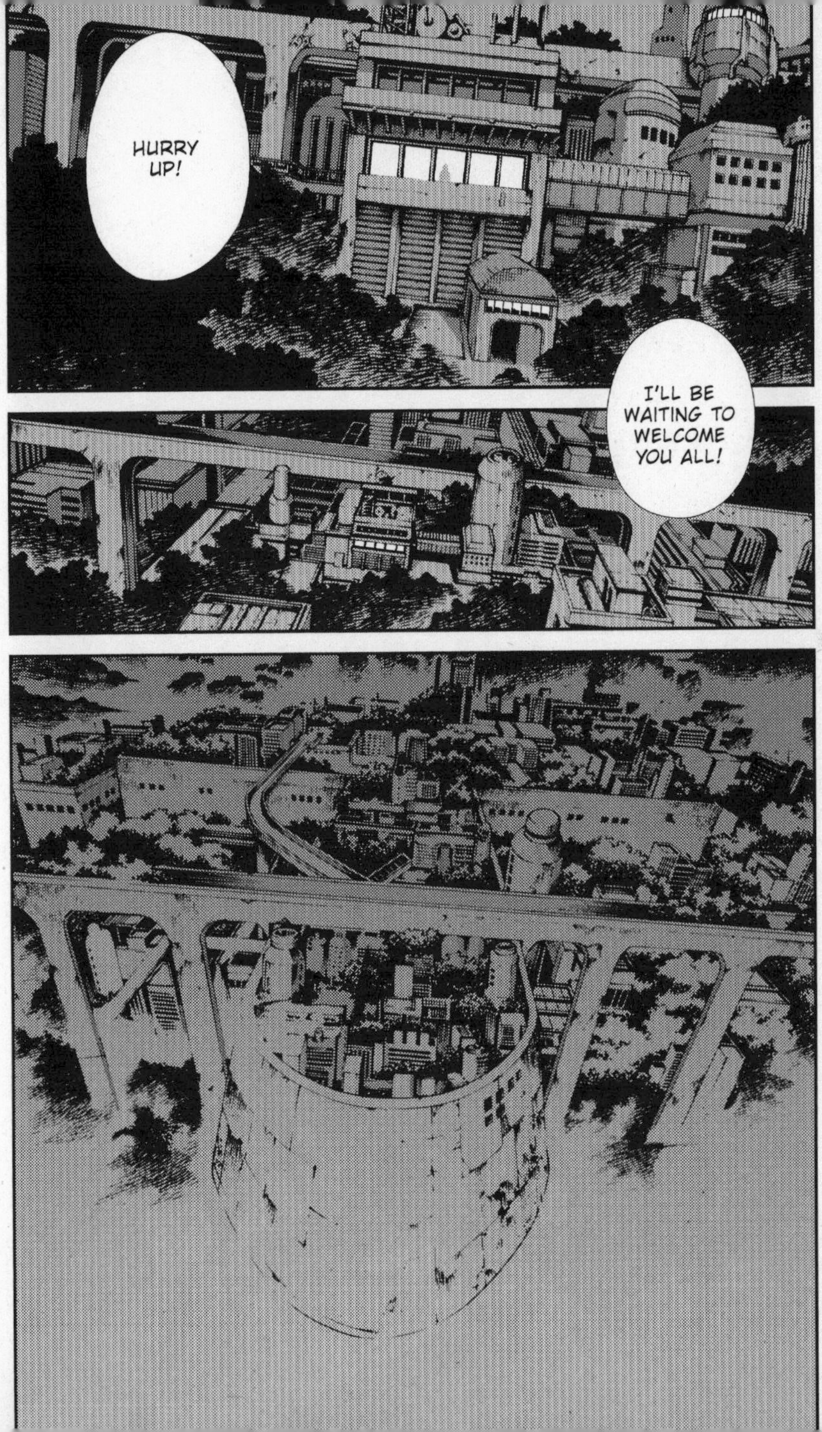
HURRY UP!
I'LL BE WAITING TO WELCOME YOU ALL!

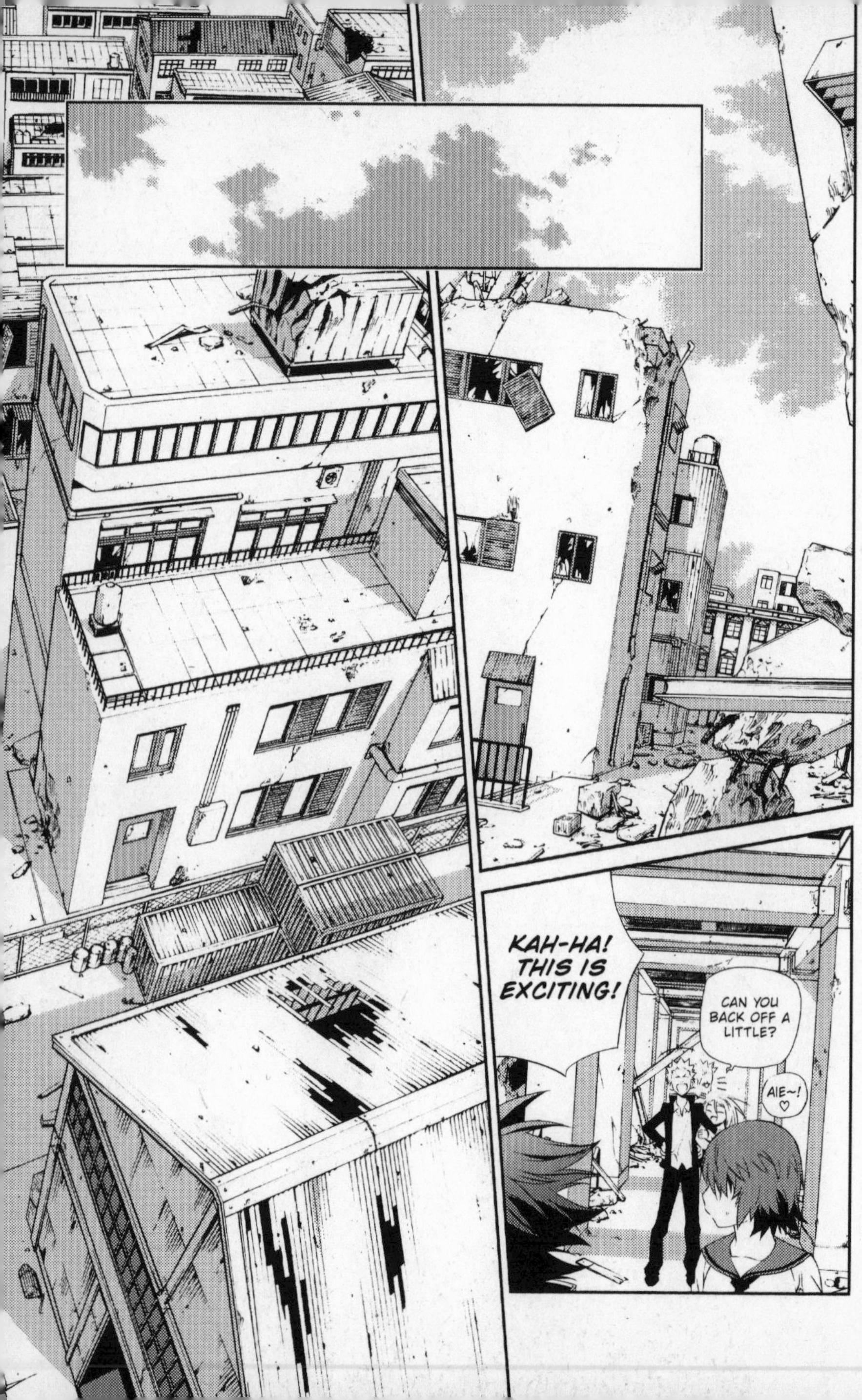
KAH-HA! THIS IS EXCITING!
CAN YOU BACK OFF A LITTLE?
AIE~! ♡

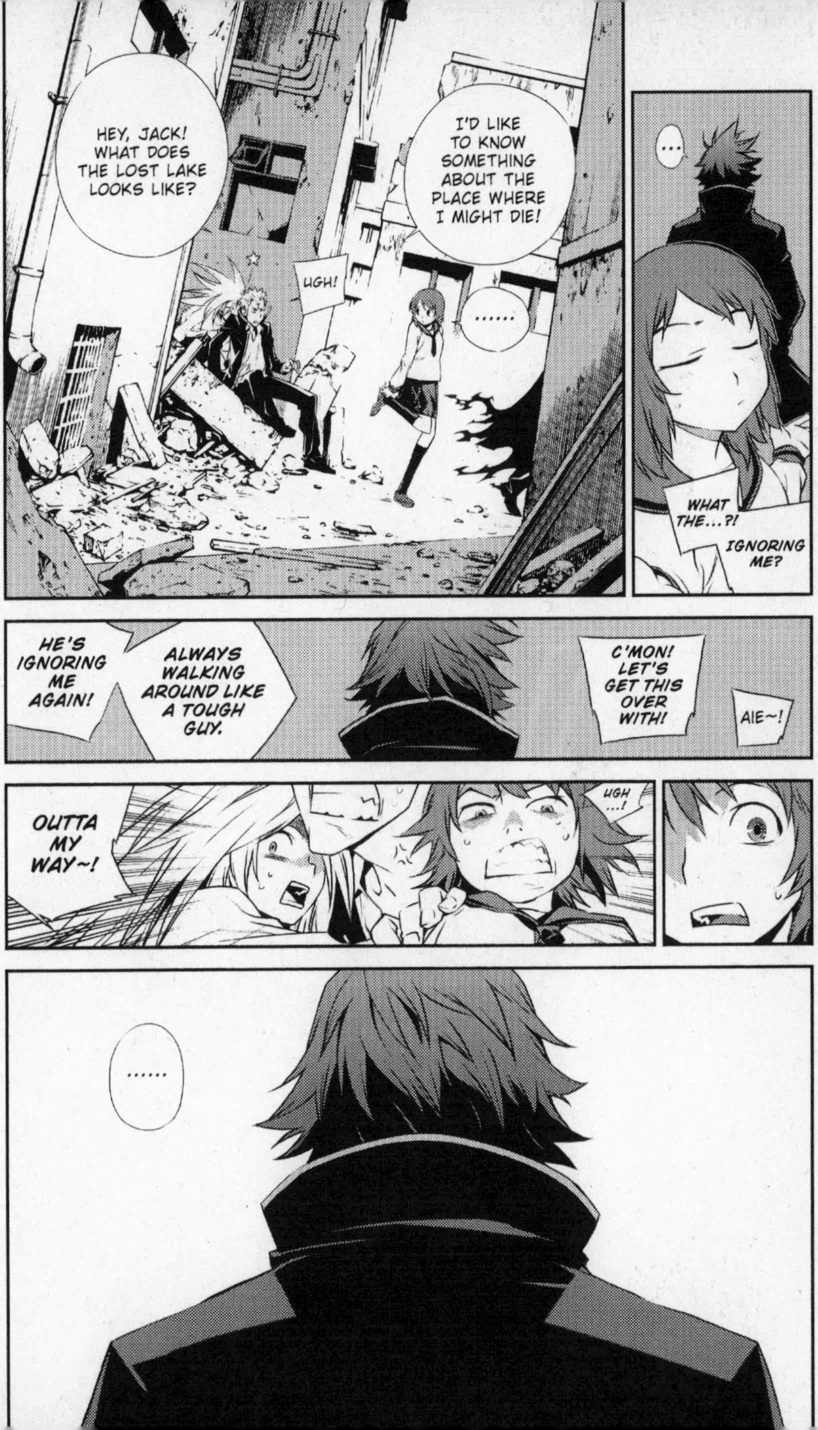
HEY, JACK! WHAT DOES THE LOST LAKE LOOKS LIKE?
I'D LIKE TO KNOW SOMETHING ABOUT THE PLACE WHERE I MIGHT DIE!
UGH!
......
...
WHAT THE...?!
IGNORING ME?
HE'S IGNORING ME AGAIN!
ALWAYS WALKING AROUND LIKE A TOUGH GUY.
C'MON! LET'S GET THIS OVER WITH!
AIE~!
OUTTA MY WAY~!
UGH ...!
......

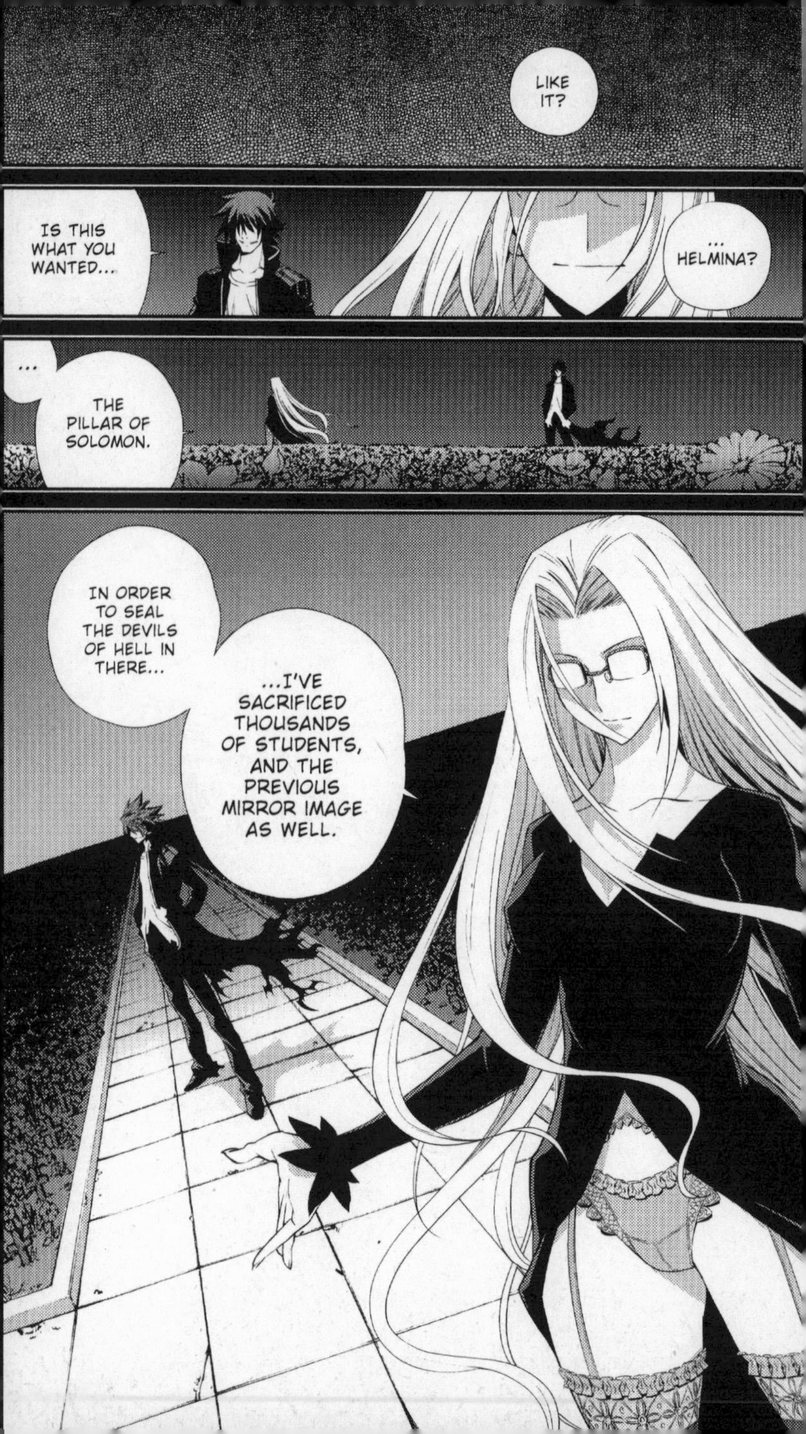
LIKE IT?
IS THIS WHAT YOU WANTED...
...HELMINA?
...
THE PILLAR OF SOLOMON.
IN ORDER TO SEAL THE DEVILS OF HELL IN THERE...
...I'VE SACRIFICED THOUSANDS OF STUDENTS, AND THE PREVIOUS MIRROR IMAGE AS WELL.

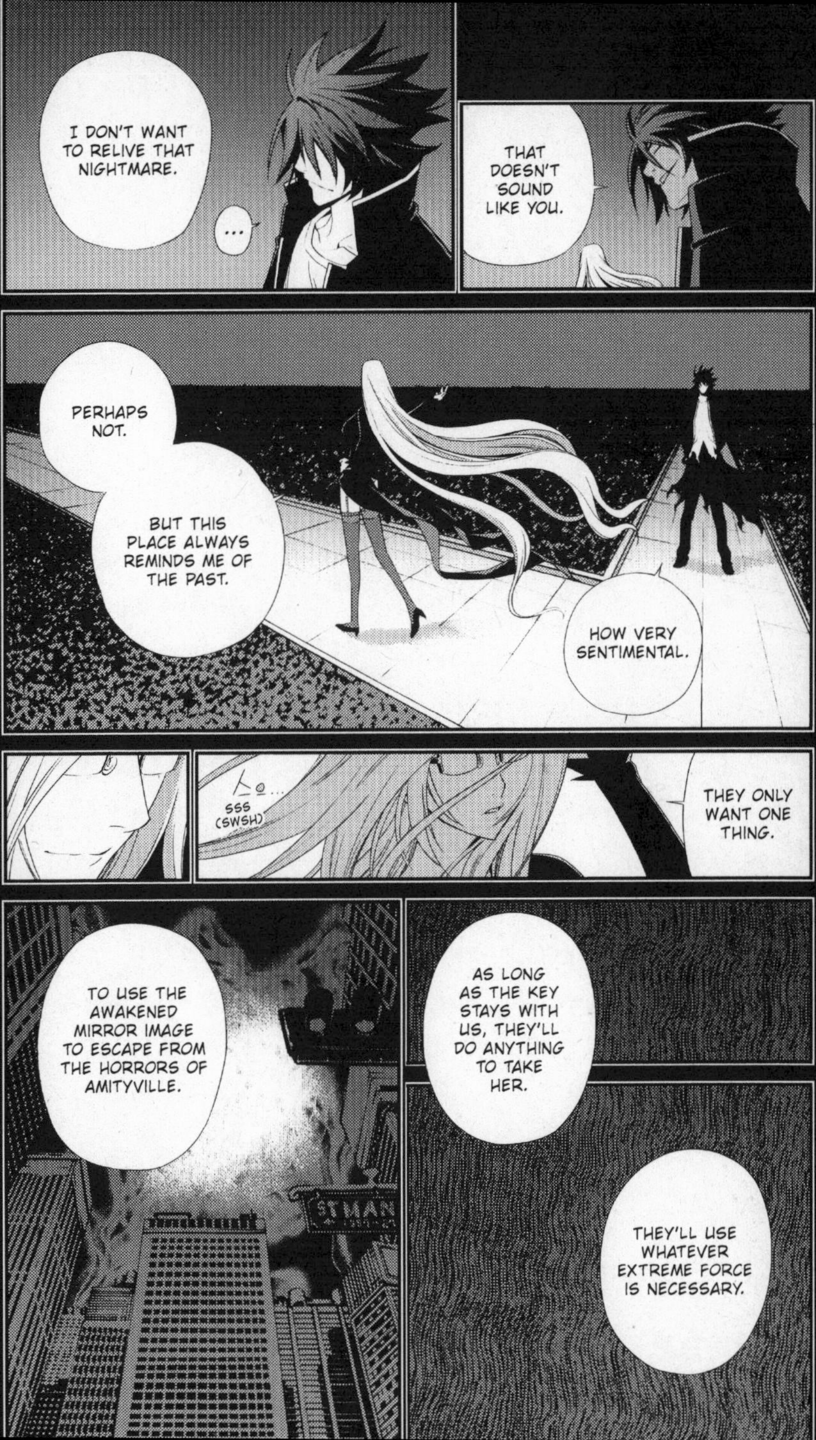

I DON'T WANT TO RELIVE THAT NIGHTMARE.
...
THAT DOESN'T SOUND LIKE YOU.
PERHAPS NOT.
BUT THIS PLACE ALWAYS REMINDS ME OF THE PAST.
HOW VERY SENTIMENTAL.
스으...
SSS (SWSH)
THEY ONLY WANT ONE THING.
TO USE THE AWAKENED MIRROR IMAGE TO ESCAPE FROM THE HORRORS OF AMITYVILLE.
AS LONG AS THE KEY STAYS WITH US, THEY'LL DO ANYTHING TO TAKE HER.
THEY'LL USE WHATEVER EXTREME FORCE IS NECESSARY.

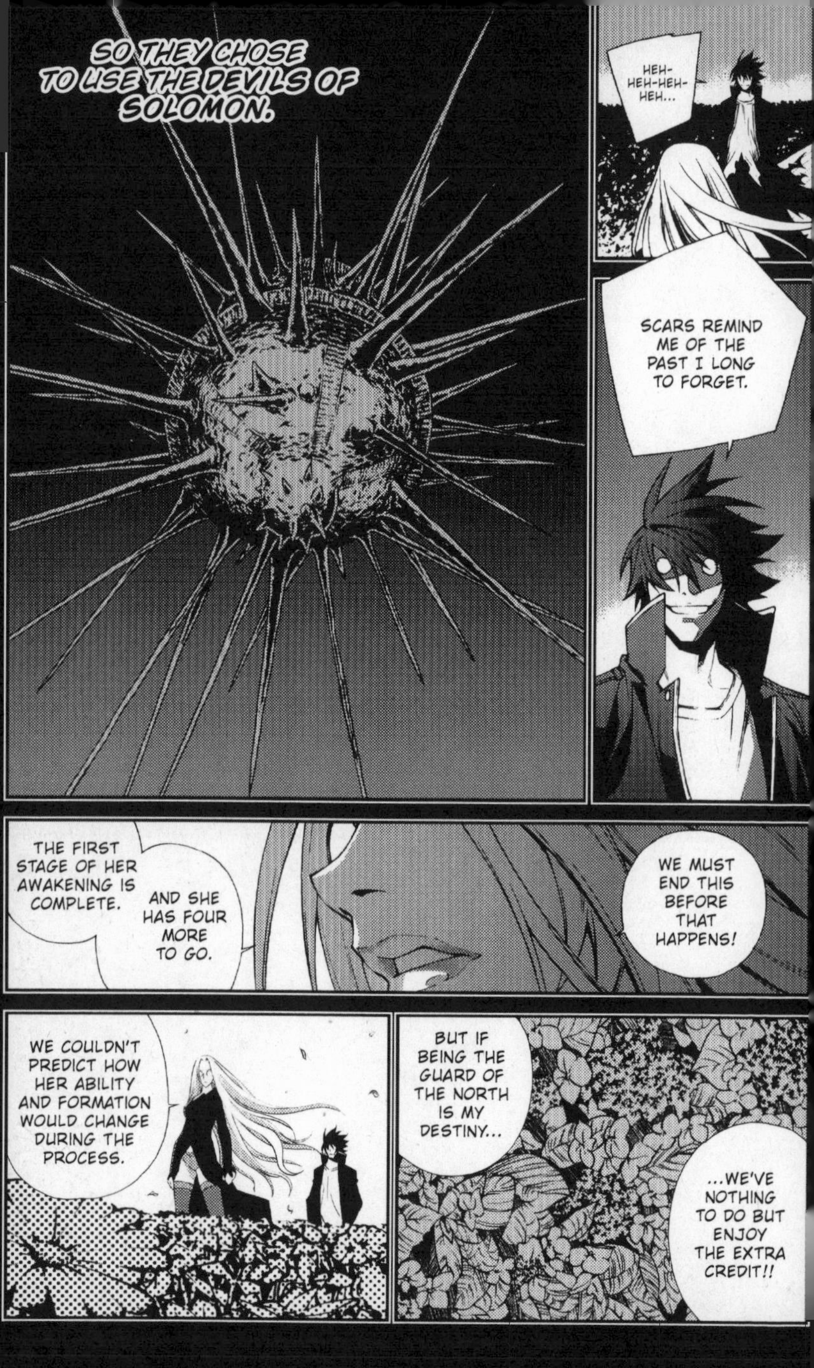
SO THEY CHOSE TO USE THE DEVILS OF SOLOMON.
HEH-HEH-HEH-HEH...
SCARS REMIND ME OF THE PAST I LONG TO FORGET.
THE FIRST STAGE OF HER AWAKENING IS COMPLETE.
AND SHE HAS FOUR MORE TO GO.
WE MUST END THIS BEFORE THAT HAPPENS!
WE COULDN'T PREDICT HOW HER ABILITY AND FORMATION WOULD CHANGE DURING THE PROCESS.
BUT IF BEING THE GUARD OF THE NORTH IS MY DESTINY...
...WE'VE NOTHING TO DO BUT ENJOY THE EXTRA CREDIT!!

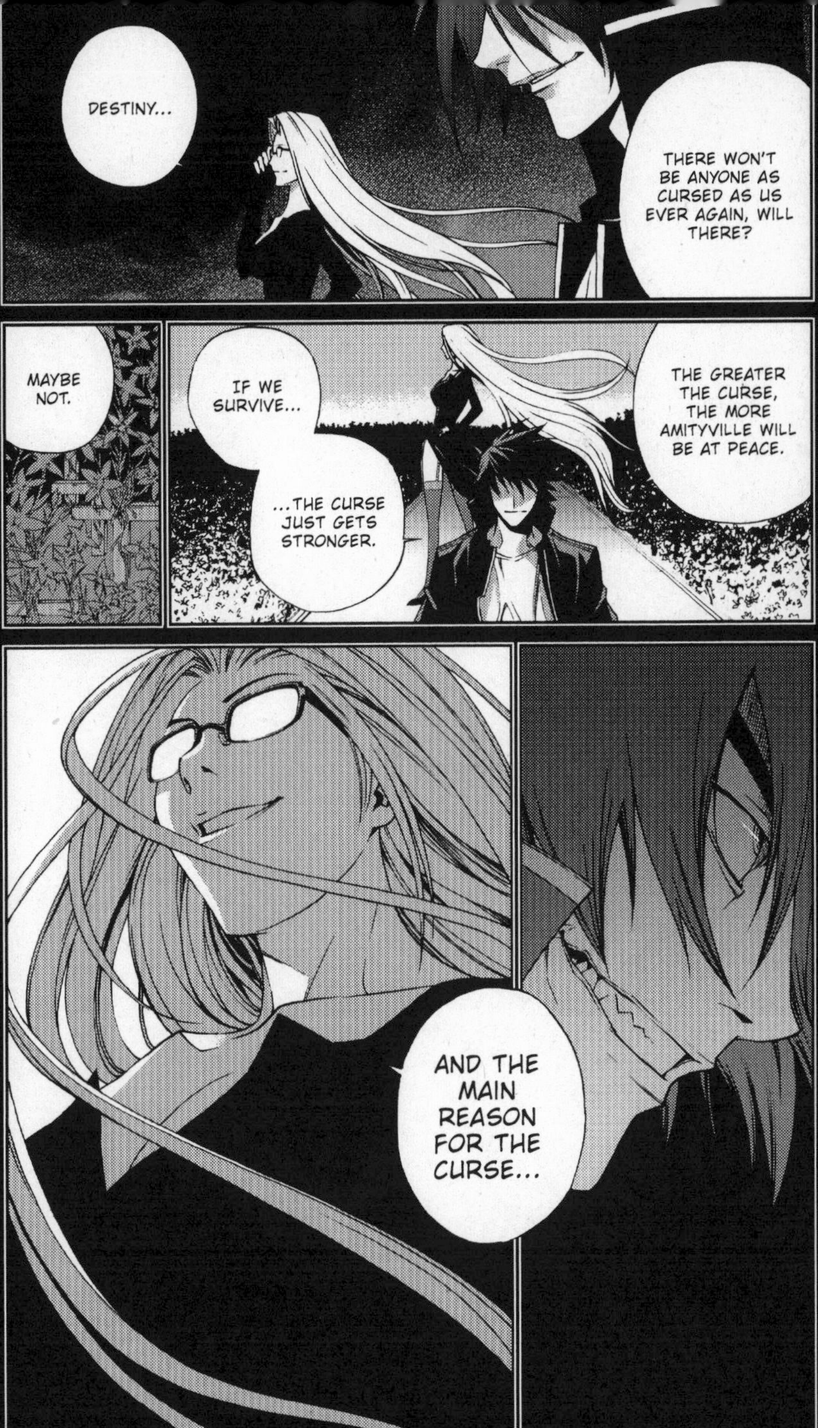
DESTINY...
THERE WON'T BE ANYONE AS CURSED AS US EVER AGAIN, WILL THERE?
MAYBE NOT.
IF WE SURVIVE...
...THE CURSE JUST GETS STRONGER.
THE GREATER THE CURSE, THE MORE AMITYVILLE WILL BE AT PEACE.
AND THE MAIN REASON FOR THE CURSE...

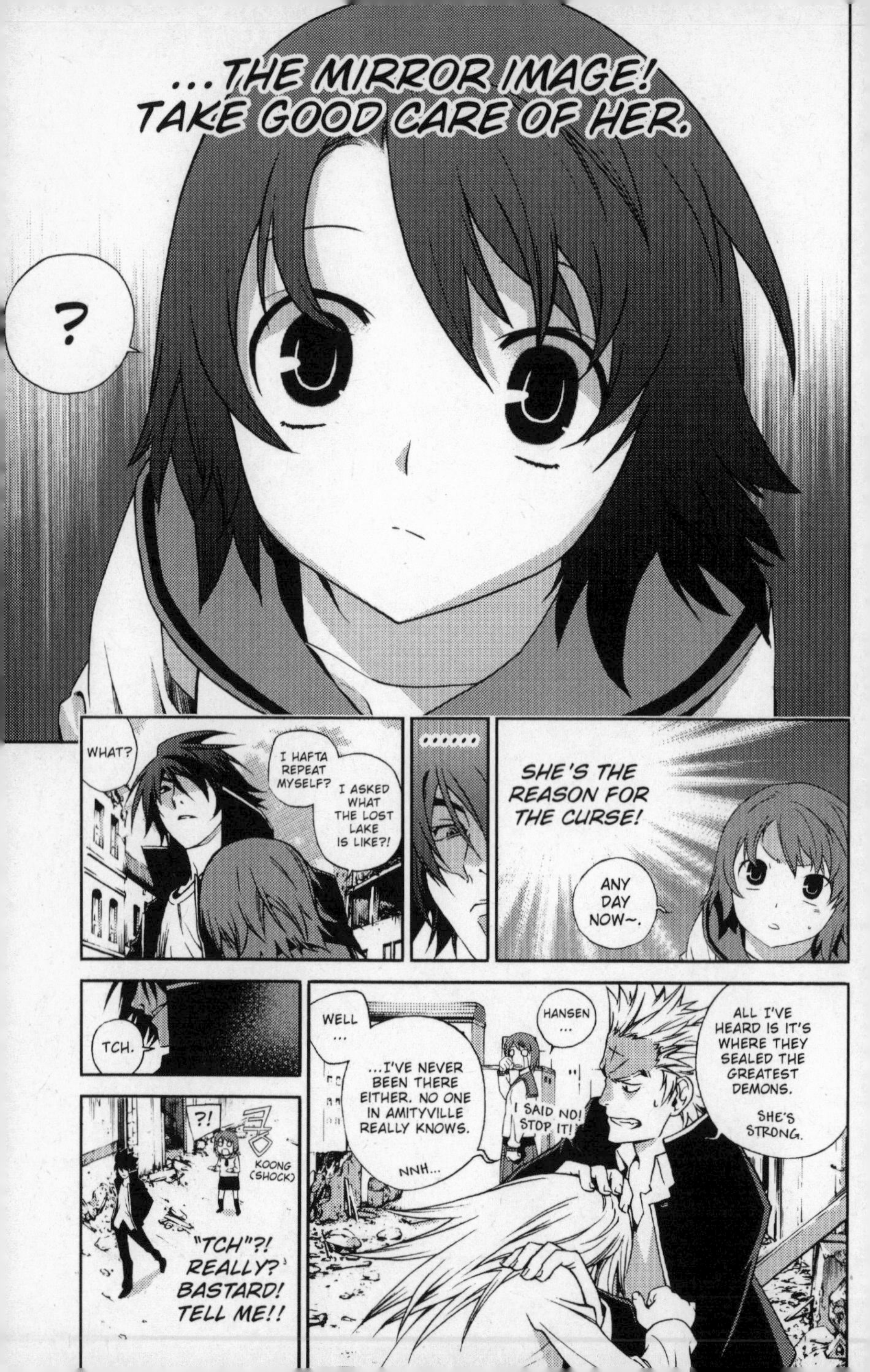
...THE MIRROR IMAGE! TAKE GOOD CARE OF HER.
?
WHAT?
I HAFTA REPEAT MYSELF?
I ASKED WHAT THE LOST LAKE IS LIKE?!
......
SHE'S THE REASON FOR THE CURSE!
ANY DAY NOW~.
TCH.
?!
KOONG (SHOCK)
"TCH"?! REALLY? BASTARD! TELL ME!!
WELL ...
...I'VE NEVER BEEN THERE EITHER. NO ONE IN AMITYVILLE REALLY KNOWS.
NNH...
HANSEN ...
I SAID STOP IT!
NO!
ALL I'VE HEARD IS IT'S WHERE THEY SEALED THE GREATEST DEMONS.
SHE'S STRONG.

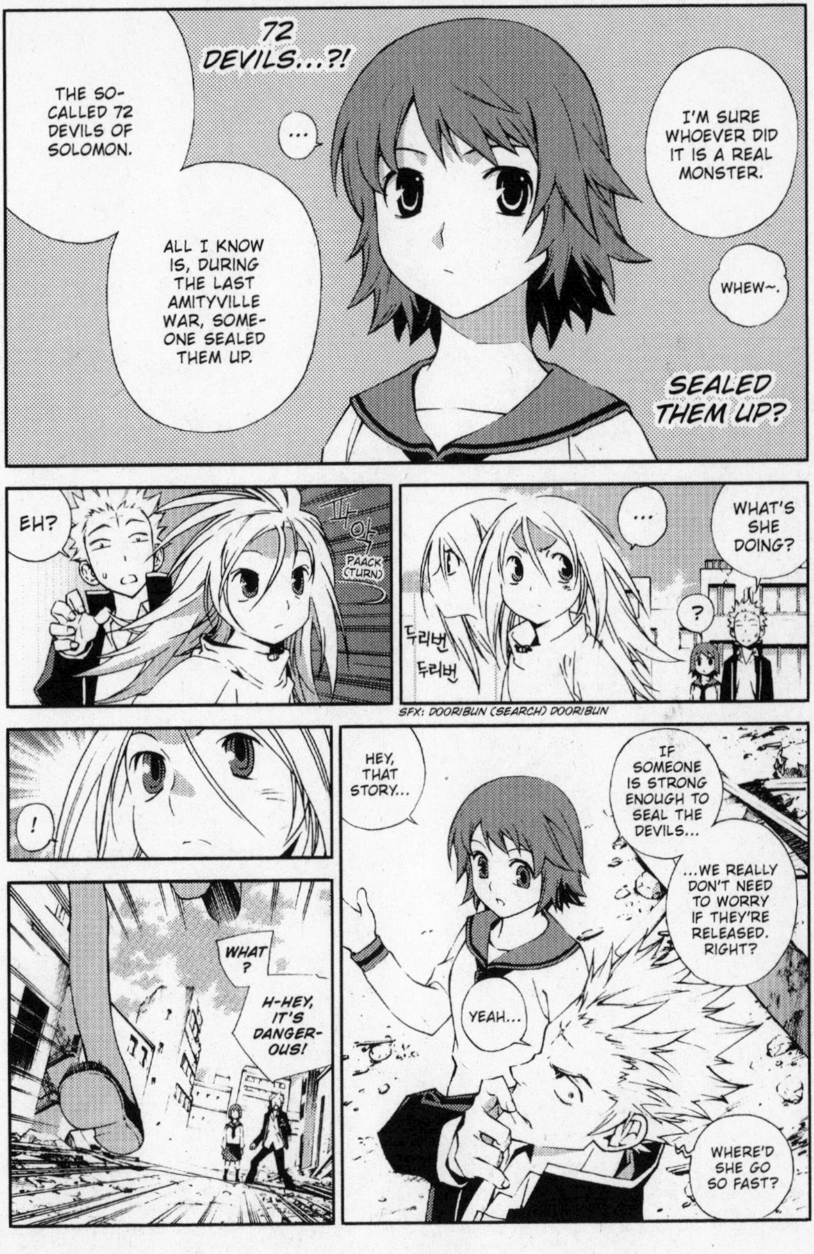
THE SO-CALLED 72 DEVILS OF SOLOMON.
72 DEVILS...?!
...
ALL I KNOW IS, DURING THE LAST AMITYVILLE WAR, SOMEONE SEALED THEM UP.
I'M SURE WHOEVER DID IT IS A REAL MONSTER.
WHEW~.
SEALED THEM UP?
EH?
파악
PAACK (TURN)
...
WHAT'S SHE DOING?
?
두리번
두리번
SFX: DOORIBUN (SEARCH) DOORIBUN
!
WHAT?
H-HEY, IT'S DANGEROUS!
HEY, THAT STORY...
IF SOMEONE IS STRONG ENOUGH TO SEAL THE DEVILS...
...WE REALLY DON'T NEED TO WORRY IF THEY'RE RELEASED. RIGHT?
YEAH...
WHERE'D SHE GO SO FAST?

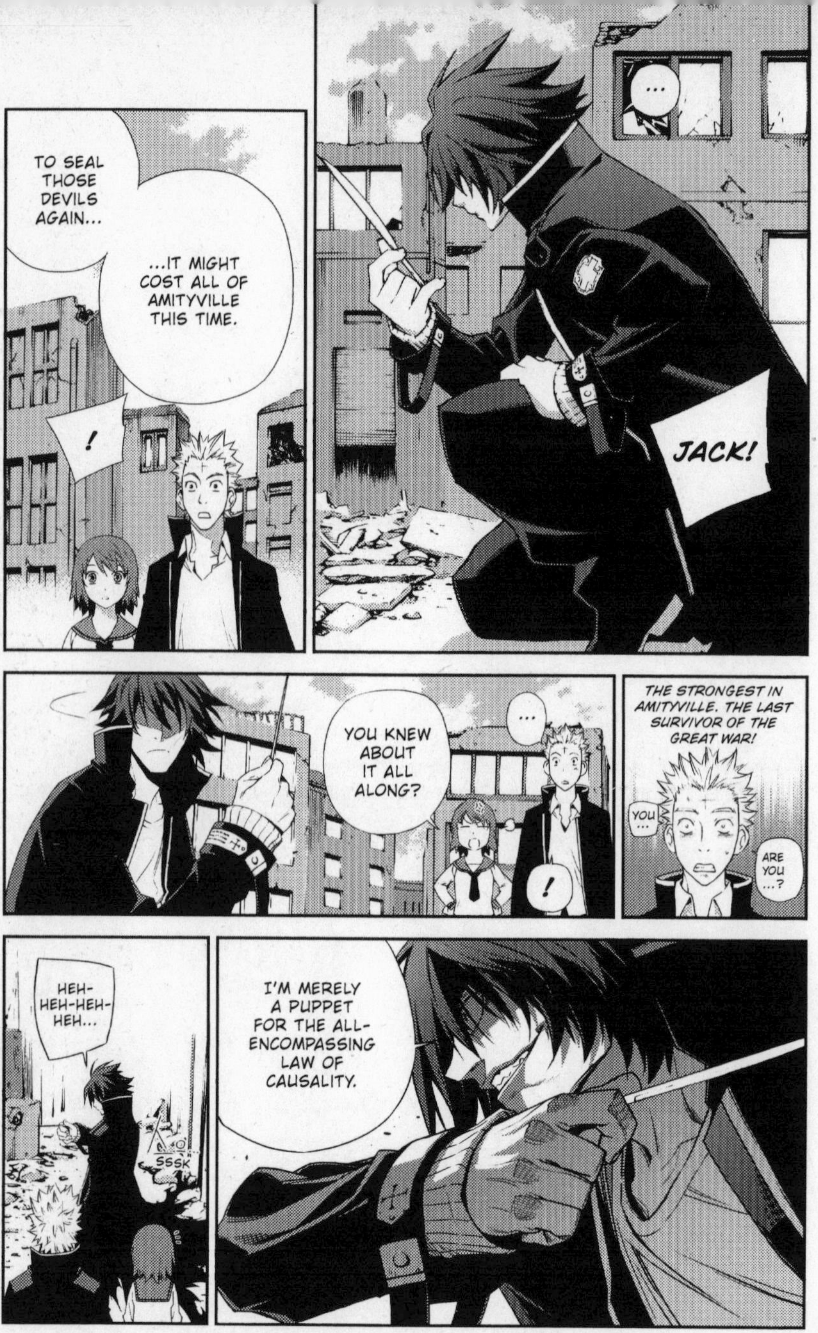
TO SEAL THOSE DEVILS AGAIN...
...IT MIGHT COST ALL OF AMITYVILLE THIS TIME.
!
...
JACK!
YOU KNEW ABOUT IT ALL ALONG?
...
!
THE STRONGEST IN AMITYVILLE. THE LAST SURVIVOR OF THE GREAT WAR!
YOU ...
ARE YOU ...?
HEH-HEH-HEH-HEH...
SSSK
I'M MERELY A PUPPET FOR THE ALL-ENCOMPASSING LAW OF CAUSALITY.

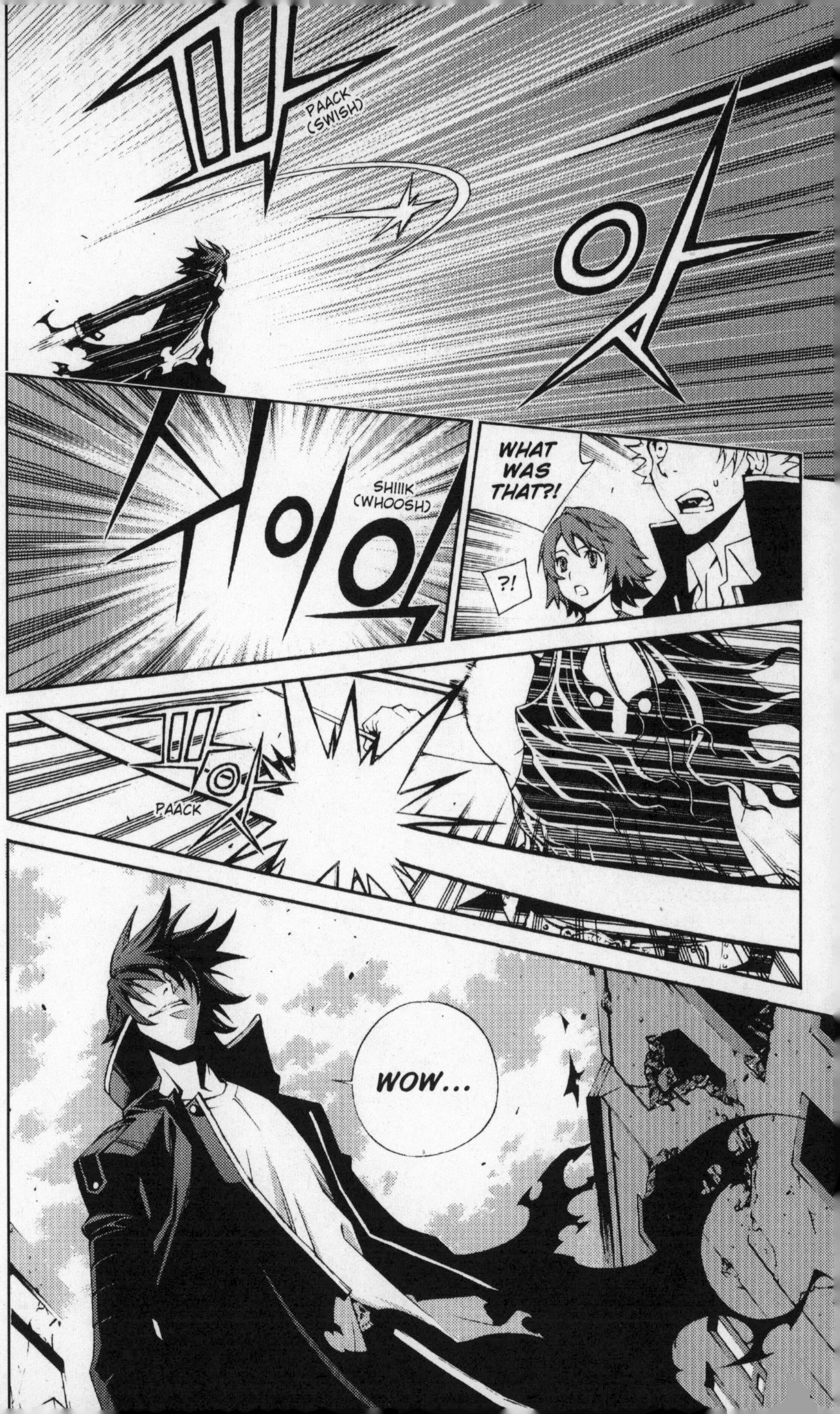
PAACK (SWISH)
SHIIIK (WHOOSH)
WHAT WAS THAT?!
?!
PAACK
WOW...

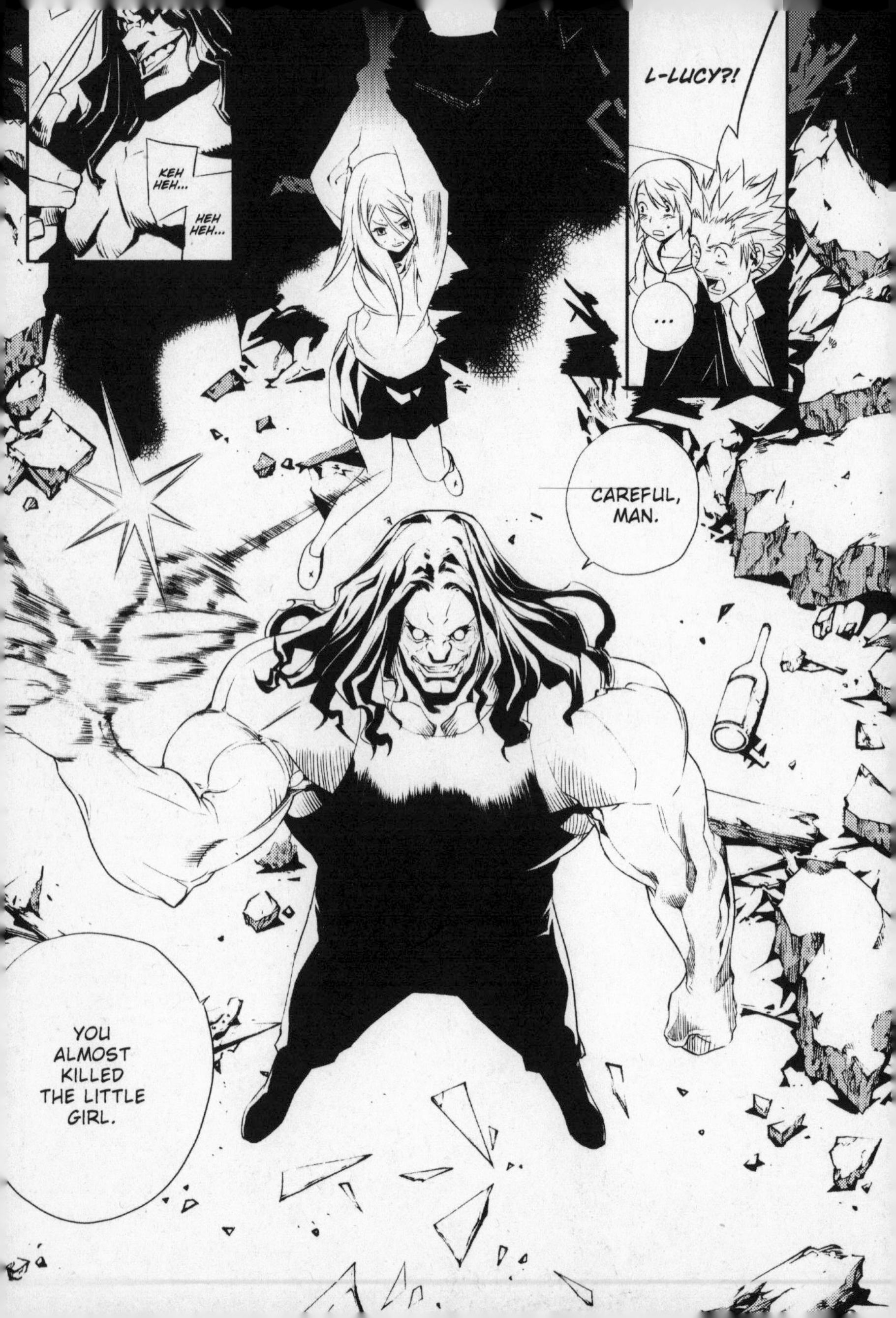
KEH HEH...
HEH HEH...
L-LUCY?!
...
CAREFUL, MAN.
YOU ALMOST KILLED THE LITTLE GIRL.

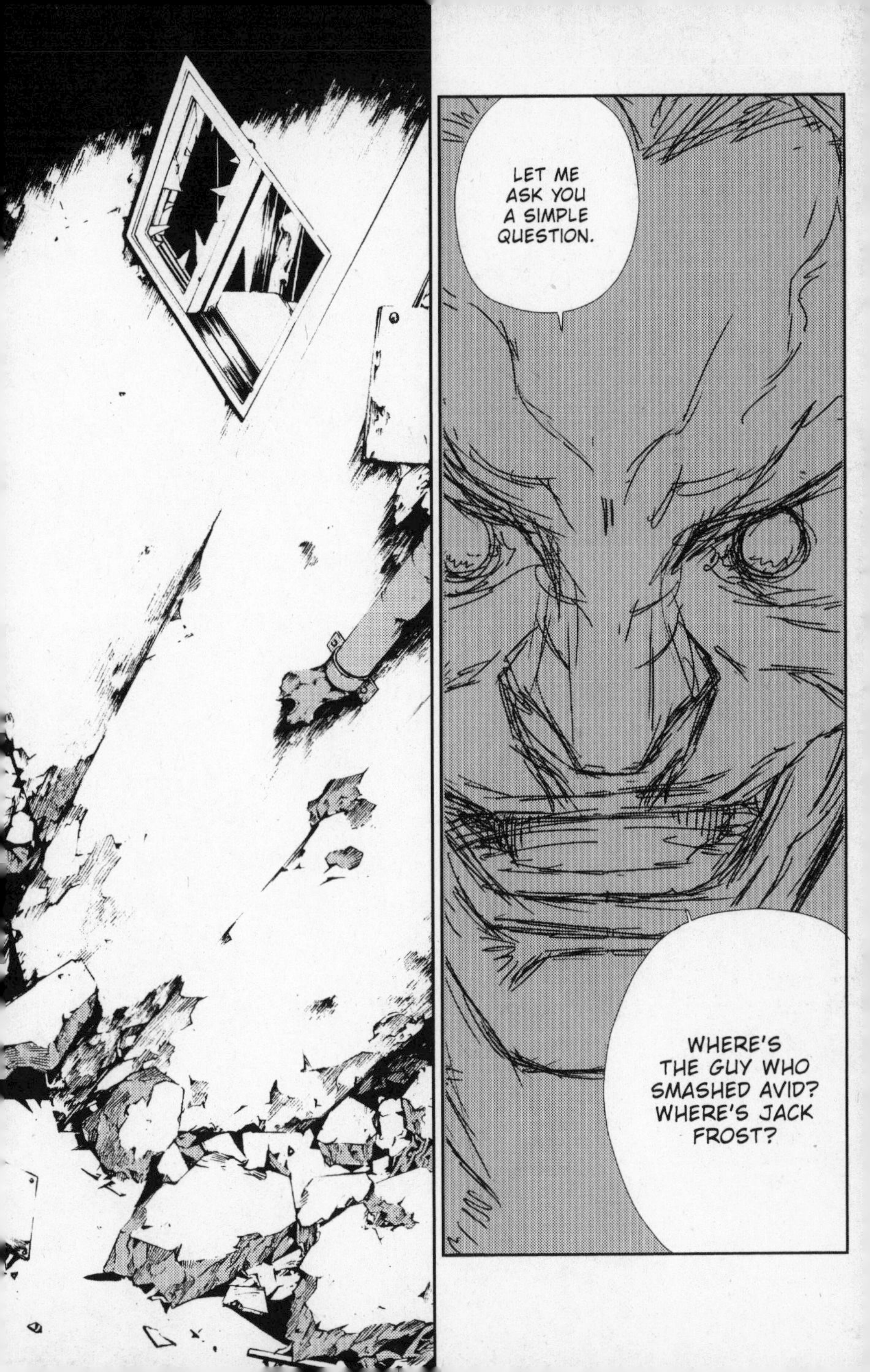
LET ME ASK YOU A SIMPLE QUESTION.
WHERE'S THE GUY WHO SMASHED AVID? WHERE'S JACK FROST?

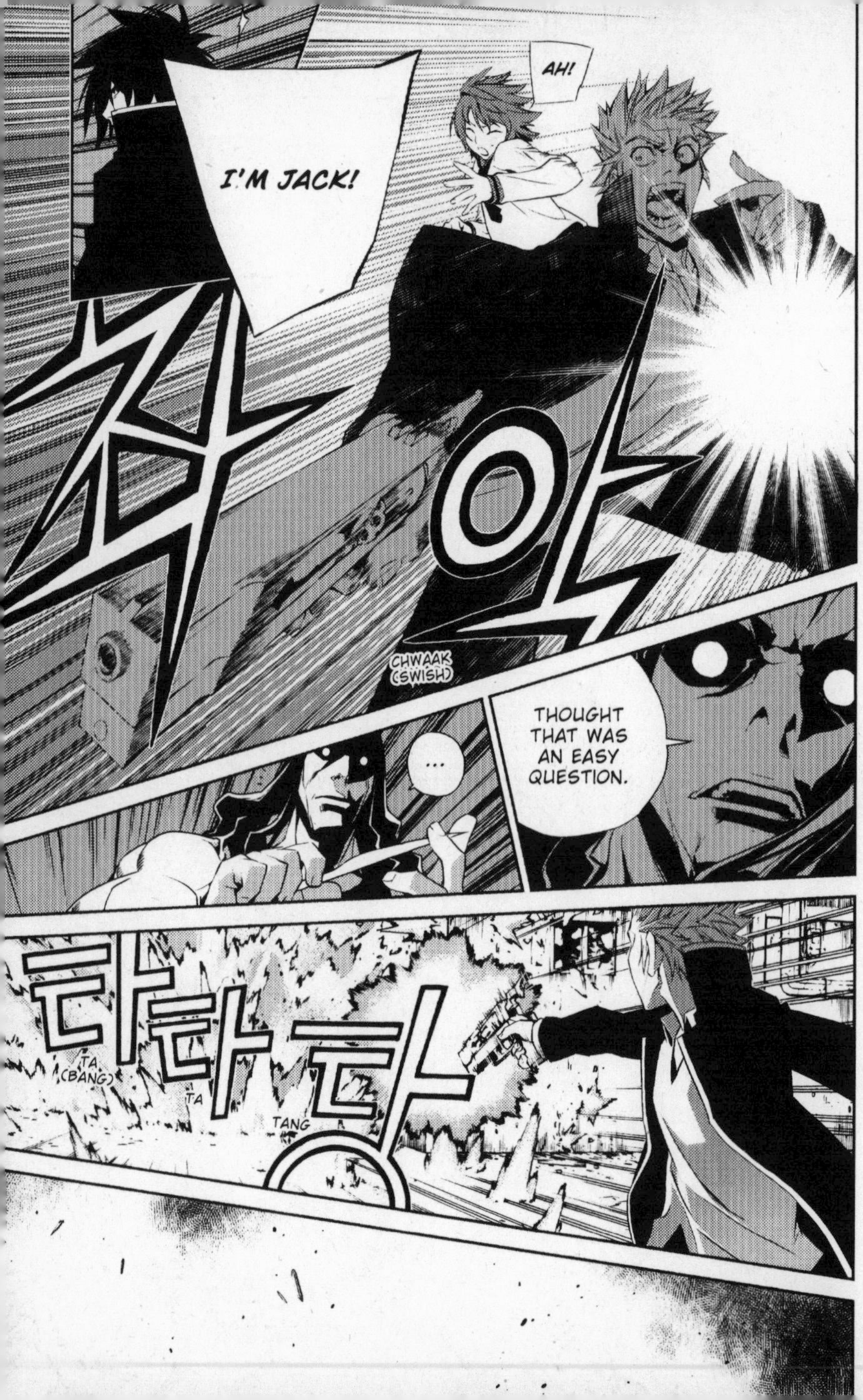
I'M JACK!
AH!
CHWAAK (SWISH)
...
THOUGHT THAT WAS AN EASY QUESTION.
타타탕
TA (BANG)
TA
TANG

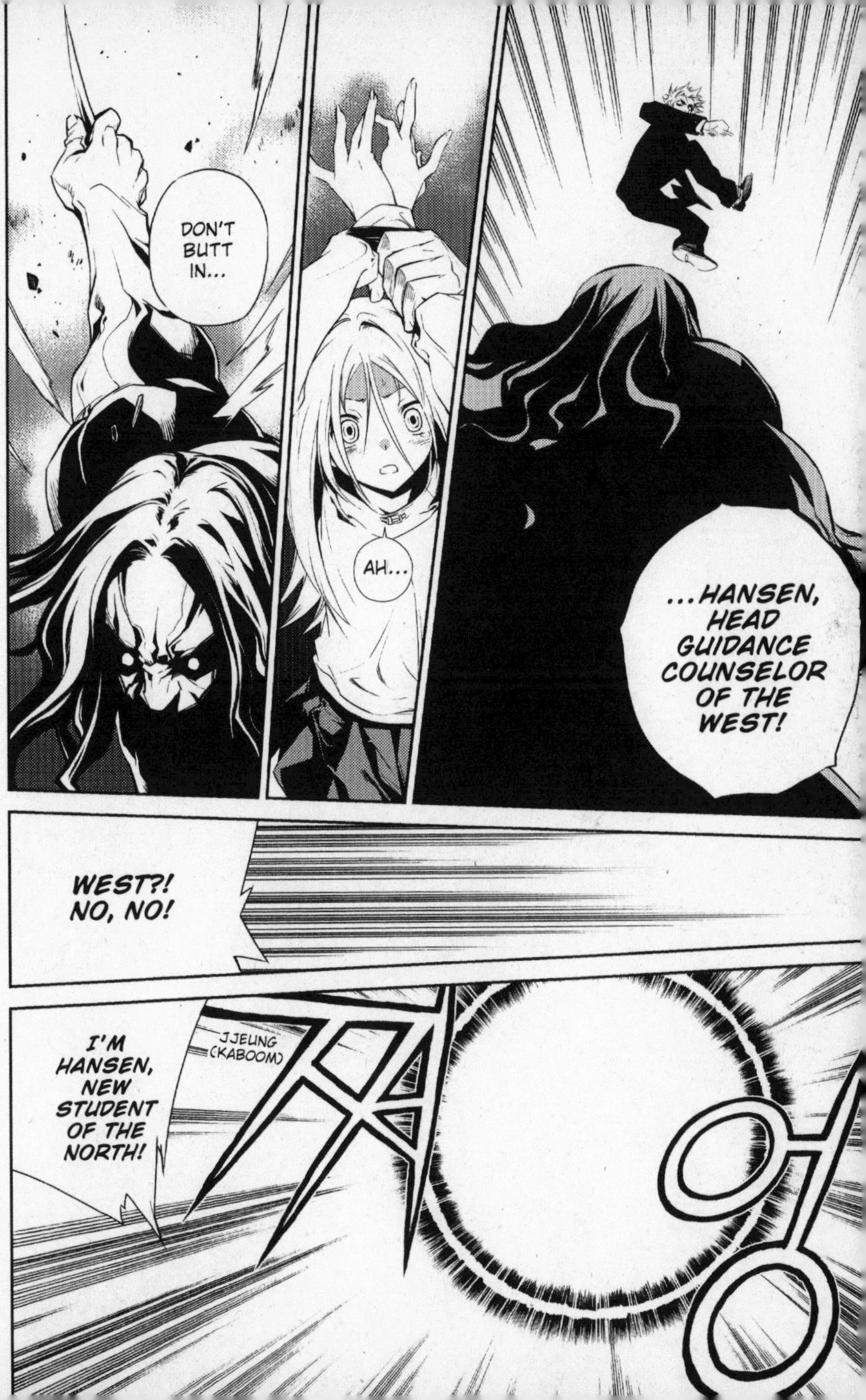
DON'T BUTT IN...
AH...
...HANSEN, HEAD GUIDANCE COUNSELOR OF THE WEST!
WEST?! NO, NO!
I'M HANSEN, NEW STUDENT OF THE NORTH!
JJEUNG (KABOOM)

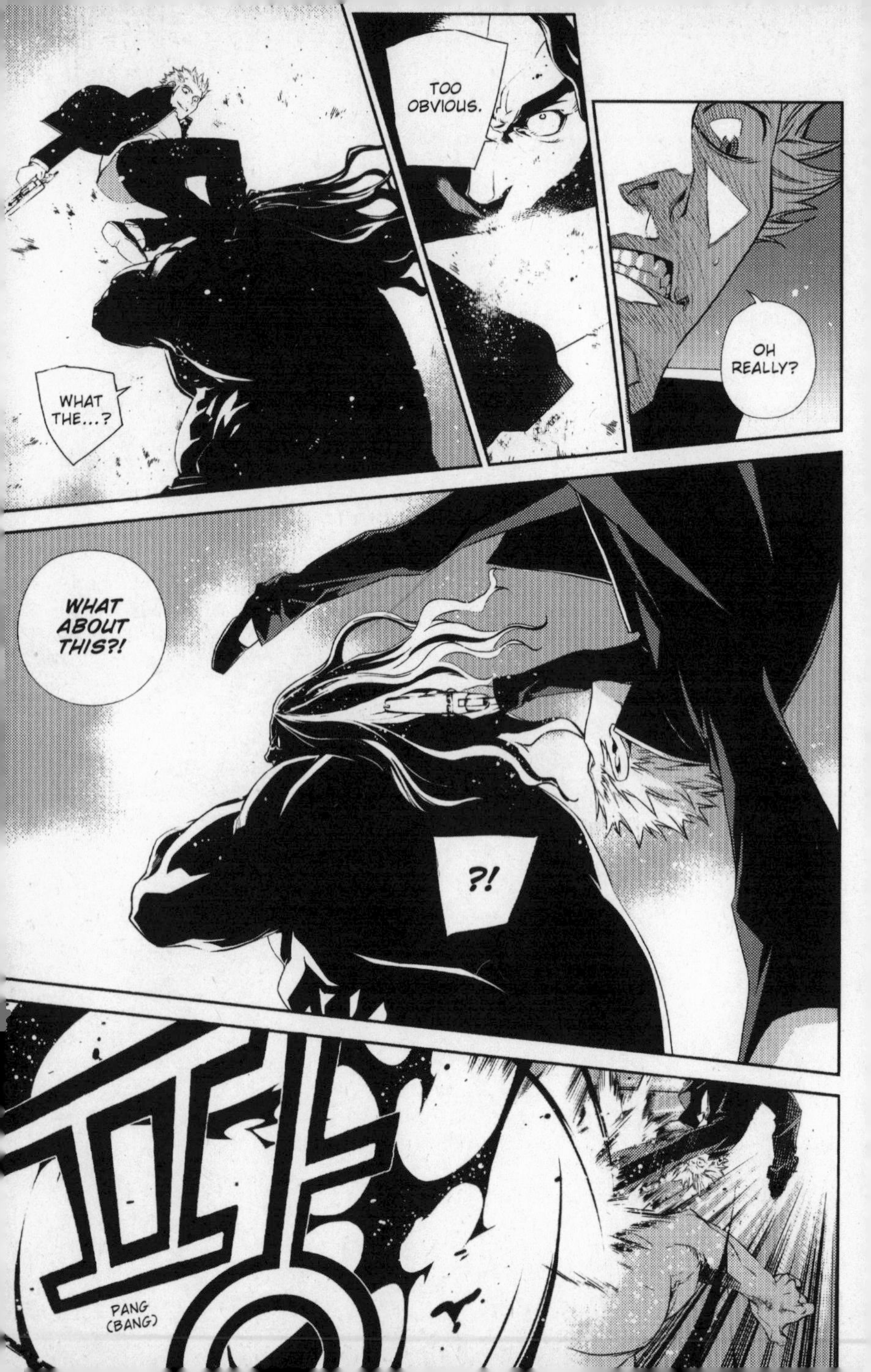
WHAT THE...?
TOO OBVIOUS.
OH REALLY?
WHAT ABOUT THIS?!
?!
PANG (BANG)

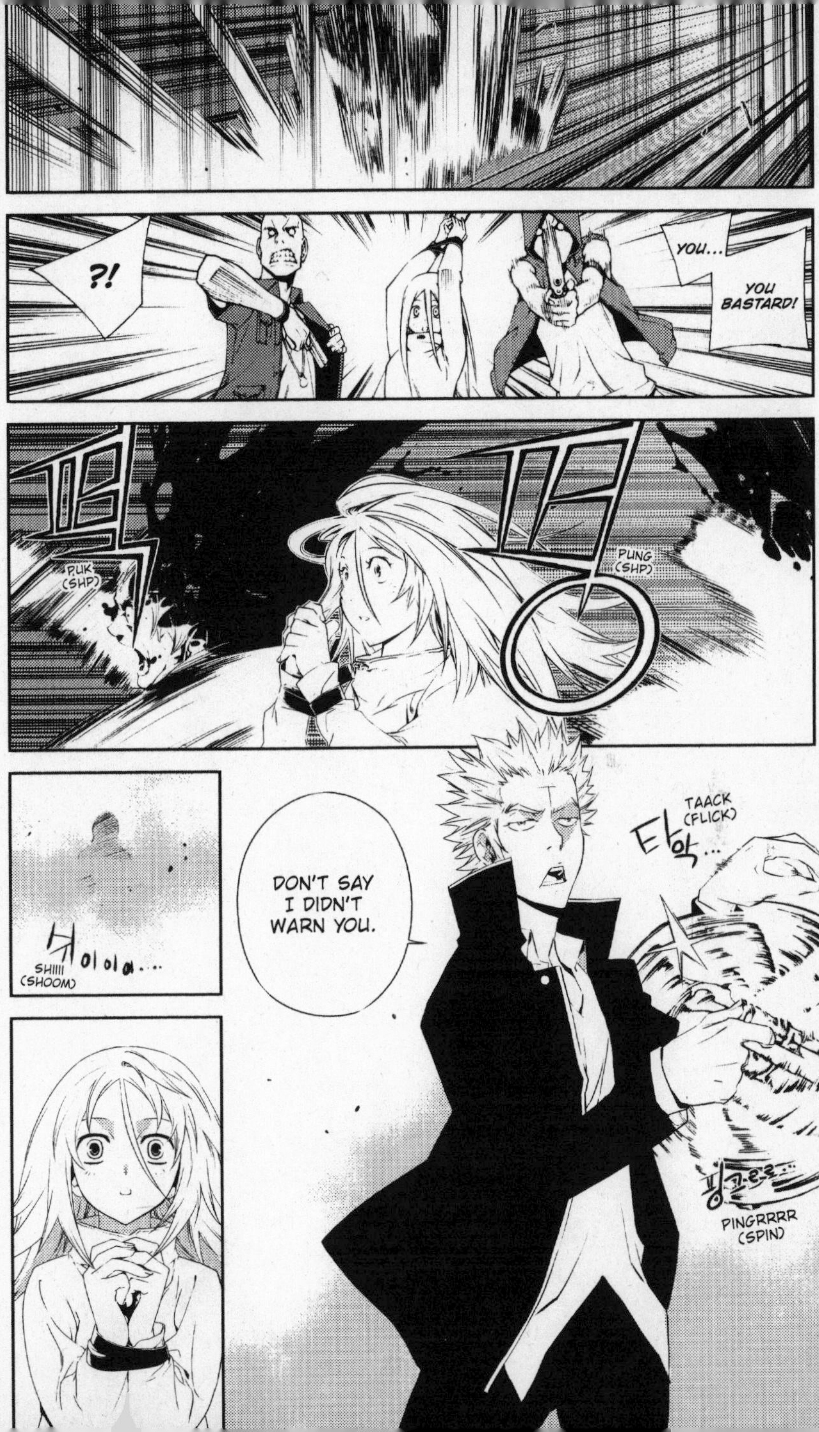
?!
YOU...
YOU BASTARD!
퍽
PUK (SHP)
펑
PUNG (SHP)
쉬이이이....
SHIIII (SHOOM)
DON'T SAY I DIDN'T WARN YOU.
타악...
TAACK (FLICK)
핑그르르...
PINGRRRR (SPIN)

AIEE~! ♡

... IMPRESSIVE. HANSEN IS A MAN... I UNDERESTIMATED HIM.

WOW.

HEH. IT STARTS NOW. EH?

YEAH~! ♡

HEH. WHAT THE...? LIP ALREADY?

?!

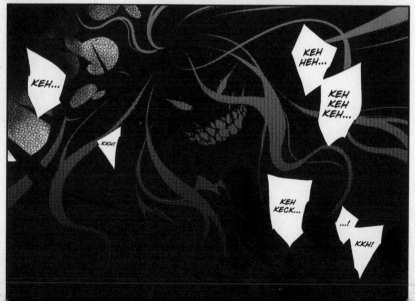

KEH HEH...

KEH KEH KEH...

KEH...

KKH!

KEH KECK...

....!

KKH!

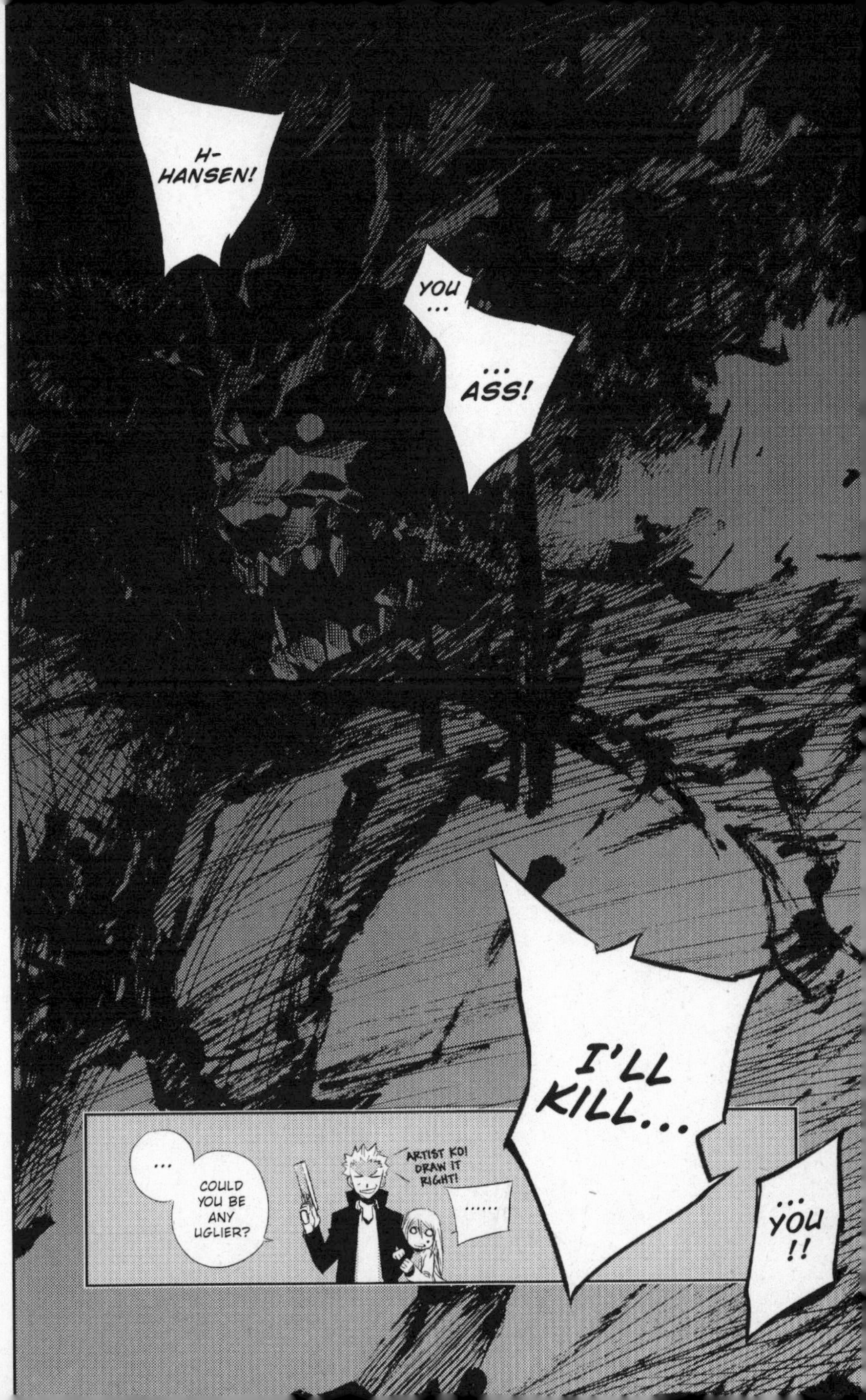
H-
HANSEN!
YOU
...
...
ASS!
I'LL
KILL...
... YOU !!
...
COULD YOU BE ANY UGLIER?
ARTIST KOI DRAW IT RIGHT!
......

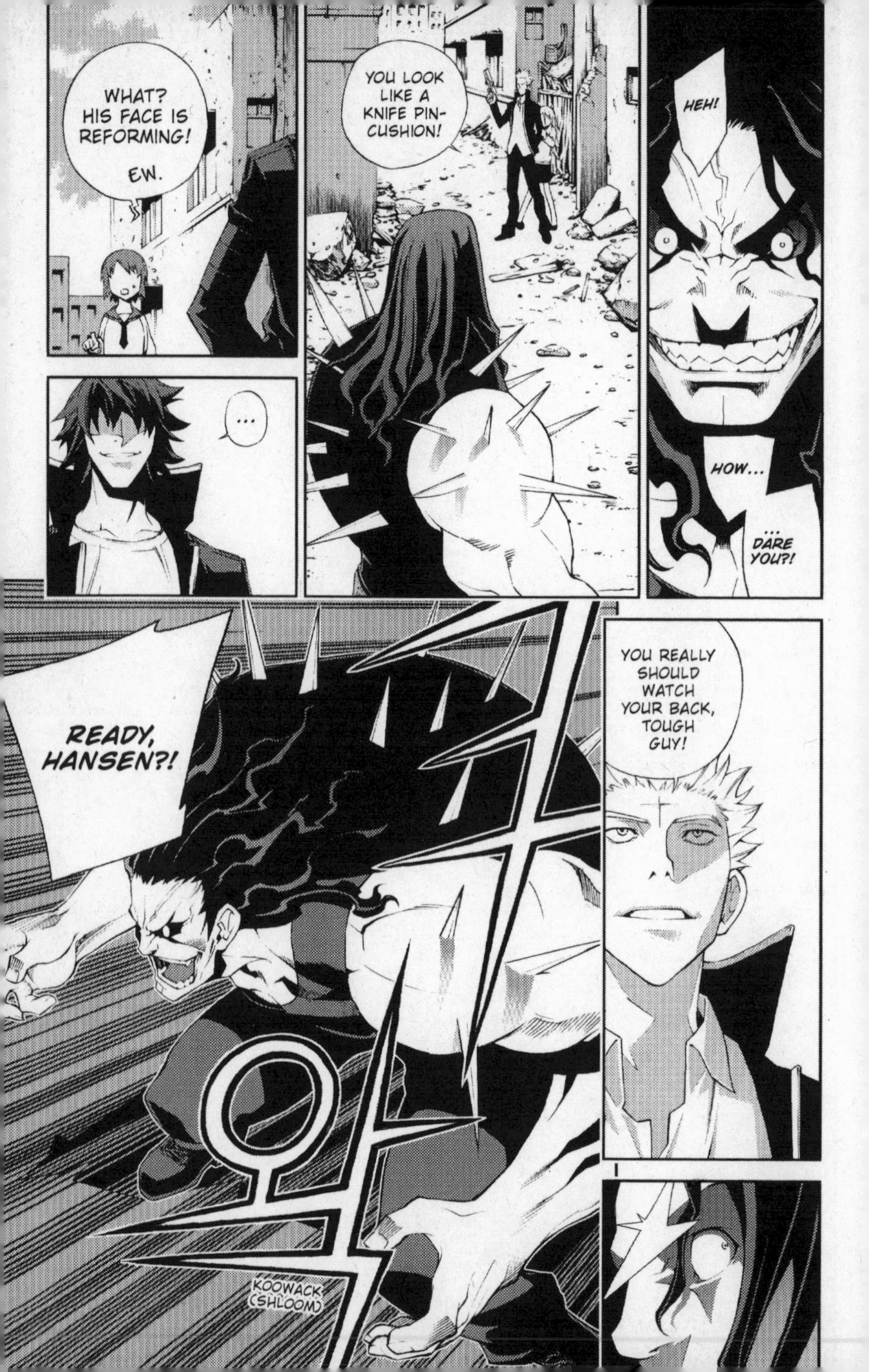
HEH!
HOW...
...DARE YOU?!
YOU LOOK LIKE A KNIFE PIN-CUSHION!
WHAT? HIS FACE IS REFORMING!
EW.
...
YOU REALLY SHOULD WATCH YOUR BACK, TOUGH GUY!
READY, HANSEN?!
KOOWACK (SHLOOM)

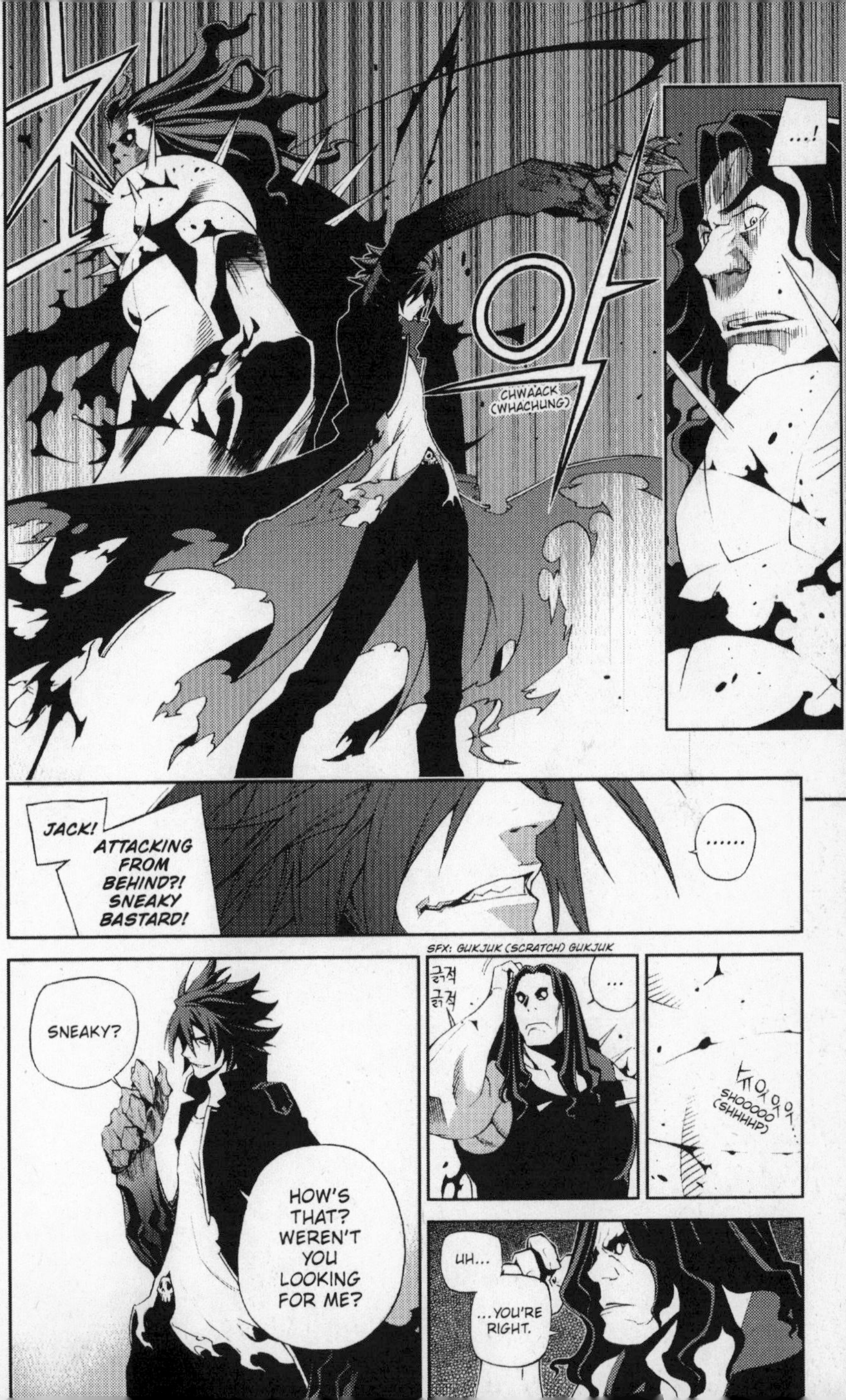
CHWAACK (WHACHUNG)
...!
JACK! ATTACKING FROM BEHIND?! SNEAKY BASTARD!
......
SFX: GUKJUK (SCRATCH) GUKJUK
SNEAKY?
HOW'S THAT? WEREN'T YOU LOOKING FOR ME?
긁적 긁적
...
SHOOOOO (SHHHHP)
UH...
...YOU'RE RIGHT.

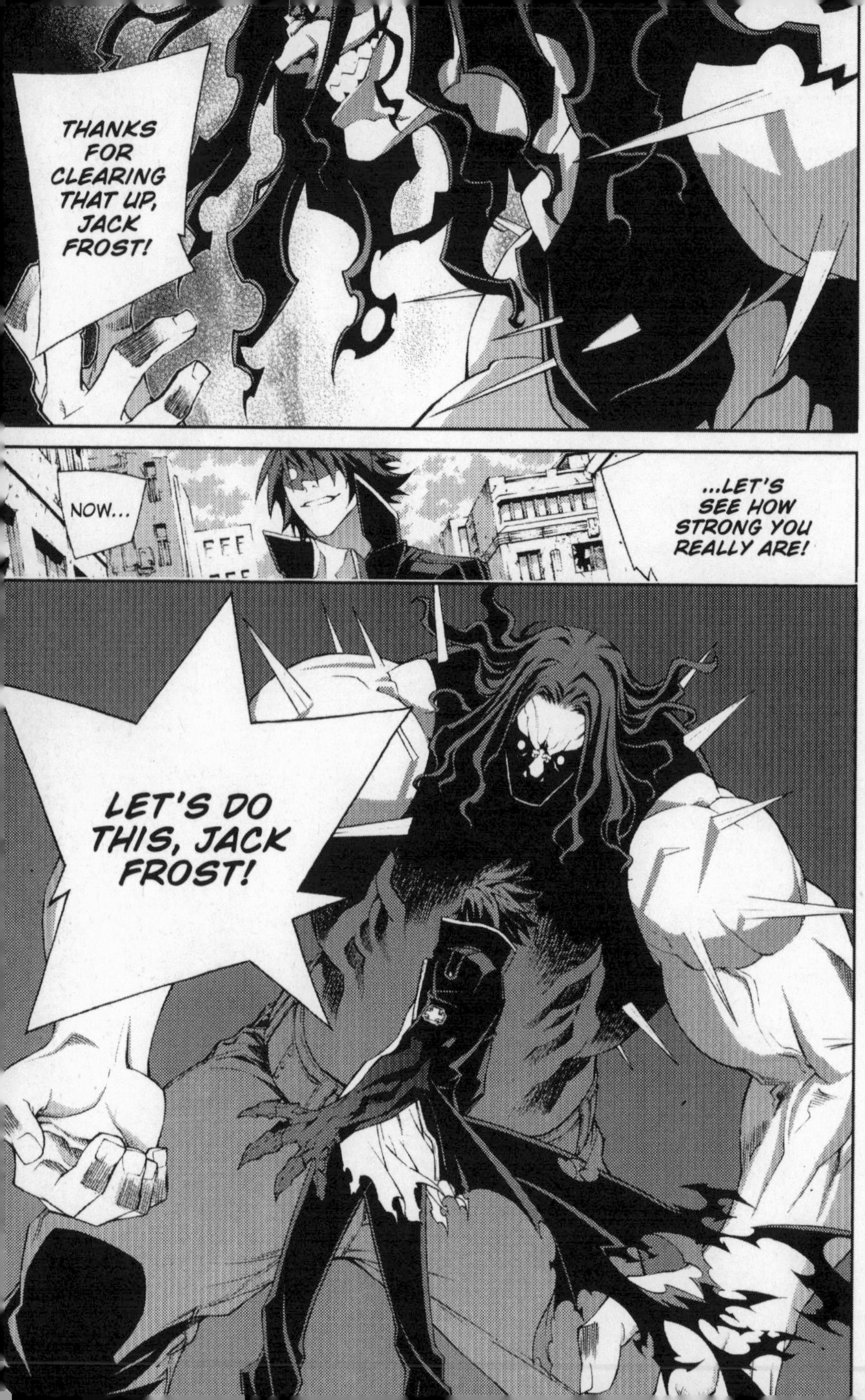
THANKS FOR CLEARING THAT UP, JACK FROST!
NOW...
...LET'S SEE HOW STRONG YOU REALLY ARE!
LET'S DO THIS, JACK FROST!

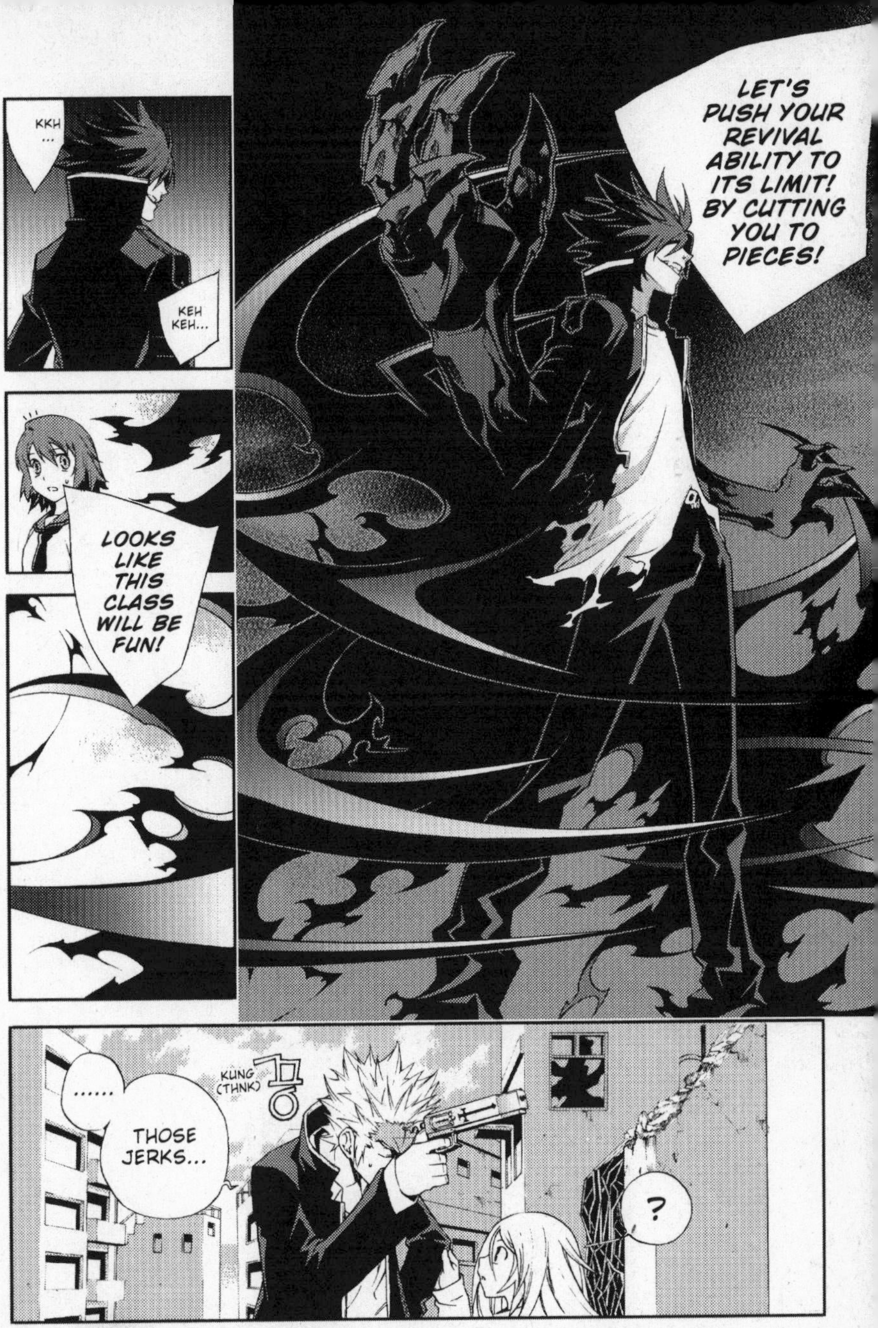
KKH ...
KEH KEH...
LOOKS LIKE THIS CLASS WILL BE FUN!
LET'S PUSH YOUR REVIVAL ABILITY TO ITS LIMIT! BY CUTTING YOU TO PIECES!
......
THOSE JERKS...
꿍 KUNG (THNK)
?

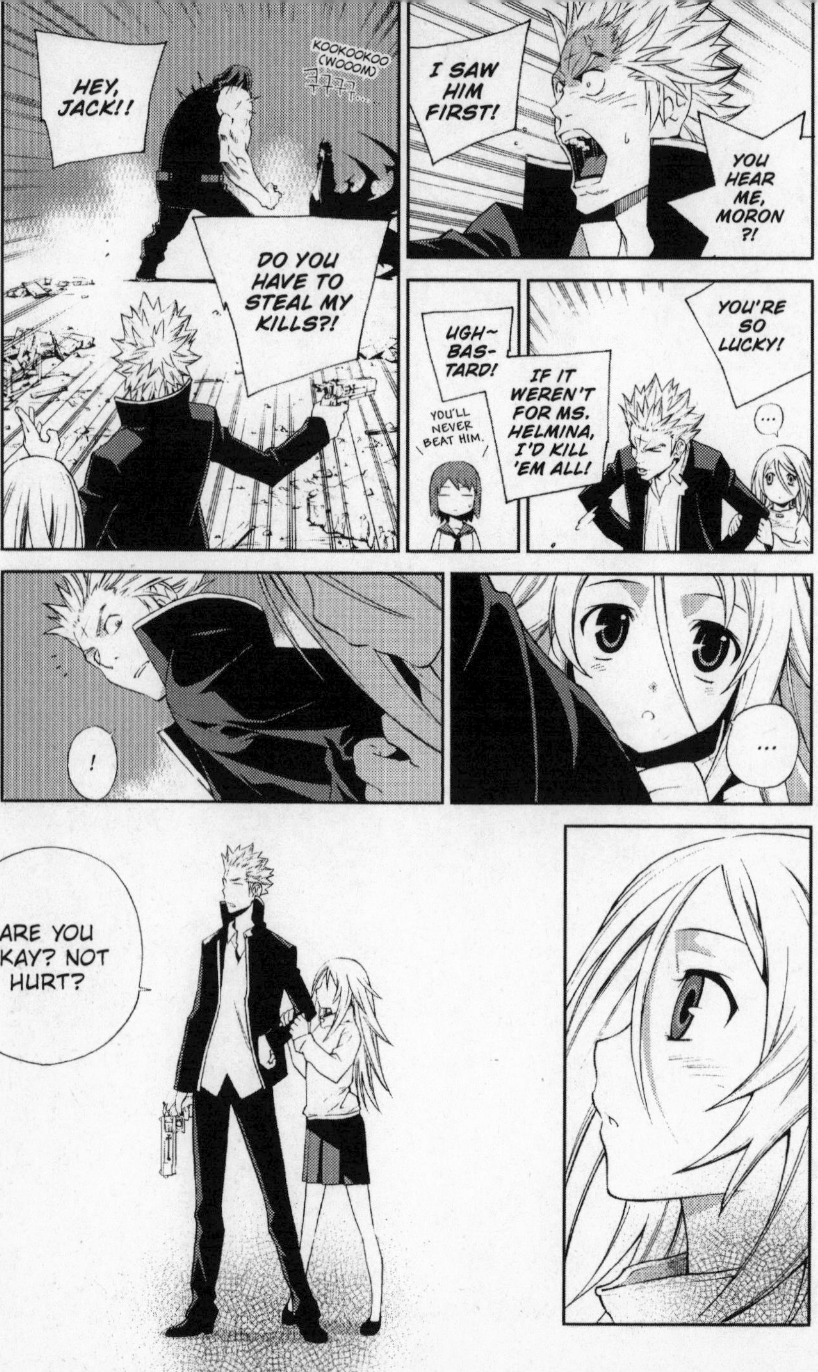
HEY, JACK!!
KOOKOOKOO (WOOOM)
쿠구구구...
DO YOU HAVE TO STEAL MY KILLS?!
I SAW HIM FIRST!
YOU HEAR ME, MORON?!
UGH~ BASTARD!
YOU'LL NEVER BEAT HIM.
IF IT WEREN'T FOR MS. HELMINA, I'D KILL 'EM ALL!
YOU'RE SO LUCKY!
...
!
...
ARE YOU OKAY? NOT HURT?

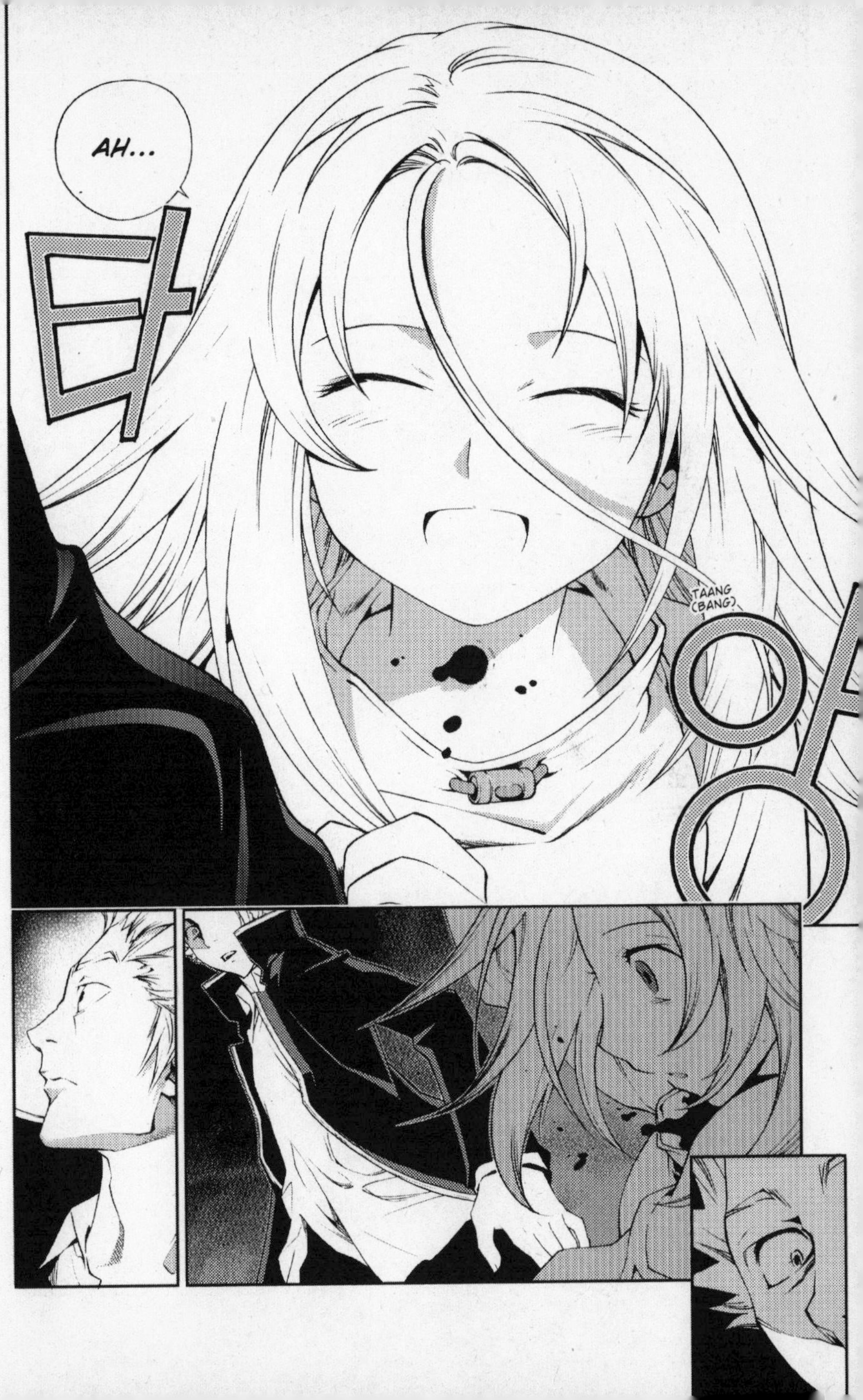
AH...
타
TAANG (BANG)
앙

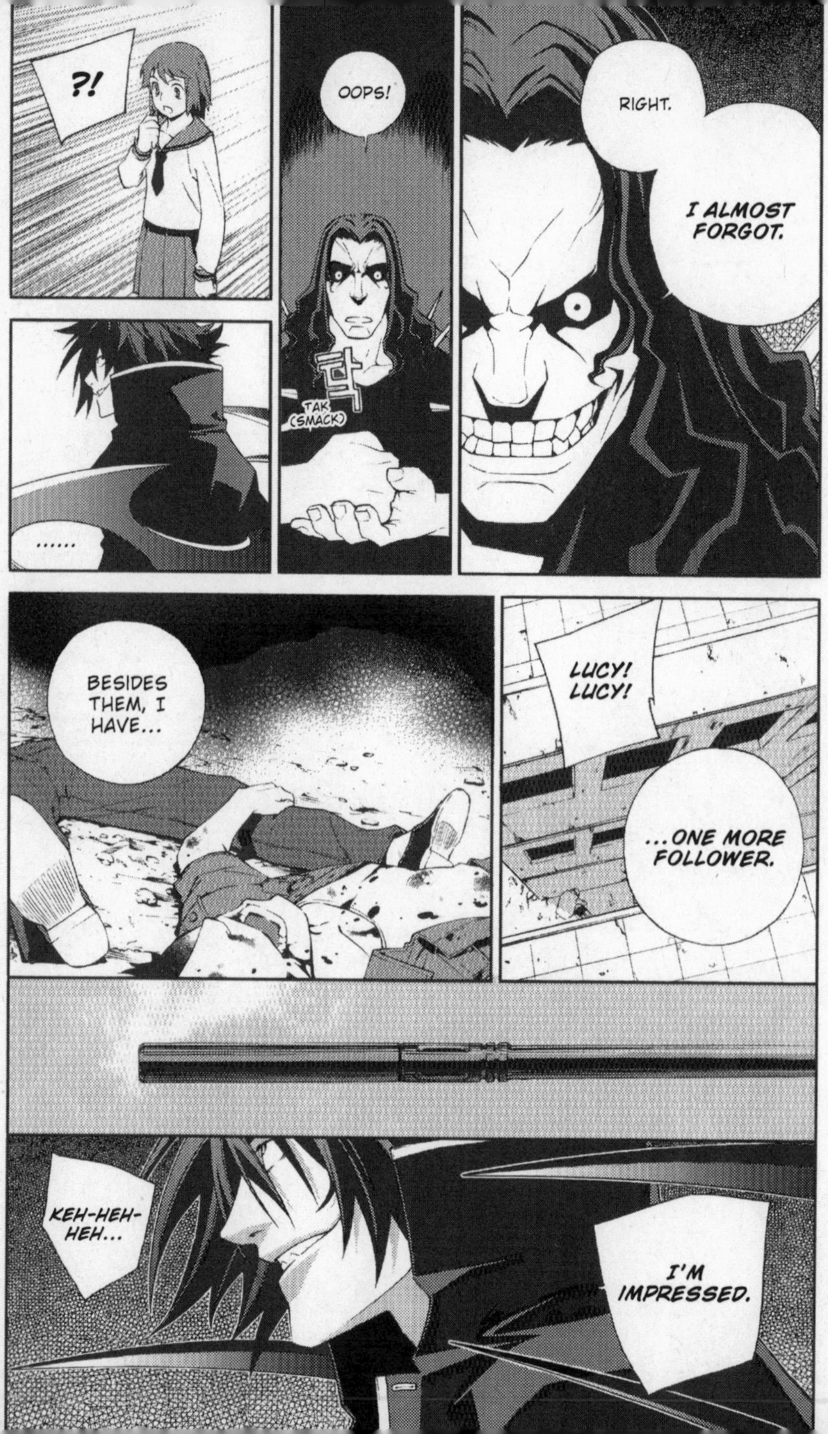
?!
......
OOPS!
TAK (SMACK)
RIGHT.
I ALMOST FORGOT.
BESIDES THEM, I HAVE...
LUCY! LUCY!
...ONE MORE FOLLOWER.
KEH-HEH-HEH...
I'M IMPRESSED.

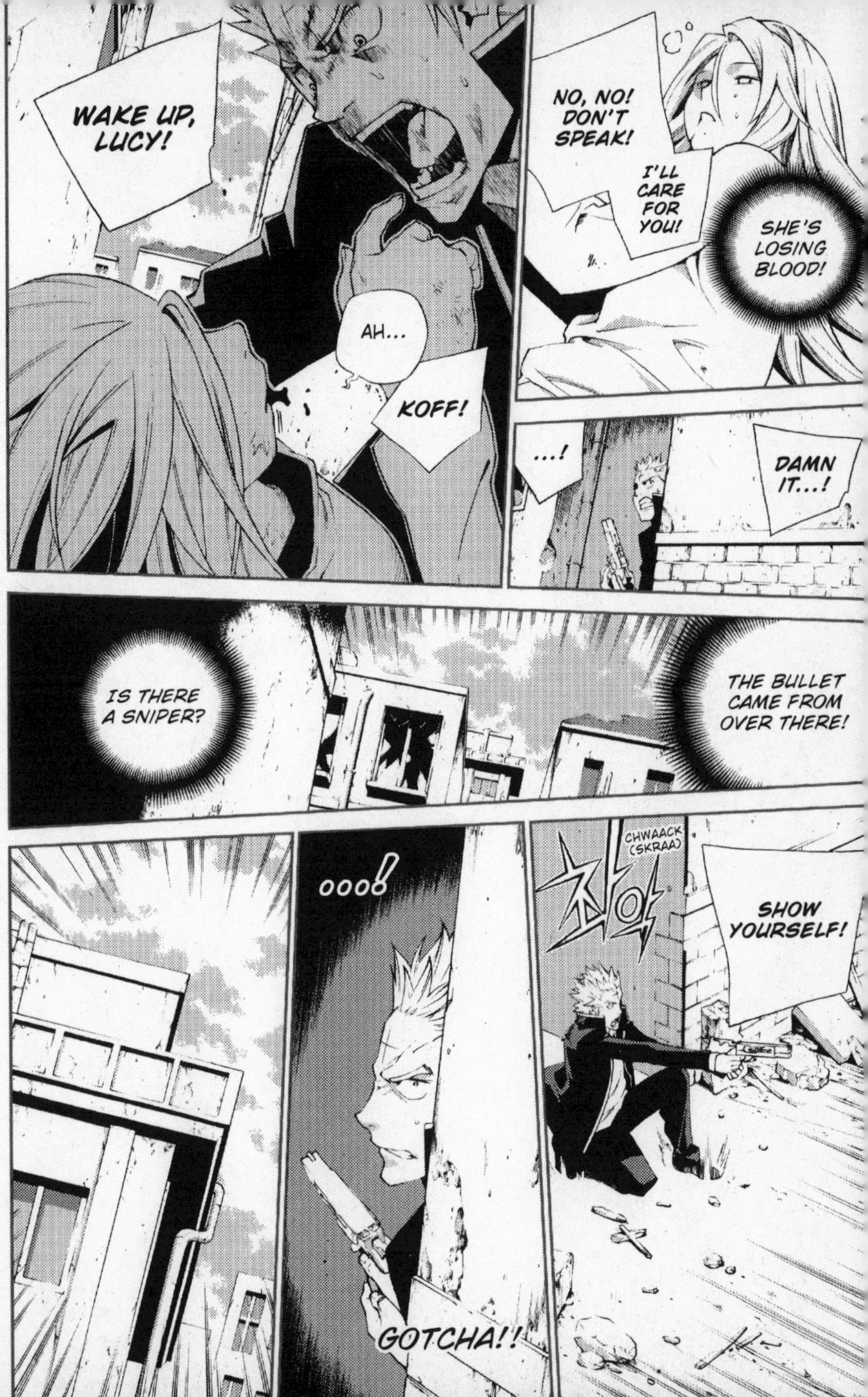
WAKE UP, LUCY!
AH...
KOFF!
NO, NO! DON'T SPEAK!
I'LL CARE FOR YOU!
SHE'S LOSING BLOOD!
...!
DAMN IT...!
IS THERE A SNIPER?
THE BULLET CAME FROM OVER THERE!
ooo!
GOTCHA!!
CHWAACK (SKRAA)
SHOW YOURSELF!

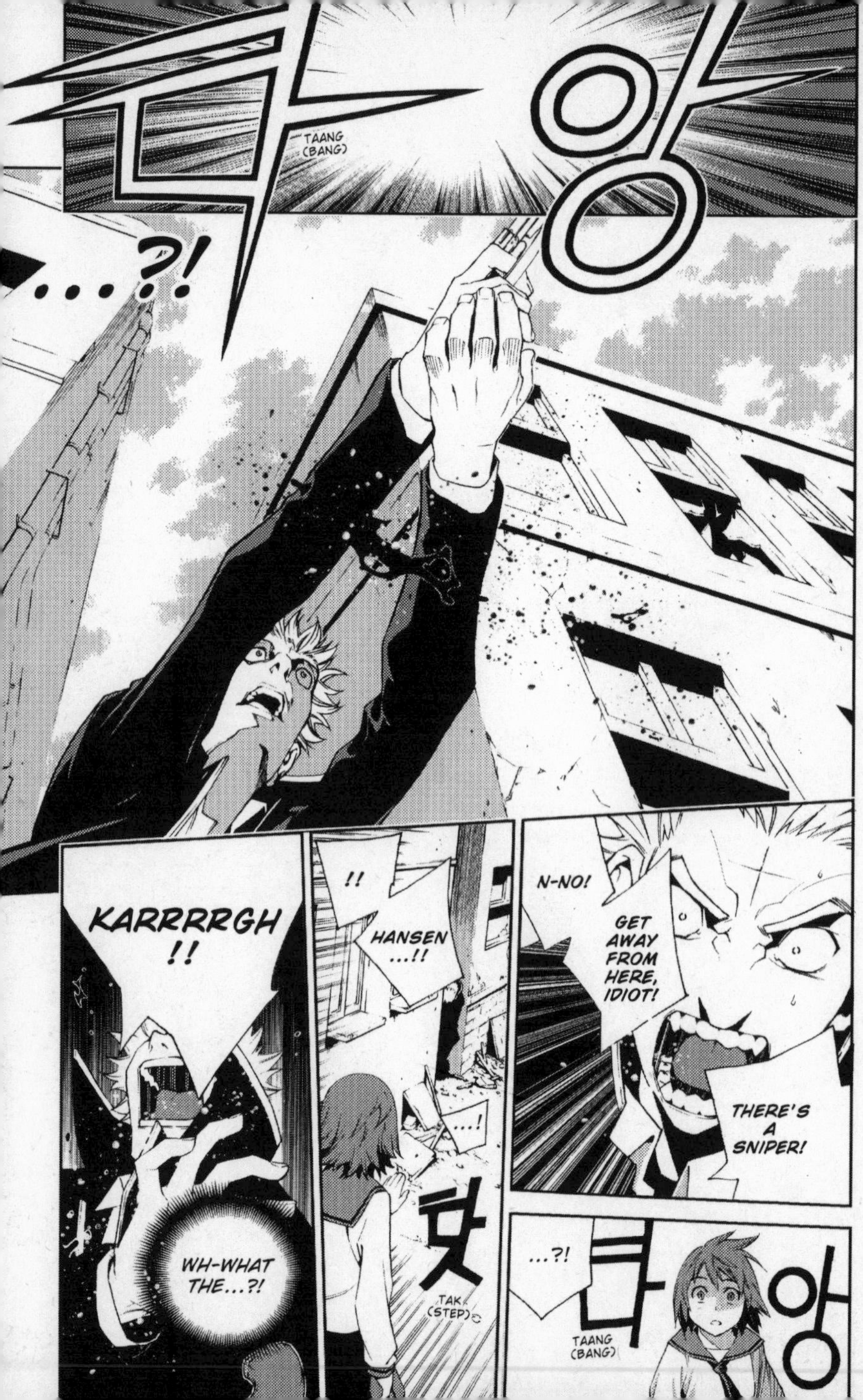

TAANG
(BANG)
...?!
KARRRRGH !!
WH-WHAT THE...?!
!!
HANSEN ...!!
...!
TAK
(STEP)
N-NO!
GET AWAY FROM HERE, IDIOT!
THERE'S A SNIPER!
...?!
TAANG
(BANG)

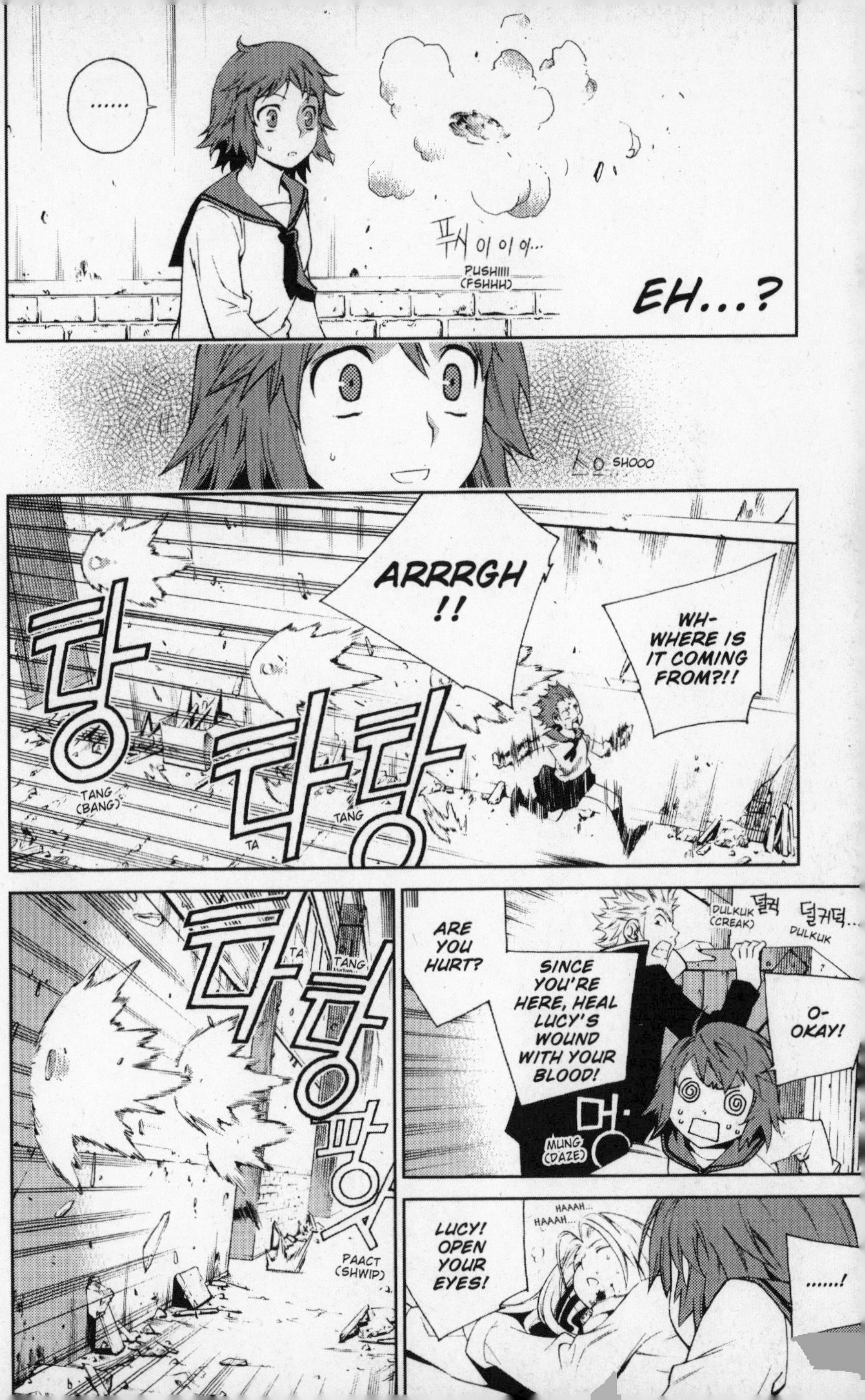
......
푸시이이이...
PUSHIIII (FSHHH)
EH...?
스으 SHOOO
ARRRGH !!
WH- WHERE IS IT COMING FROM?!!
탕
TANG (BANG)
타당
TA
TANG
타당
TA
TANG
팡
PAACT (SHWIP)
ARE YOU HURT?
SINCE YOU'RE HERE, HEAL LUCY'S WOUND WITH YOUR BLOOD!
덜컥
DULKUK (CREAK)
덜커덕...
DULKUK
O- OKAY!
멍
MUNG (DAZE)
HAAAH... HAAAH...
LUCY! OPEN YOUR EYES!
......!

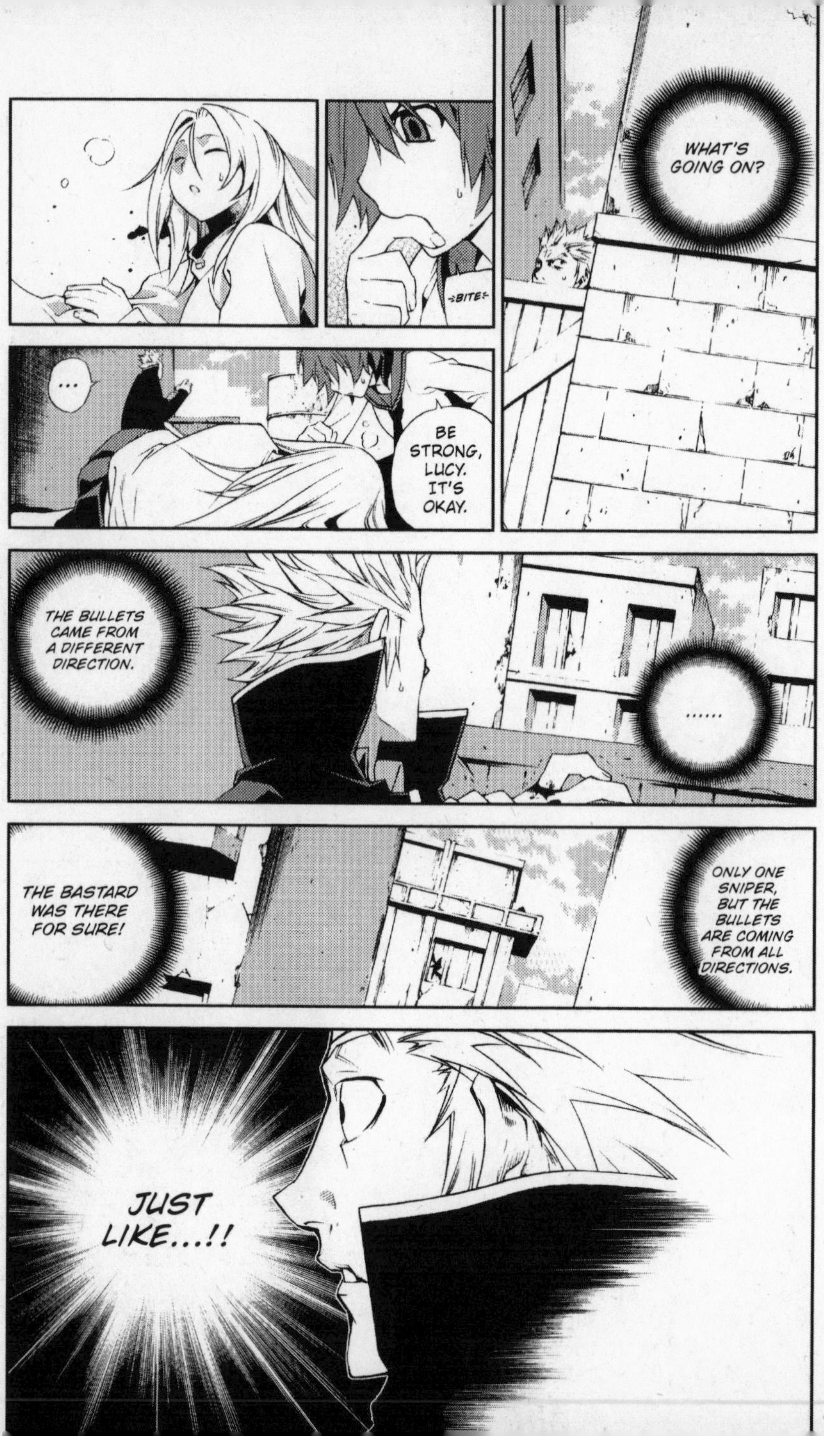
BITE
...
BE STRONG, LUCY. IT'S OKAY.
WHAT'S GOING ON?
THE BULLETS CAME FROM A DIFFERENT DIRECTION.
......
THE BASTARD WAS THERE FOR SURE!
ONLY ONE SNIPER, BUT THE BULLETS ARE COMING FROM ALL DIRECTIONS.
JUST LIKE...!!

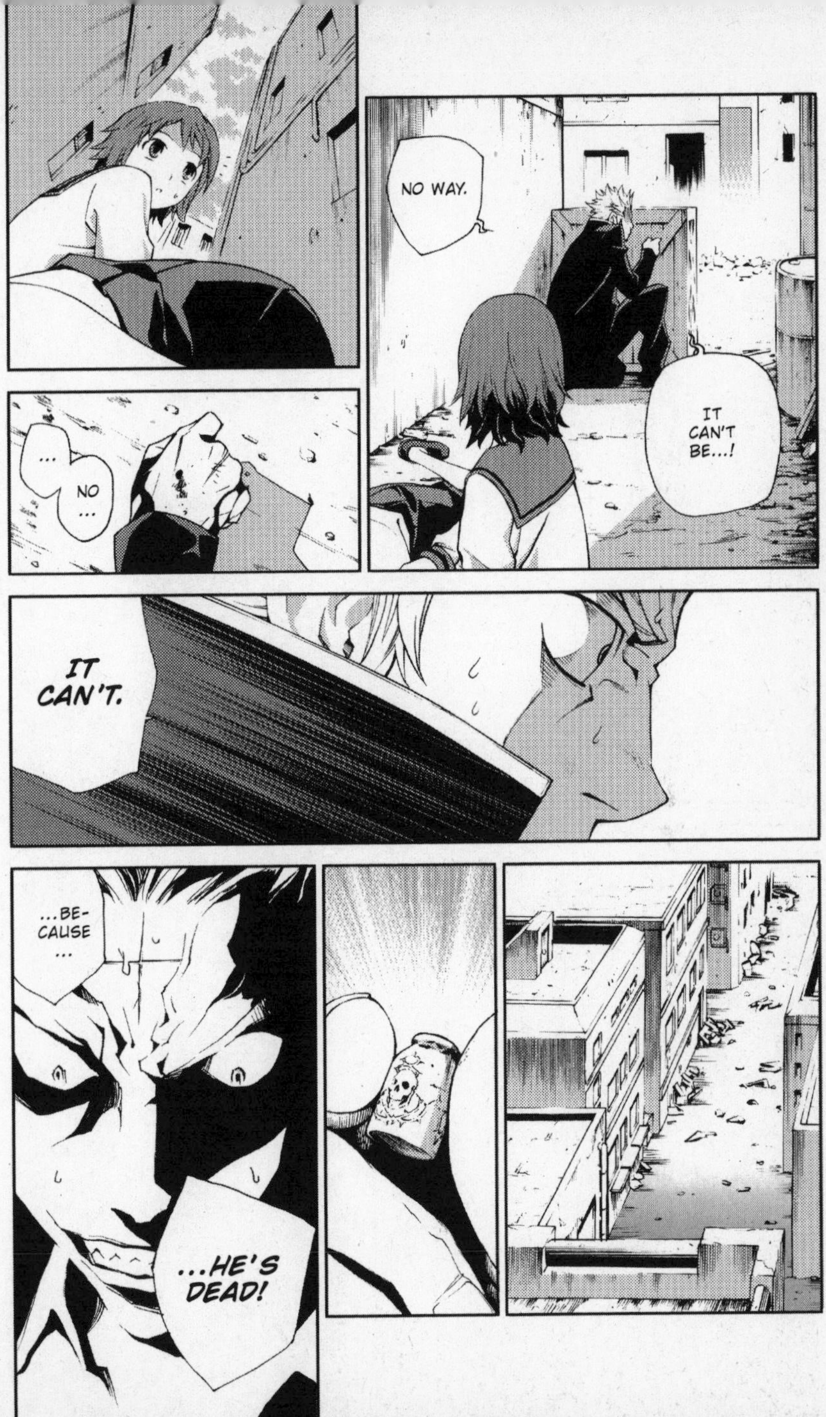
... NO ...
NO WAY.
IT CAN'T BE...!
IT CAN'T.
...BE- CAUSE ...
...HE'S DEAD!

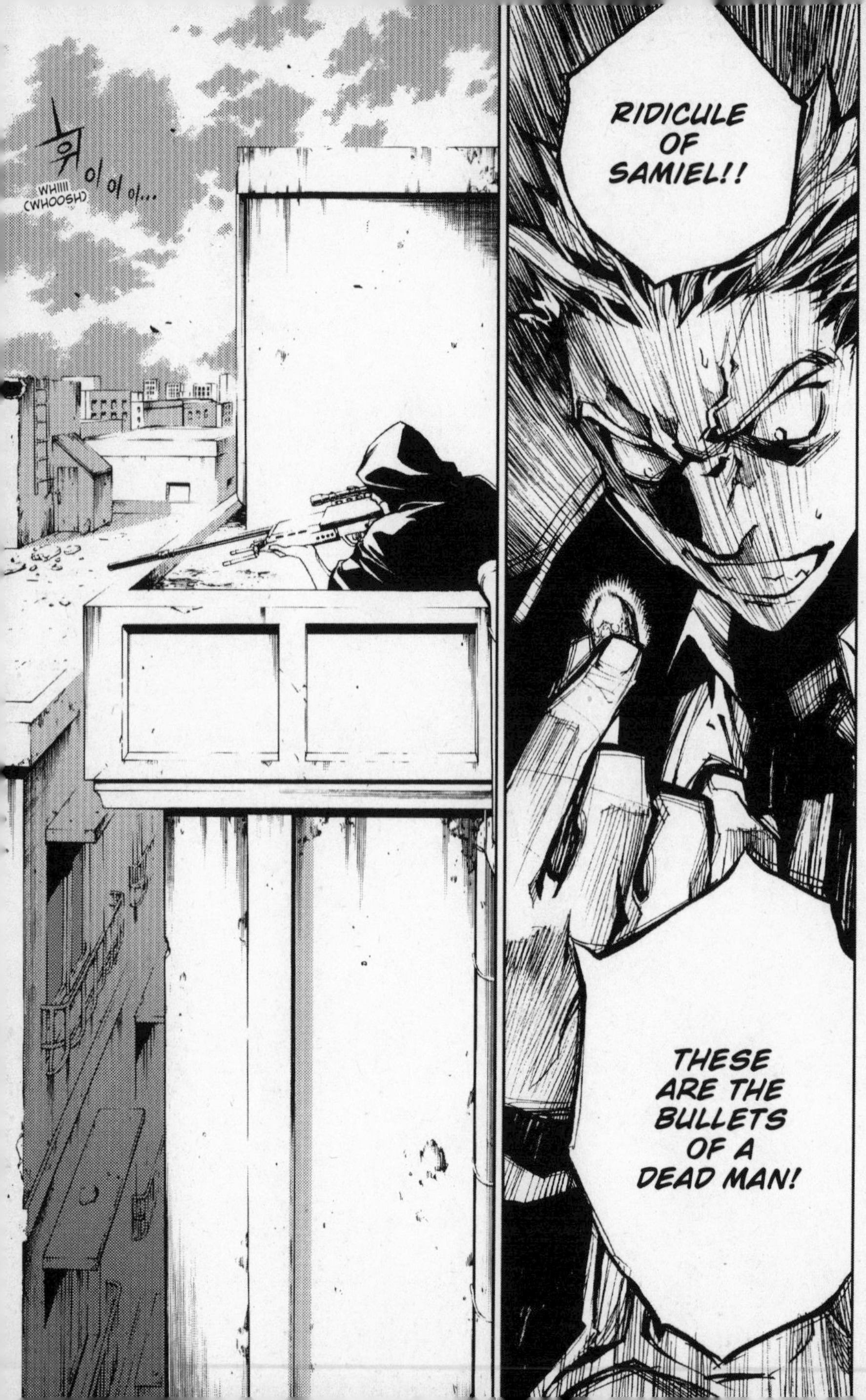
휘이이이...
WHIIIII (WHOOSH)
RIDICULE OF SAMIEL!!
THESE ARE THE BULLETS OF A DEAD MAN!

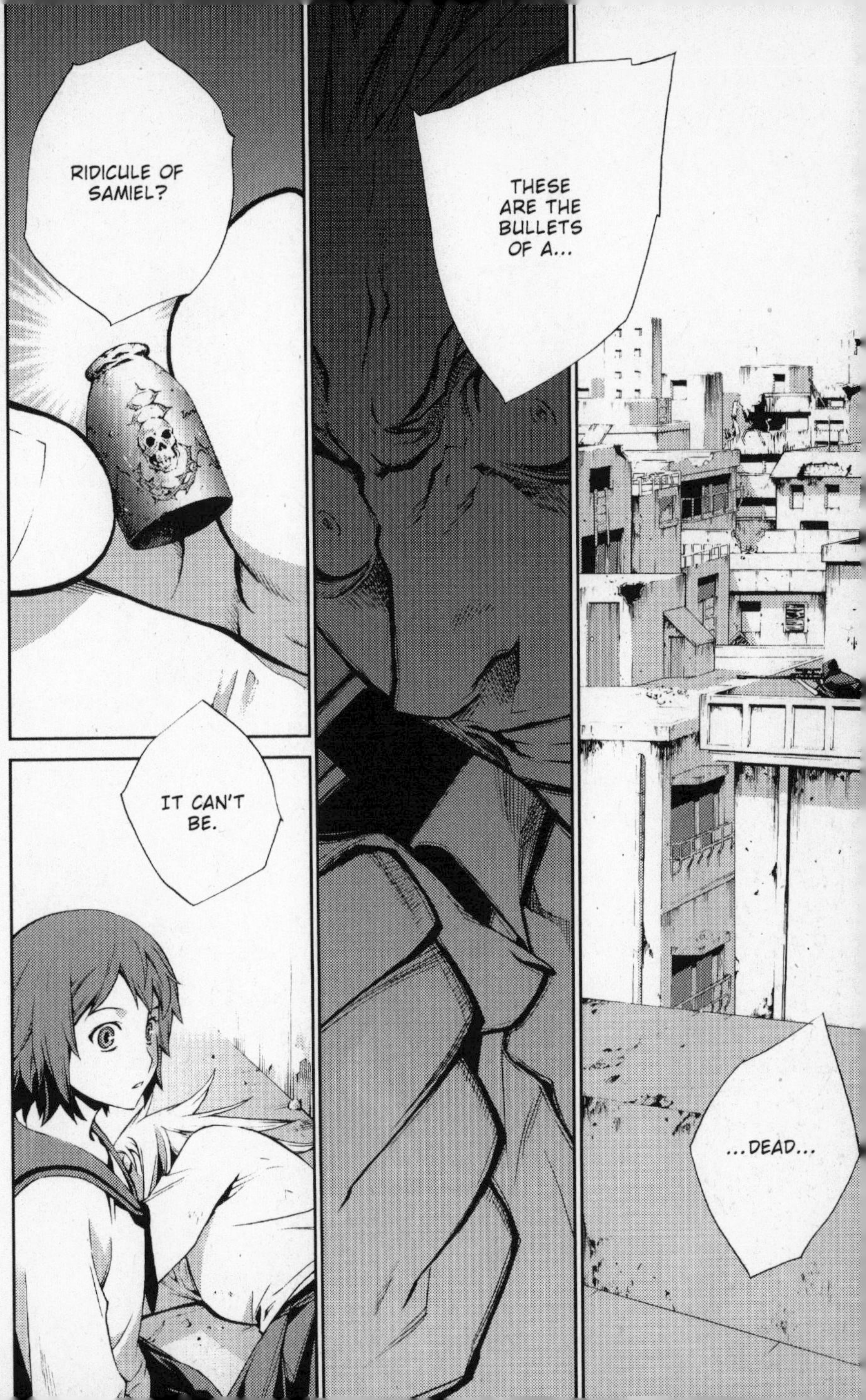
RIDICULE OF SAMIEL?
IT CAN'T BE.
THESE ARE THE BULLETS OF A...
...DEAD...

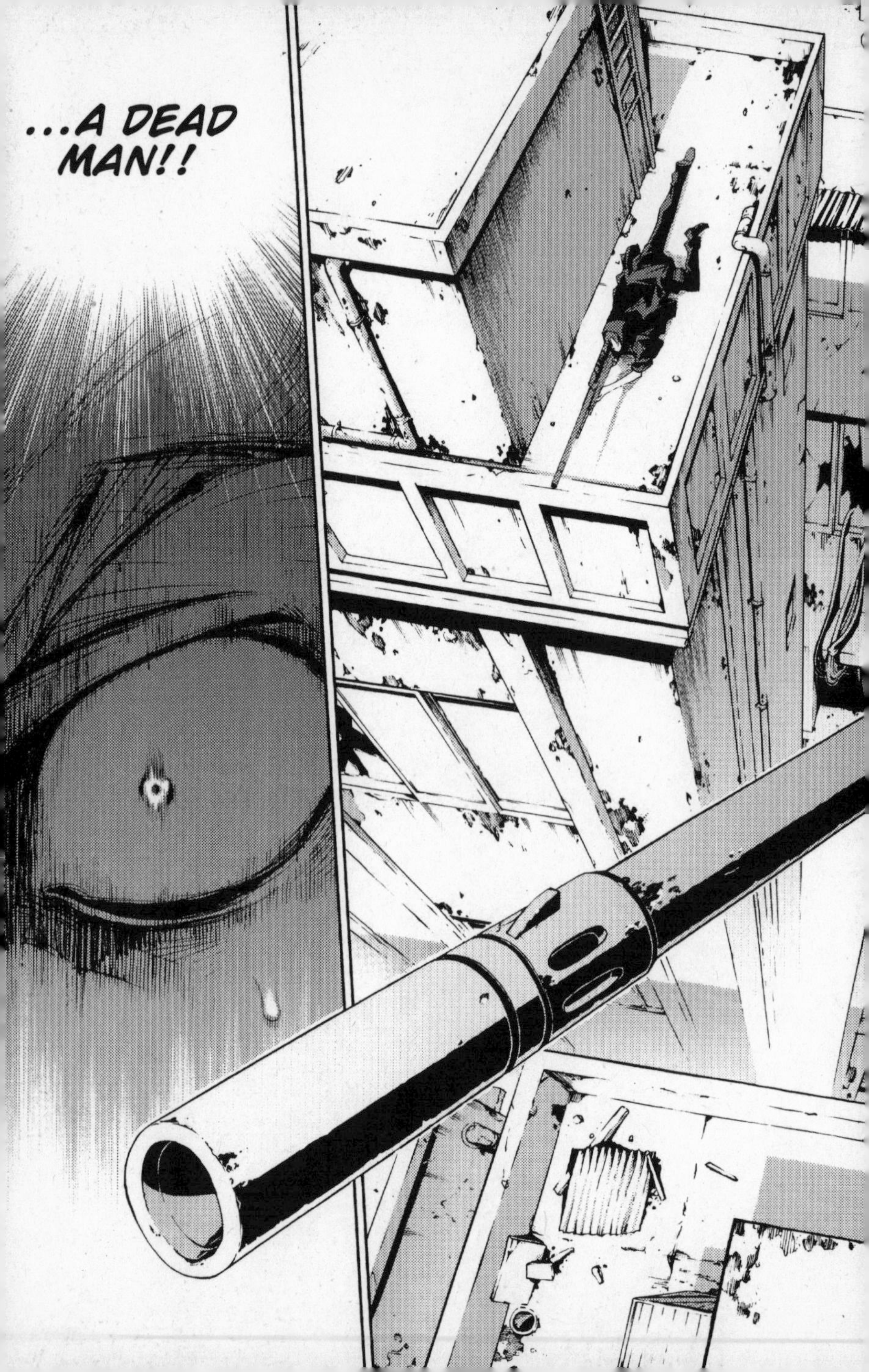
...A DEAD MAN!!

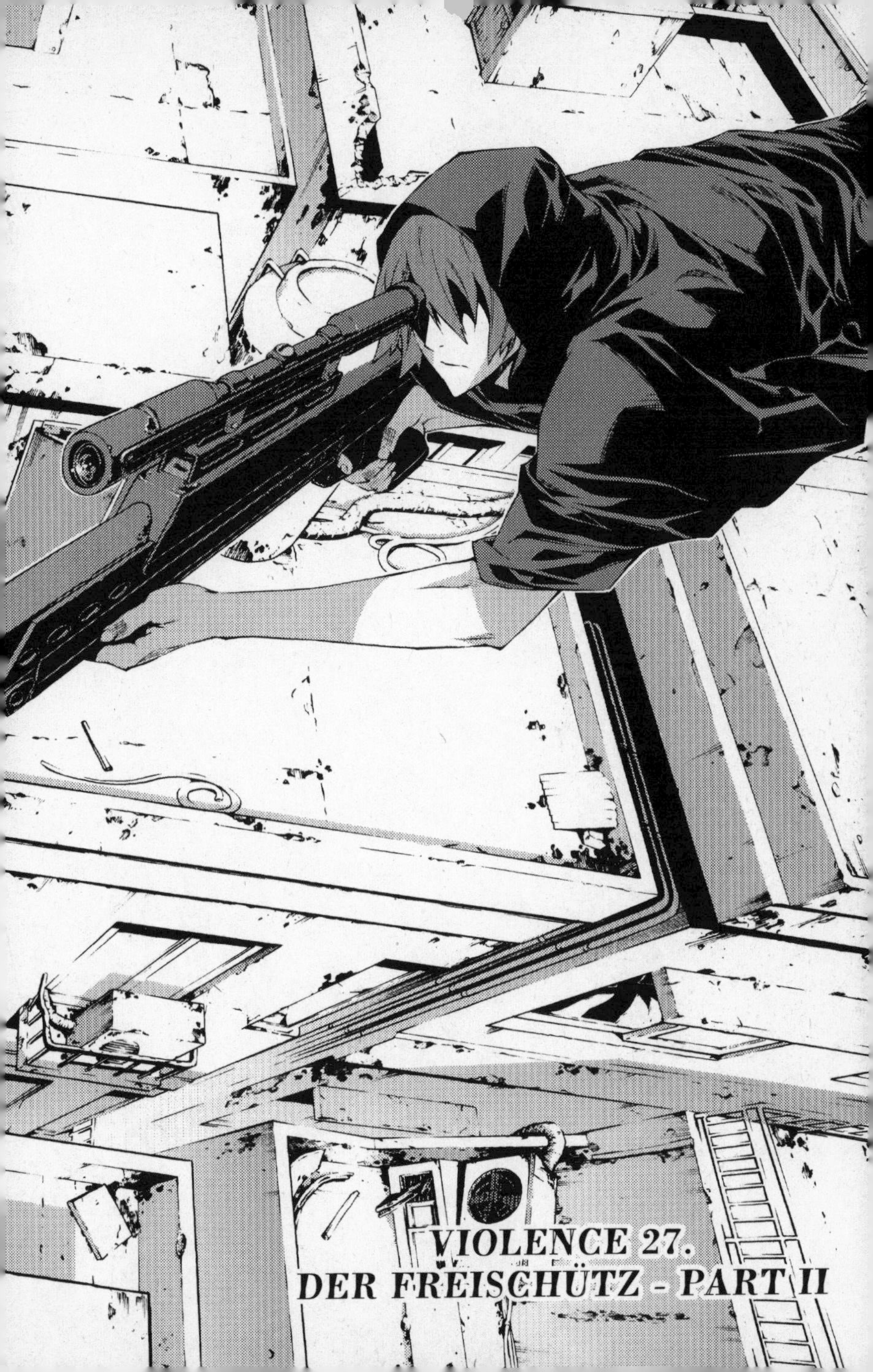
VIOLENCE 27.
DER FREISCHÜTZ - PART II

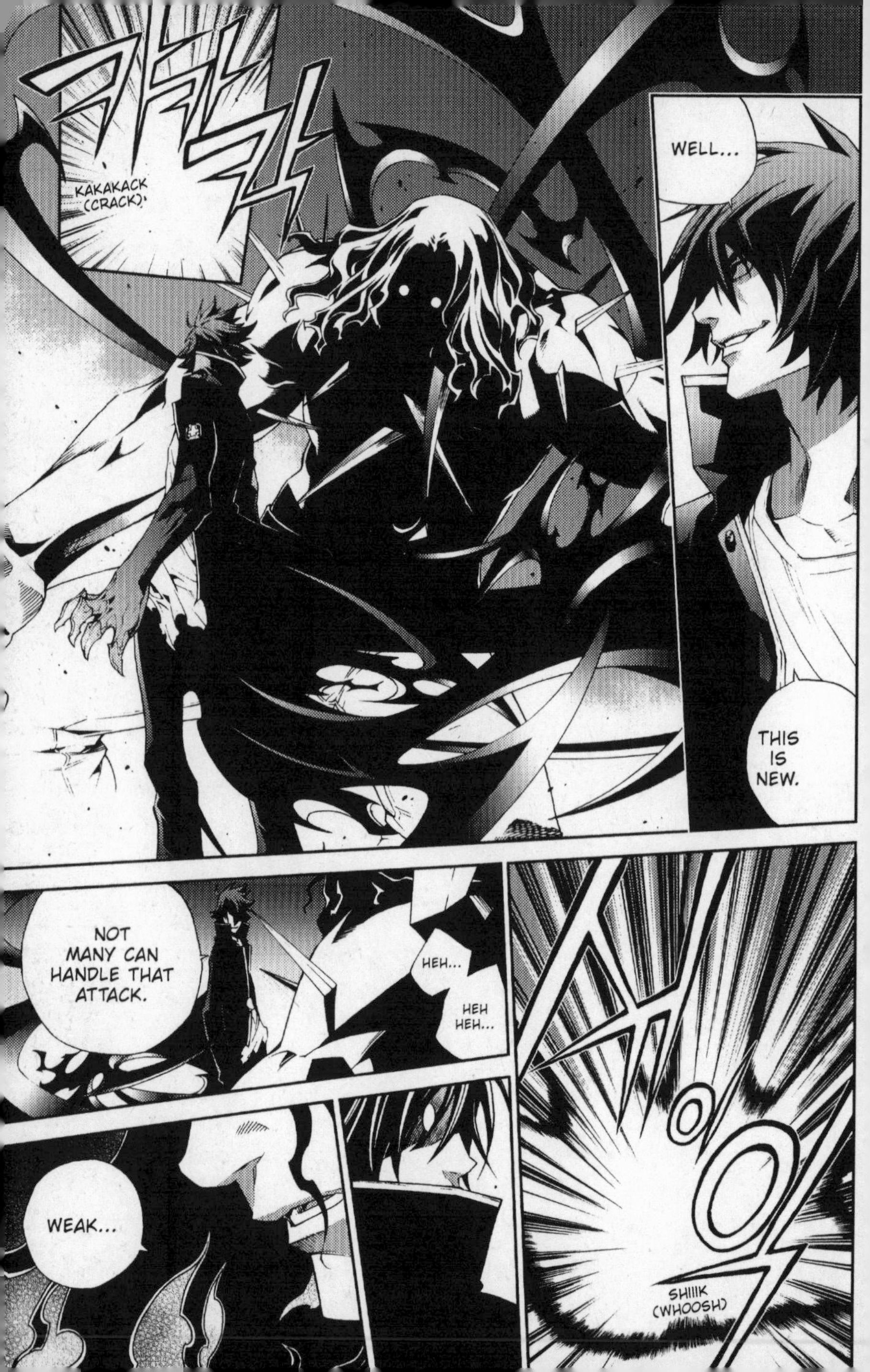

KAKAKACK (CRACK)!
WELL...
THIS IS NEW.
NOT MANY CAN HANDLE THAT ATTACK.
HEH...
HEH HEH...
WEAK...
SHIIIK (WHOOSH)

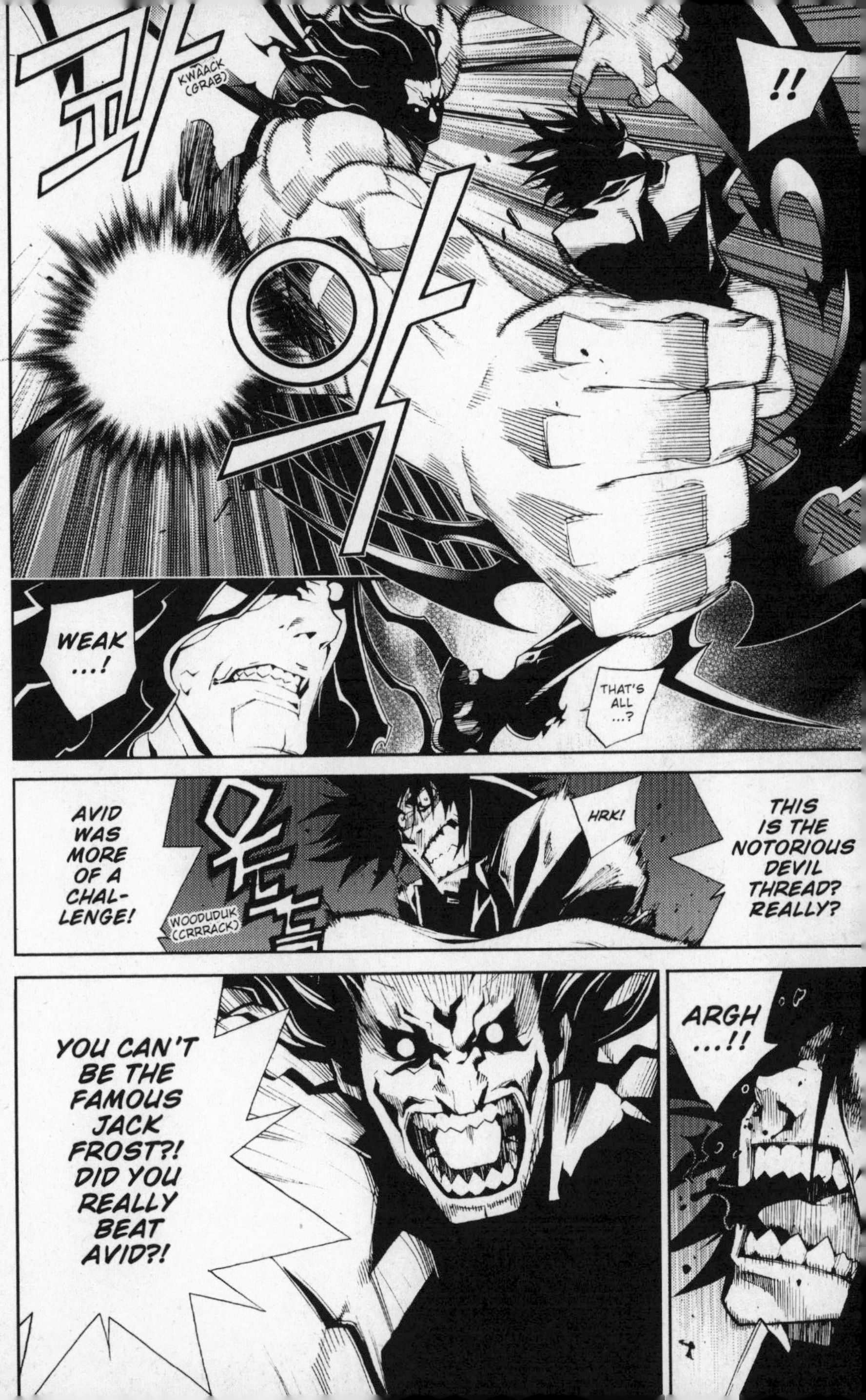
KWAACK (GRAB)
!!
WEAK ...!
THAT'S ALL ...?
AVID WAS MORE OF A CHAL-LENGE!
WOODUDUK (CRRRACK)
HRK!
THIS IS THE NOTORIOUS DEVIL THREAD? REALLY?
YOU CAN'T BE THE FAMOUS JACK FROST?! DID YOU REALLY BEAT AVID?!
ARGH ...!!

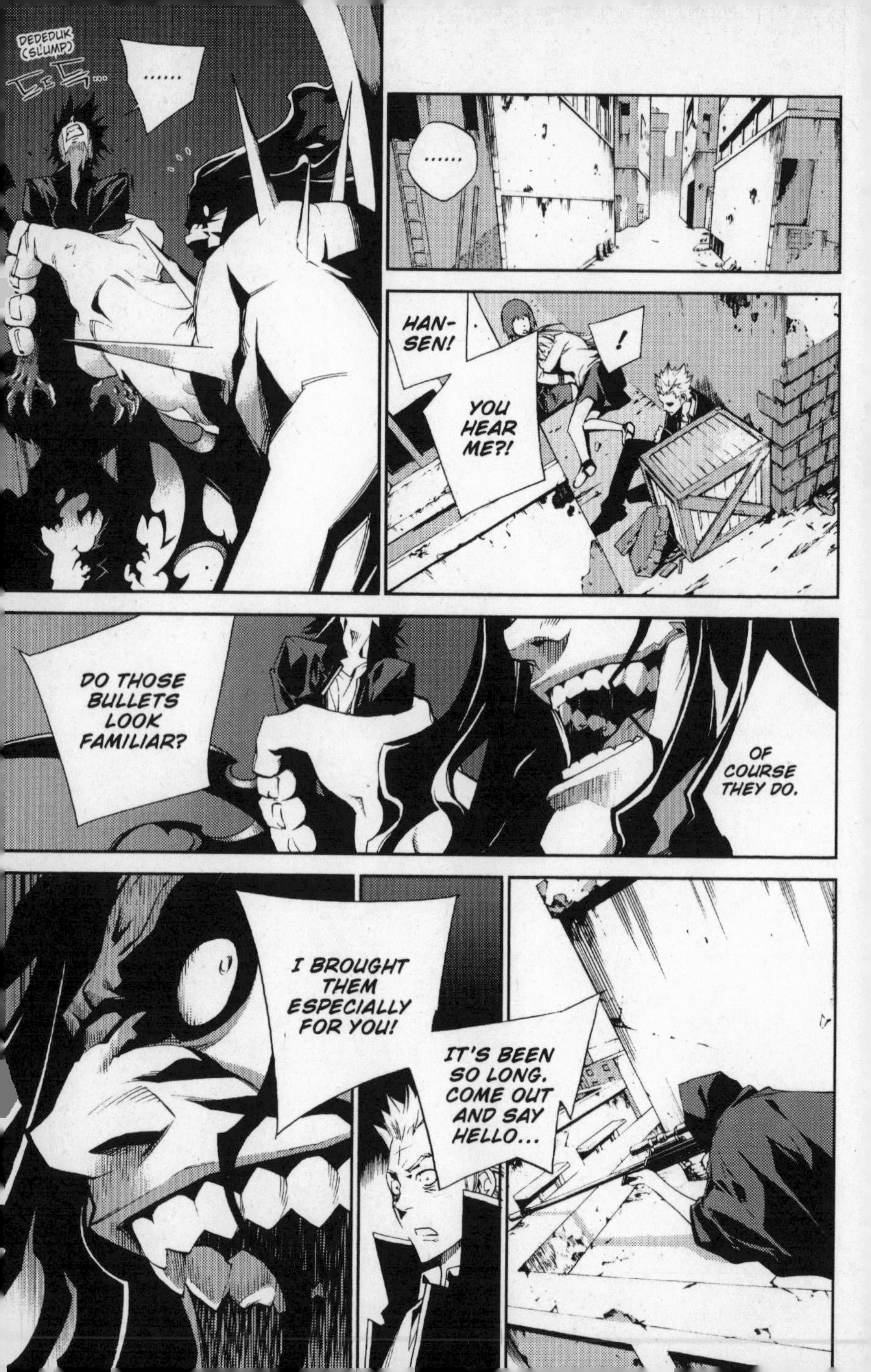
DEDEDUK (SLUMP)
......
......
HAN-SEN!
YOU HEAR ME?!
!
DO THOSE BULLETS LOOK FAMILIAR?
OF COURSE THEY DO.
I BROUGHT THEM ESPECIALLY FOR YOU!
IT'S BEEN SO LONG. COME OUT AND SAY HELLO...

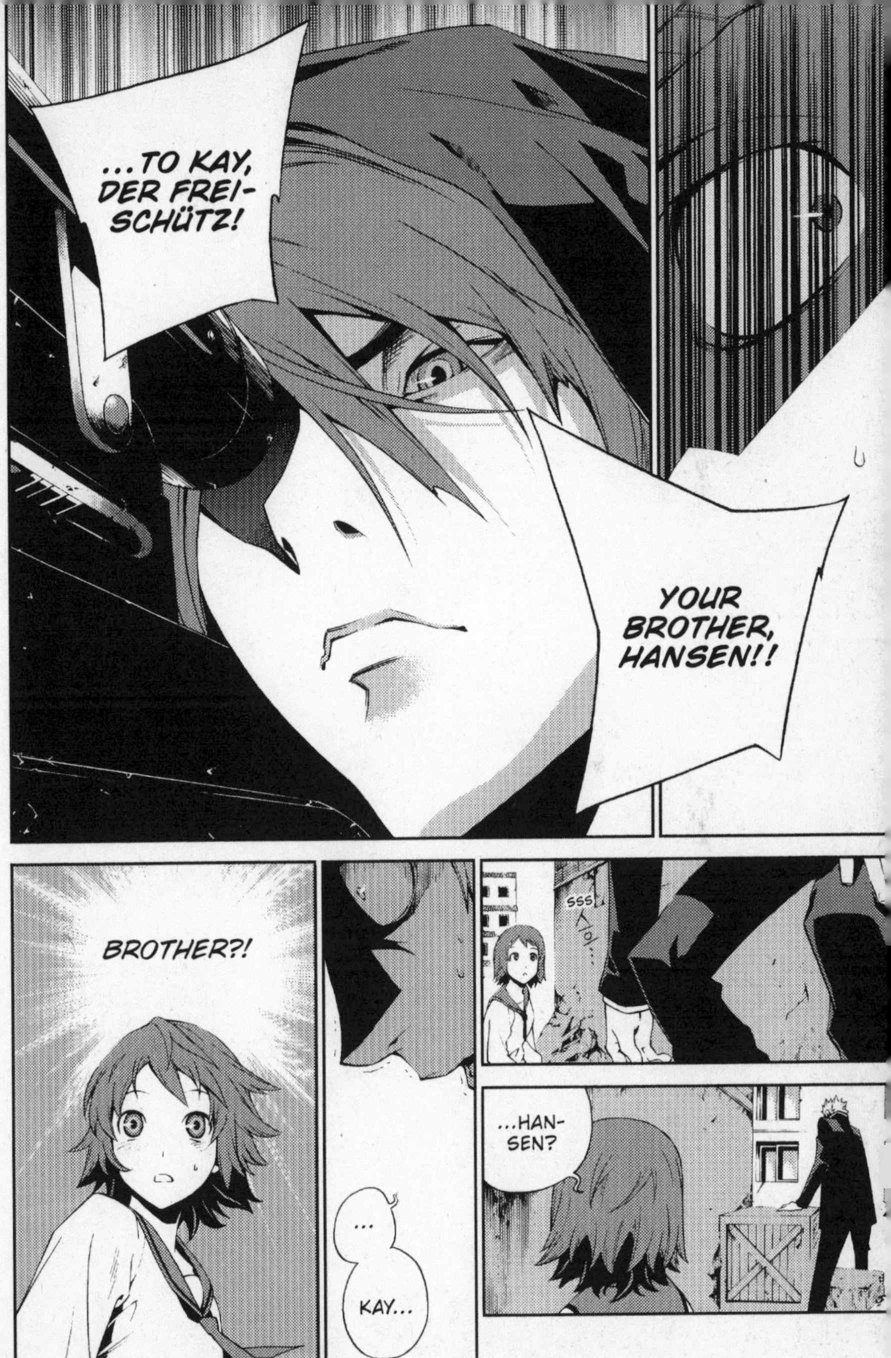
...TO KAY, DER FREI-SCHÜTZ!
YOUR BROTHER, HANSEN!!
BROTHER?!
...
KAY...
SSS
...HAN-SEN?

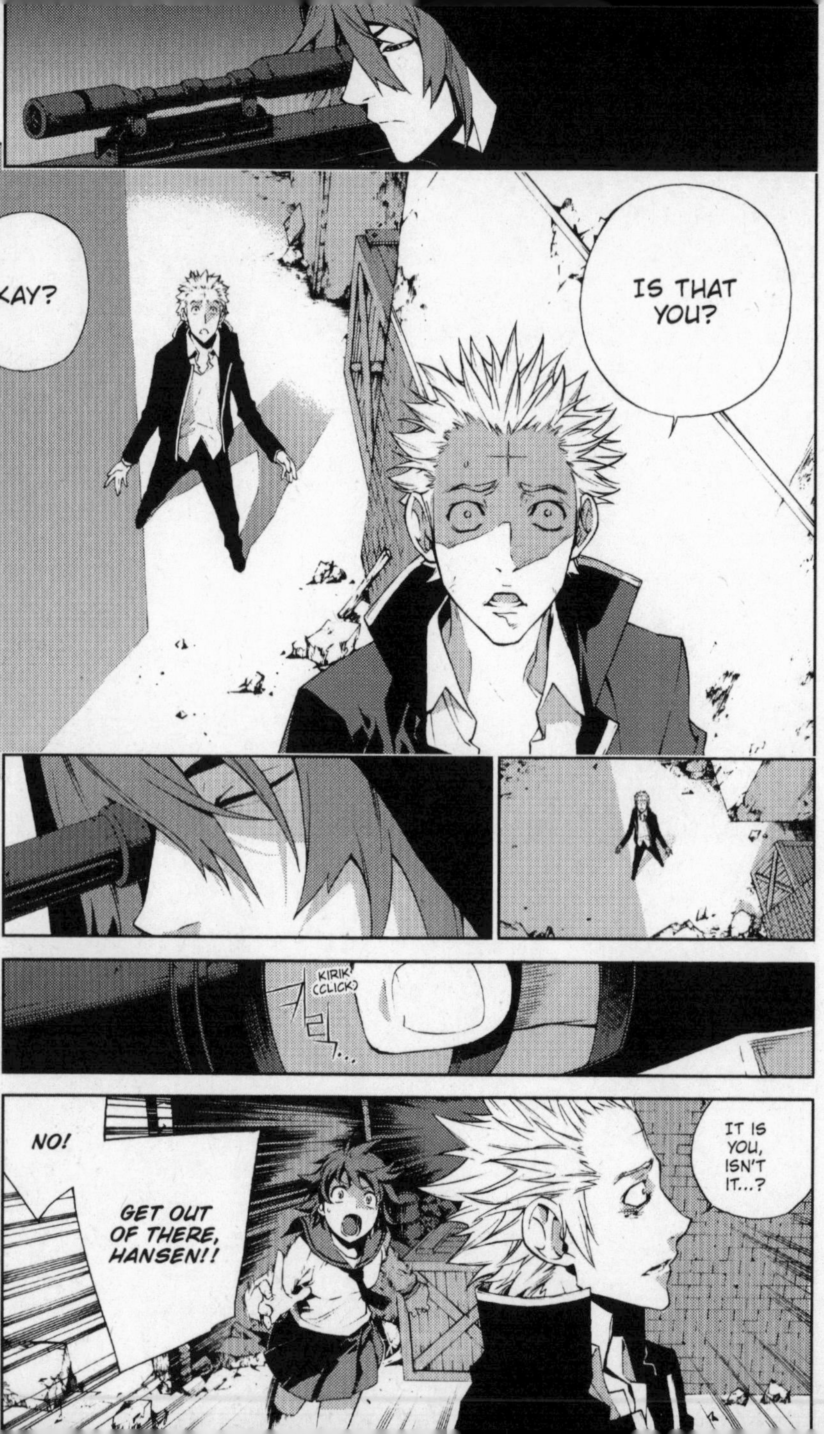
KAY?
IS THAT YOU?
KIRIK (CLICK)
NO!
GET OUT OF THERE, HANSEN!!
IT IS YOU, ISN'T IT...?

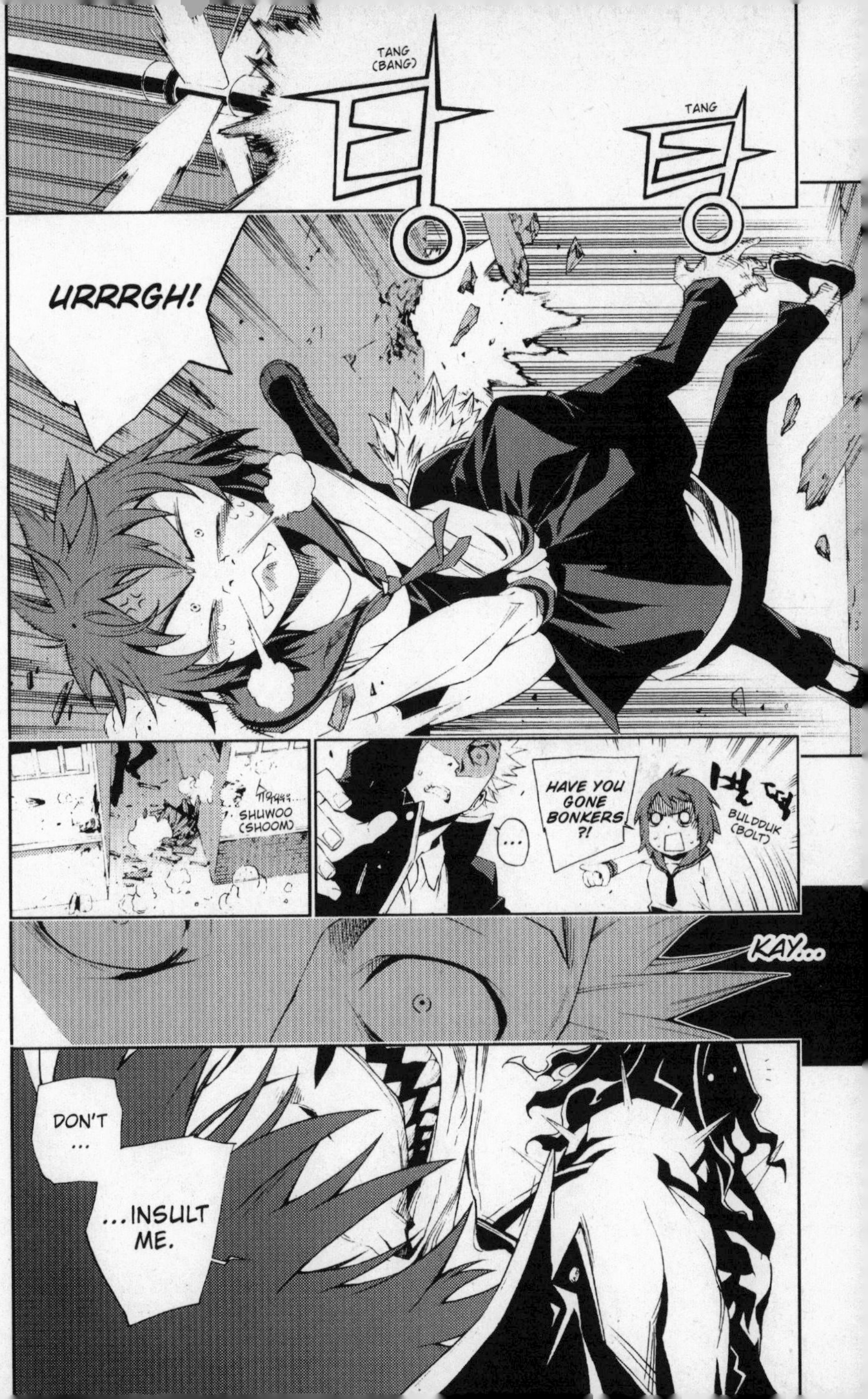

TANG (BANG)
탕
TANG
탕
URRRGH!
SHUWOO (SHOOM)
HAVE YOU GONE BONKERS?!
...
벌떡
BULDDUK (BOLT)
KAY...
DON'T ...
...INSULT ME.

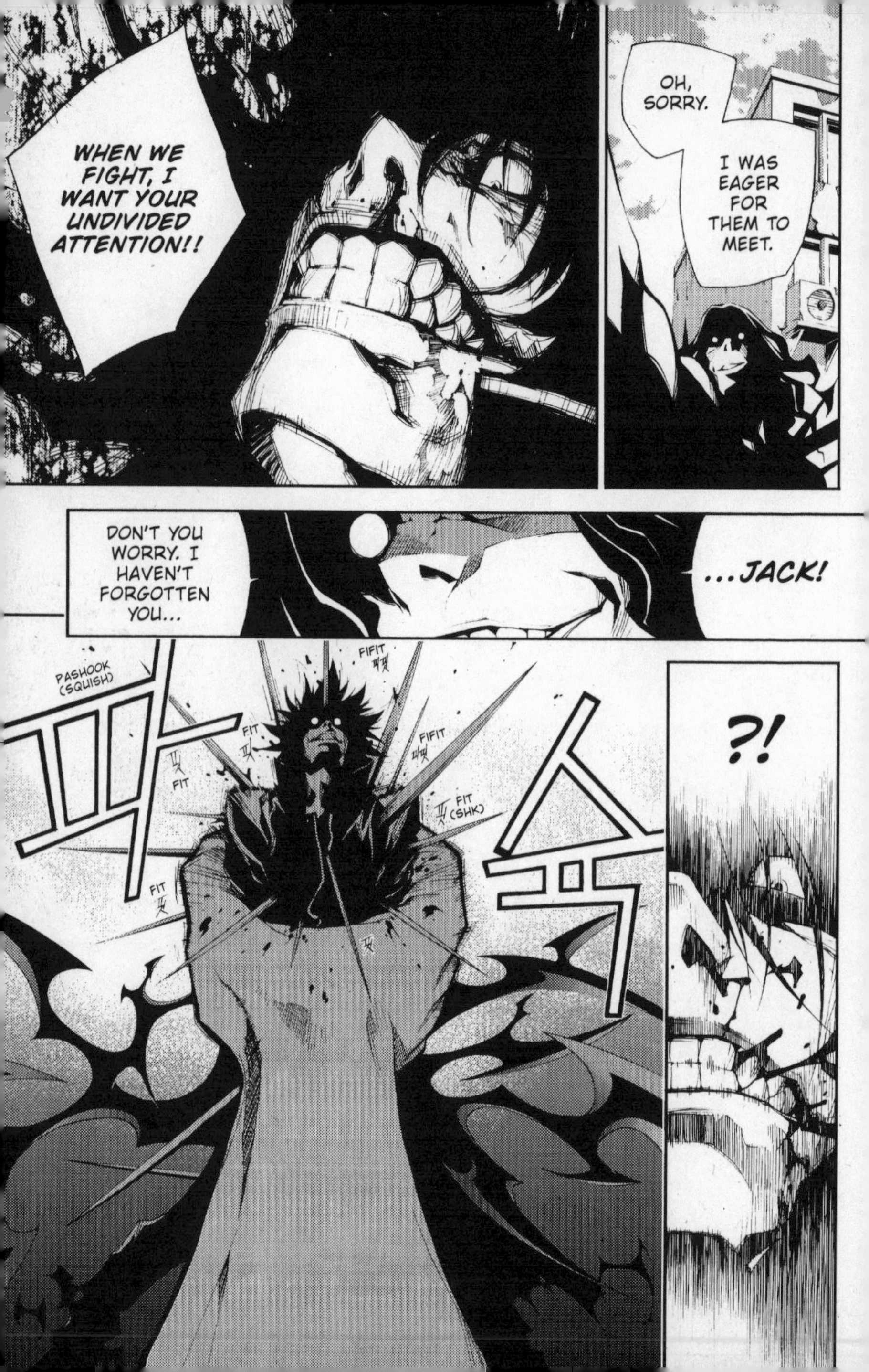
WHEN WE FIGHT, I WANT YOUR UNDIVIDED ATTENTION!!
OH, SORRY.
I WAS EAGER FOR THEM TO MEET.
DON'T YOU WORRY. I HAVEN'T FORGOTTEN YOU...
...JACK!
PASHOOK (SQUISH)
FIFIT
FIT
FIT
FIFIT
FIT (SHK)
FIT
?!

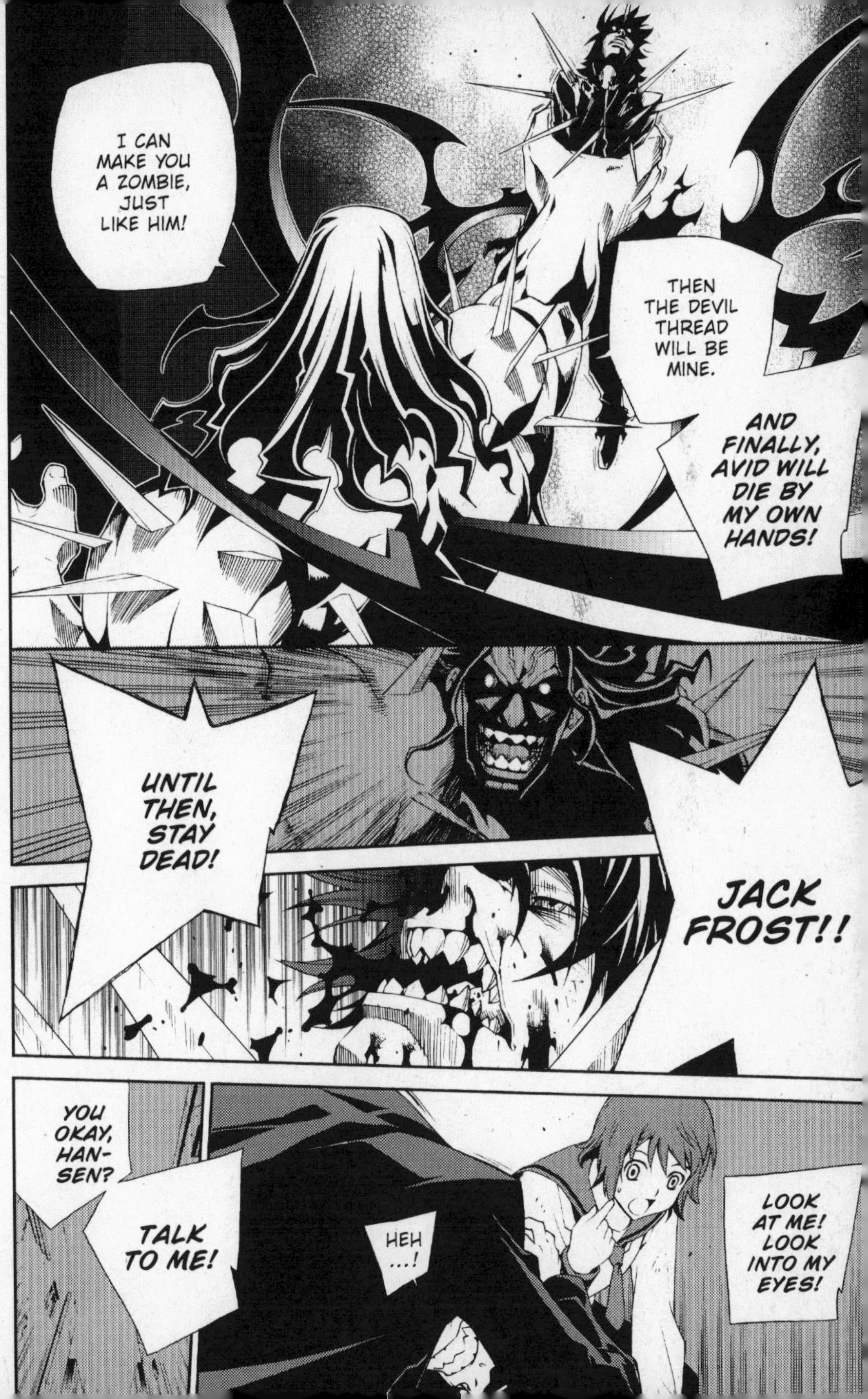
I CAN MAKE YOU A ZOMBIE, JUST LIKE HIM!
THEN THE DEVIL THREAD WILL BE MINE.
AND FINALLY, AVID WILL DIE BY MY OWN HANDS!
UNTIL THEN, STAY DEAD!
JACK FROST!!
YOU OKAY, HAN-SEN?
TALK TO ME!
HEH ...!
LOOK AT ME! LOOK INTO MY EYES!

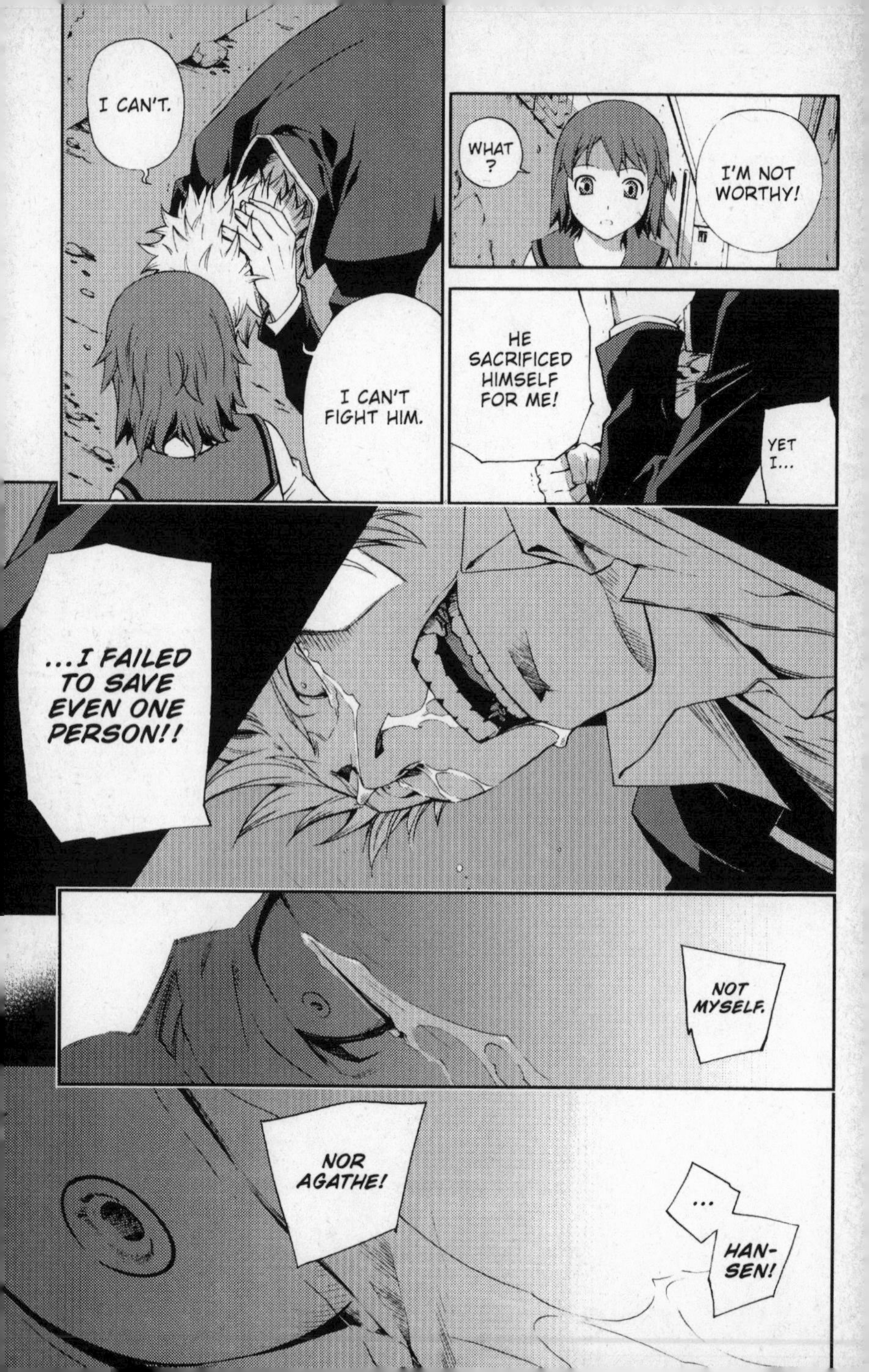

I CAN'T.
I CAN'T FIGHT HIM.
WHAT ?
I'M NOT WORTHY!
HE SACRIFICED HIMSELF FOR ME!
YET I...
...I FAILED TO SAVE EVEN ONE PERSON!!
NOT MYSELF.
NOR AGATHE!
...
HAN-SEN!

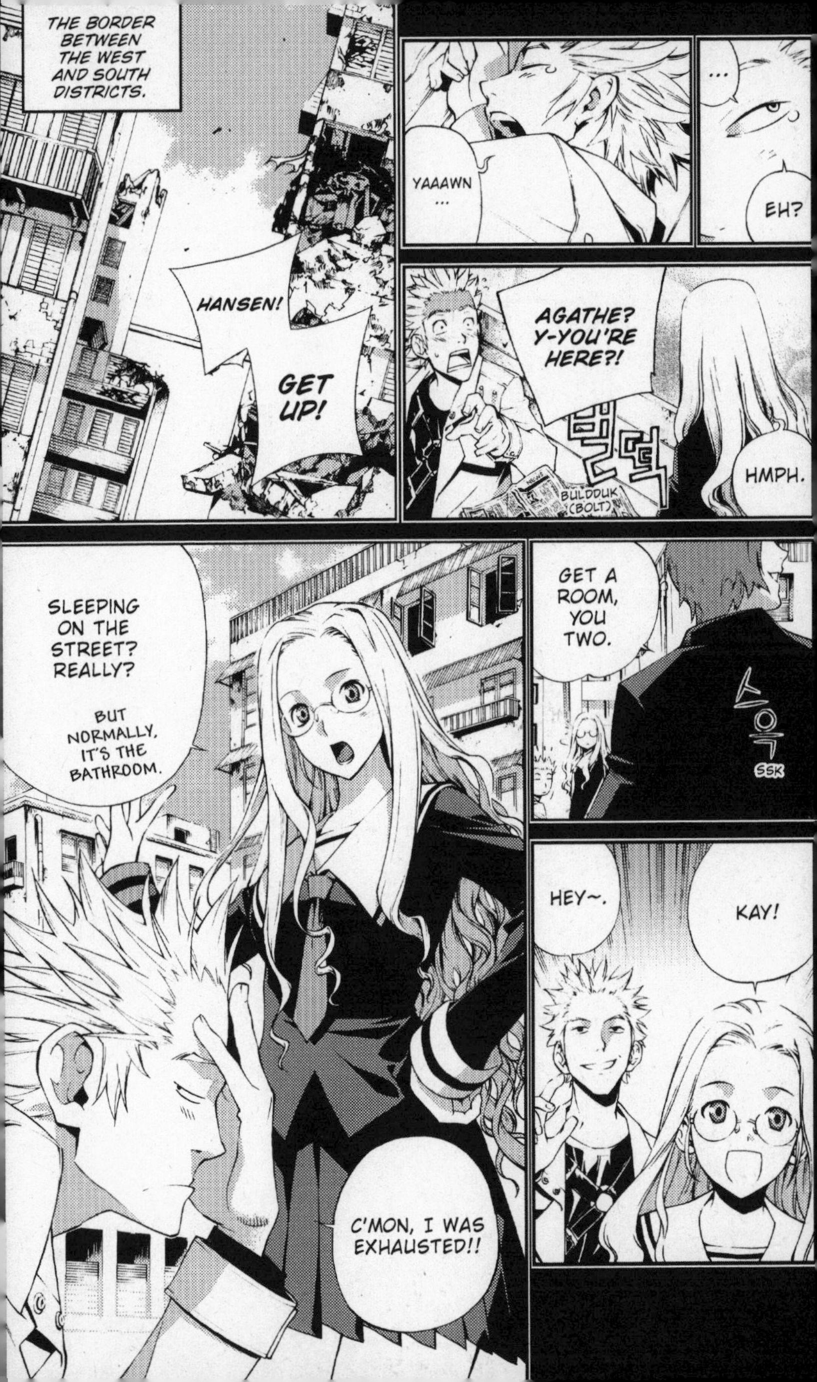
THE BORDER BETWEEN THE WEST AND SOUTH DISTRICTS.
HANSEN!
GET UP!
YAAAWN ...
...
EH?
AGATHE? Y-YOU'RE HERE?!
BULDDUK (BOLT)
HMPH.
SLEEPING ON THE STREET? REALLY?
BUT NORMALLY, IT'S THE BATHROOM.
C'MON, I WAS EXHAUSTED!!
GET A ROOM, YOU TWO.
SSK
HEY~.
KAY!

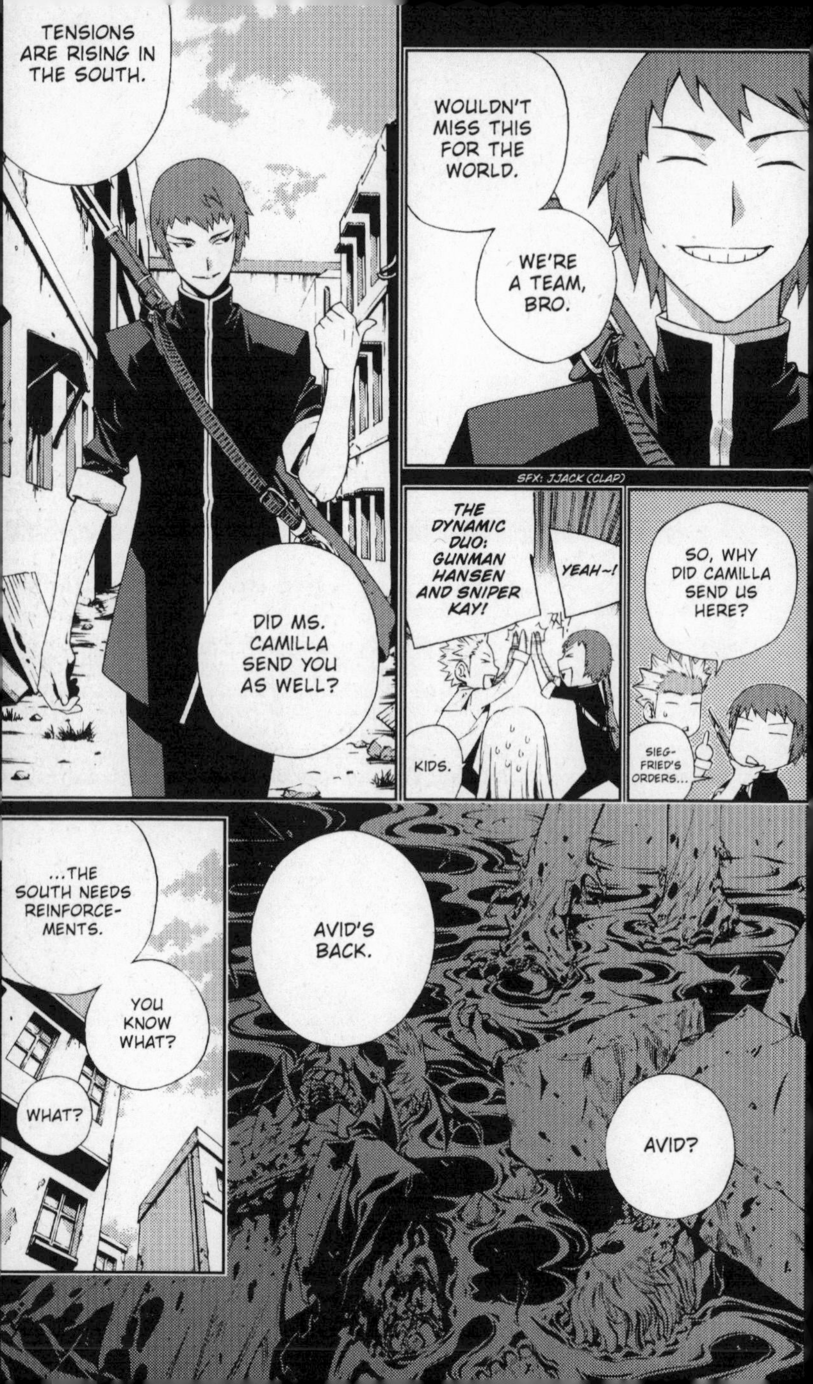
TENSIONS ARE RISING IN THE SOUTH.
DID MS. CAMILLA SEND YOU AS WELL?
WOULDN'T MISS THIS FOR THE WORLD.
WE'RE A TEAM, BRO.
SFX: JJACK (CLAP)
THE DYNAMIC DUO: GUNMAN HANSEN AND SNIPER KAY!
YEAH~!
KIDS.
SO, WHY DID CAMILLA SEND US HERE?
SIEG-FRIED'S ORDERS...
...THE SOUTH NEEDS REINFORCE-MENTS.
YOU KNOW WHAT?
WHAT?
AVID'S BACK.
AVID?

DON'T KNOW WHY, BUT HE'S AFTER SIEGFRIED NOW.

AND HE SOMEHOW CAME BACK AS A VAMPIRE!

VAMPIRE?

REALLY? I THOUGHT VAMPIRES WERE EXTINCT!

APPARENTLY NOT.

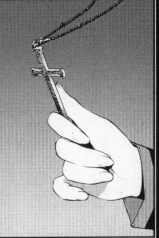

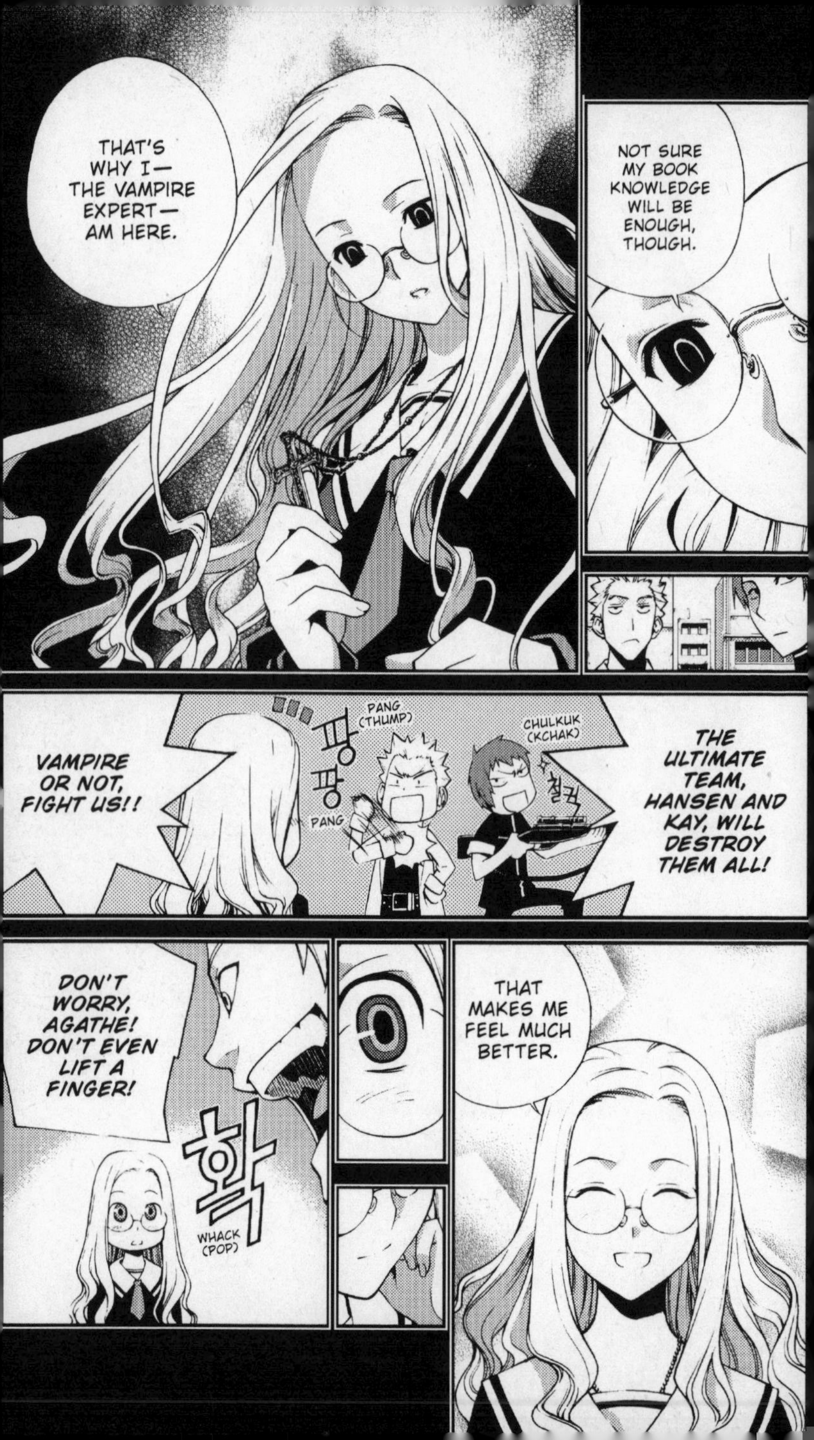

THAT'S WHY I— THE VAMPIRE EXPERT— AM HERE.
NOT SURE MY BOOK KNOWLEDGE WILL BE ENOUGH, THOUGH.
VAMPIRE OR NOT, FIGHT US!!
팡 팡
PANG (THUMP)
PANG
철컥
CHULKUK (KCHAK)
THE ULTIMATE TEAM, HANSEN AND KAY, WILL DESTROY THEM ALL!
DON'T WORRY, AGATHE! DON'T EVEN LIFT A FINGER!
확
WHACK (POP)
THAT MAKES ME FEEL MUCH BETTER.

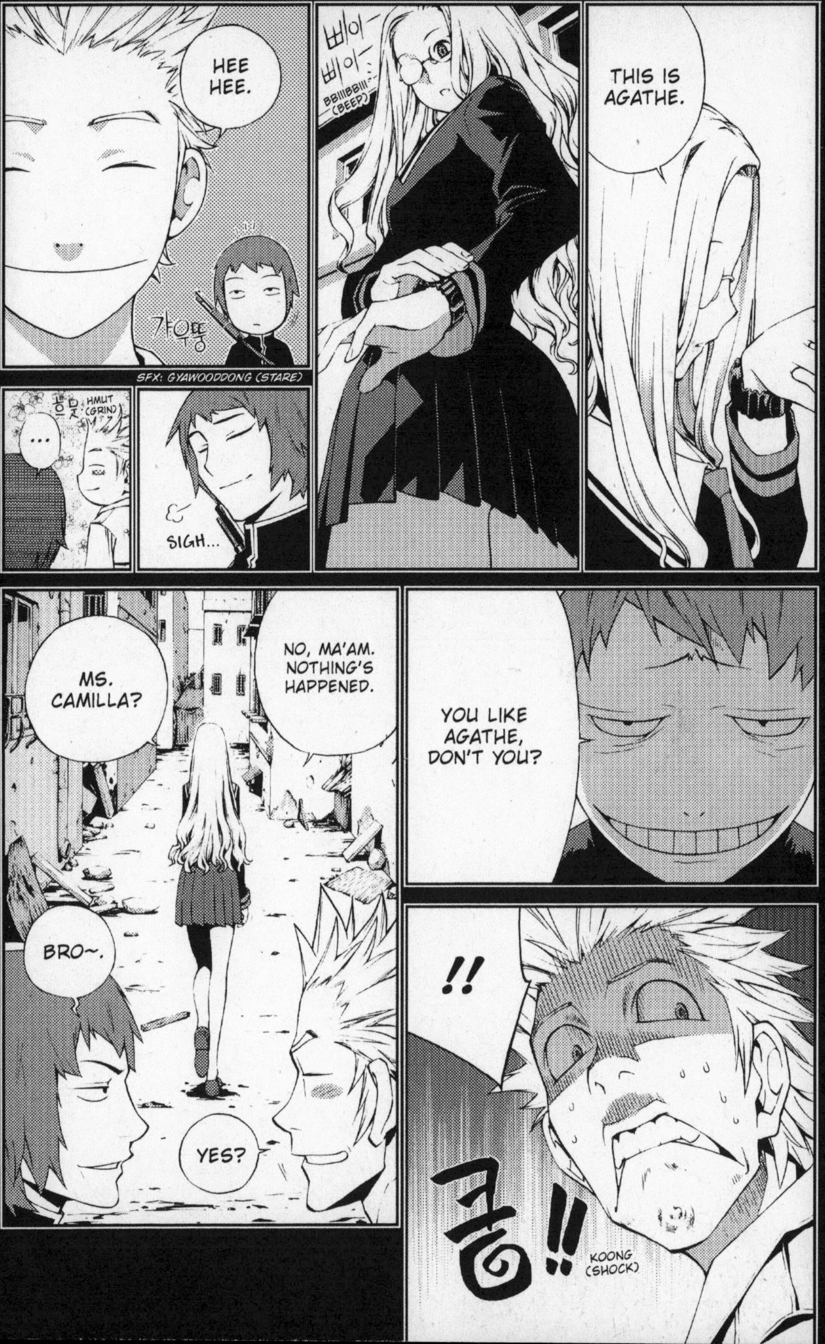
HEE HEE.
갸우뚱
SFX: GYAWOODDONG (STARE)
흐뭇
HMUT (GRIND)
...
SIGH...
삐이- 삐이-
BBIIIBBIII (BEEP)
THIS IS AGATHE.
MS. CAMILLA?
NO, MA'AM. NOTHING'S HAPPENED.
BRO~.
YES?
YOU LIKE AGATHE, DON'T YOU?
!!
쿵!!
KOONG (SHOCK)

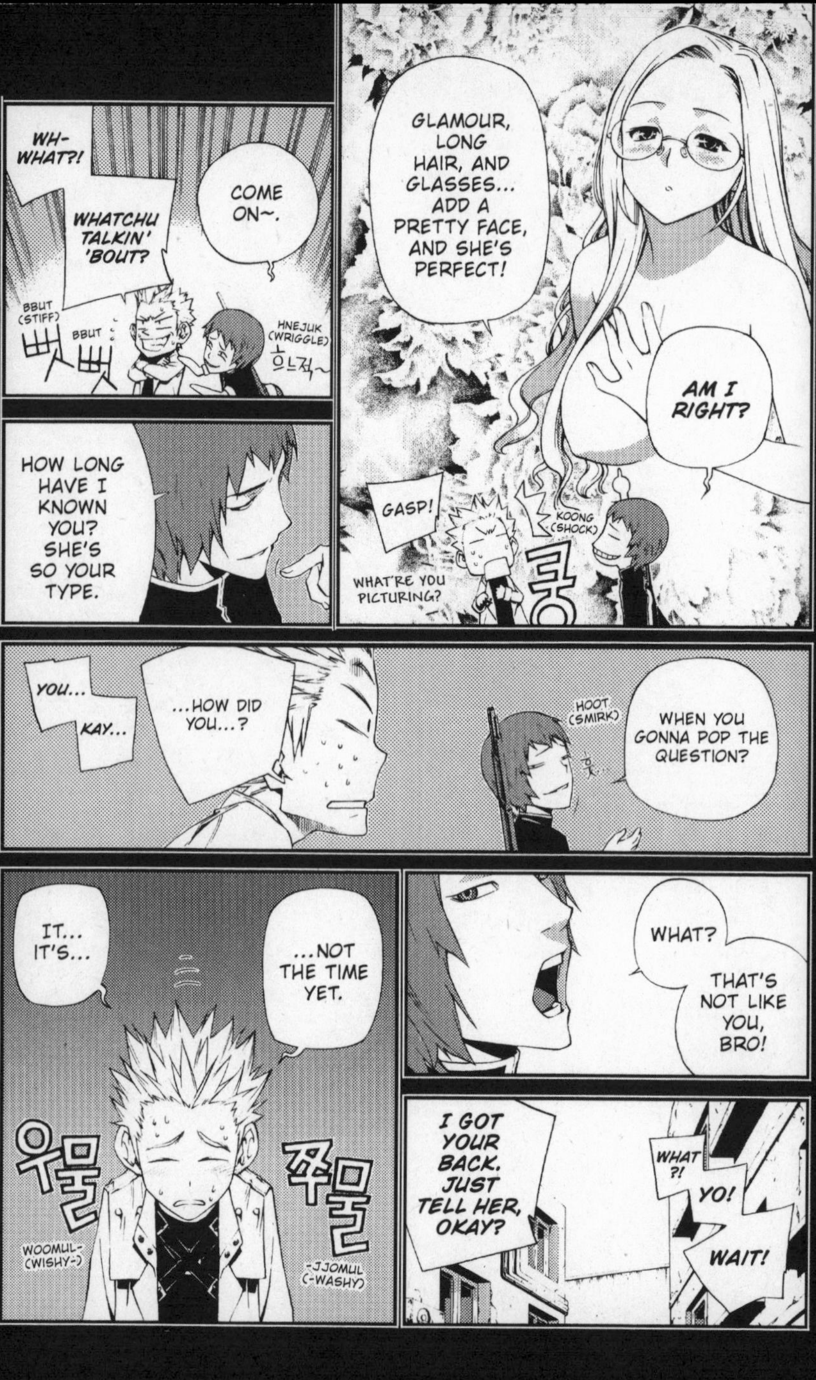
WH-WHAT?!
WHATCHU TALKIN' 'BOUT?
COME ON~.
BBUT (STIFF)
BBUT
빳빳
HNEJUK (WRIGGLE)
흐느적~
HOW LONG HAVE I KNOWN YOU? SHE'S SO YOUR TYPE.
GLAMOUR, LONG HAIR, AND GLASSES... ADD A PRETTY FACE, AND SHE'S PERFECT!
AM I RIGHT?
GASP!
KOONG (SHOCK)
쿵
WHAT'RE YOU PICTURING?
YOU...
KAY...
...HOW DID YOU...?
HOOT (SMIRK)
훗
WHEN YOU GONNA POP THE QUESTION?
IT... IT'S...
...NOT THE TIME YET.
우물
쭈물
WOOMUL- (WISHY-)
-JJOMUL (-WASHY)
WHAT?
THAT'S NOT LIKE YOU, BRO!
I GOT YOUR BACK. JUST TELL HER, OKAY?
WHAT?!
YO!
WAIT!

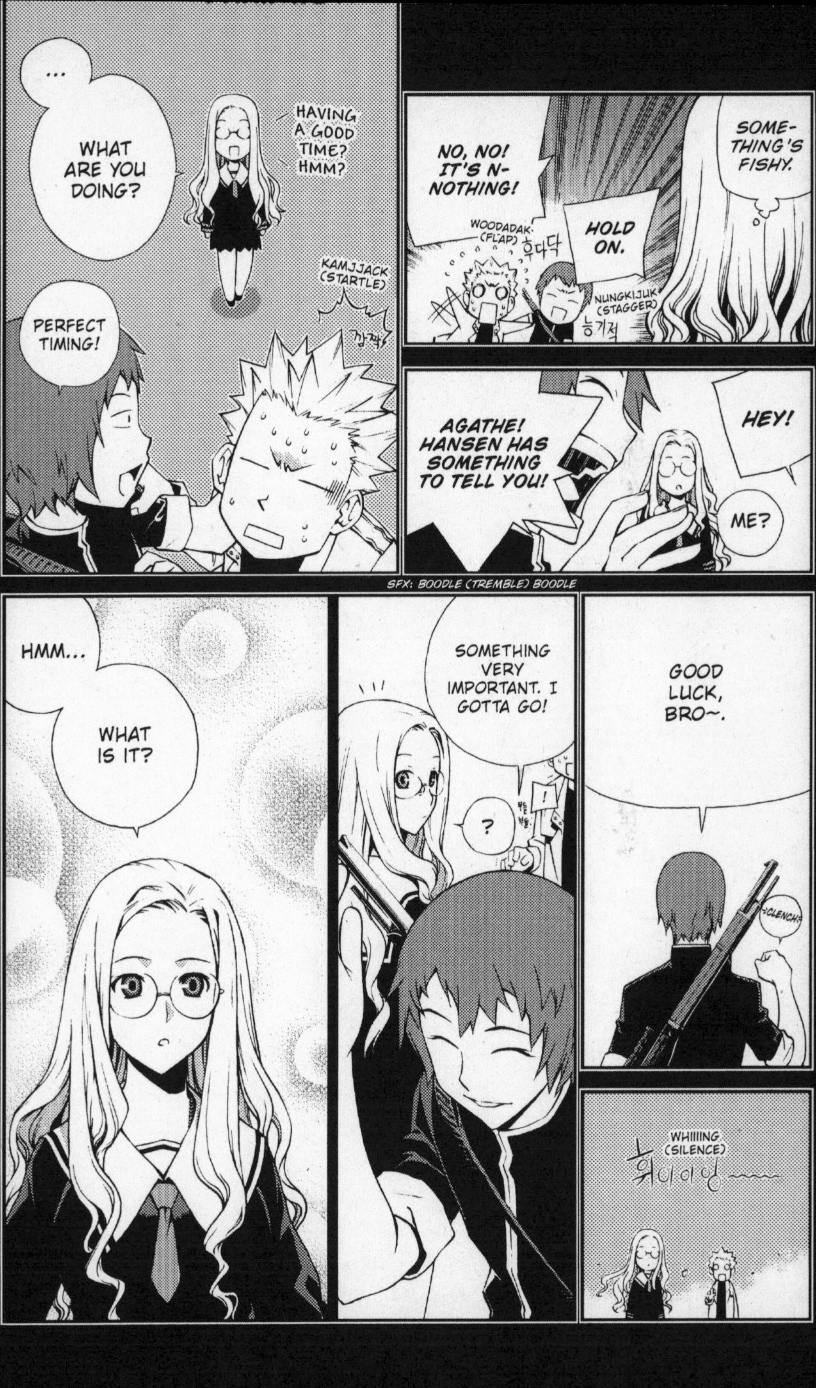
...
WHAT ARE YOU DOING?
HAVING A GOOD TIME? HMM?
KAMJJACK (STARTLE)
깜짝
PERFECT TIMING!
NO, NO! IT'S N-NOTHING!
WOODADAK (FLAP)
후다닥
HOLD ON.
NUNGKIJUK (STAGGER)
능기적
SOME-THING'S FISHY.
AGATHE! HANSEN HAS SOMETHING TO TELL YOU!
HEY!
ME?
SFX: BOODLE (TREMBLE) BOODLE
HMM...
WHAT IS IT?
SOMETHING VERY IMPORTANT. I GOTTA GO!
?
!
GOOD LUCK, BRO~.
CLENCH
WHIIIING (SILENCE)

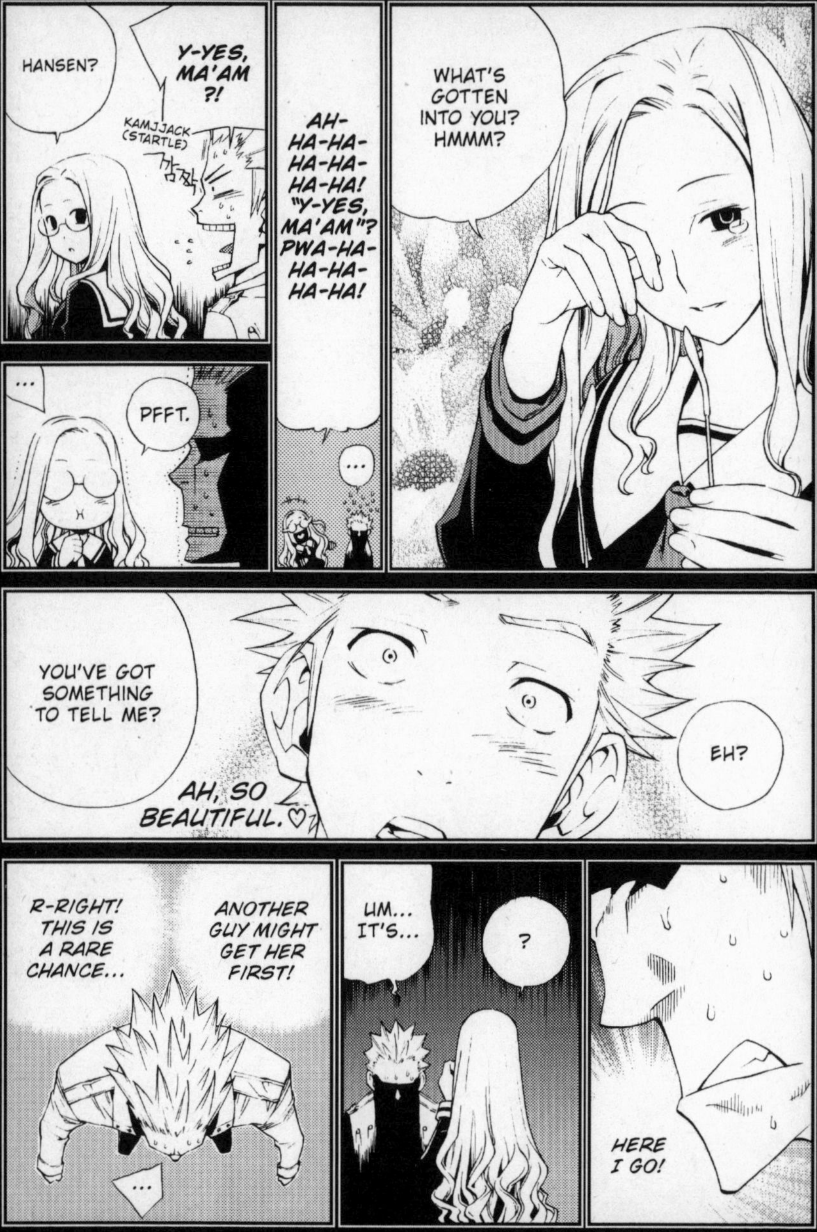
HANSEN?
Y-YES, MA'AM?!
KAMJJACK (STARTLE)
깜짝
...
PFFT.
AH-HA-HA-HA-HA-HA-HA! "Y-YES, MA'AM"? PWA-HA-HA-HA-HA-HA-HA!
...
WHAT'S GOTTEN INTO YOU? HMMM?
YOU'VE GOT SOMETHING TO TELL ME?
EH?
AH, SO BEAUTIFUL.♡
R-RIGHT! THIS IS A RARE CHANCE...
ANOTHER GUY MIGHT GET HER FIRST!
...
UM... IT'S...
?
HERE I GO!

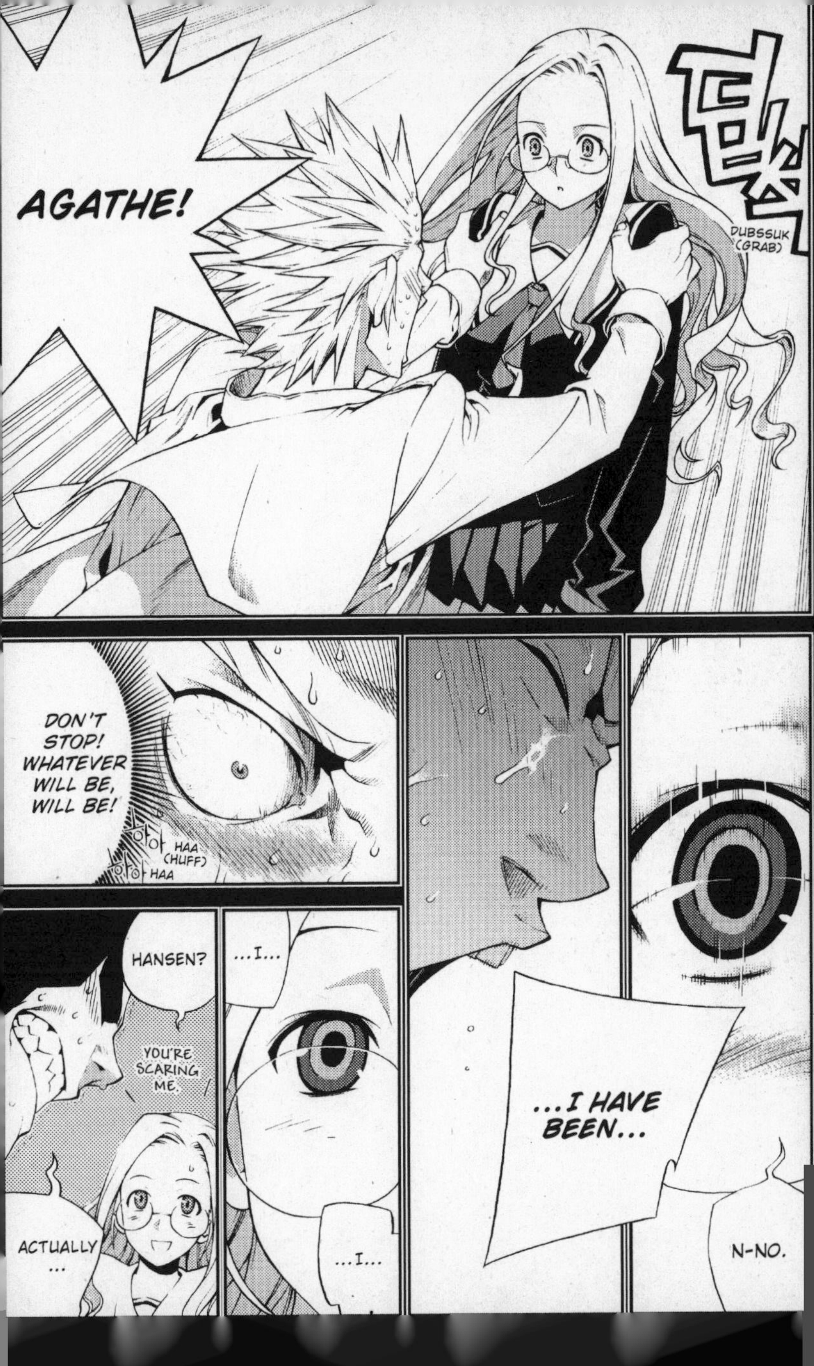
AGATHE!
DUBSSUK (GRAB)
DON'T STOP! WHATEVER WILL BE, WILL BE!
HAA (HUFF)
HAA
HANSEN?
YOU'RE SCARING ME.
ACTUALLY ...
...I...
...I...
...I HAVE BEEN...
N-NO.

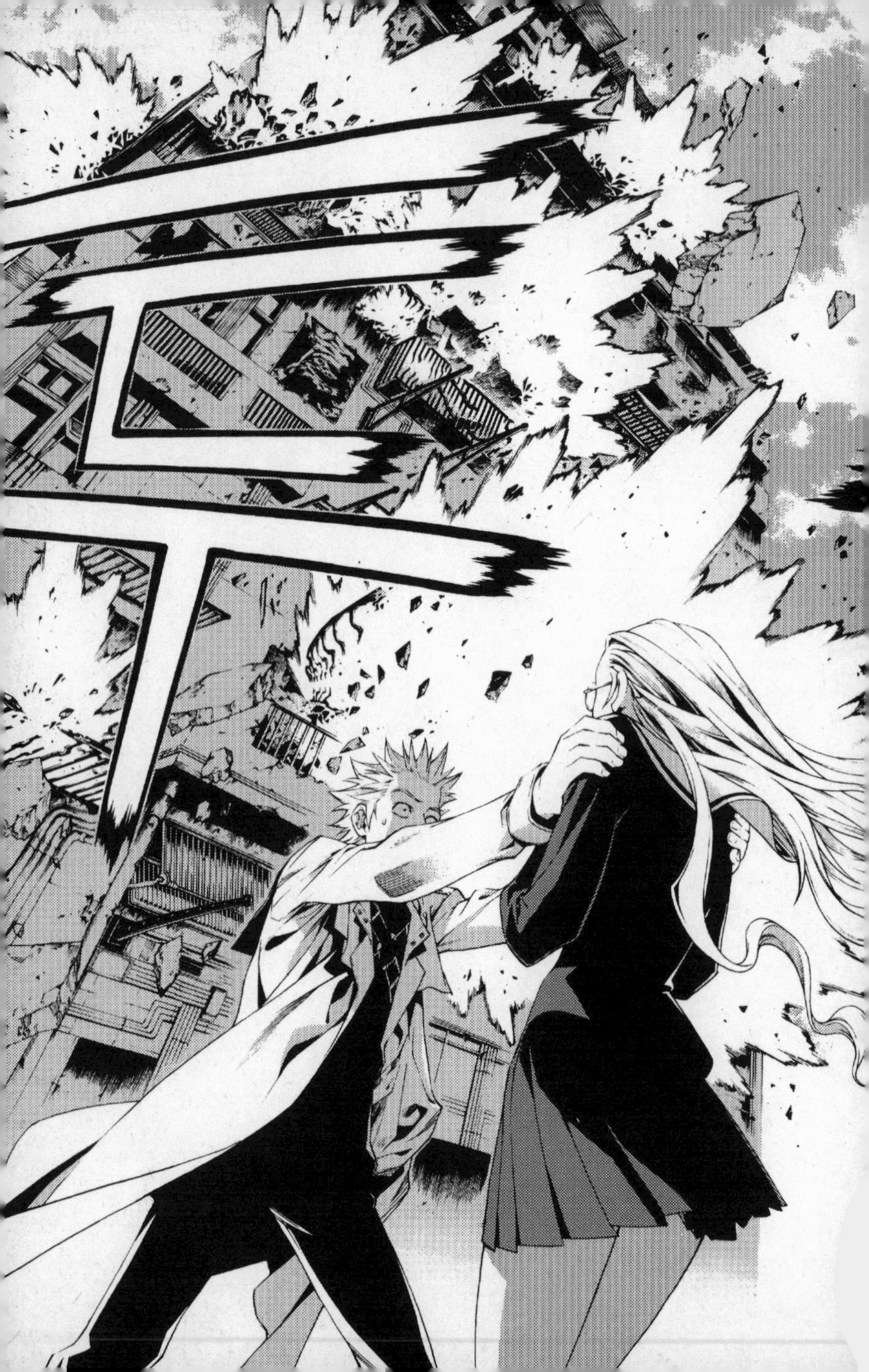

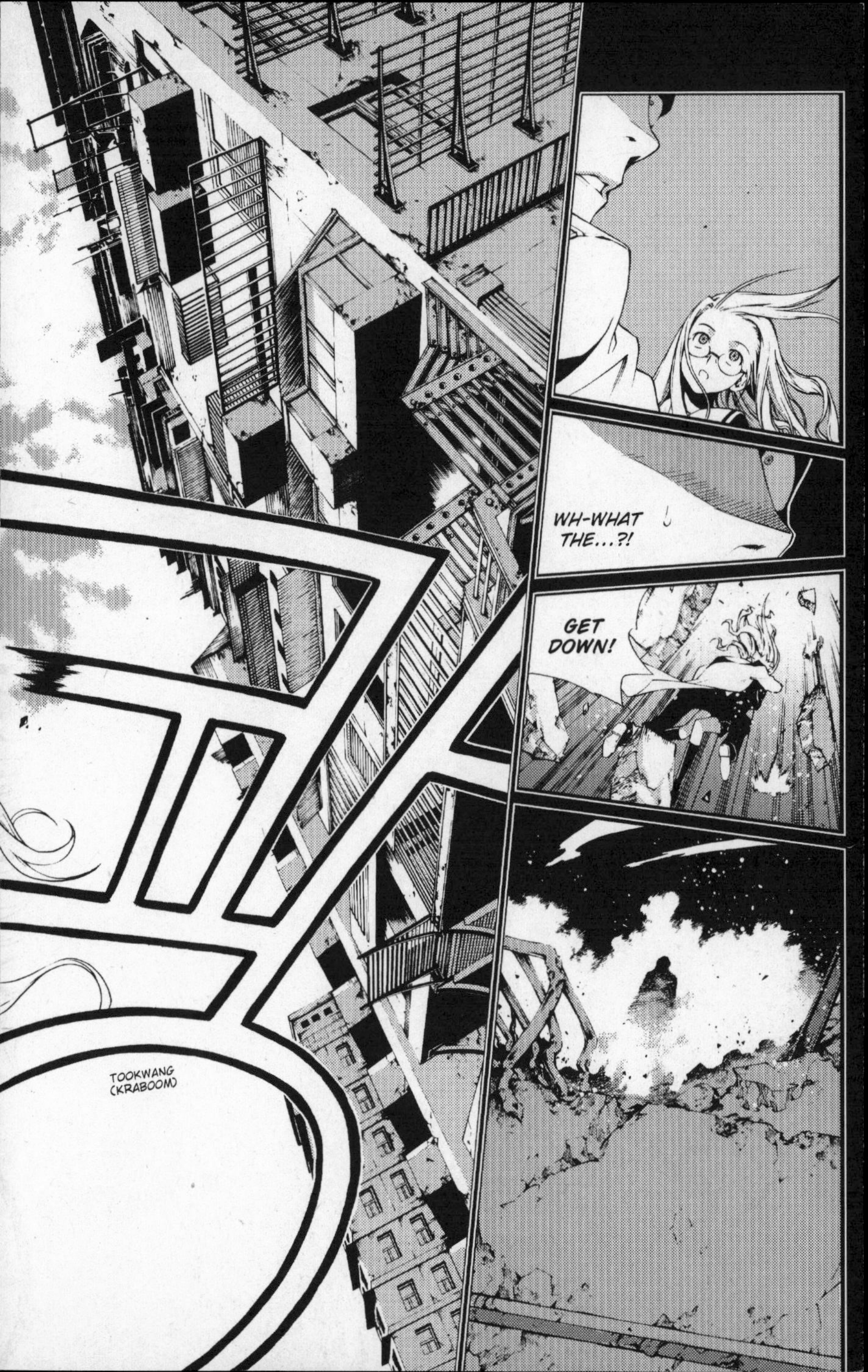
TOOKWANG
(KRABOOM)
WH-WHAT THE...?!
GET DOWN!

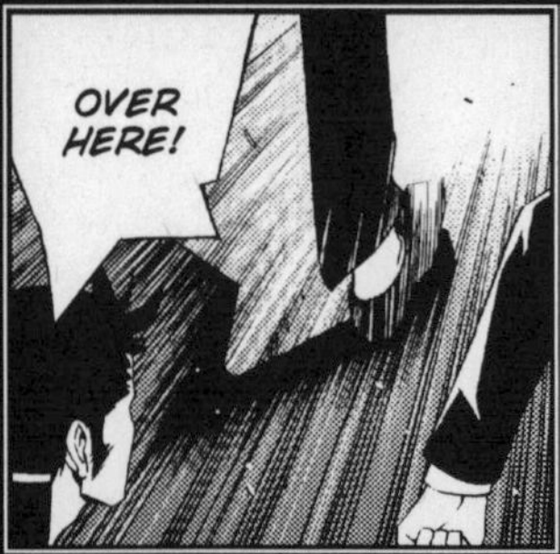
OVER HERE!

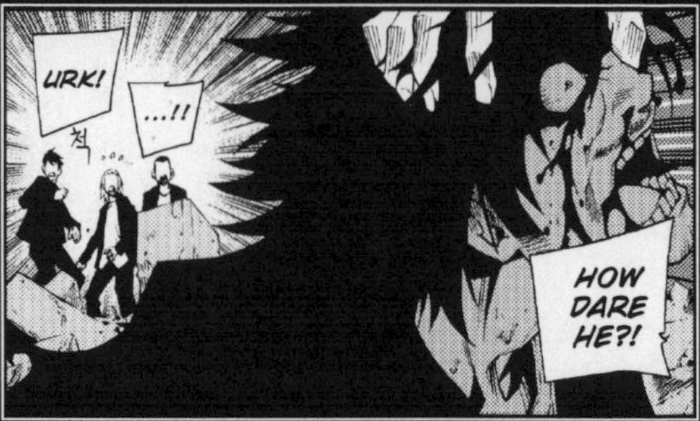
URK!
...!!
척
HOW DARE HE?!

SFX: CHUK (SCUFF)

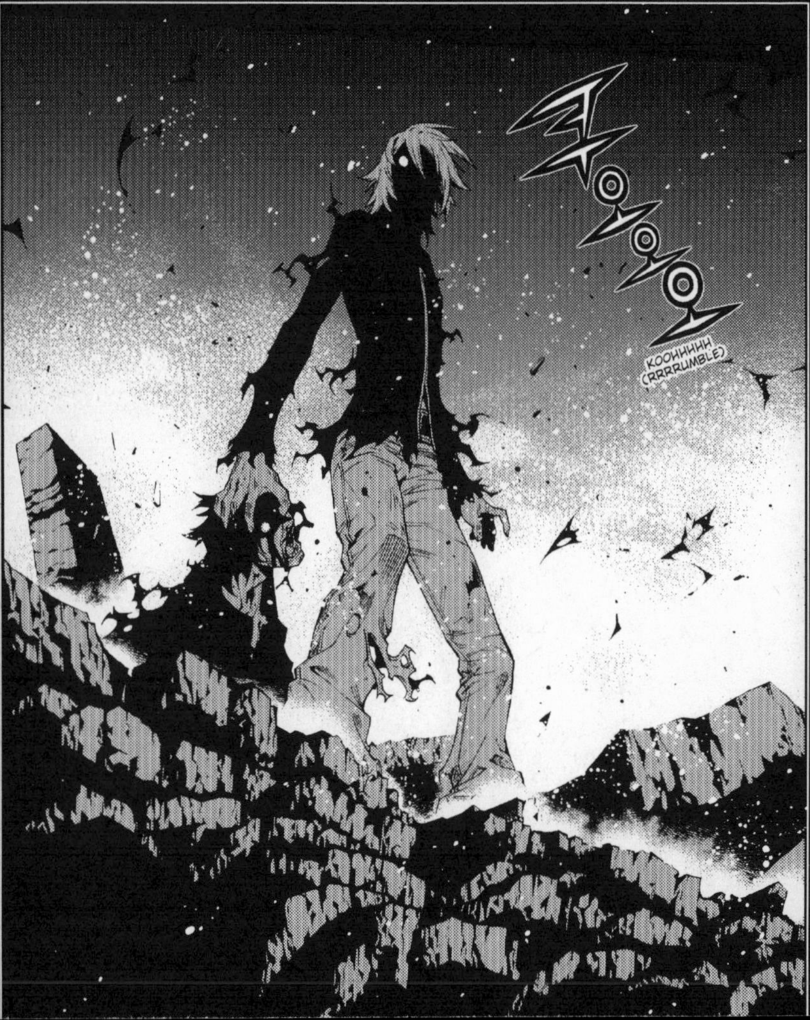
KOOHHHHH (RRRRUMBLE)

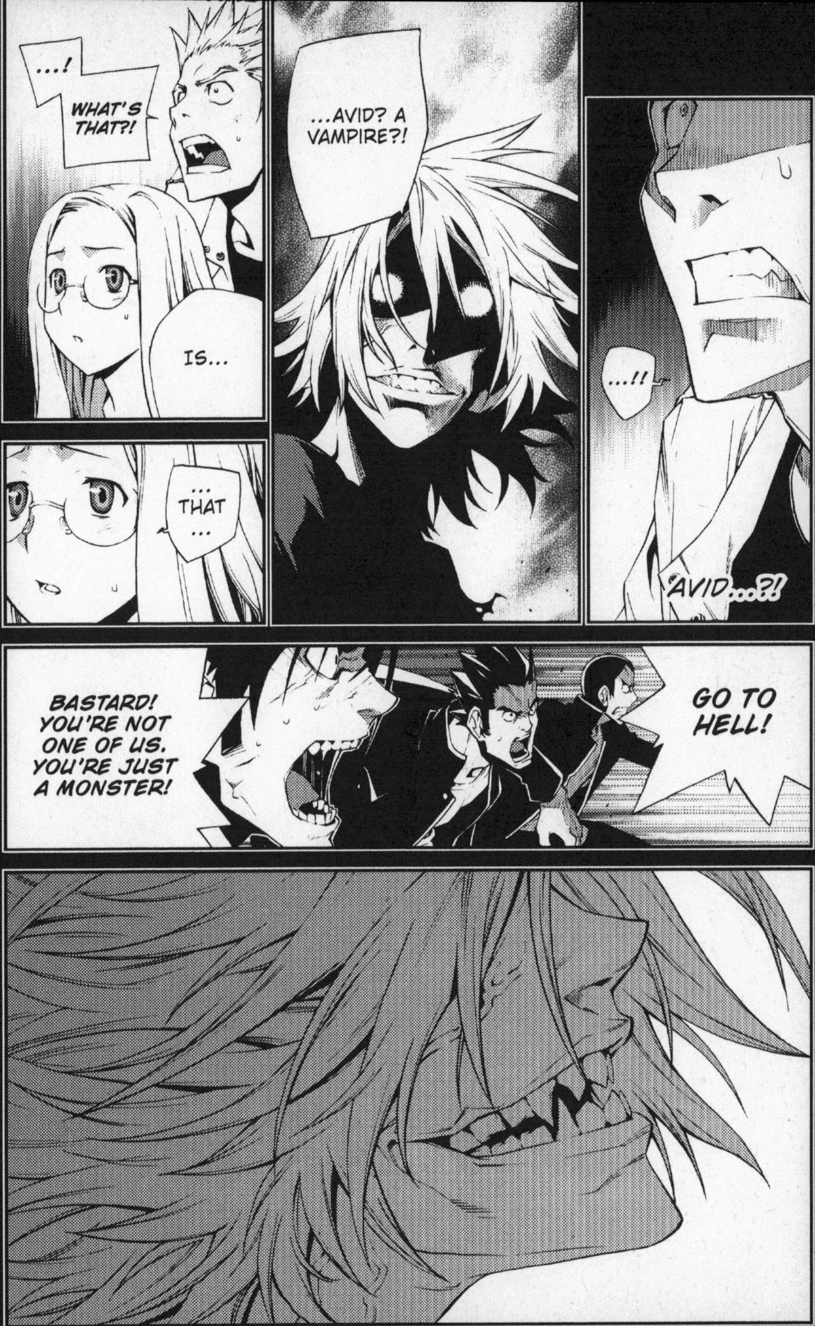
...!
WHAT'S THAT?!
IS...
... THAT ...
...AVID? A VAMPIRE?!
...!!
AVID...?!
BASTARD! YOU'RE NOT ONE OF US. YOU'RE JUST A MONSTER!
GO TO HELL!

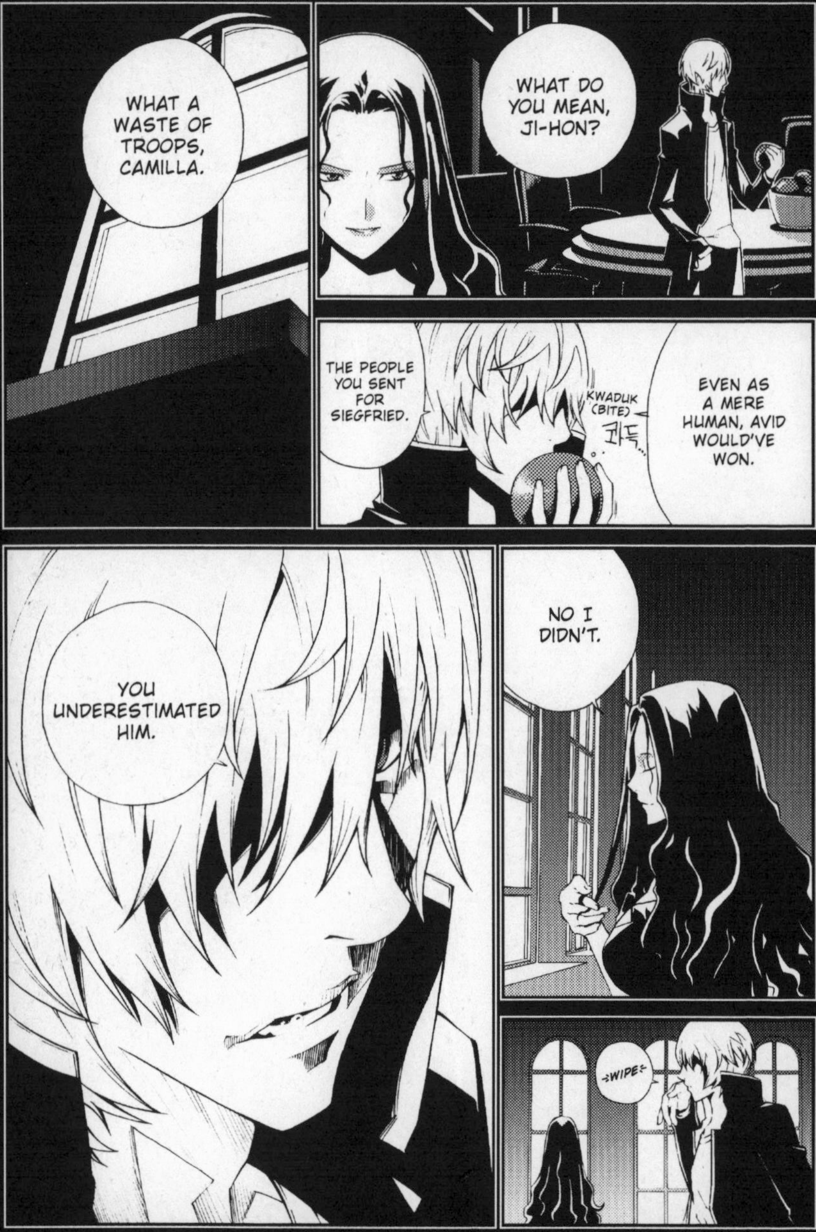
WHAT A WASTE OF TROOPS, CAMILLA.
WHAT DO YOU MEAN, JI-HON?
THE PEOPLE YOU SENT FOR SIEGFRIED.
KWADUK (BITE)
콰득
EVEN AS A MERE HUMAN, AVID WOULD'VE WON.
YOU UNDERESTIMATED HIM.
NO I DIDN'T.
WIPE

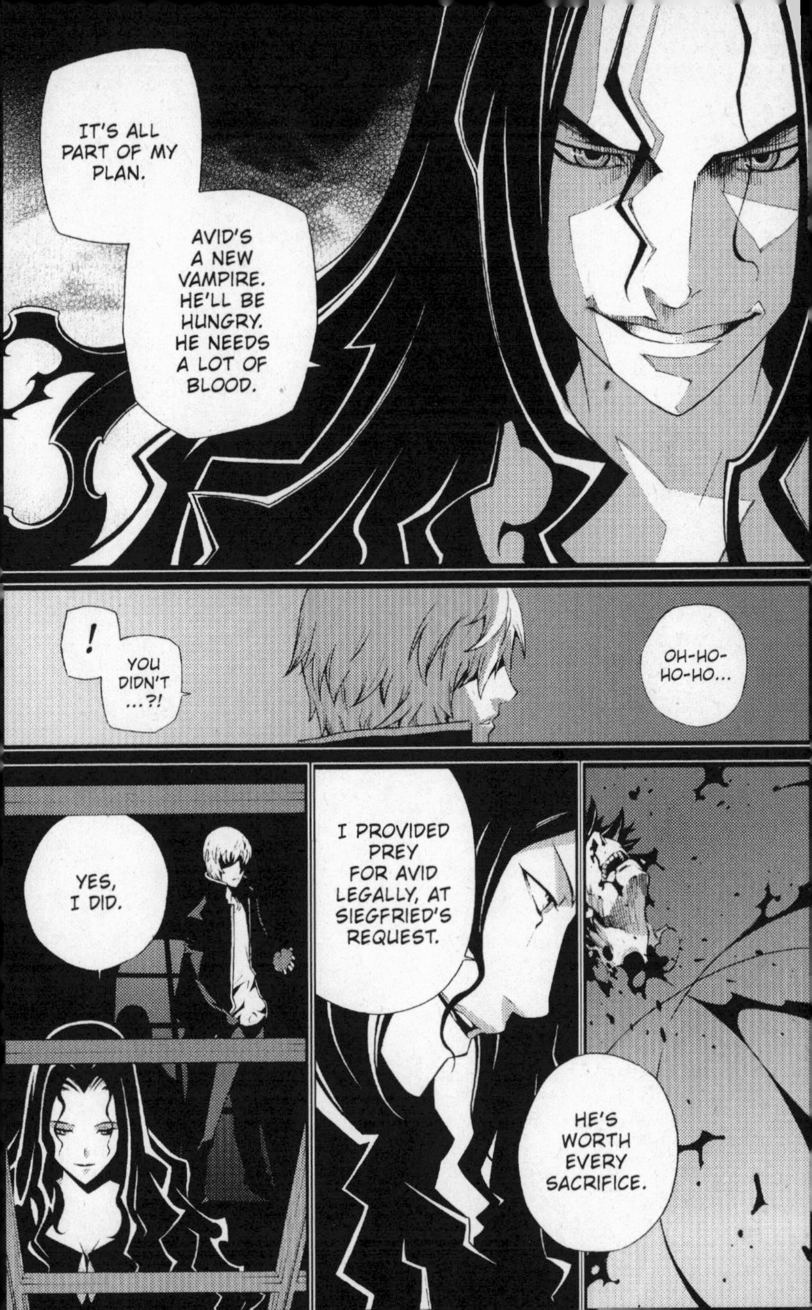
IT'S ALL PART OF MY PLAN.
AVID'S A NEW VAMPIRE. HE'LL BE HUNGRY. HE NEEDS A LOT OF BLOOD.
!
YOU DIDN'T ...?!
OH-HO-HO-HO...
YES, I DID.
I PROVIDED PREY FOR AVID LEGALLY, AT SIEGFRIED'S REQUEST.
HE'S WORTH EVERY SACRIFICE.

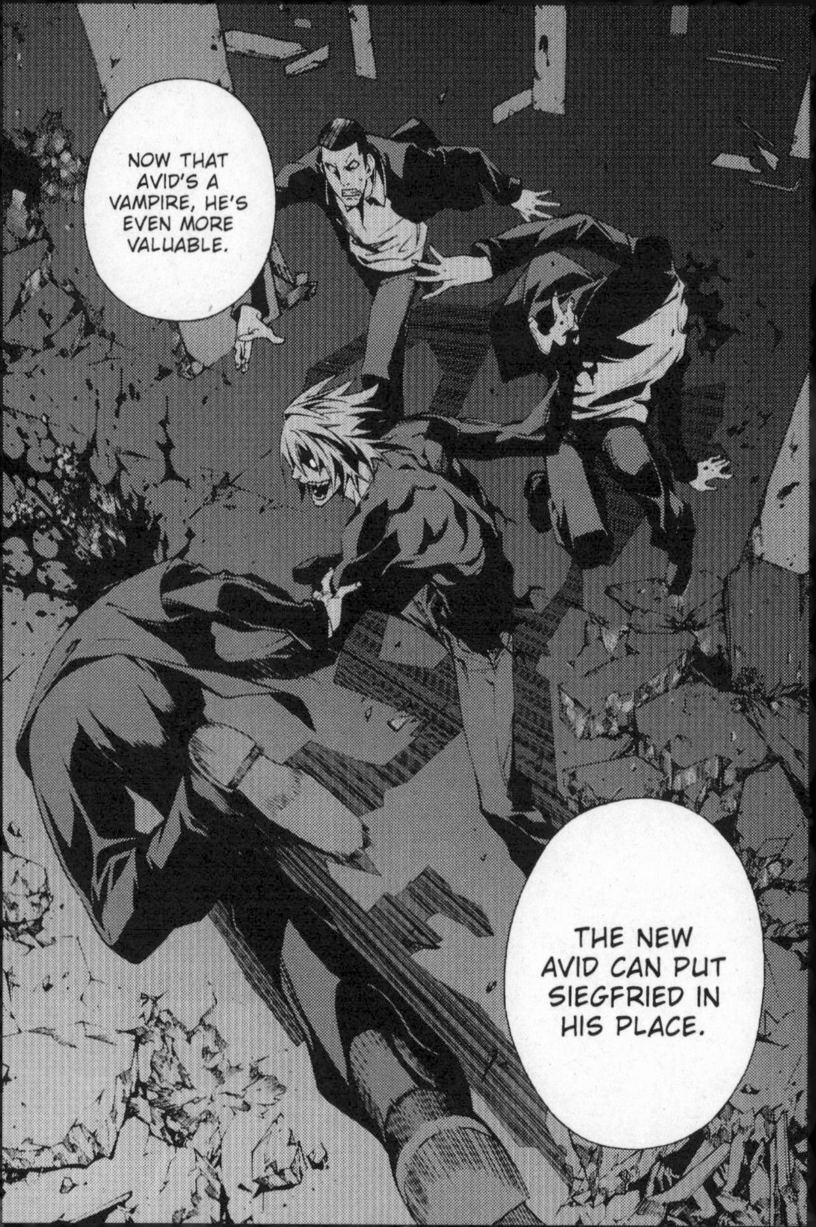
NOW THAT AVID'S A VAMPIRE, HE'S EVEN MORE VALUABLE.
THE NEW AVID CAN PUT SIEGFRIED IN HIS PLACE.

STUPID SIEGFRIED...

...HE'S MAKING ALL THE WRONG ENEMIES.

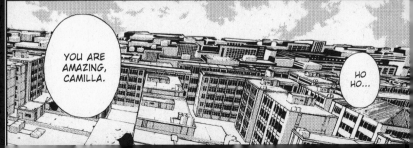

YOU ARE AMAZING, CAMILLA.

HO HO...

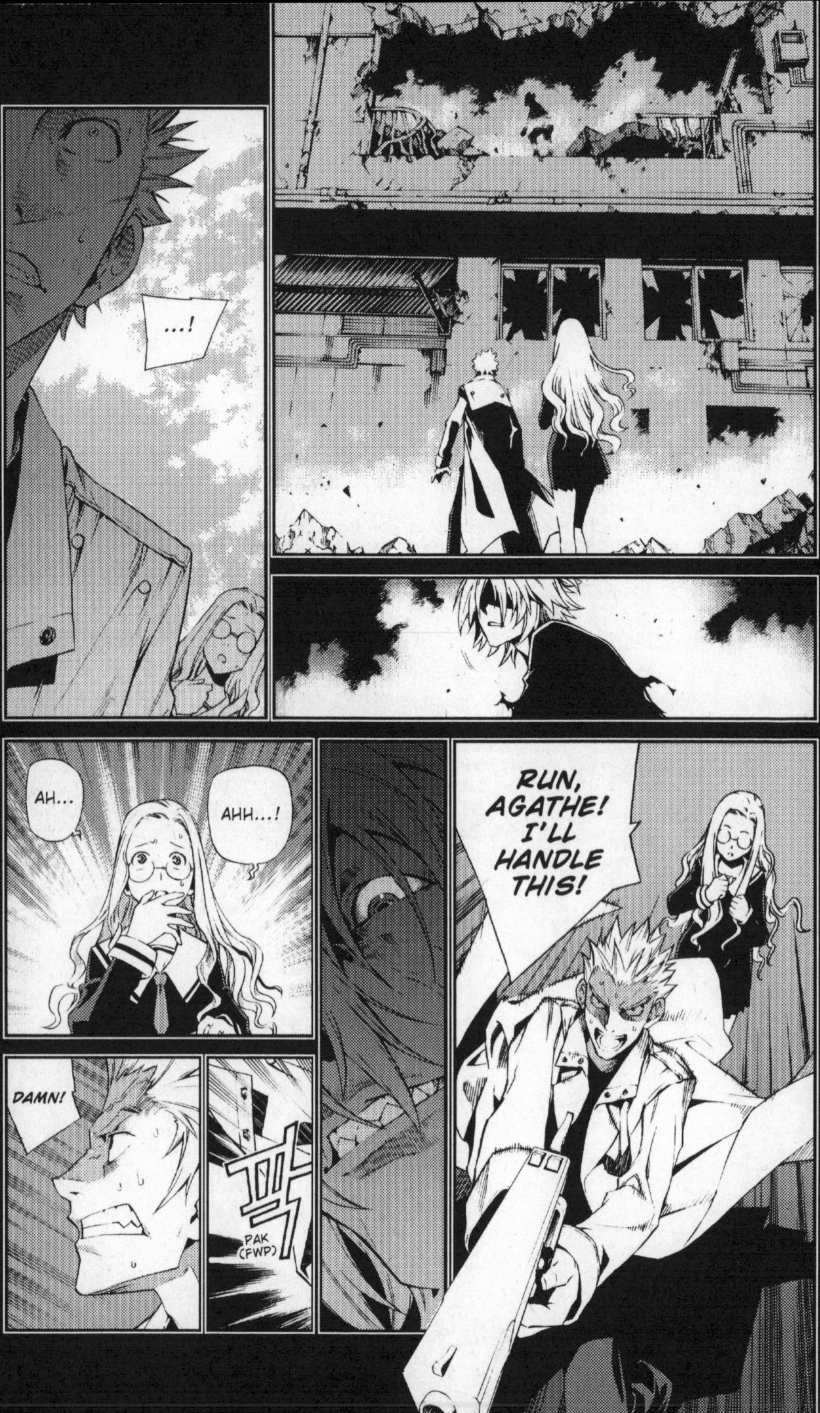

...!
AH...
AHH...!
DAMN!
팍
PAK (FWP)
RUN, AGATHE! I'LL HANDLE THIS!

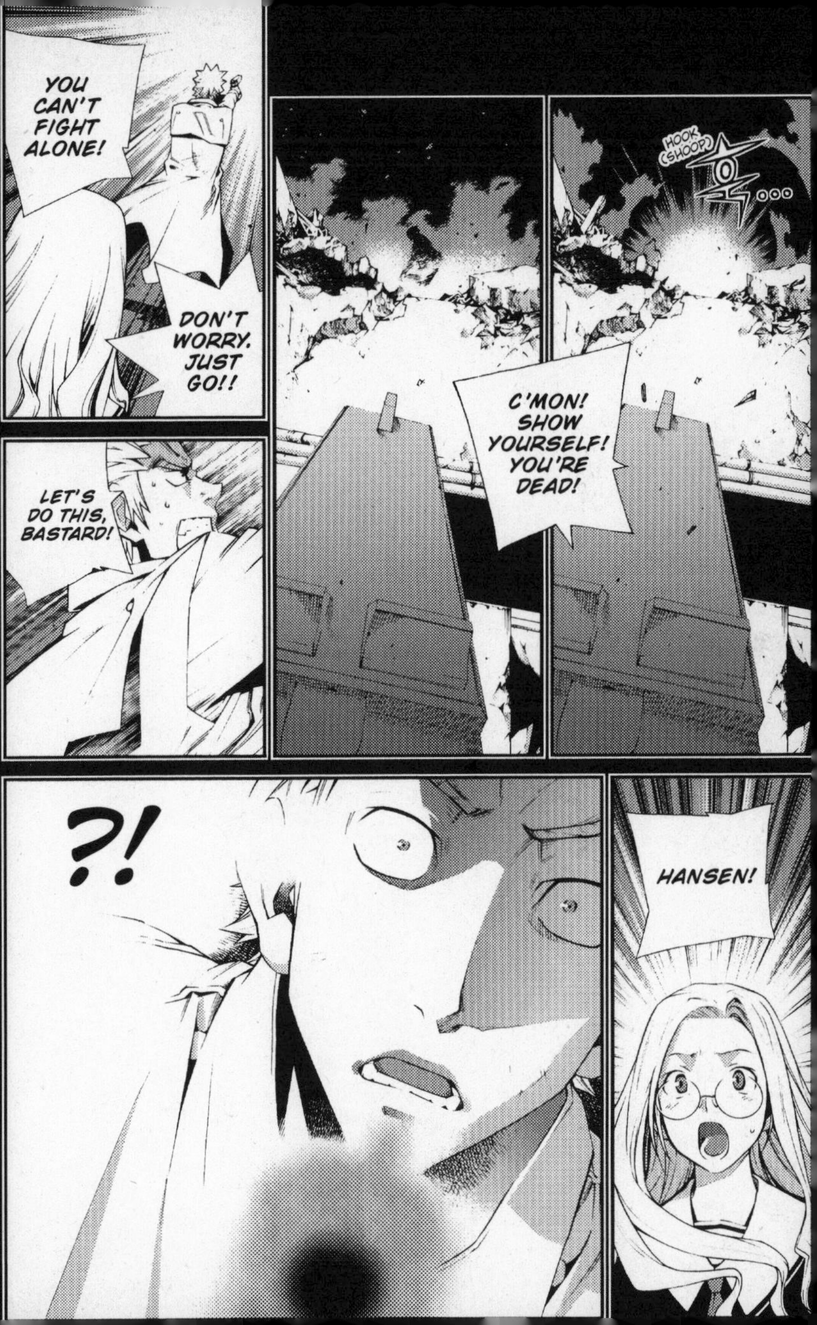

YOU CAN'T FIGHT ALONE!
DON'T WORRY. JUST GO!!
LET'S DO THIS, BASTARD!
C'MON! SHOW YOURSELF! YOU'RE DEAD!
HOOK (SHOOP)
...
?!
HANSEN!

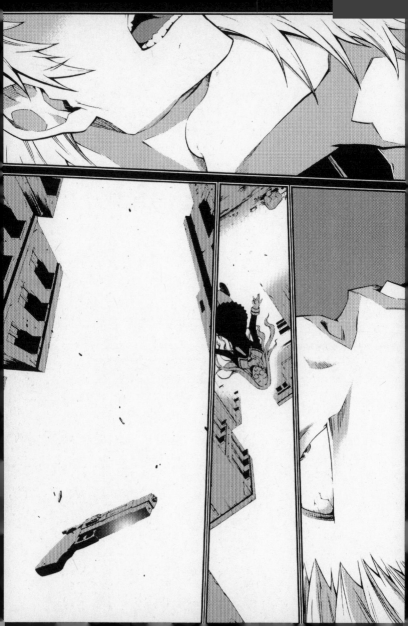

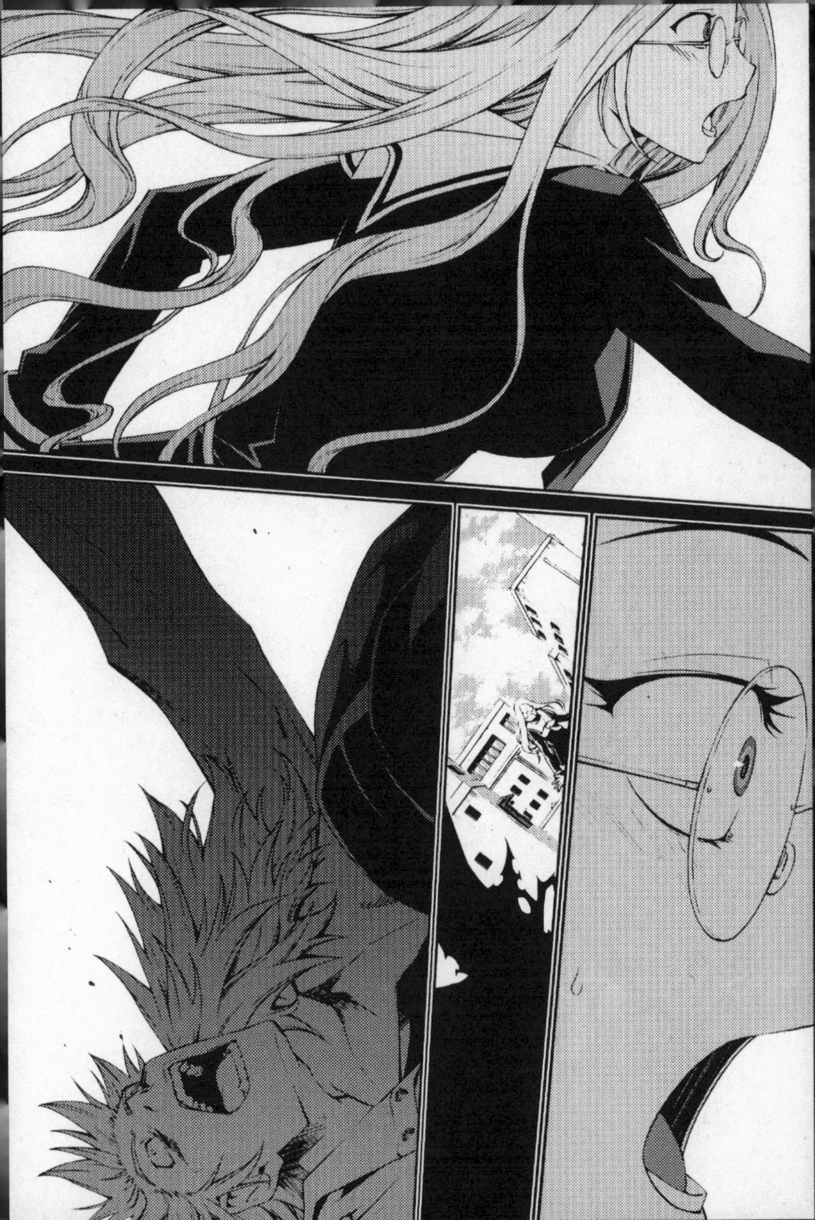

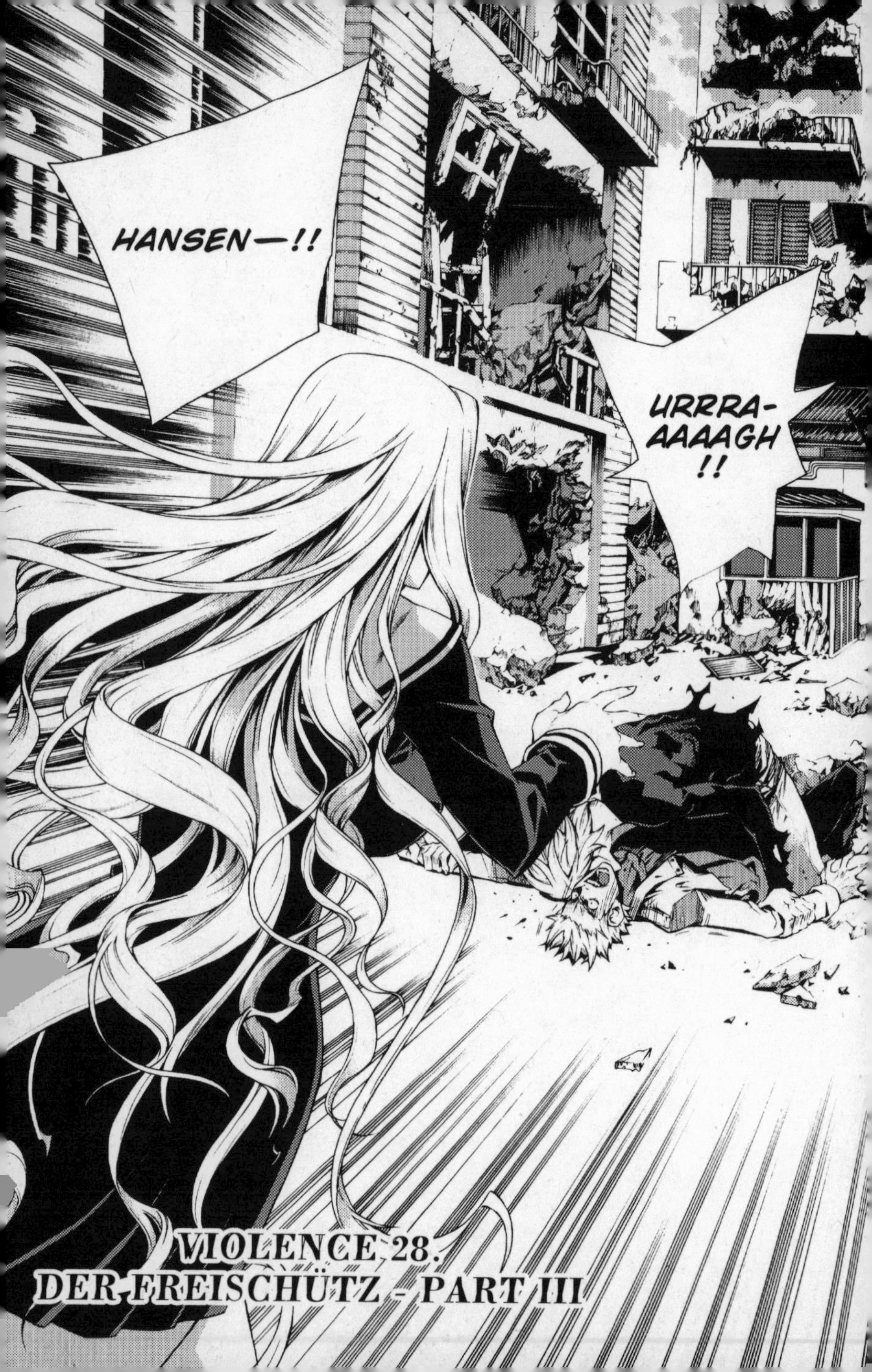
HANSEN—!!
URRRA-AAAAGH!!
VIOLENCE 28.
DER FREISCHÜTZ - PART III

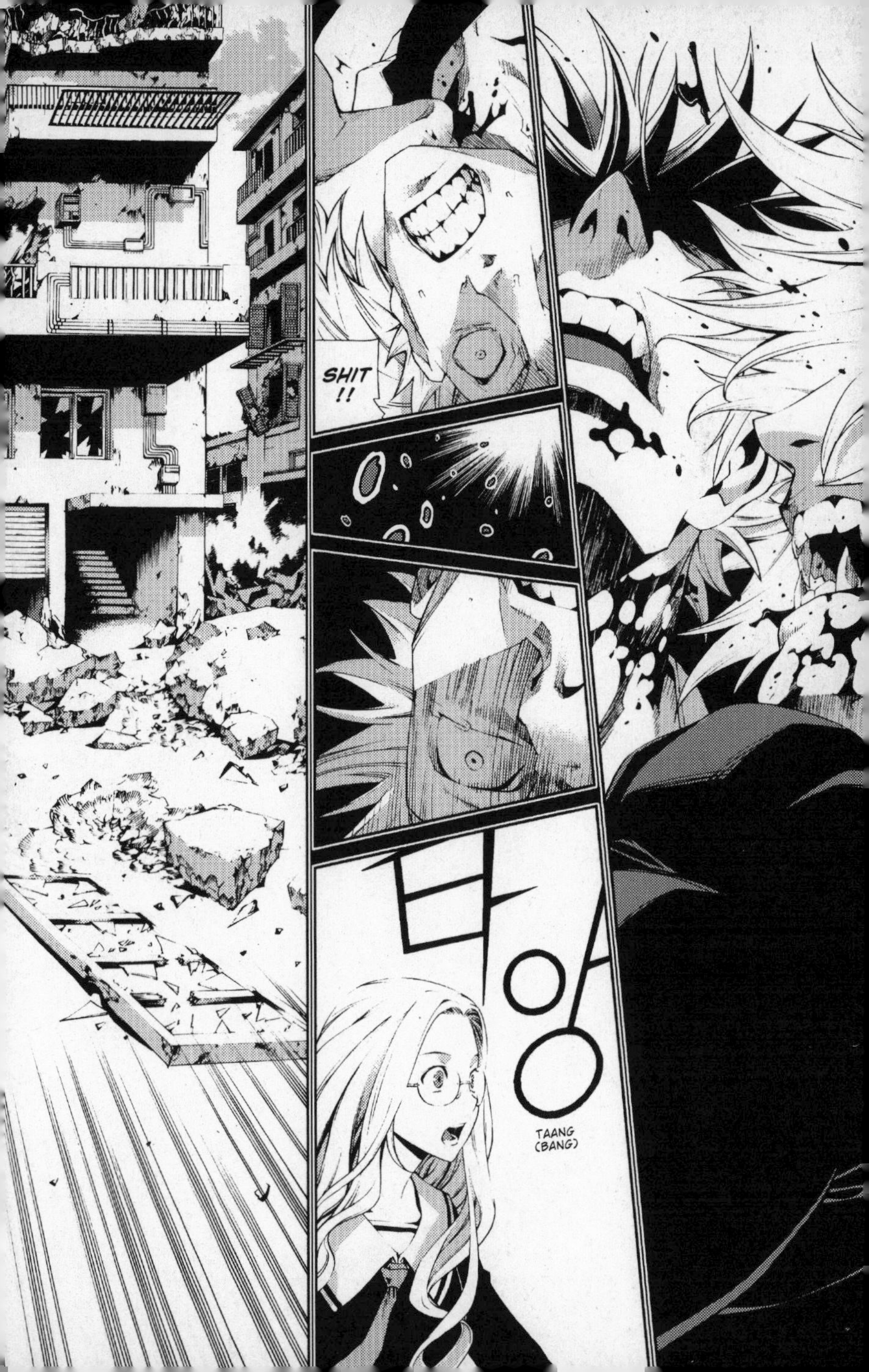
SHIT !!
TAANG (BANG)

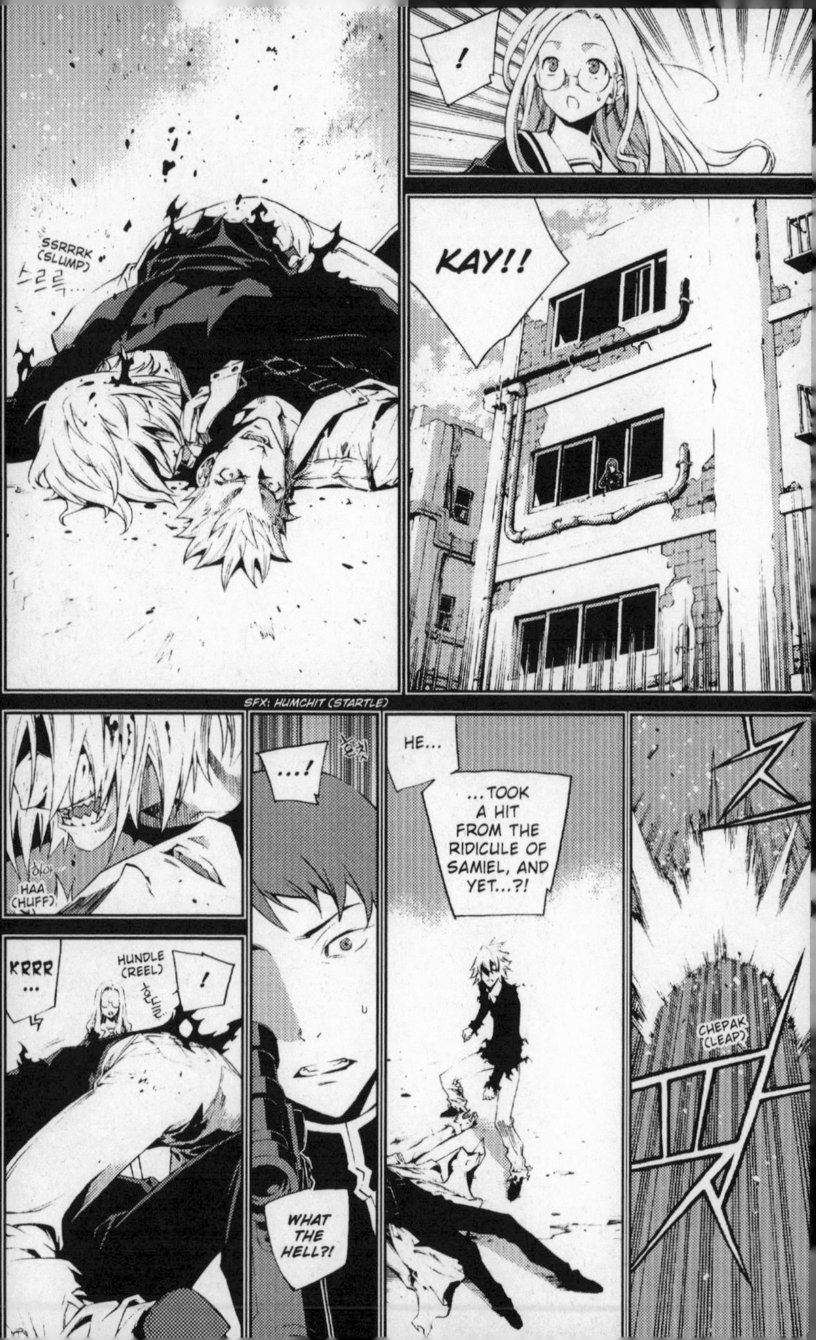
SSRRRK (SLUMP)
스르륵...
!
KAY!!
SFX: HUMCHIT (STARTLE)
하아
HAA (CHUFF)
KRRR...
HUNDLE (REEL)
!
...!
WHAT THE HELL?!
HE...
...TOOK A HIT FROM THE RIDICULE OF SAMIEL, AND YET...?!
CHEPAK (LEAP)

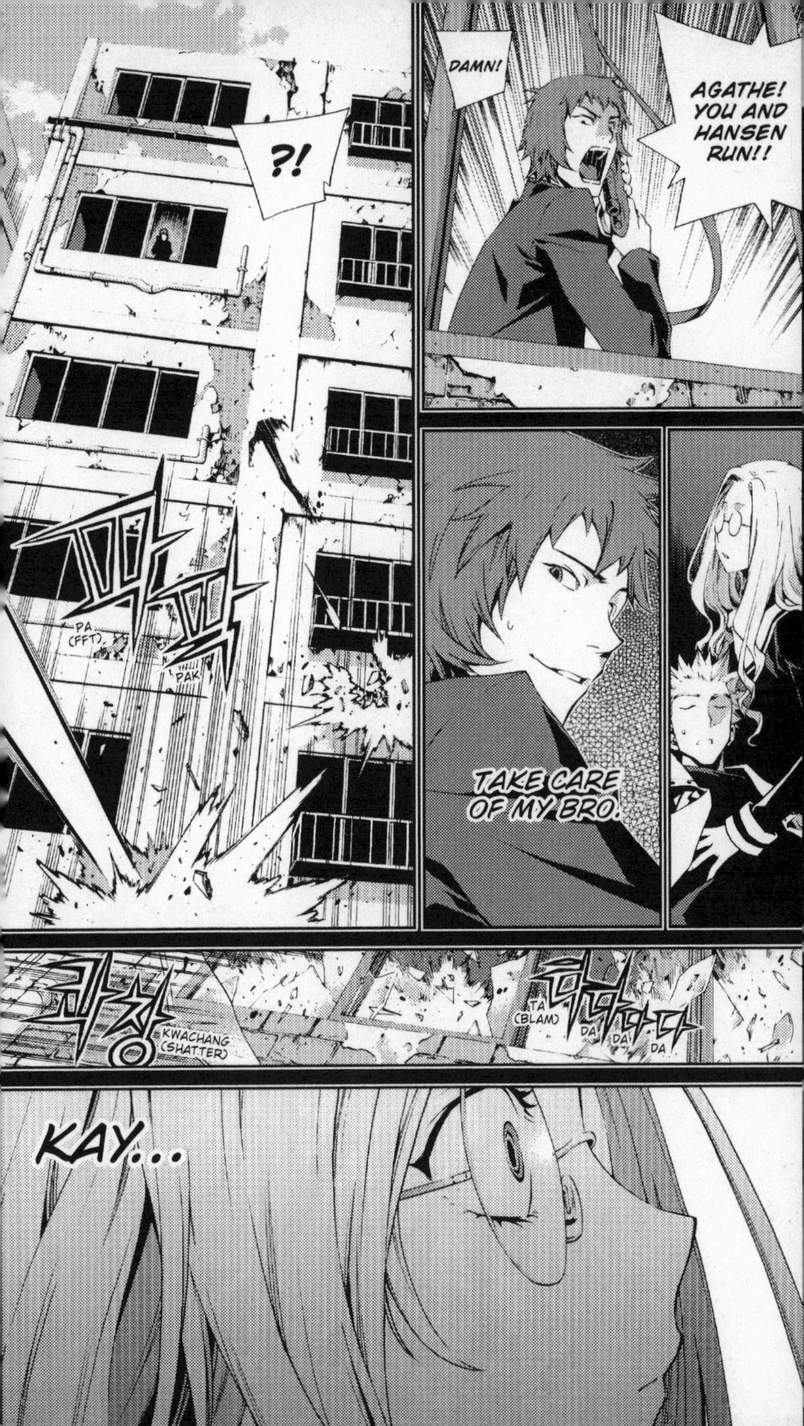
?!
PA (FFT)
PAK
DAMN!
AGATHE! YOU AND HANSEN RUN!!
TAKE CARE OF MY BRO.
KWACHANG (SHATTER)
TA (BLAM)
DA
DA
DA
KAY...

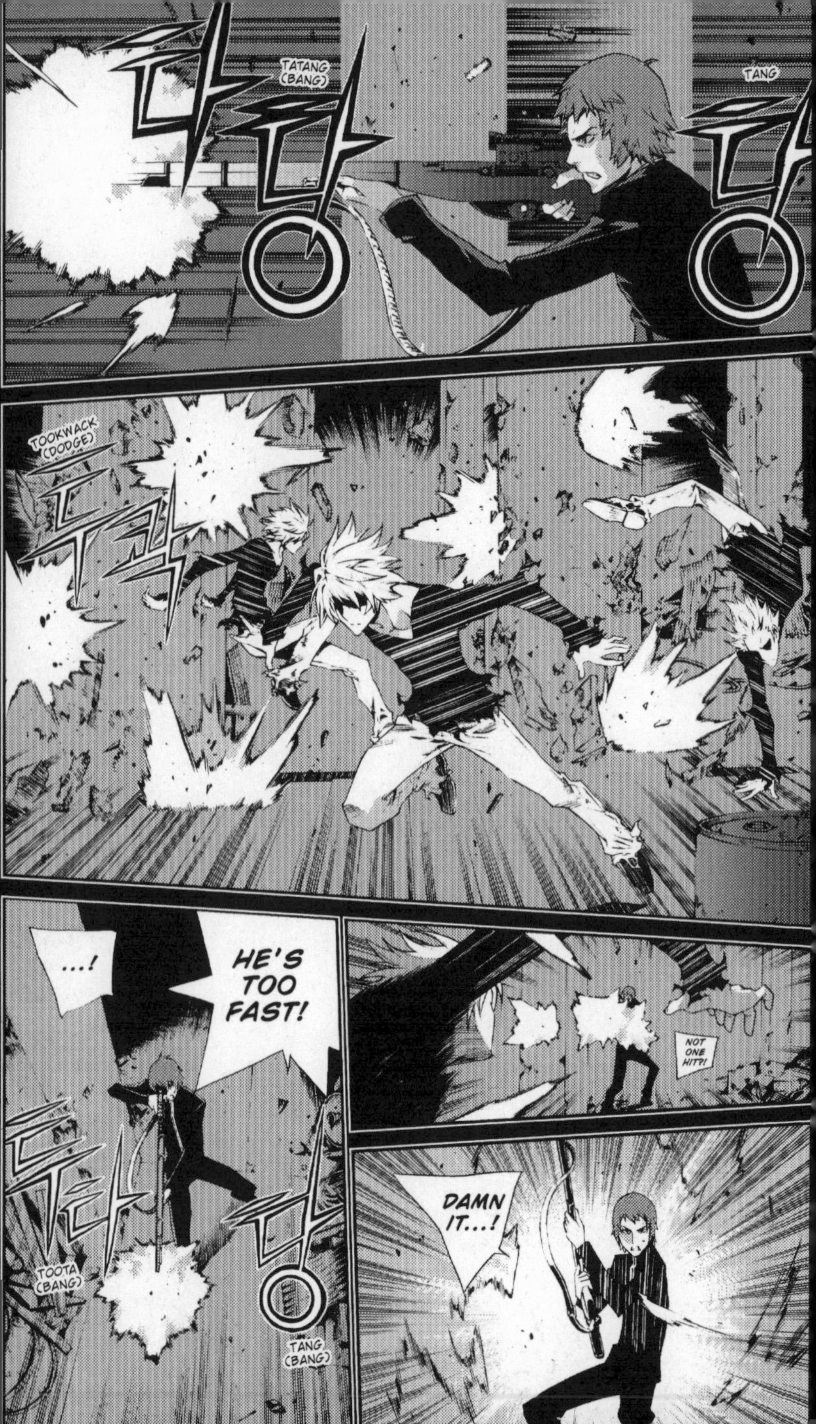
TATANG (BANG)
TANG
TOOKWACK (DODGE)
...!
HE'S TOO FAST!
TOOTA (BANG)
TANG (BANG)
NOT ONE HIT?!
DAMN IT...!

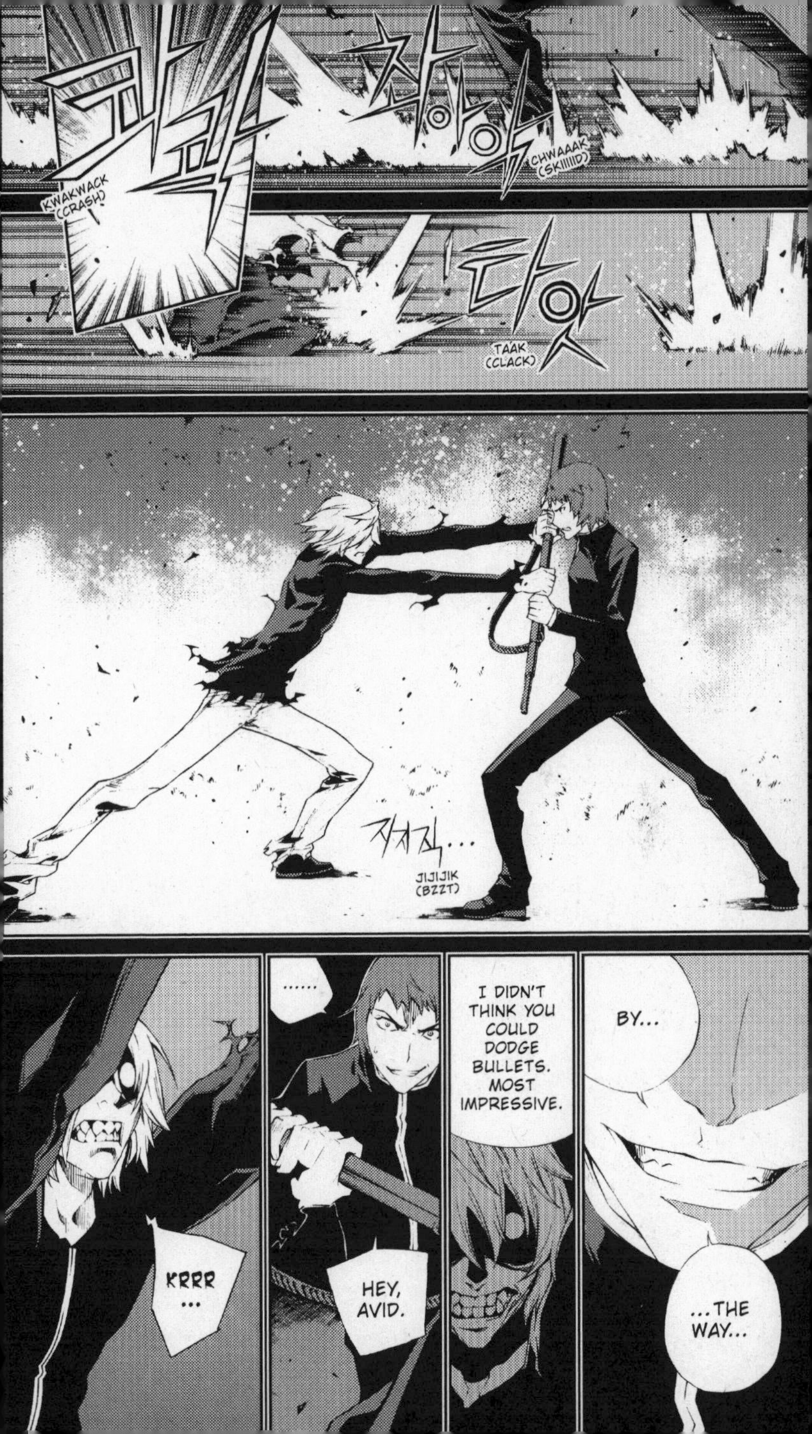
KWAKWACK (CRASH)
CHWAAAK (SKIIIIID)
TAAK (CLACK)
JIJIJIK (BZZT)
KRRR ...
......
HEY, AVID.
I DIDN'T THINK YOU COULD DODGE BULLETS. MOST IMPRESSIVE.
BY...
...THE WAY...

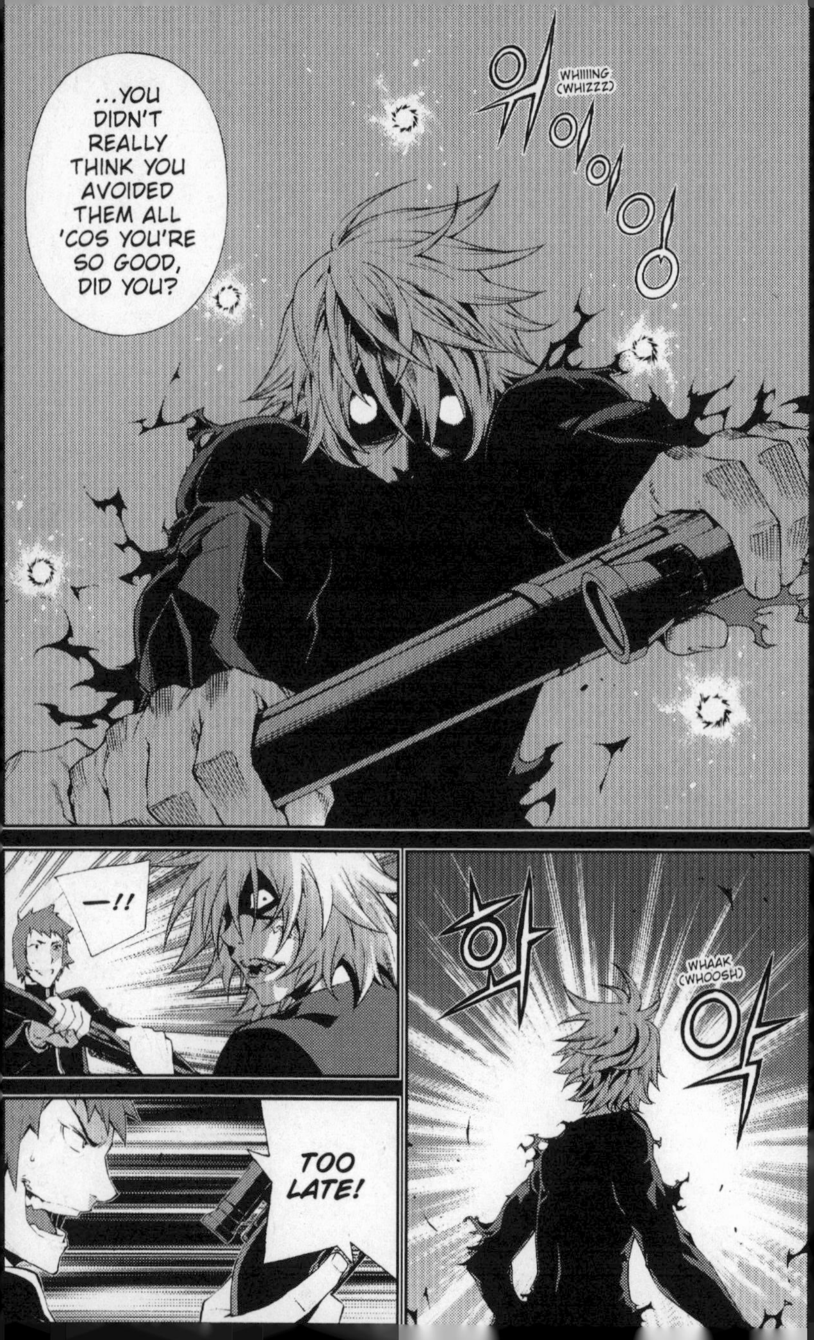
...YOU DIDN'T REALLY THINK YOU AVOIDED THEM ALL 'COS YOU'RE SO GOOD, DID YOU?
WHIIIING (WHIZZZ)
—!!
WHAAK (WHOOSH)
TOO LATE!

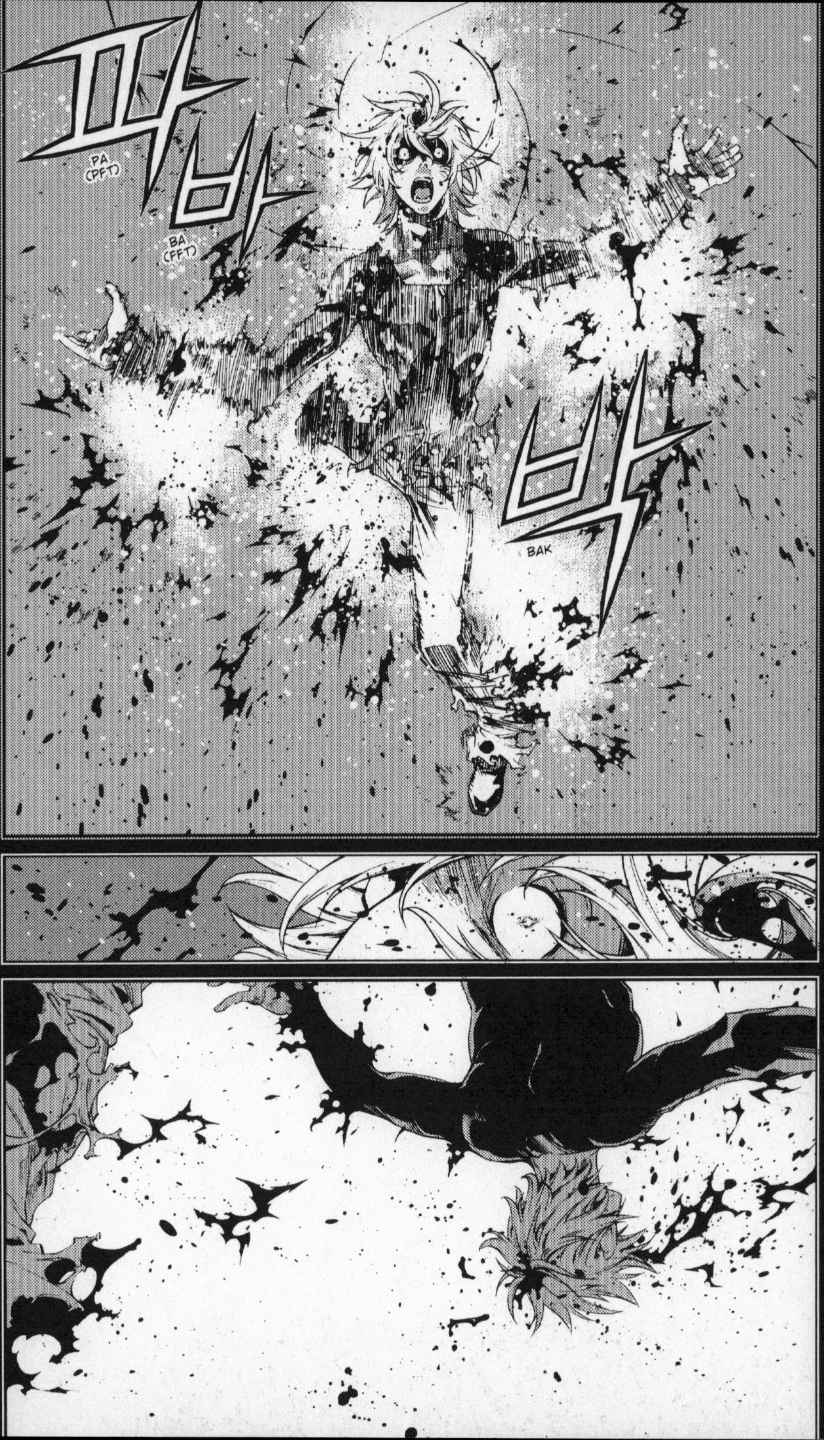
파
PA
(PFFT)
바
BA
(PFFT)
박
BAK

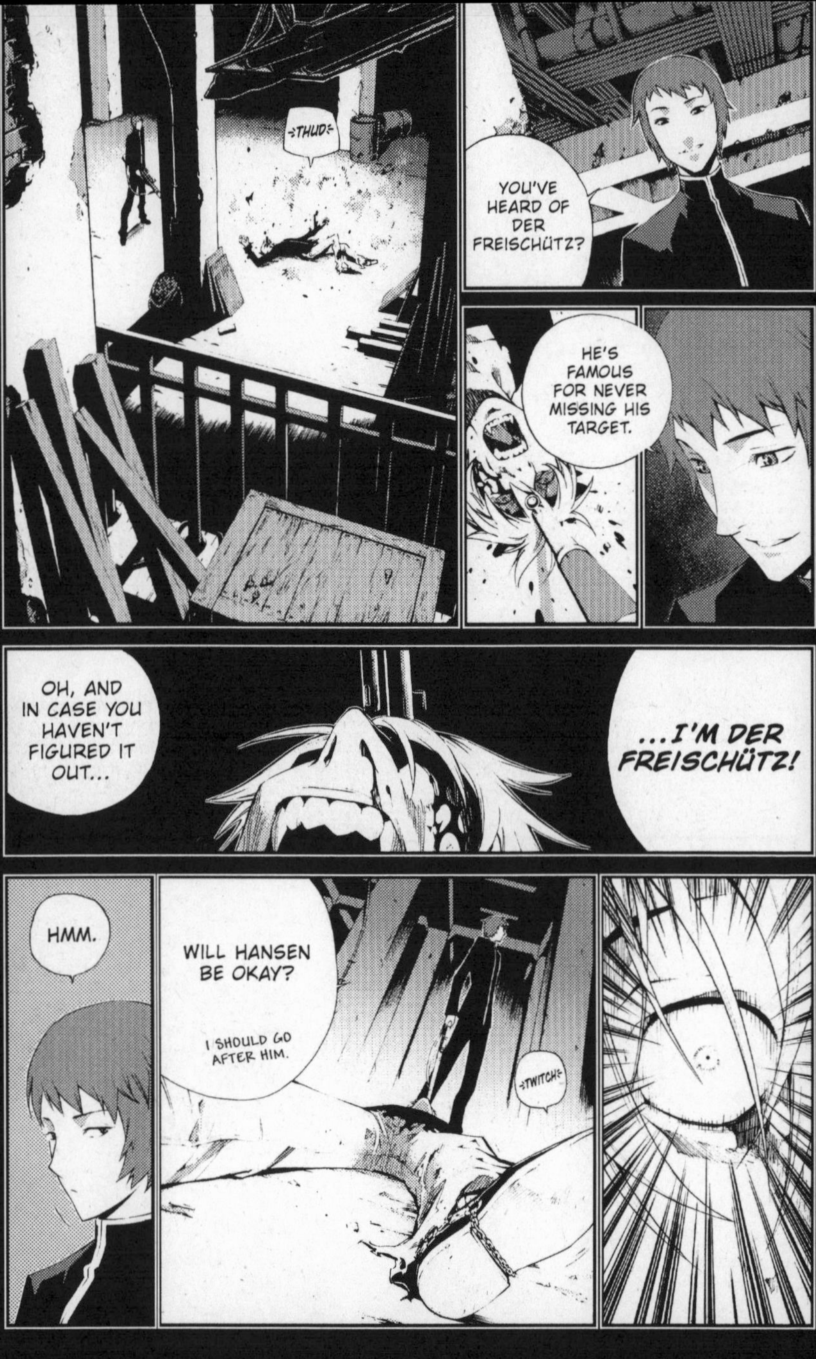
THUD
YOU'VE HEARD OF DER FREISCHÜTZ?
HE'S FAMOUS FOR NEVER MISSING HIS TARGET.
OH, AND IN CASE YOU HAVEN'T FIGURED IT OUT...
...I'M DER FREISCHÜTZ!
HMM.
WILL HANSEN BE OKAY?
I SHOULD GO AFTER HIM.
TWITCH

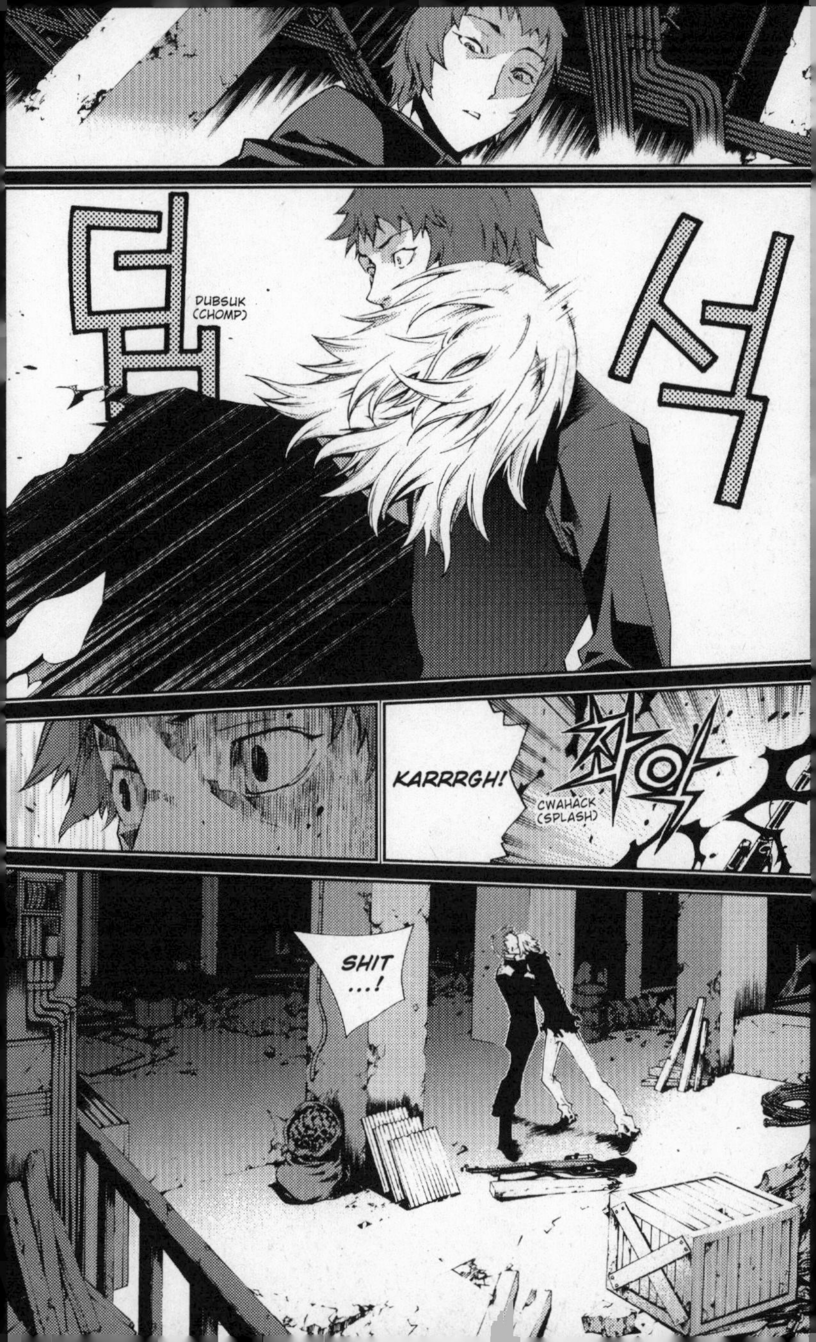
덥석
DUBSUK
(CHOMP)
KARRRGH!
CWAHACK
(SPLASH)
SHIT
...!

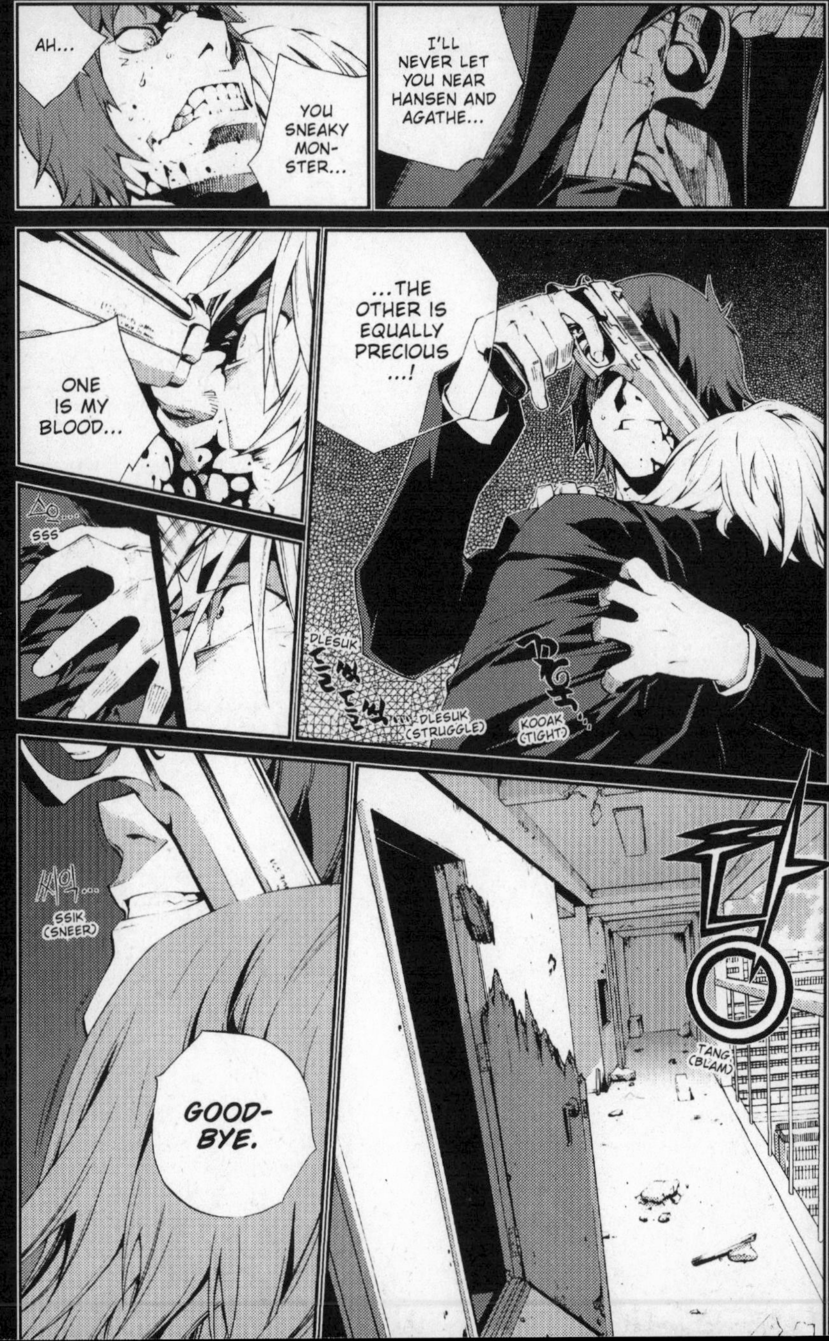
AH...
YOU SNEAKY MON-STER...
I'LL NEVER LET YOU NEAR HANSEN AND AGATHE...
ONE IS MY BLOOD...
SSS
...THE OTHER IS EQUALLY PRECIOUS ...!
DLESUK
DLESUK (STRUGGLE)
KOOAK (TIGHT)
SSIK (SNEER)
GOOD-BYE.
TANG (BLAM)

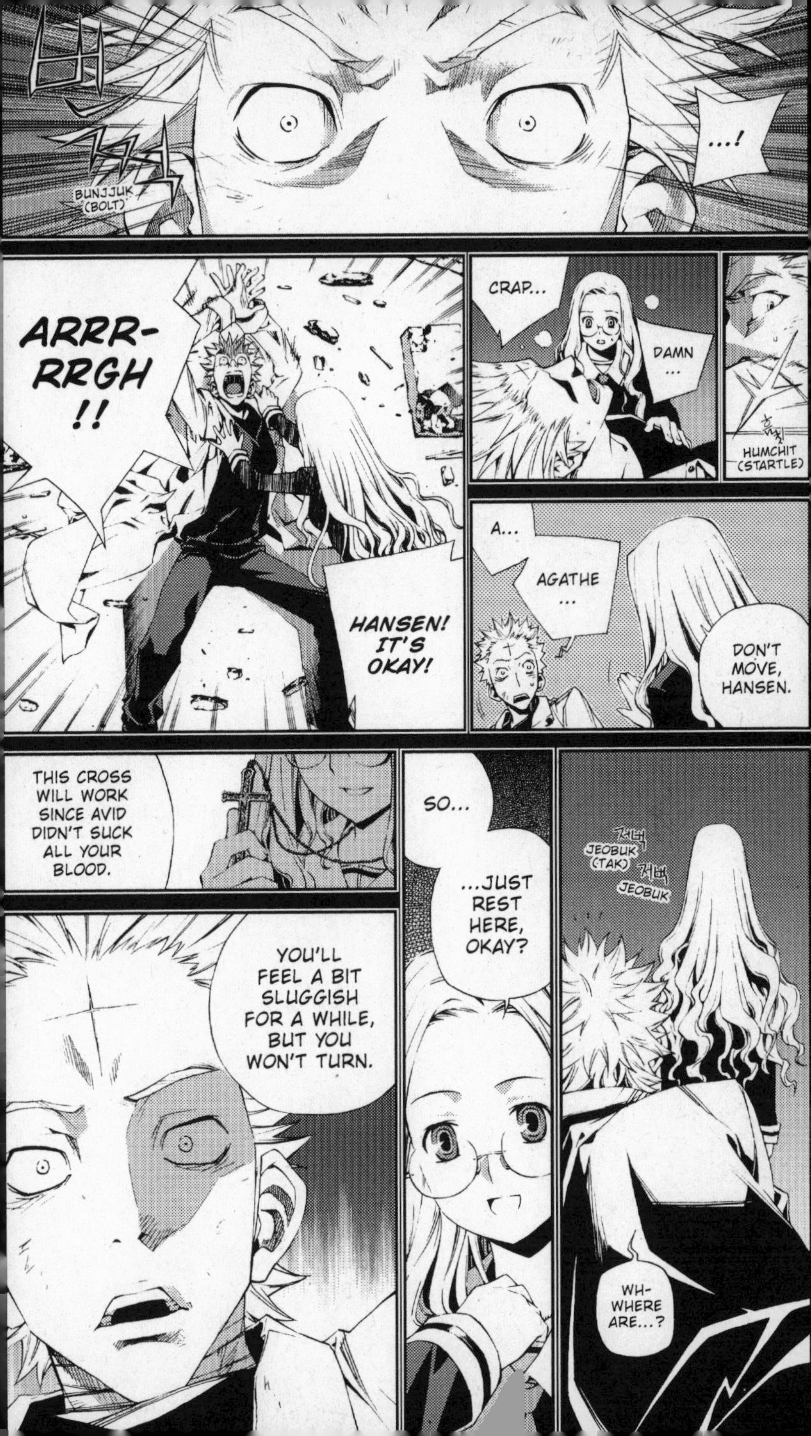
BUNJJUK (BOLT)
...!
ARRR-RRGH!!
HANSEN! IT'S OKAY!
CRAP...
DAMN...
흠칫
HUMCHIT (STARTLE)
A...
AGATHE...
DON'T MOVE, HANSEN.
THIS CROSS WILL WORK SINCE AVID DIDN'T SUCK ALL YOUR BLOOD.
YOU'LL FEEL A BIT SLUGGISH FOR A WHILE, BUT YOU WON'T TURN.
SO...
...JUST REST HERE, OKAY?
저벅
JEOBUK (TAK)
저벅
JEOBUK
WH-WHERE ARE...?

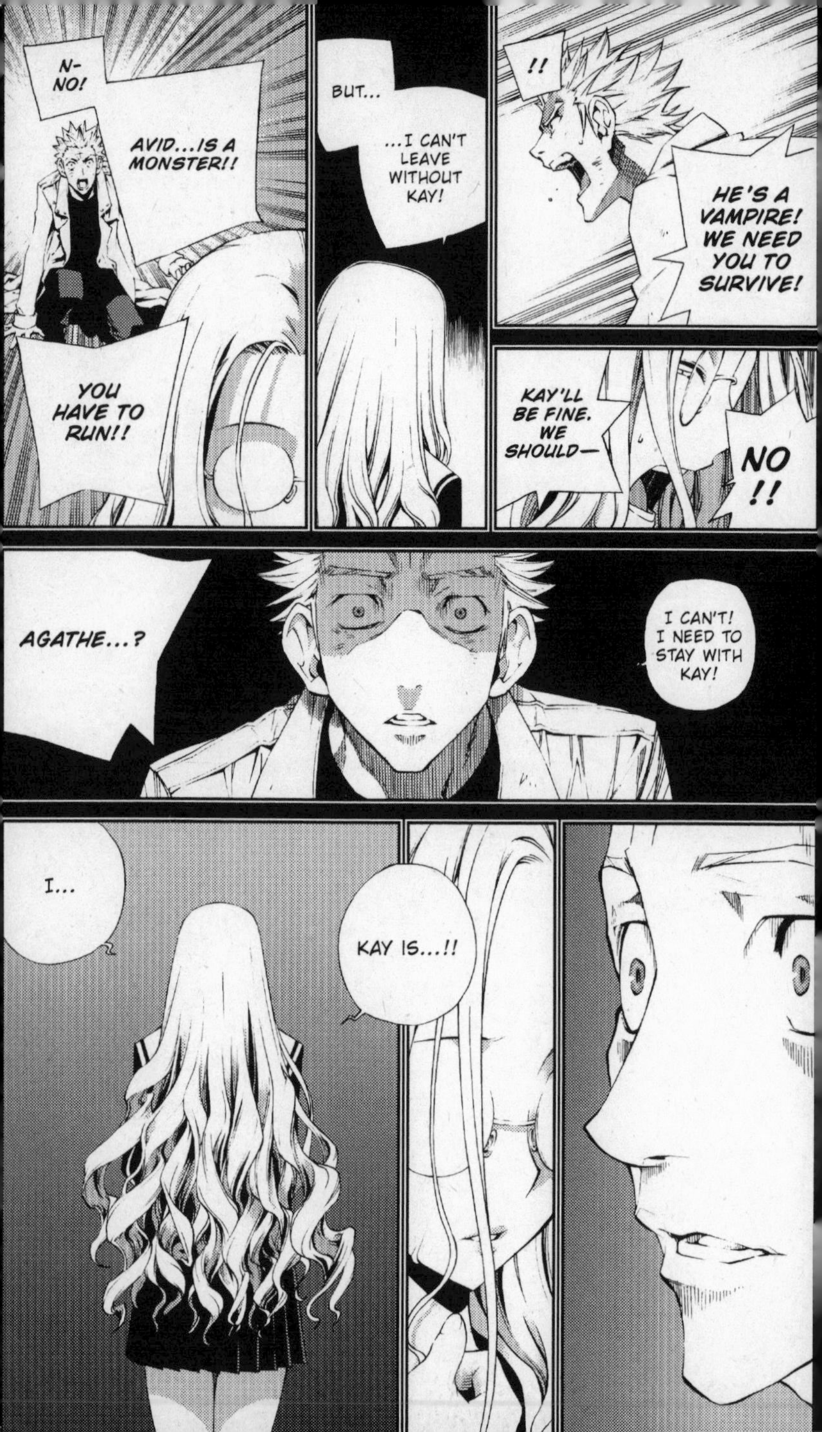
N-NO!
AVID...IS A MONSTER!!
YOU HAVE TO RUN!!
BUT...
...I CAN'T LEAVE WITHOUT KAY!
!!
HE'S A VAMPIRE! WE NEED YOU TO SURVIVE!
KAY'LL BE FINE. WE SHOULD—
NO !!
AGATHE...?
I CAN'T! I NEED TO STAY WITH KAY!
I...
KAY IS...!!

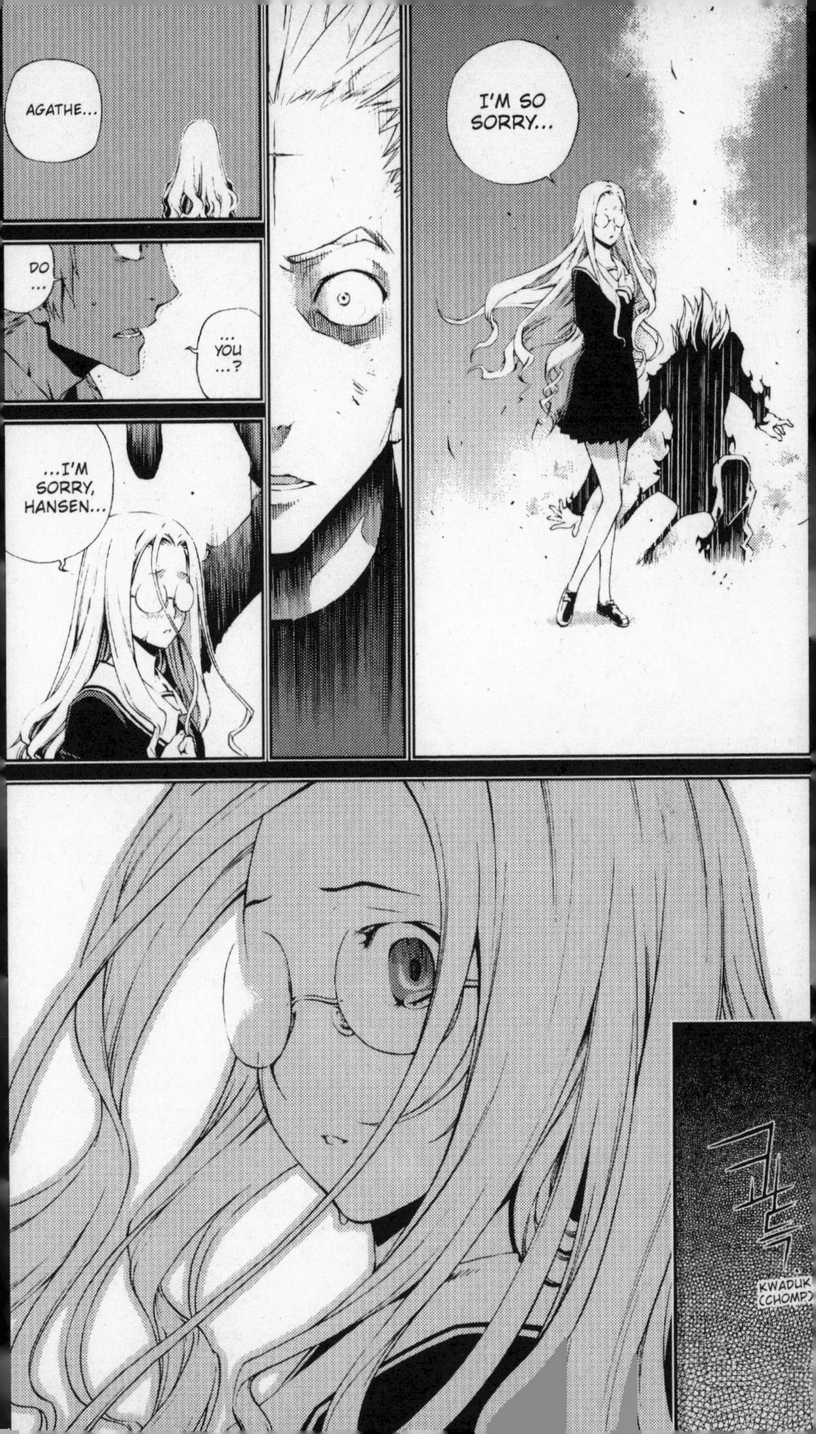
AGATHE...
DO ...
... YOU ...?
...I'M SORRY, HANSEN...
I'M SO SORRY...
KWADUK (CHOMP)

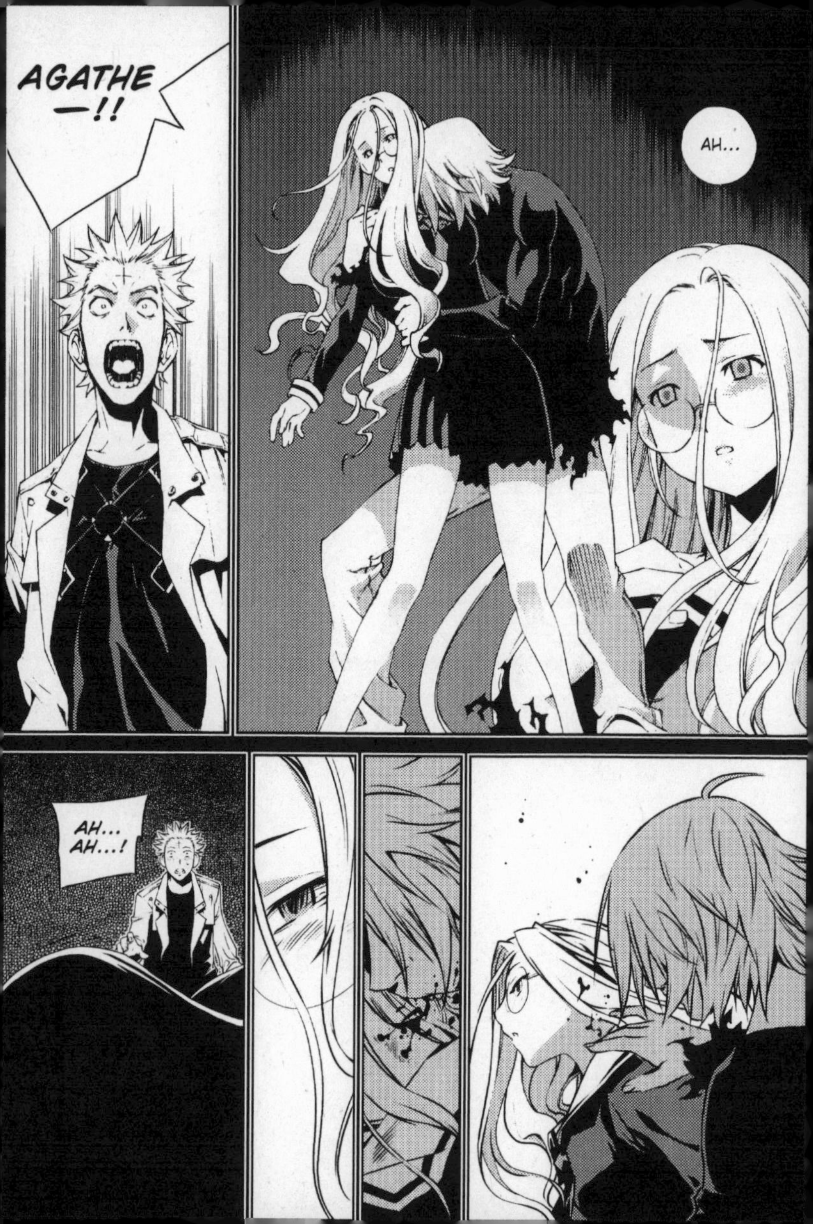
AGATHE —!!
AH...
AH... AH...!

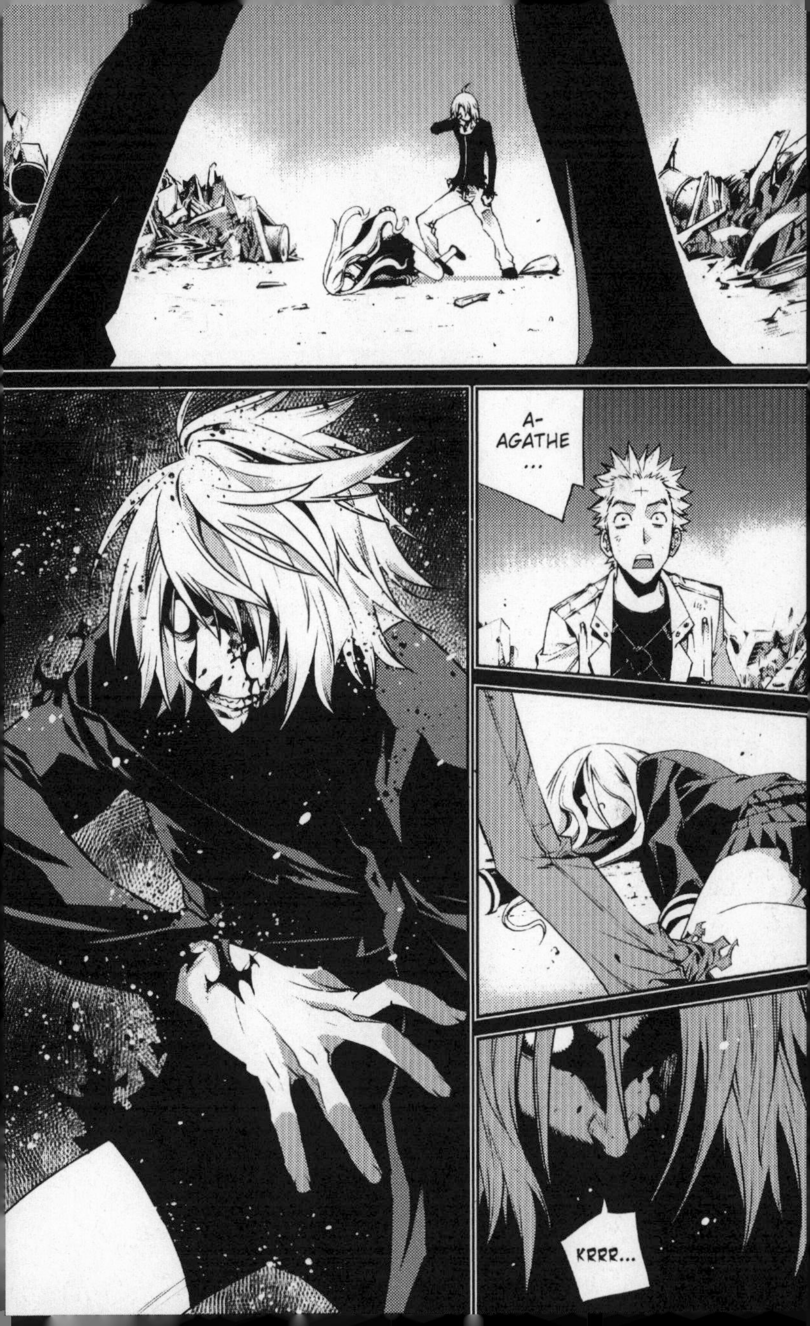
A-
AGATHE
...
KRRR...

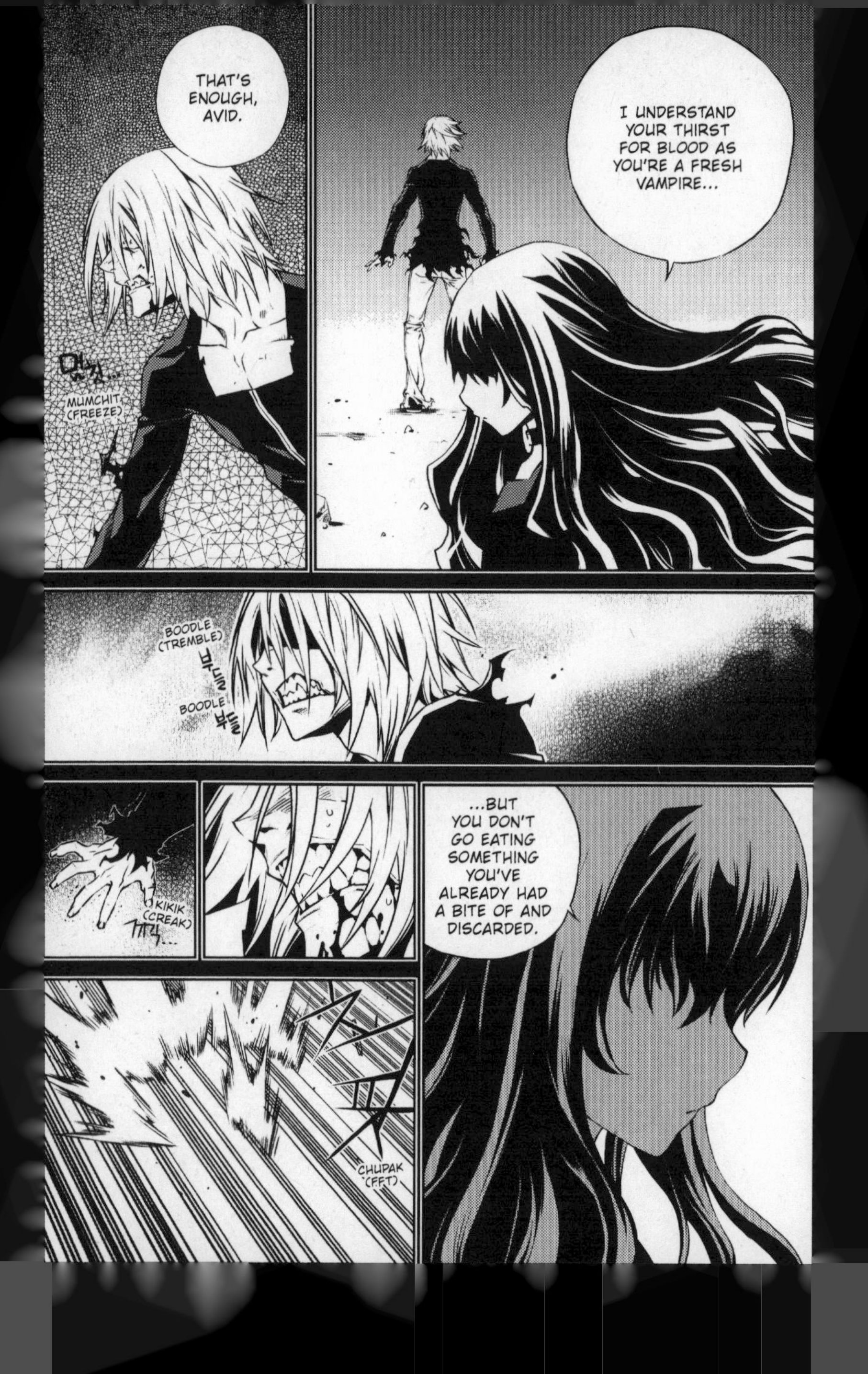
THAT'S ENOUGH, AVID.
MUMCHIT (FREEZE)
I UNDERSTAND YOUR THIRST FOR BLOOD AS YOU'RE A FRESH VAMPIRE...
BOODLE (TREMBLE)
BOODLE
KIKIK (CREAK)
...BUT YOU DON'T GO EATING SOMETHING YOU'VE ALREADY HAD A BITE OF AND DISCARDED.
CHUPAK (CFFT)

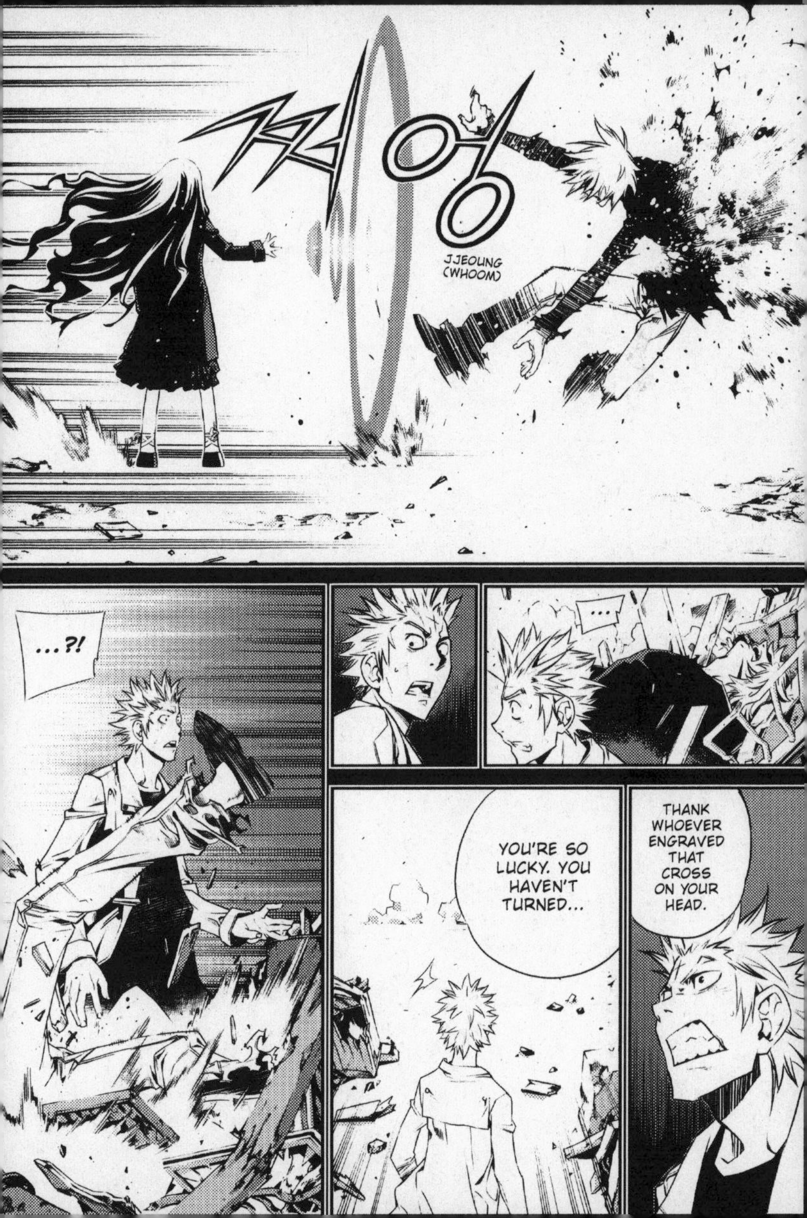
JJEOUNG
(WHOOM)
...?!
...
YOU'RE SO LUCKY. YOU HAVEN'T TURNED...
THANK WHOEVER ENGRAVED THAT CROSS ON YOUR HEAD.

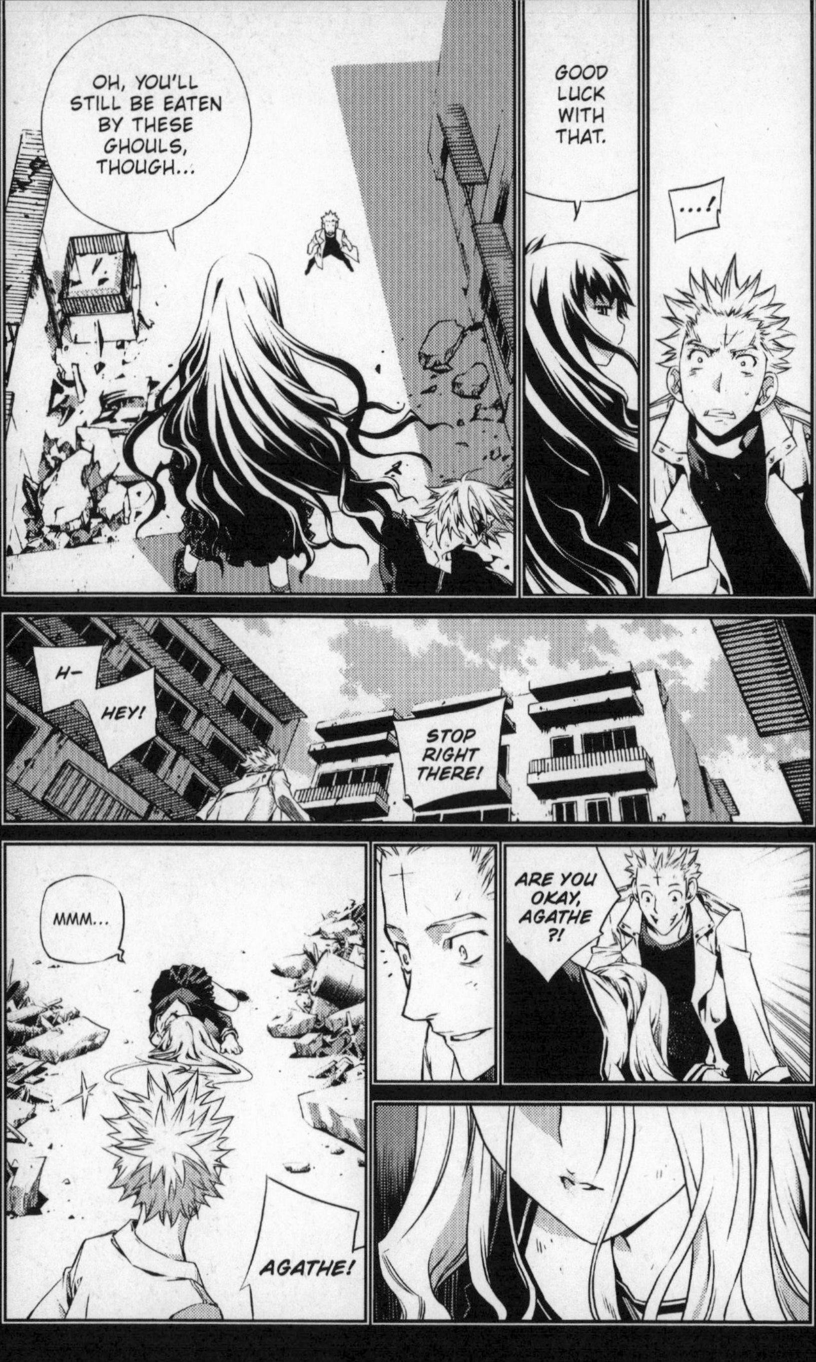
OH, YOU'LL STILL BE EATEN BY THESE GHOULS, THOUGH...
GOOD LUCK WITH THAT.
...!
H-
HEY!
STOP RIGHT THERE!
MMM...
AGATHE!
ARE YOU OKAY, AGATHE ?!

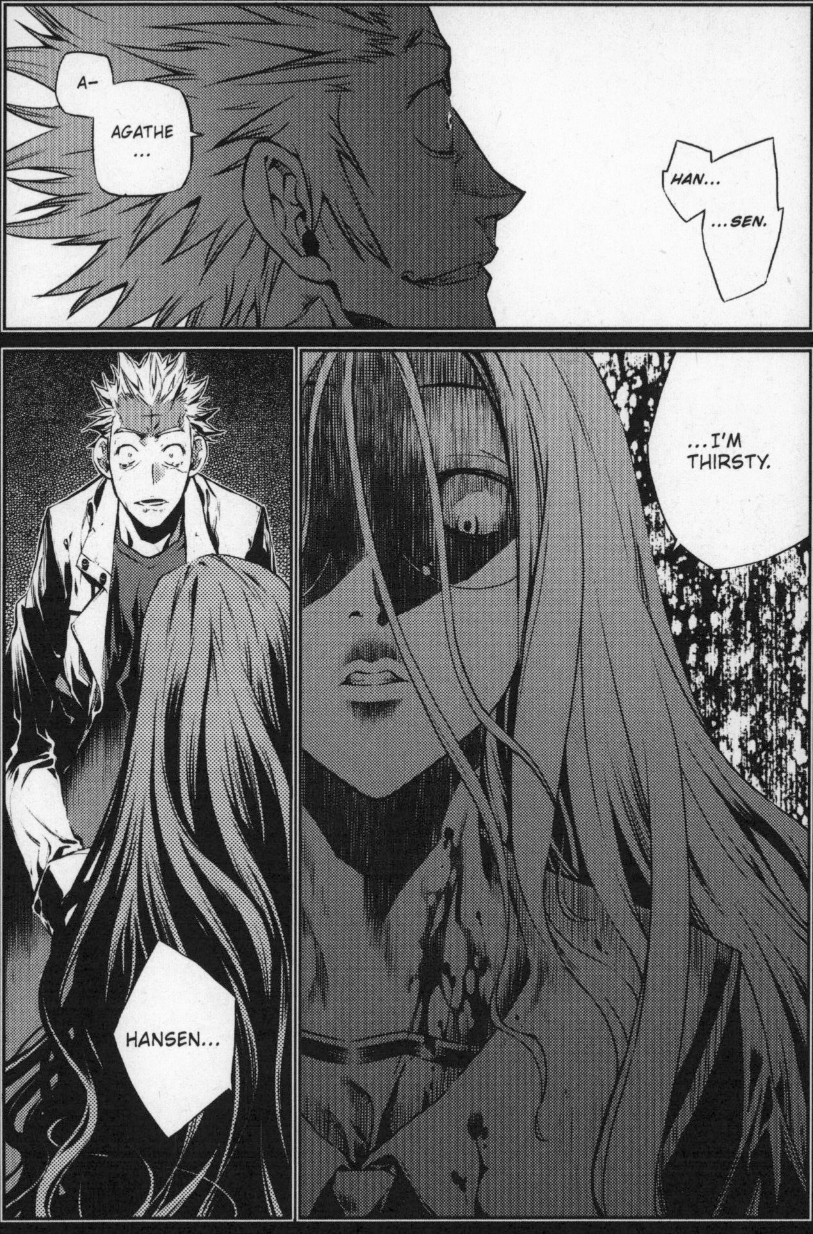
A-
AGATHE ...
HAN...
...SEN.
HANSEN...
...I'M THIRSTY.

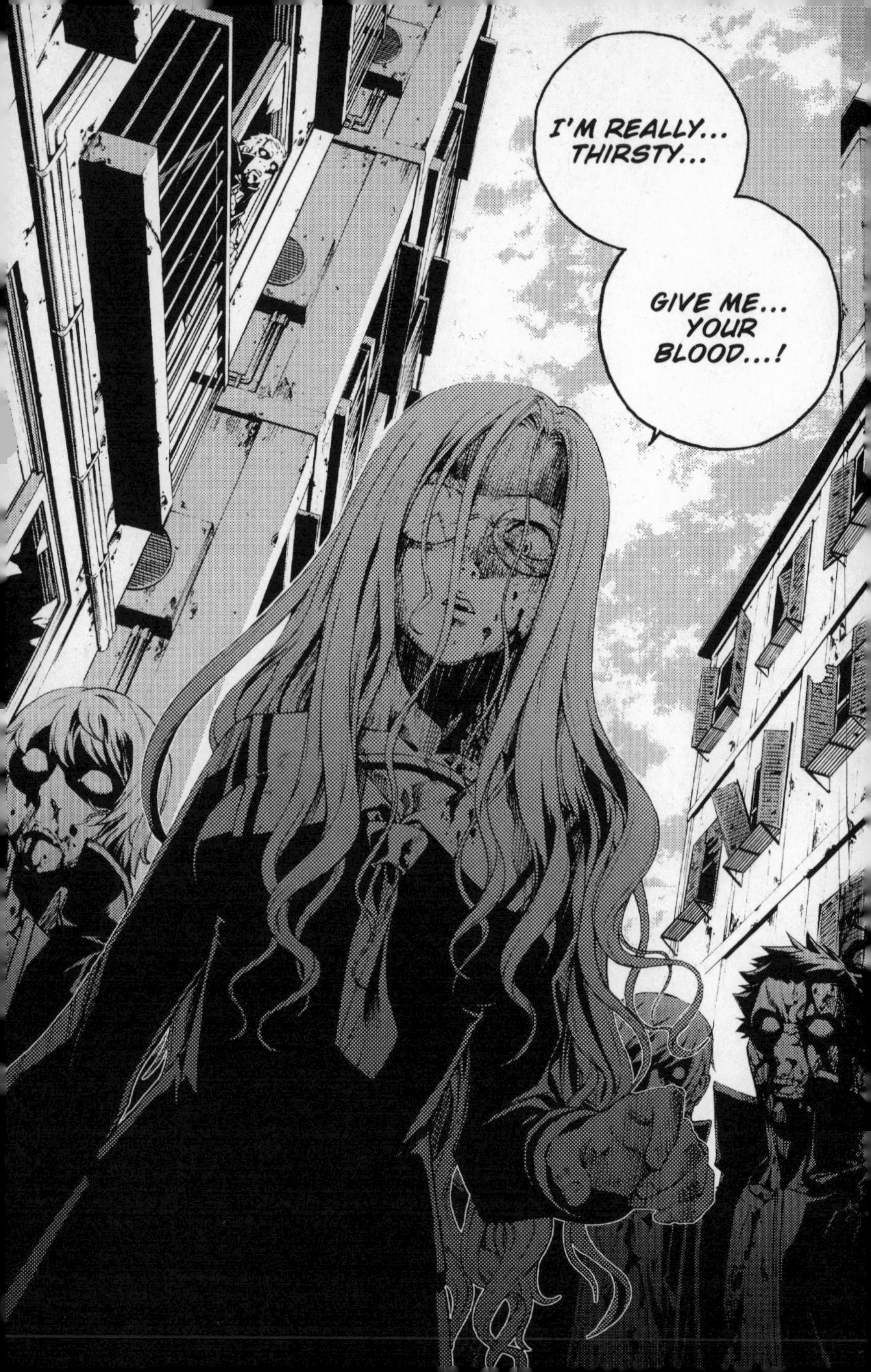
I'M REALLY... THIRSTY...
GIVE ME... YOUR BLOOD...!

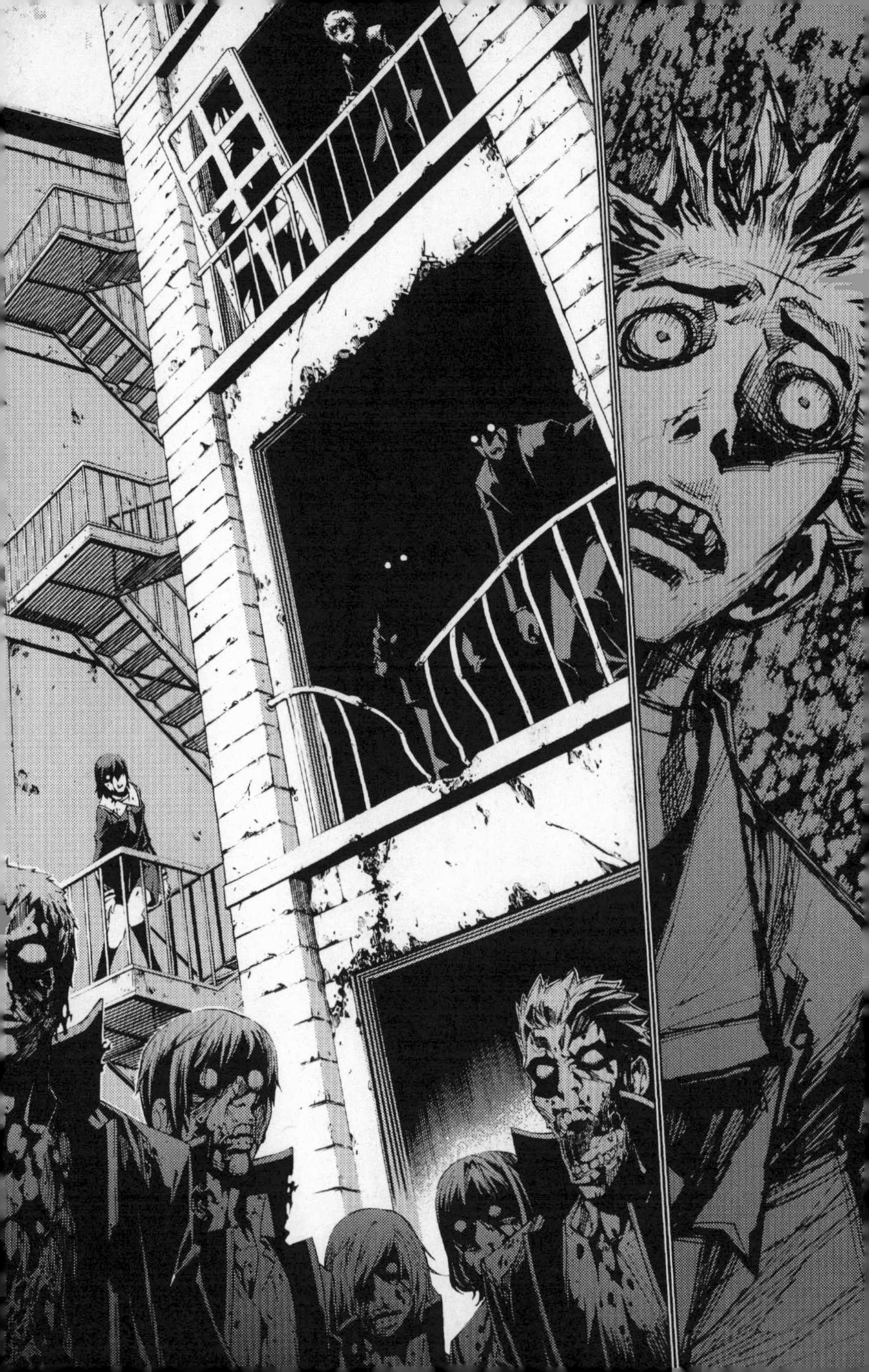

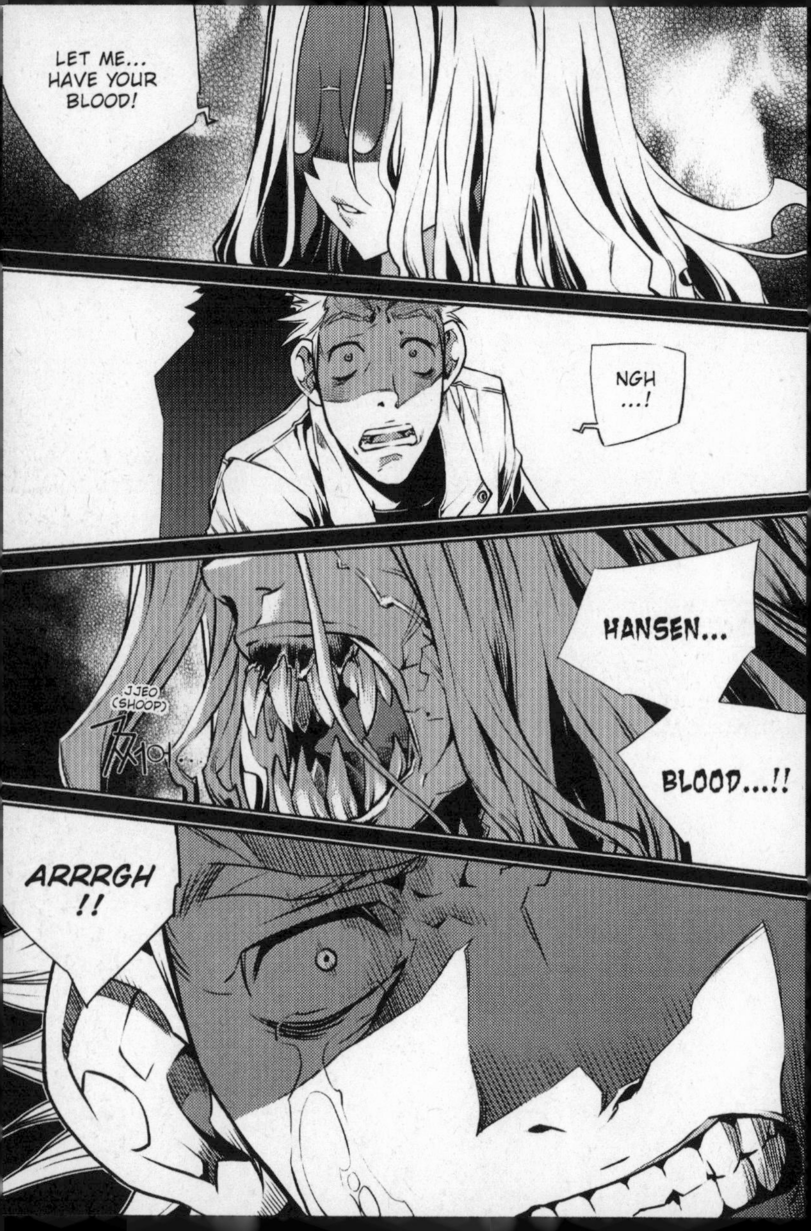
LET ME... HAVE YOUR BLOOD!
NGH ...!
JJEO (SHOOP)
HANSEN...
BLOOD...!!
ARRRGH !!

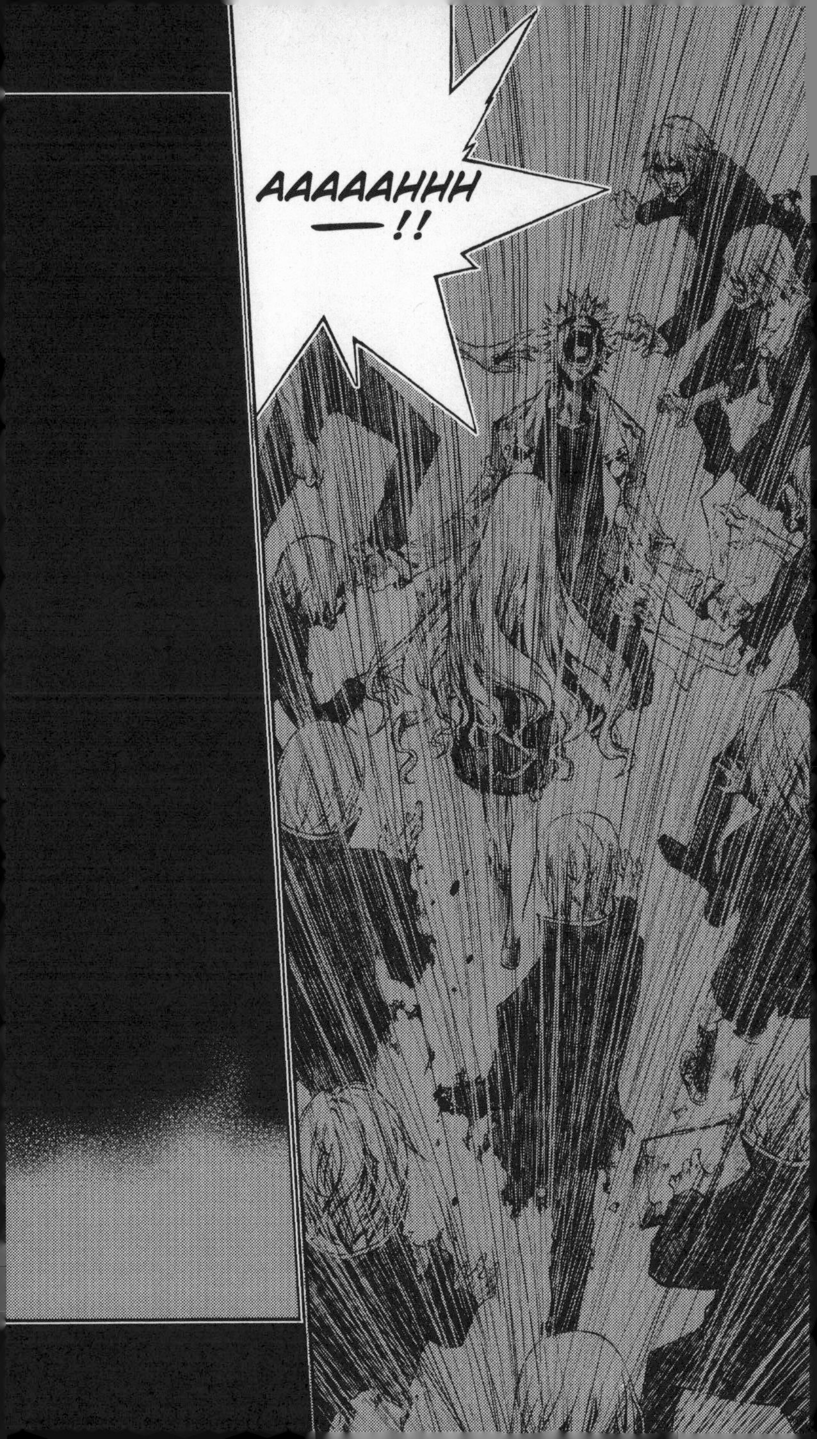
AAAAAHHH—!!

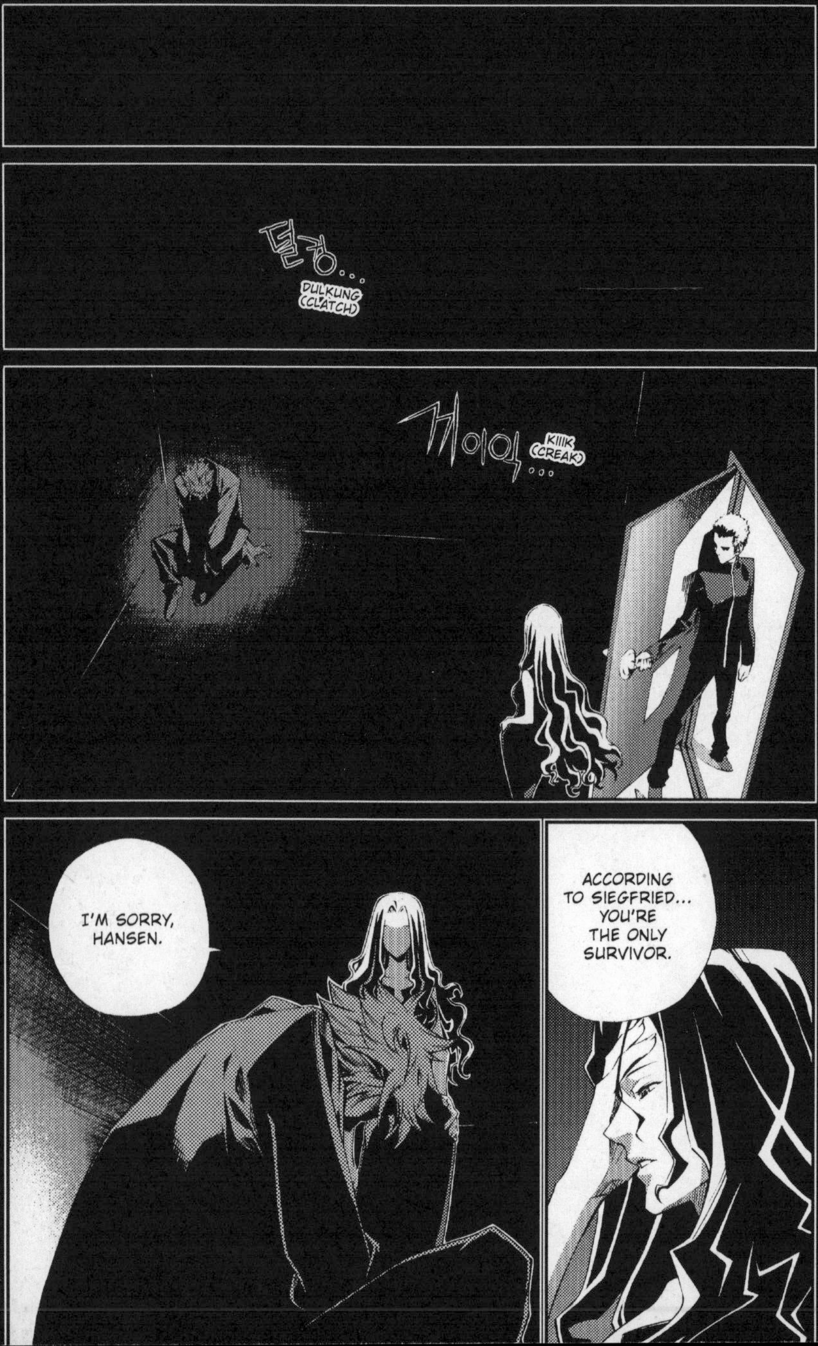
덜컹...
DULKUNG (CLATCH)
끼이익...
KIIIK (CREAK)
I'M SORRY, HANSEN.
ACCORDING TO SIEGFRIED... YOU'RE THE ONLY SURVIVOR.

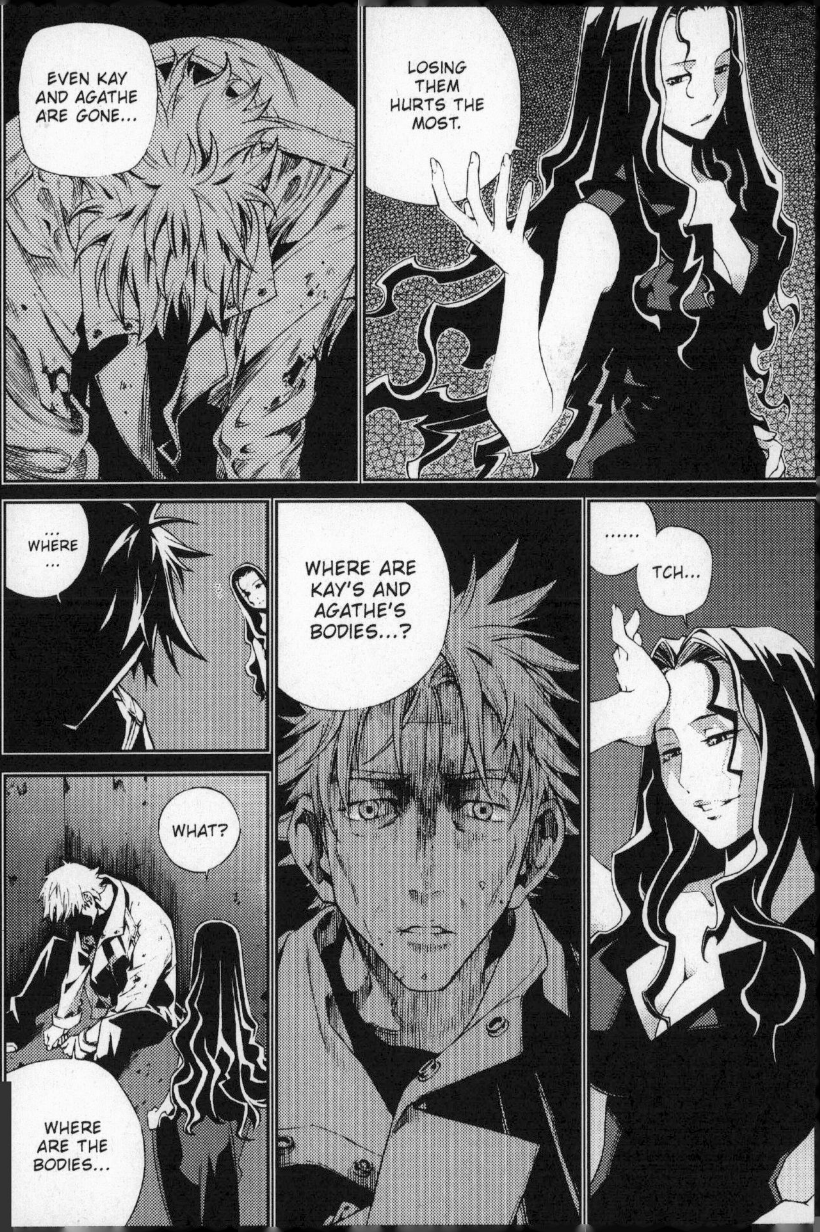
EVEN KAY AND AGATHE ARE GONE...
LOSING THEM HURTS THE MOST.
... WHERE ...
WHAT?
WHERE ARE THE BODIES...
WHERE ARE KAY'S AND AGATHE'S BODIES...?
......
TCH...

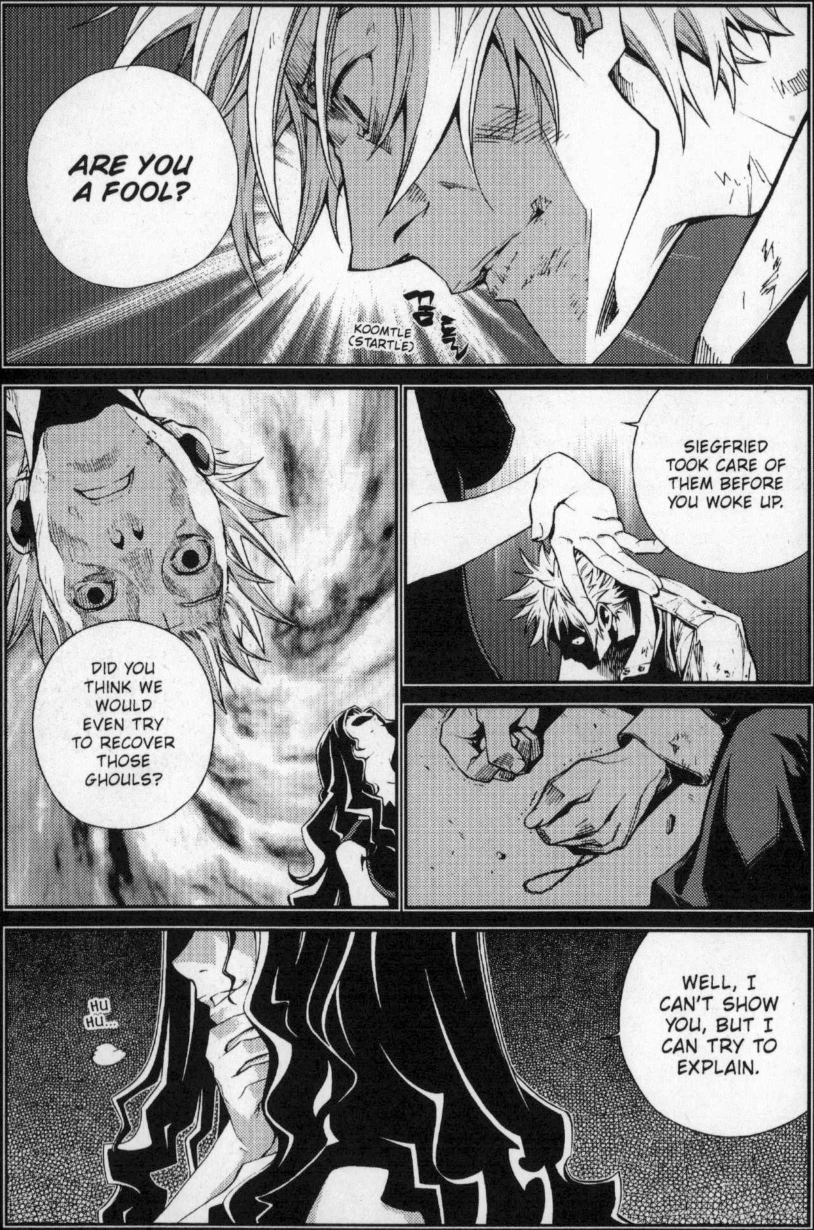
ARE YOU A FOOL?
KOOMTLE (STARTLE)
DID YOU THINK WE WOULD EVEN TRY TO RECOVER THOSE GHOULS?
SIEGFRIED TOOK CARE OF THEM BEFORE YOU WOKE UP.
HU HU...
WELL, I CAN'T SHOW YOU, BUT I CAN TRY TO EXPLAIN.

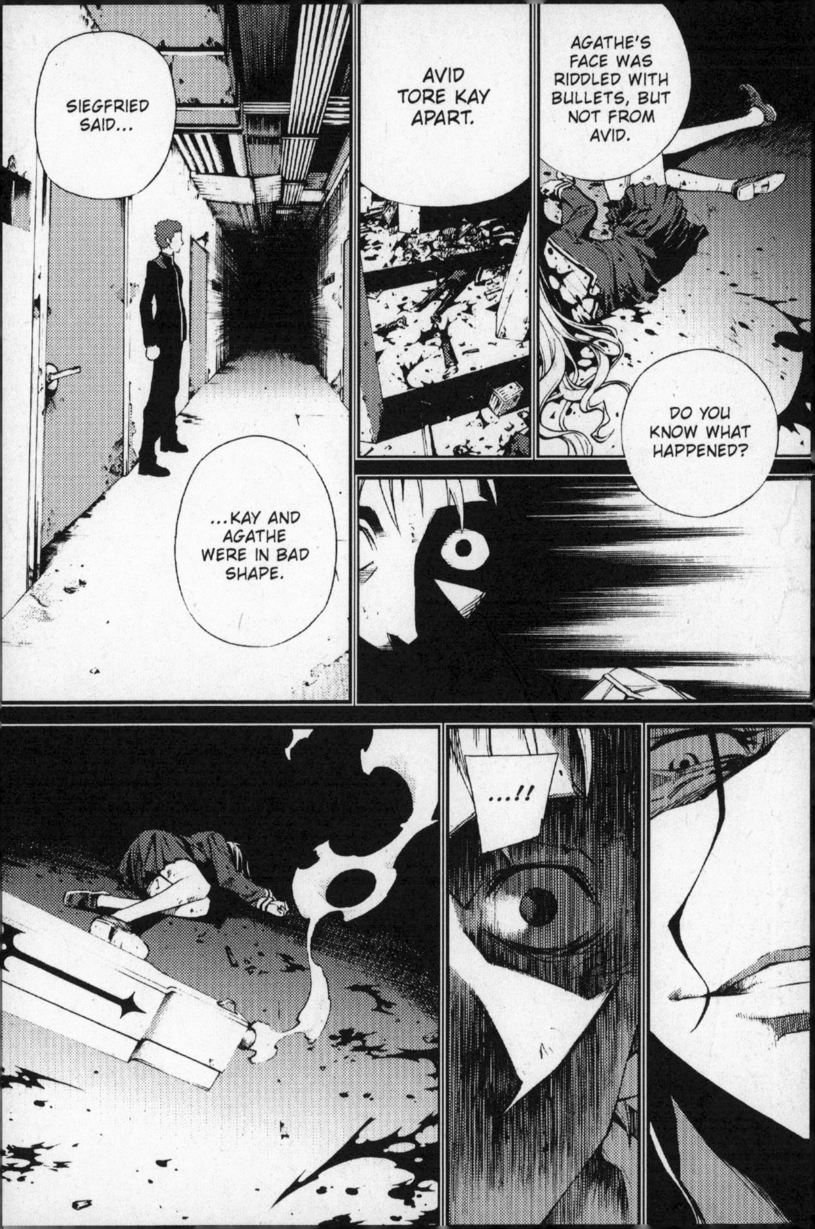
SIEGFRIED SAID...
...KAY AND AGATHE WERE IN BAD SHAPE.
AVID TORE KAY APART.
AGATHE'S FACE WAS RIDDLED WITH BULLETS, BUT NOT FROM AVID.
DO YOU KNOW WHAT HAPPENED?
...!!

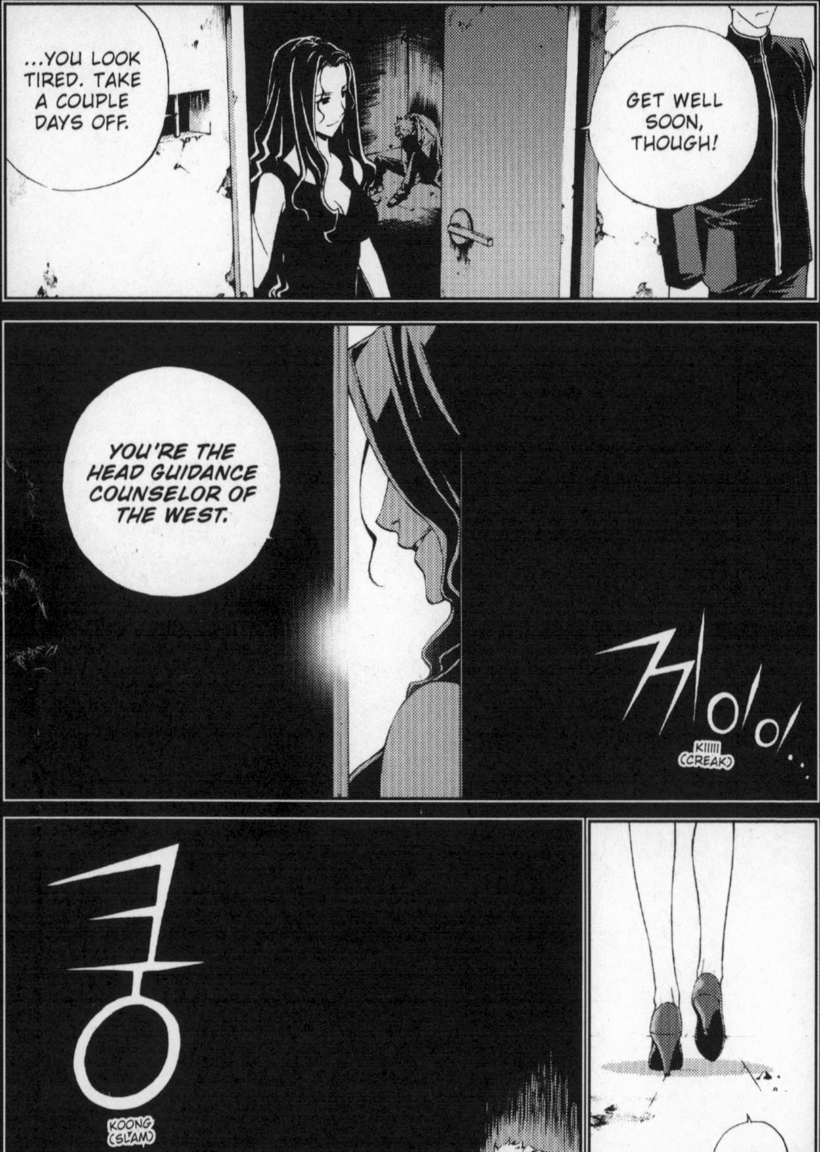
...YOU LOOK TIRED. TAKE A COUPLE DAYS OFF.
GET WELL SOON, THOUGH!
YOU'RE THE HEAD GUIDANCE COUNSELOR OF THE WEST.
KIIIII (CREAK)
KOONG (SLAM)
HMPH.

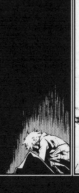

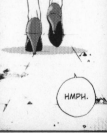

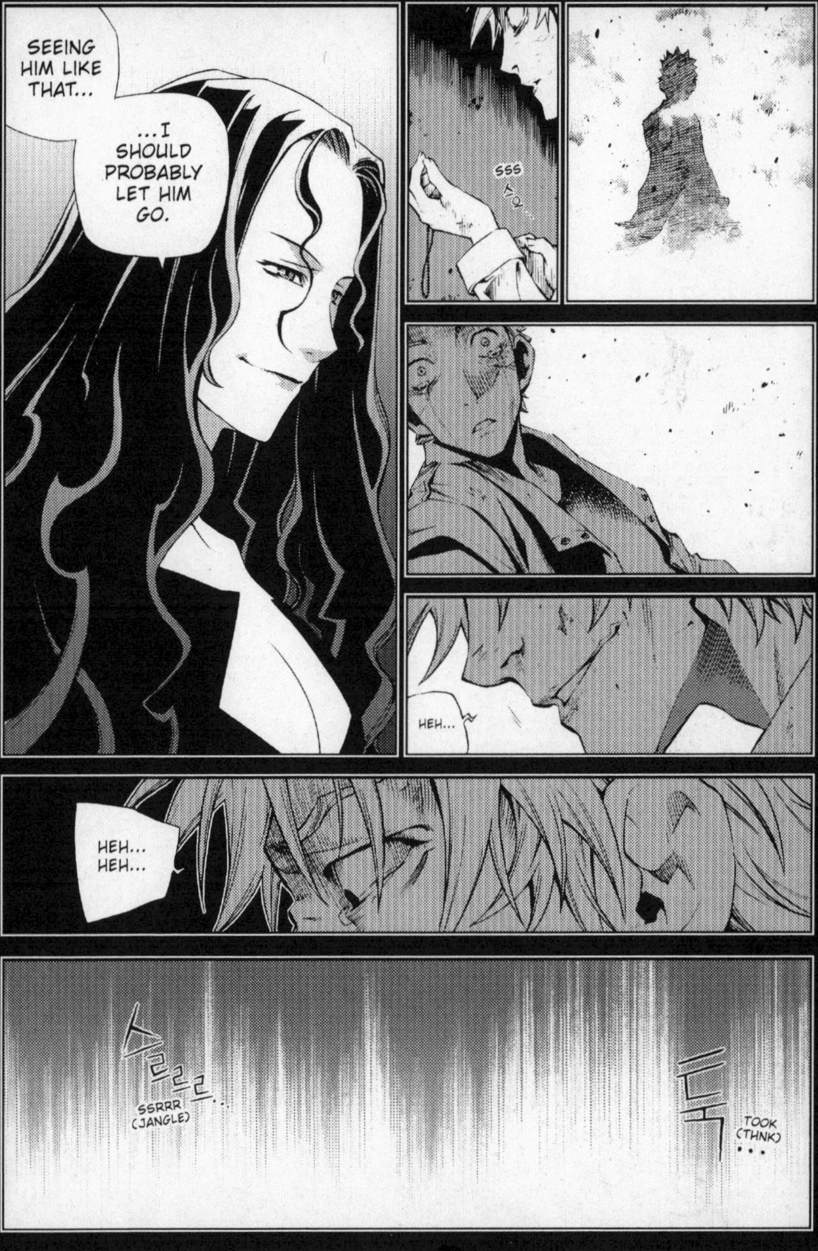
SEEING HIM LIKE THAT...
...I SHOULD PROBABLY LET HIM GO.
SSS
HEH...
HEH... HEH...
SSRRR (JANGLE)
TOOK (THNK)...

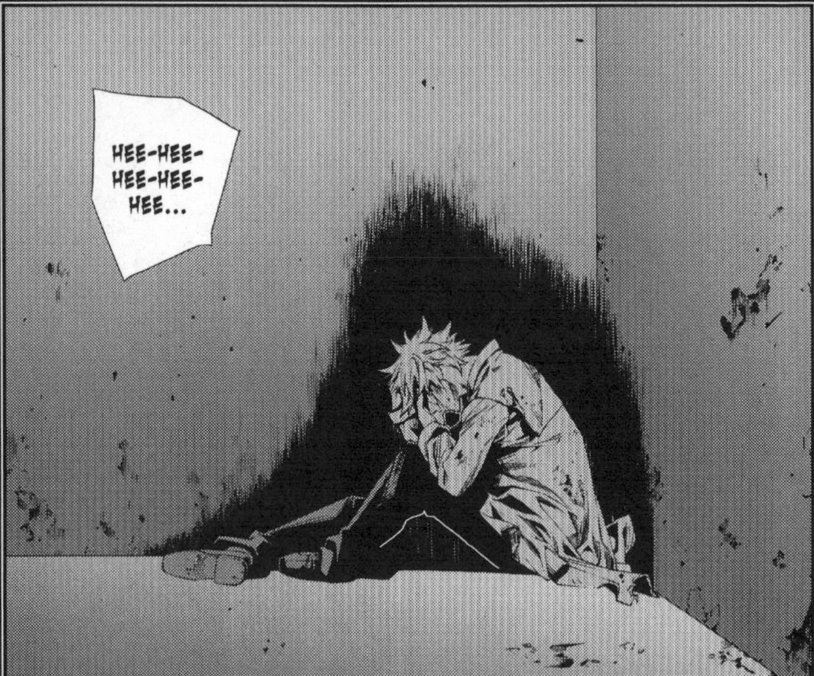
HEE-HEE-HEE-HEE-HEE...
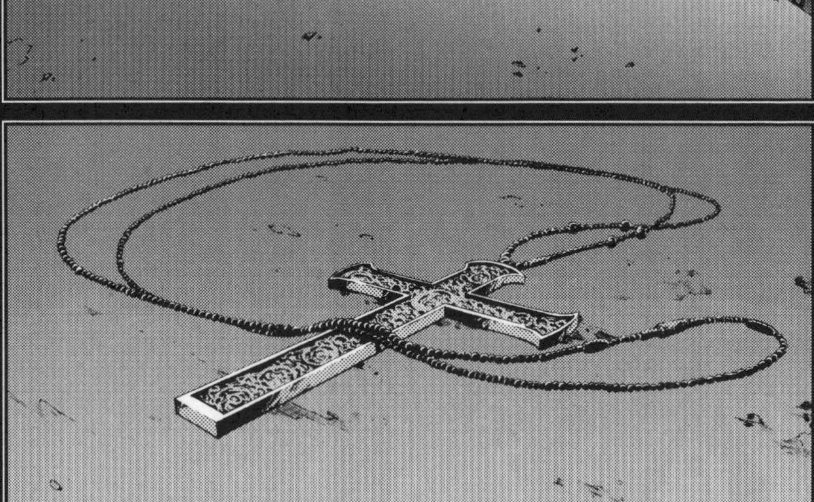

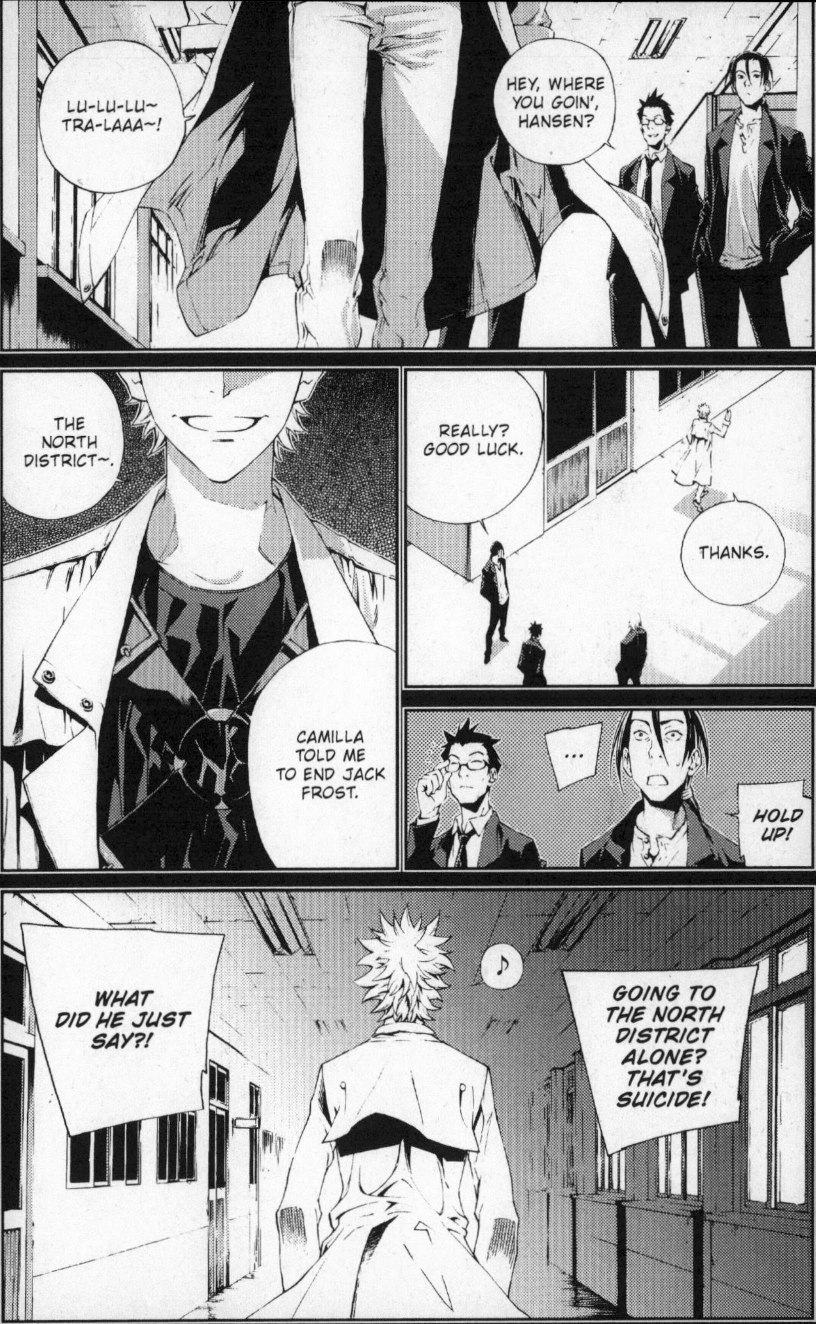
LU-LU-LU~ TRA-LAAA~!
HEY, WHERE YOU GOIN', HANSEN?
THE NORTH DISTRICT~.
CAMILLA TOLD ME TO END JACK FROST.
REALLY? GOOD LUCK.
THANKS.
...
HOLD UP!
WHAT DID HE JUST SAY?!
♪
GOING TO THE NORTH DISTRICT ALONE? THAT'S SUICIDE!

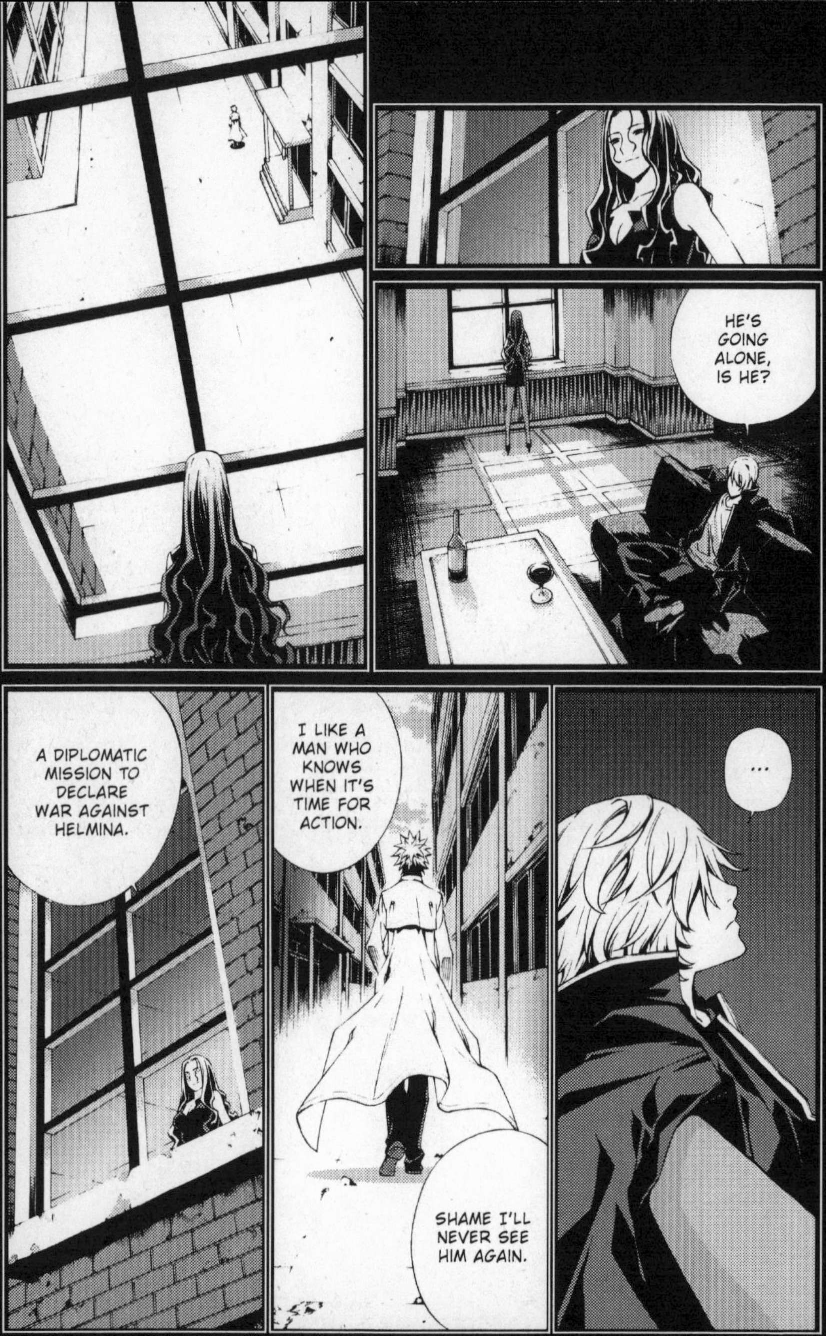
HE'S GOING ALONE, IS HE?
A DIPLOMATIC MISSION TO DECLARE WAR AGAINST HELMINA.
I LIKE A MAN WHO KNOWS WHEN IT'S TIME FOR ACTION.
SHAME I'LL NEVER SEE HIM AGAIN.
...

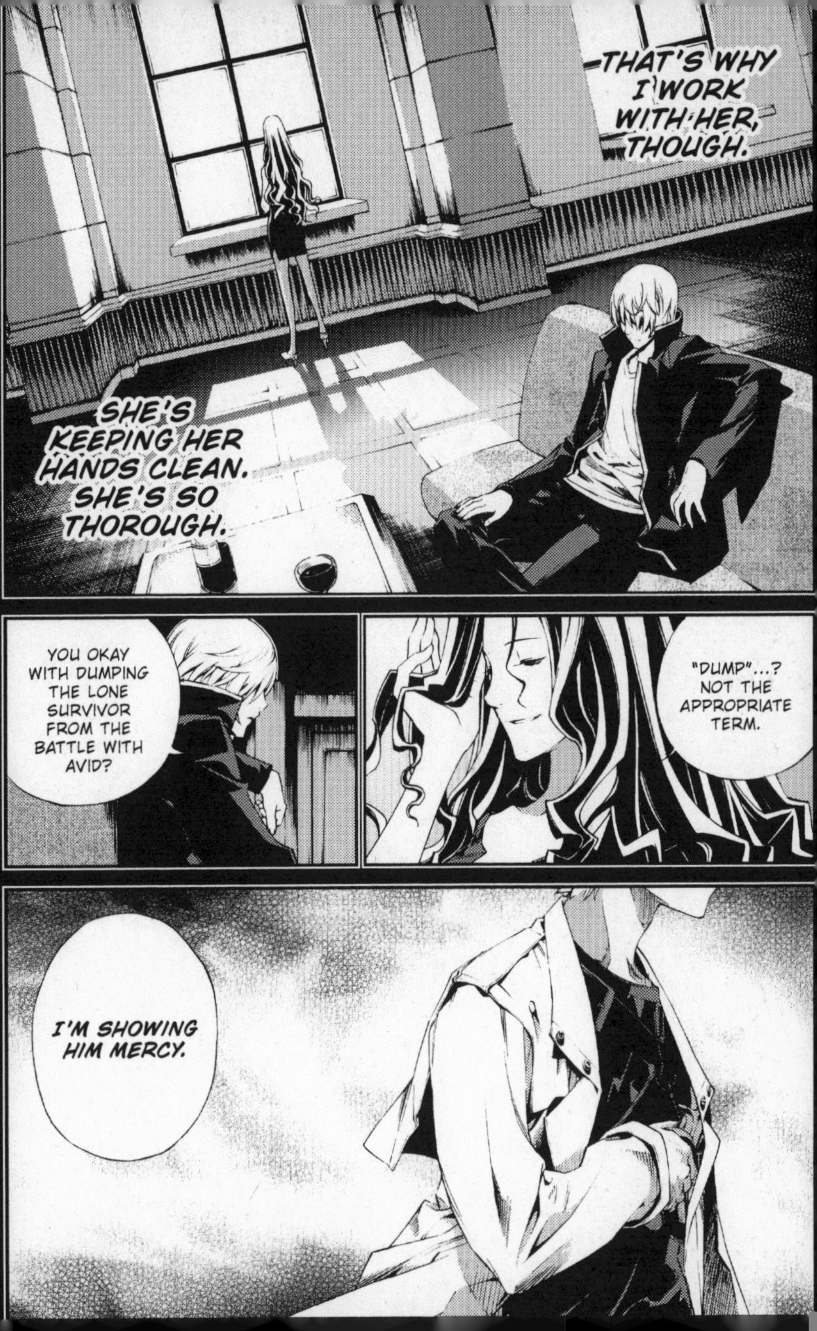

THAT'S WHY I WORK WITH HER, THOUGH.
SHE'S KEEPING HER HANDS CLEAN. SHE'S SO THOROUGH.
YOU OKAY WITH DUMPING THE LONE SURVIVOR FROM THE BATTLE WITH AVID?
"DUMP"...? NOT THE APPROPRIATE TERM.
I'M SHOWING HIM MERCY.

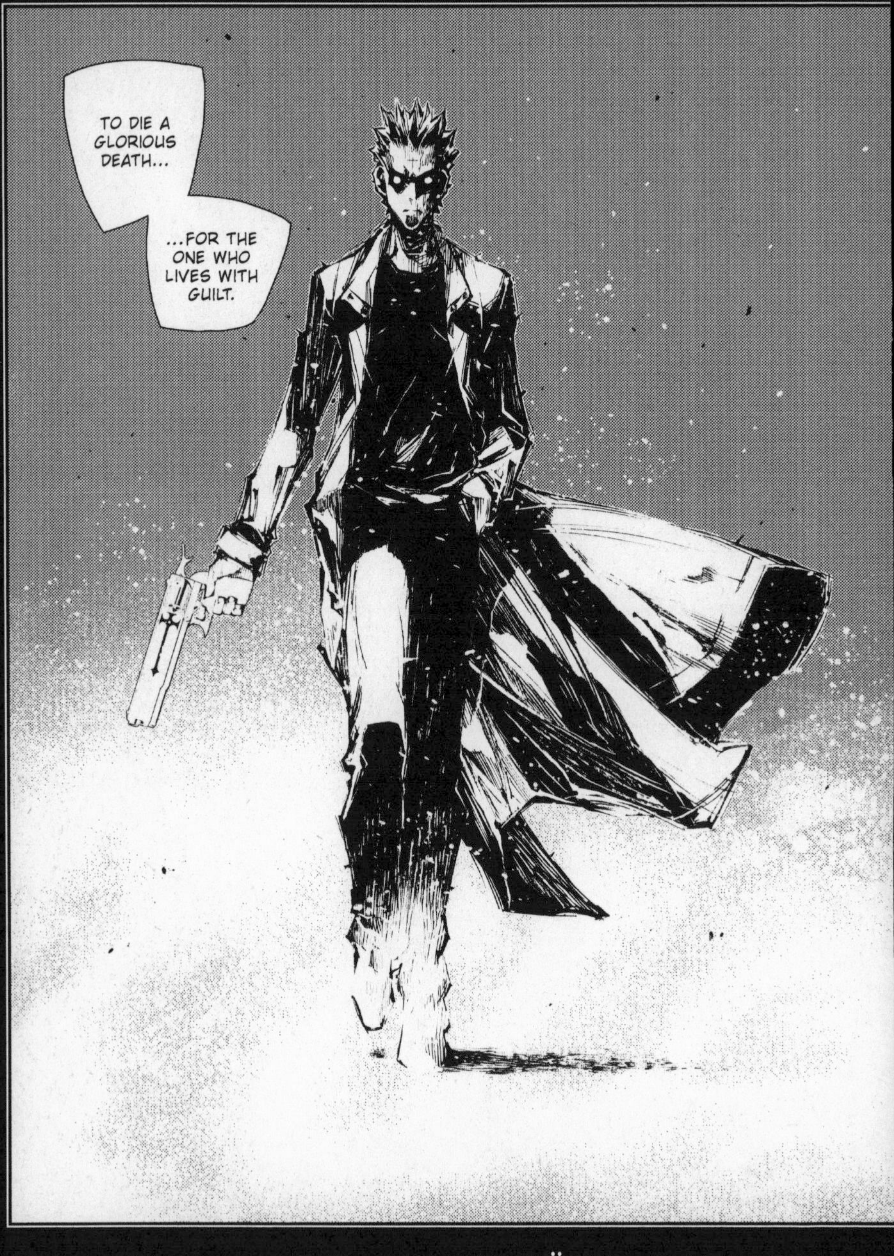
TO DIE A GLORIOUS DEATH...
...FOR THE ONE WHO LIVES WITH GUILT.

VIOLENCE 29. DER FREISCHÜTZ - PART IV

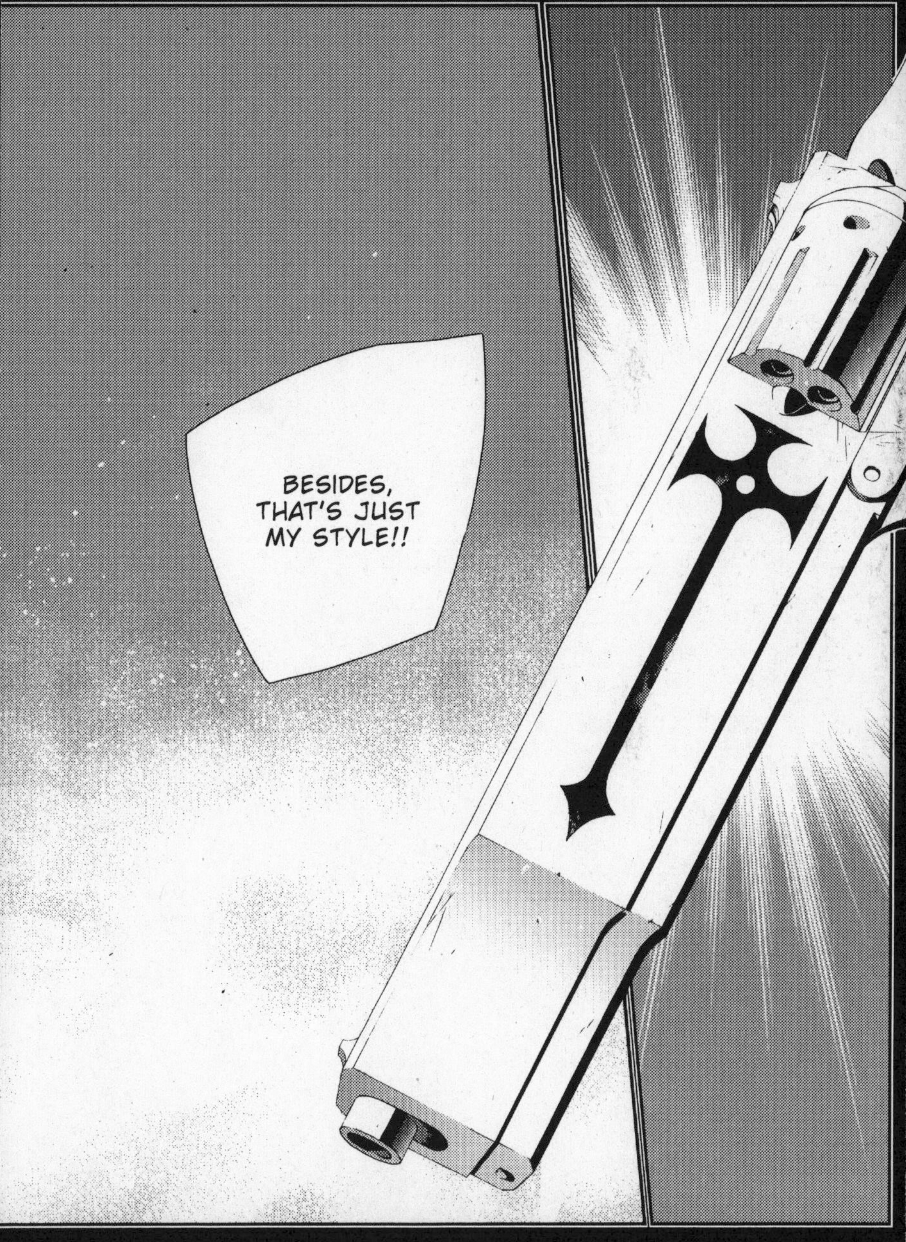
BESIDES, THAT'S JUST MY STYLE!!

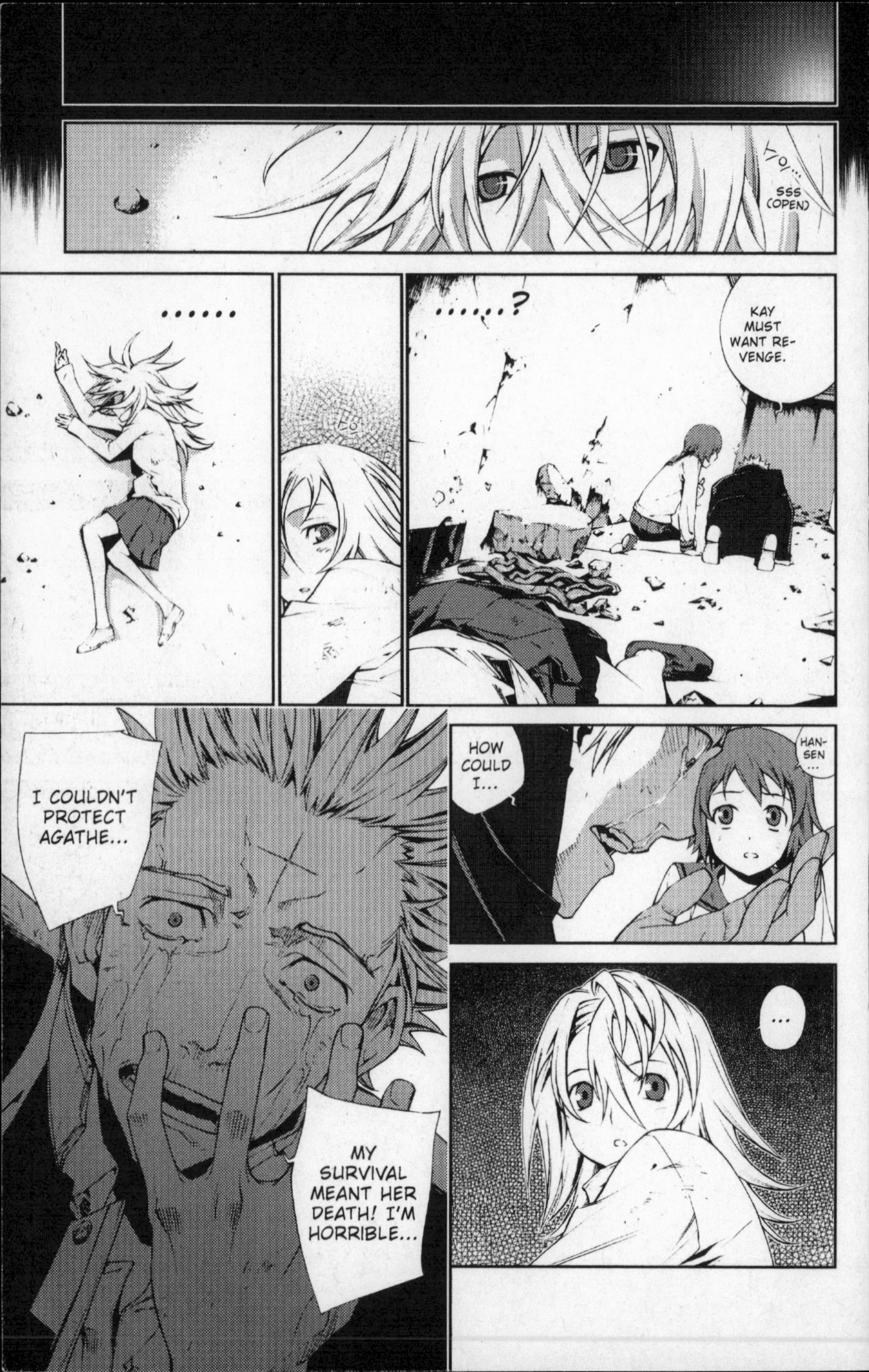
SSS (OPEN)
......
......?
KAY MUST WANT RE-VENGE.
I COULDN'T PROTECT AGATHE...
MY SURVIVAL MEANT HER DEATH! I'M HORRIBLE...
HOW COULD I...
HAN-SEN ...
...

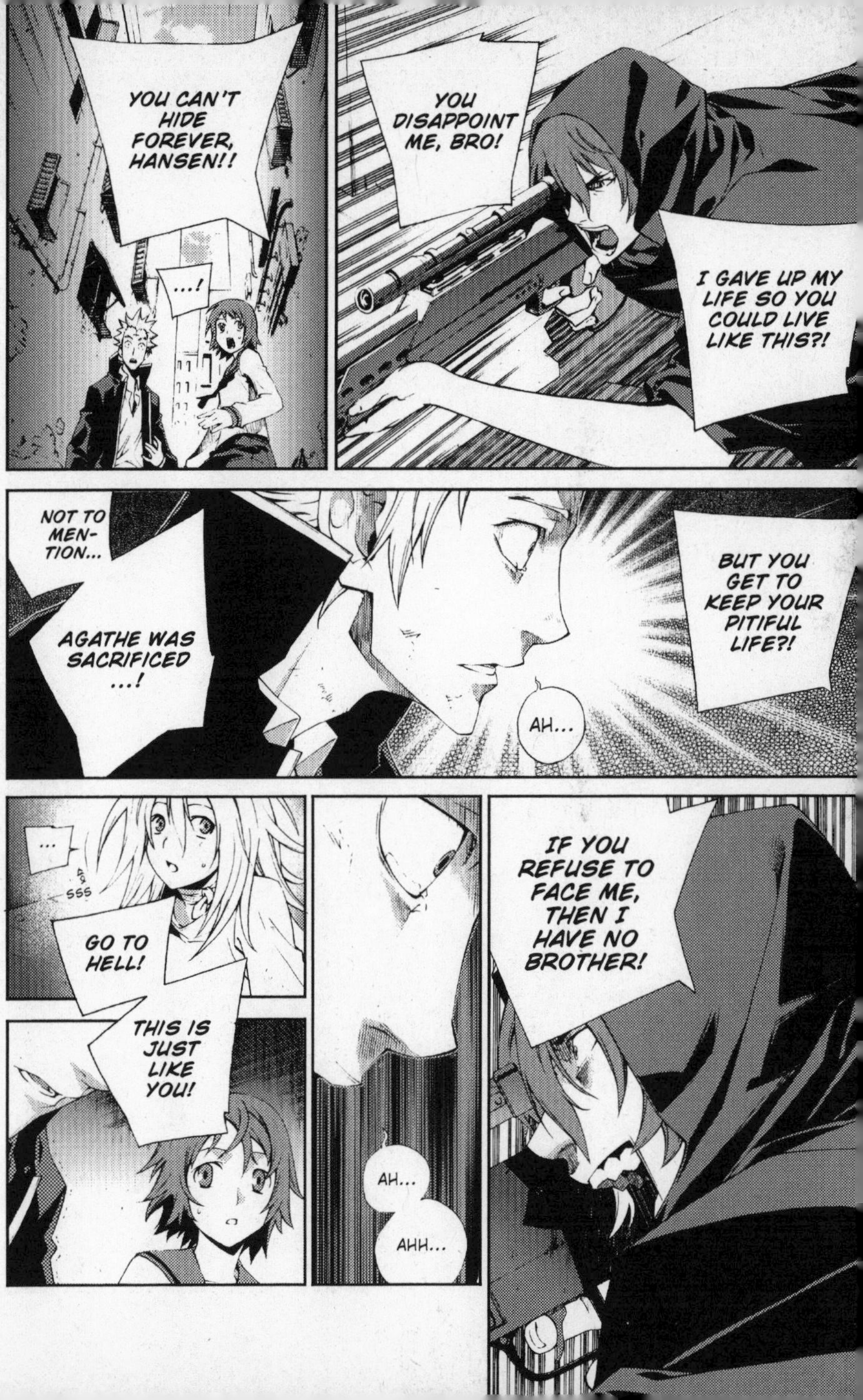
YOU CAN'T HIDE FOREVER, HANSEN!!
...!
YOU DISAPPOINT ME, BRO!
I GAVE UP MY LIFE SO YOU COULD LIVE LIKE THIS?!
NOT TO MEN-TION...
AGATHE WAS SACRIFICED ...!
BUT YOU GET TO KEEP YOUR PITIFUL LIFE?!
AH...
...
SSS
GO TO HELL!
THIS IS JUST LIKE YOU!
AH...
AHH...
IF YOU REFUSE TO FACE ME, THEN I HAVE NO BROTHER!

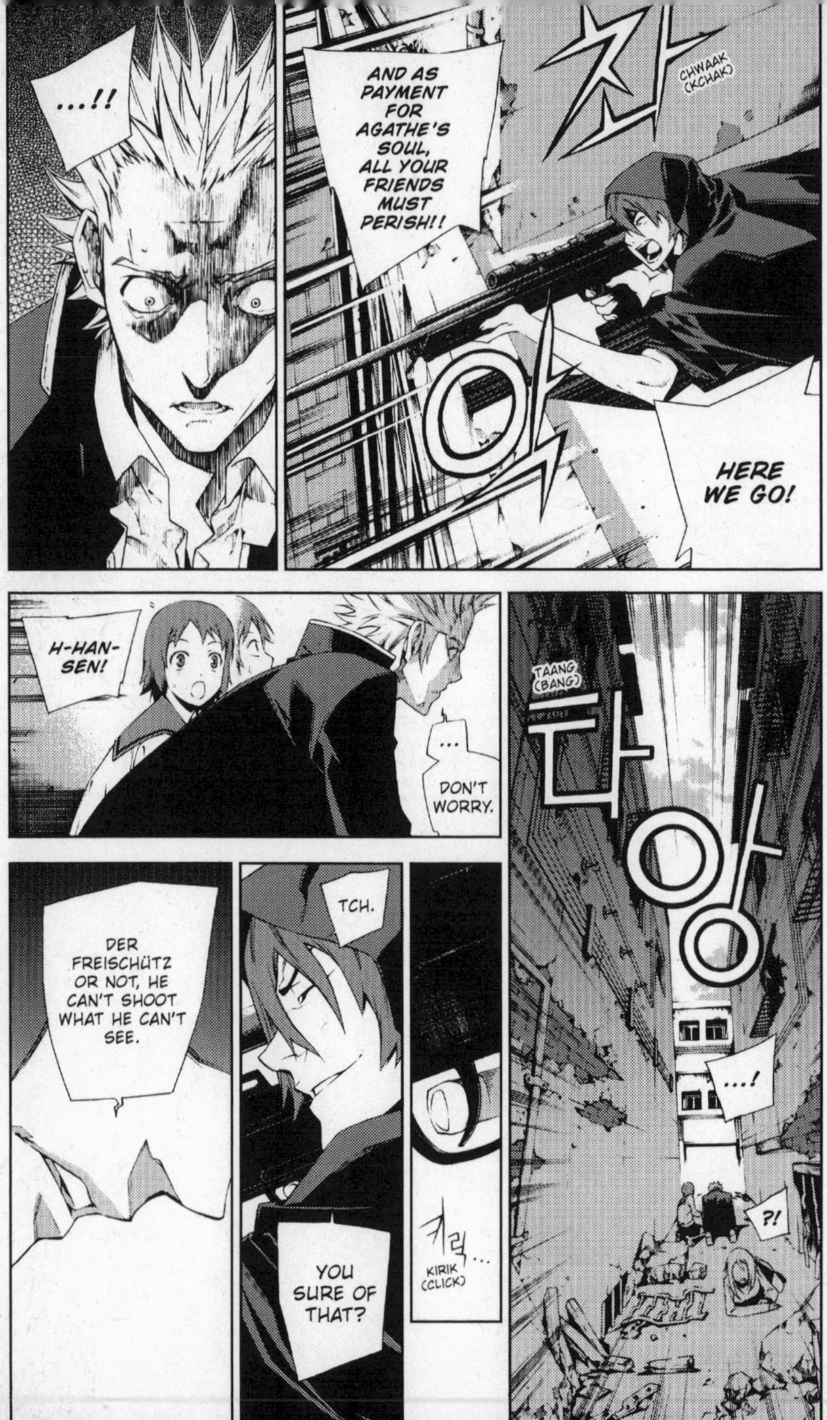
...!!
AND AS PAYMENT FOR AGATHE'S SOUL, ALL YOUR FRIENDS MUST PERISH!!
CHWAAK (KCHAK)
HERE WE GO!
H-HAN-SEN!
...
DON'T WORRY.
DER FREISCHÜTZ OR NOT, HE CAN'T SHOOT WHAT HE CAN'T SEE.
TCH.
YOU SURE OF THAT?
KIRIK (CLICK)
TAANG (BANG)
...!
?!

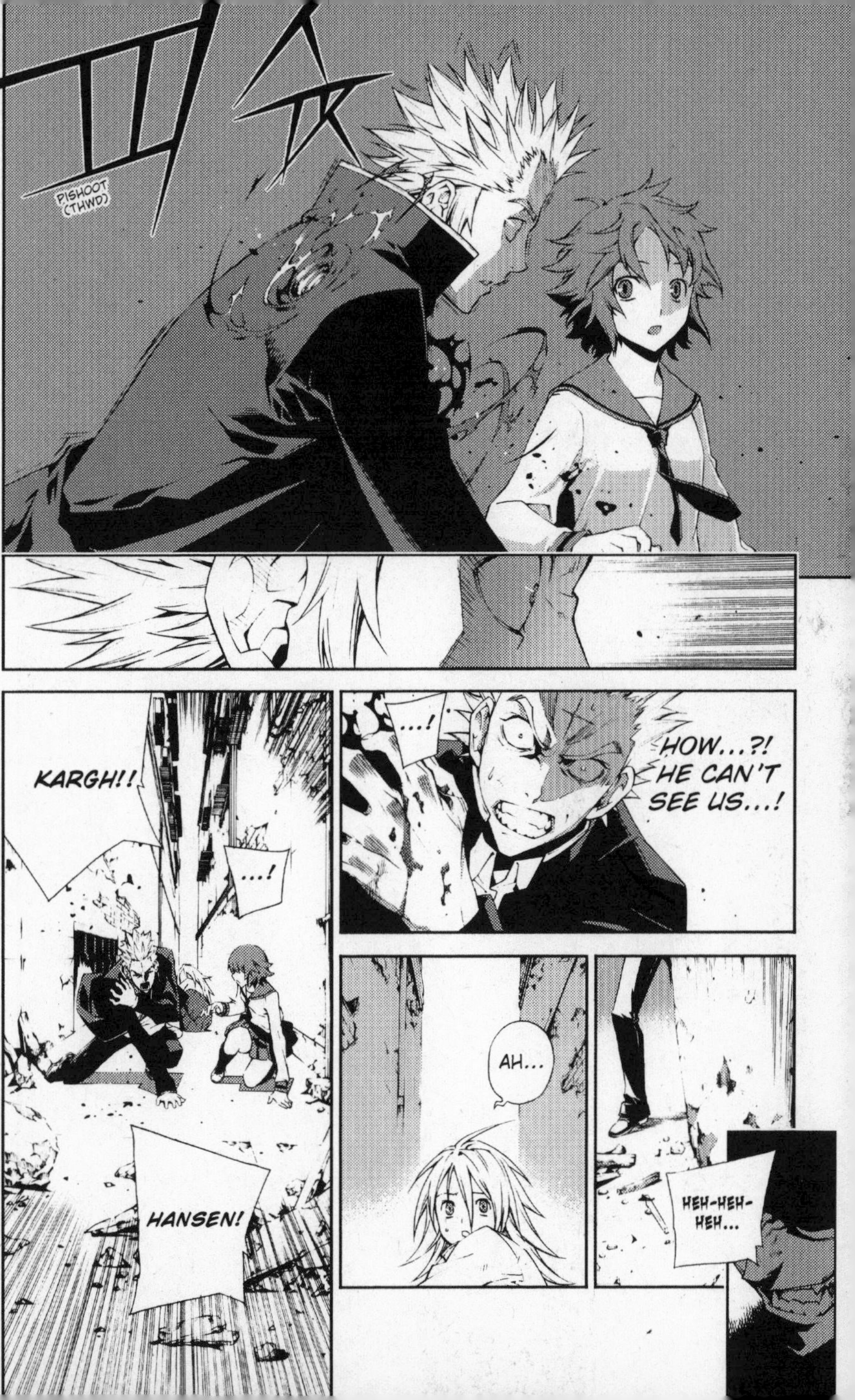
PISHOOT (THWD)
KARGH!!
...!
HANSEN!
...!
HOW...?! HE CAN'T SEE US...!
AH...
HEH-HEH-HEH...

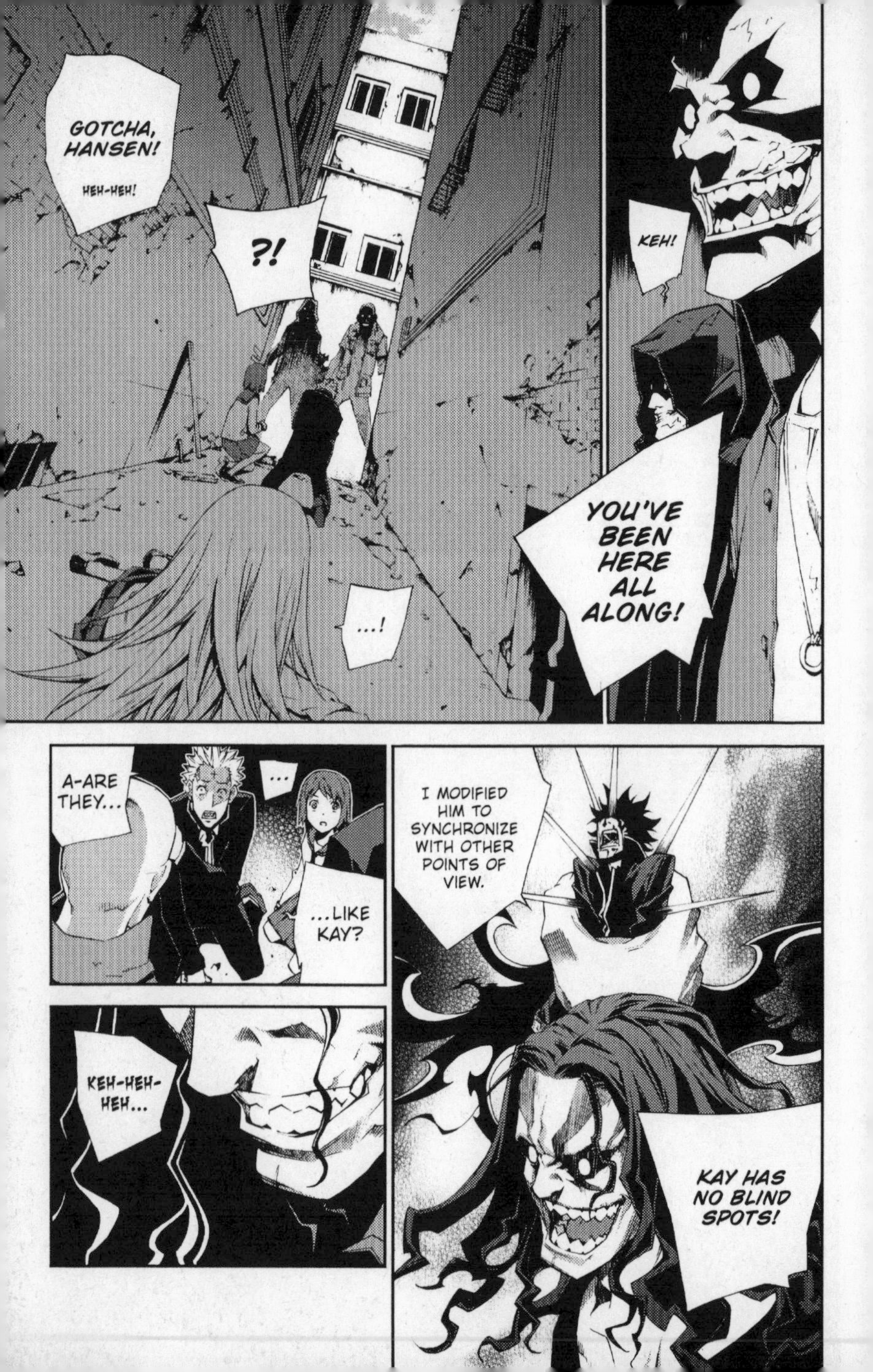
GOTCHA, HANSEN!
HEH-HEH!
?!
...!
KEH!
YOU'VE BEEN HERE ALL ALONG!
A-ARE THEY...
...
...LIKE KAY?
I MODIFIED HIM TO SYNCHRONIZE WITH OTHER POINTS OF VIEW.
KEH-HEH-HEH...
KAY HAS NO BLIND SPOTS!

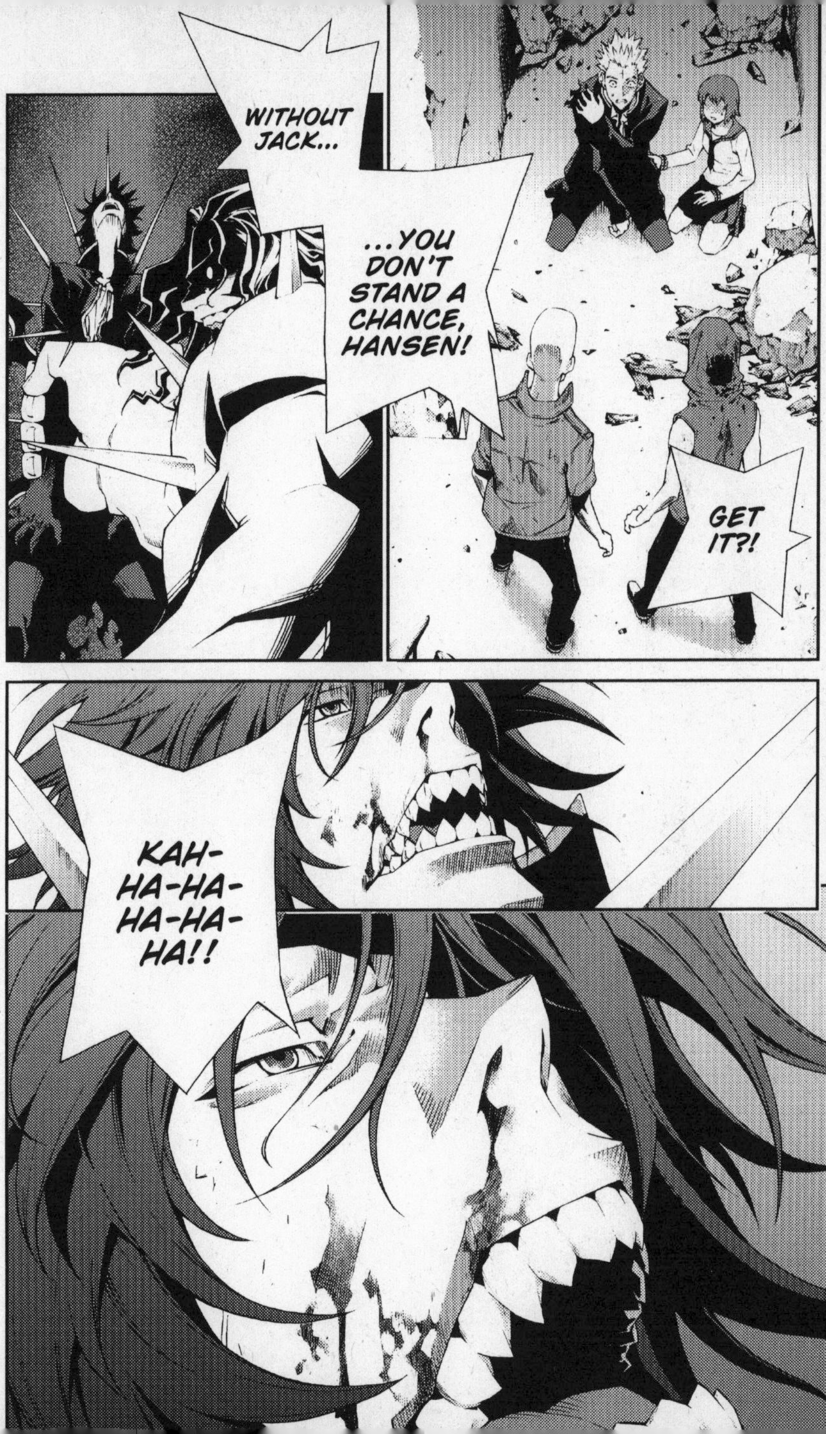
WITHOUT JACK...
...YOU DON'T STAND A CHANCE, HANSEN!
GET IT?!
KAH-HA-HA-HA-HA-HA!!

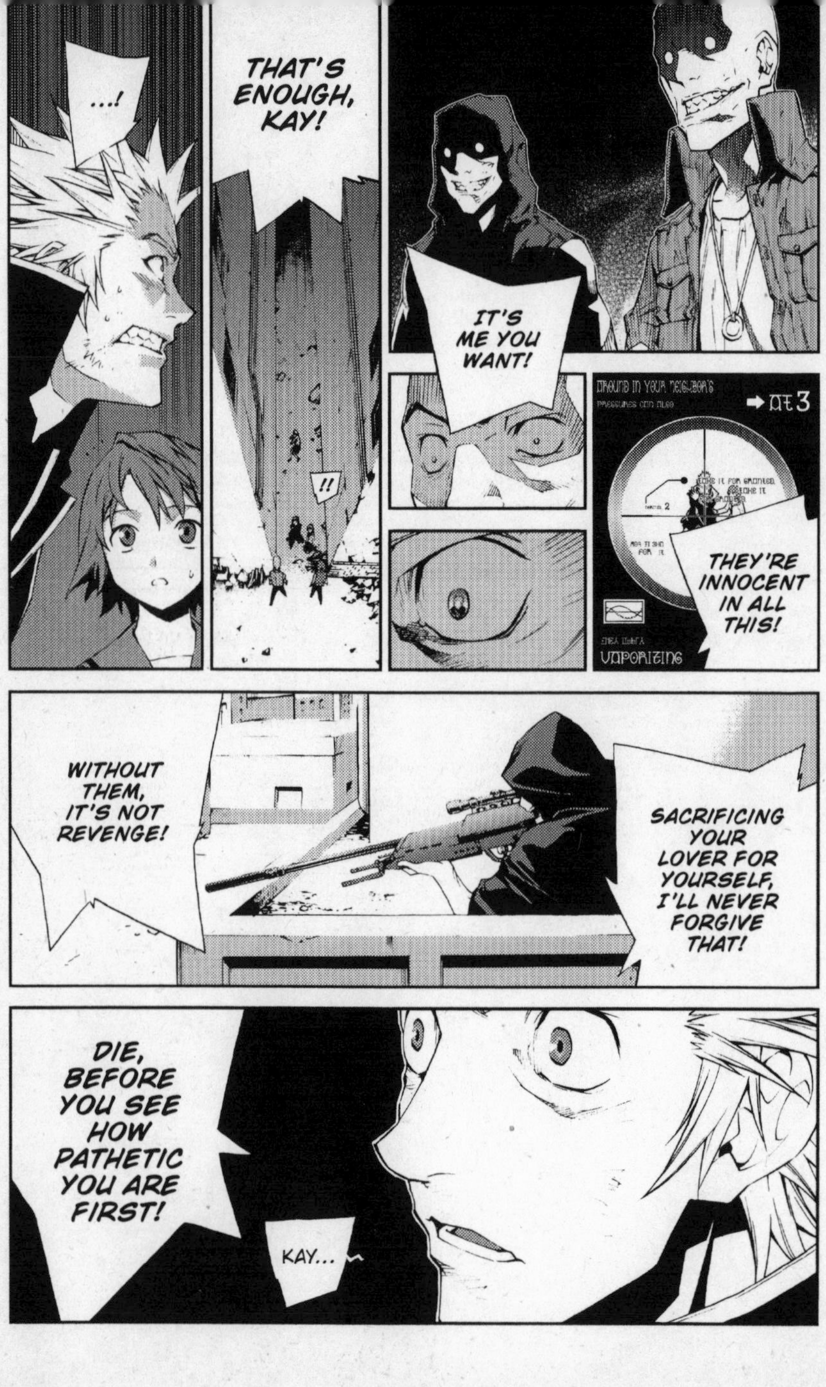
...!
THAT'S ENOUGH, KAY!
!!
IT'S ME YOU WANT!
THEY'RE INNOCENT IN ALL THIS!
WITHOUT THEM, IT'S NOT REVENGE!
SACRIFICING YOUR LOVER FOR YOURSELF, I'LL NEVER FORGIVE THAT!
DIE, BEFORE YOU SEE HOW PATHETIC YOU ARE FIRST!
KAY...

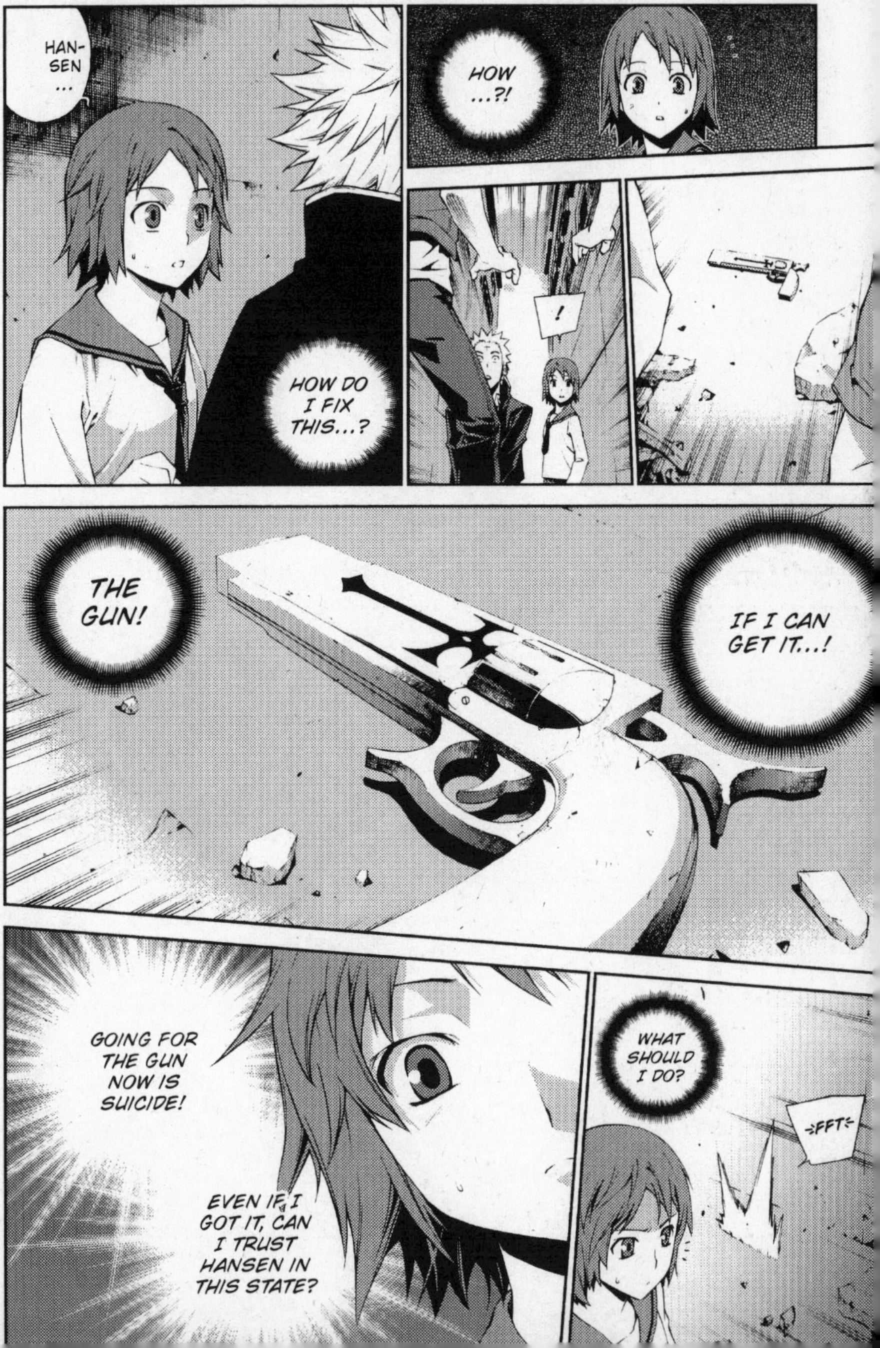
HAN-
SEN
...
HOW DO
I FIX
THIS...?
HOW
...?!
!
THE
GUN!
IF I CAN
GET IT...!
GOING FOR
THE GUN
NOW IS
SUICIDE!
EVEN IF I
GOT IT, CAN
I TRUST
HANSEN IN
THIS STATE?
WHAT
SHOULD
I DO?
FFT

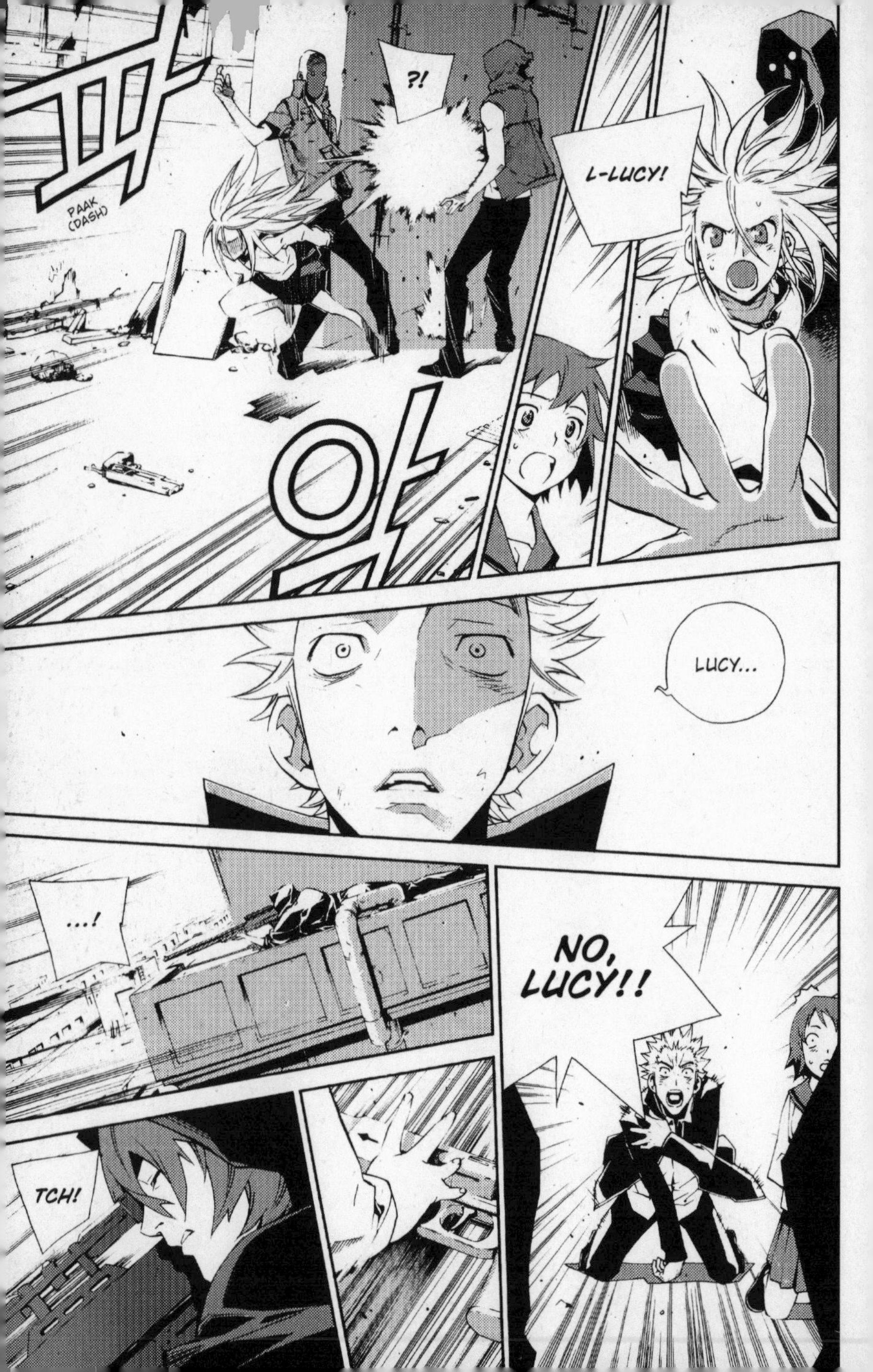
PAAK
(DASH)
?!
L-LUCY!
LUCY...
...!
TCH!
NO, LUCY!!

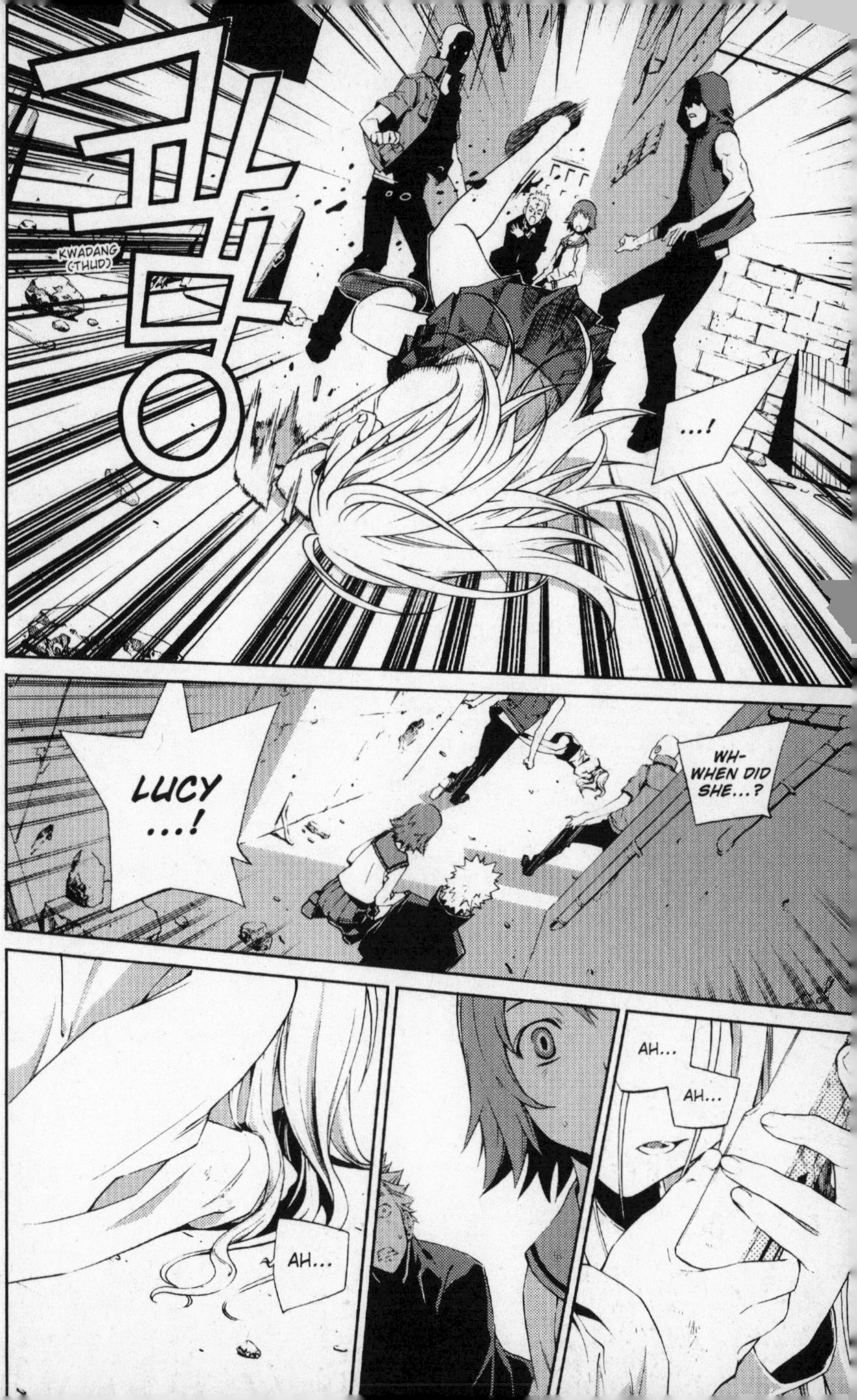
KWADANG (THUD)
...!
LUCY ...!
WH-WHEN DID SHE...?
AH...
AH...
AH...

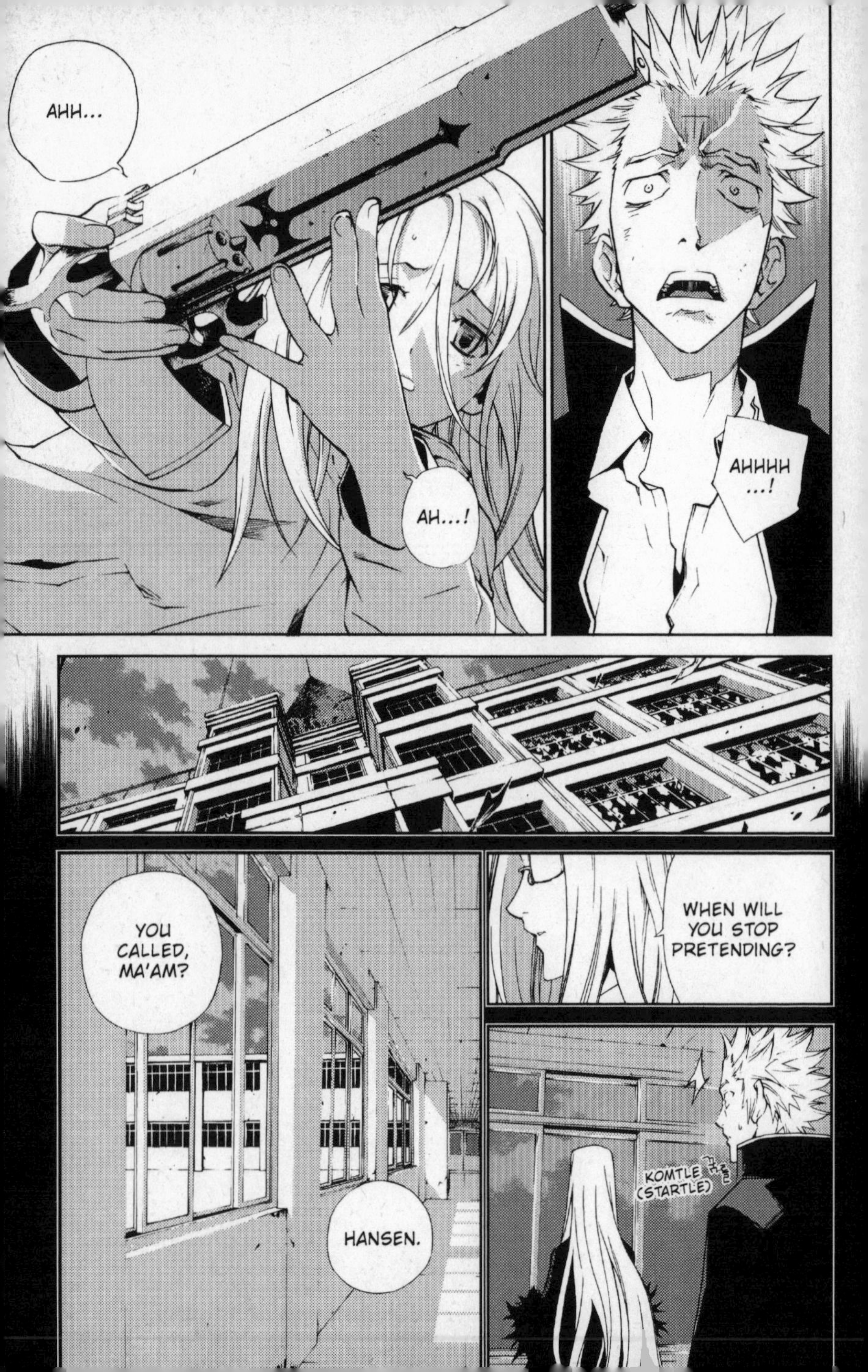
AHH...
AH...!
AHHHH ...!
YOU CALLED, MA'AM?
HANSEN.
WHEN WILL YOU STOP PRETENDING?
KOMTLE (STARTLE)

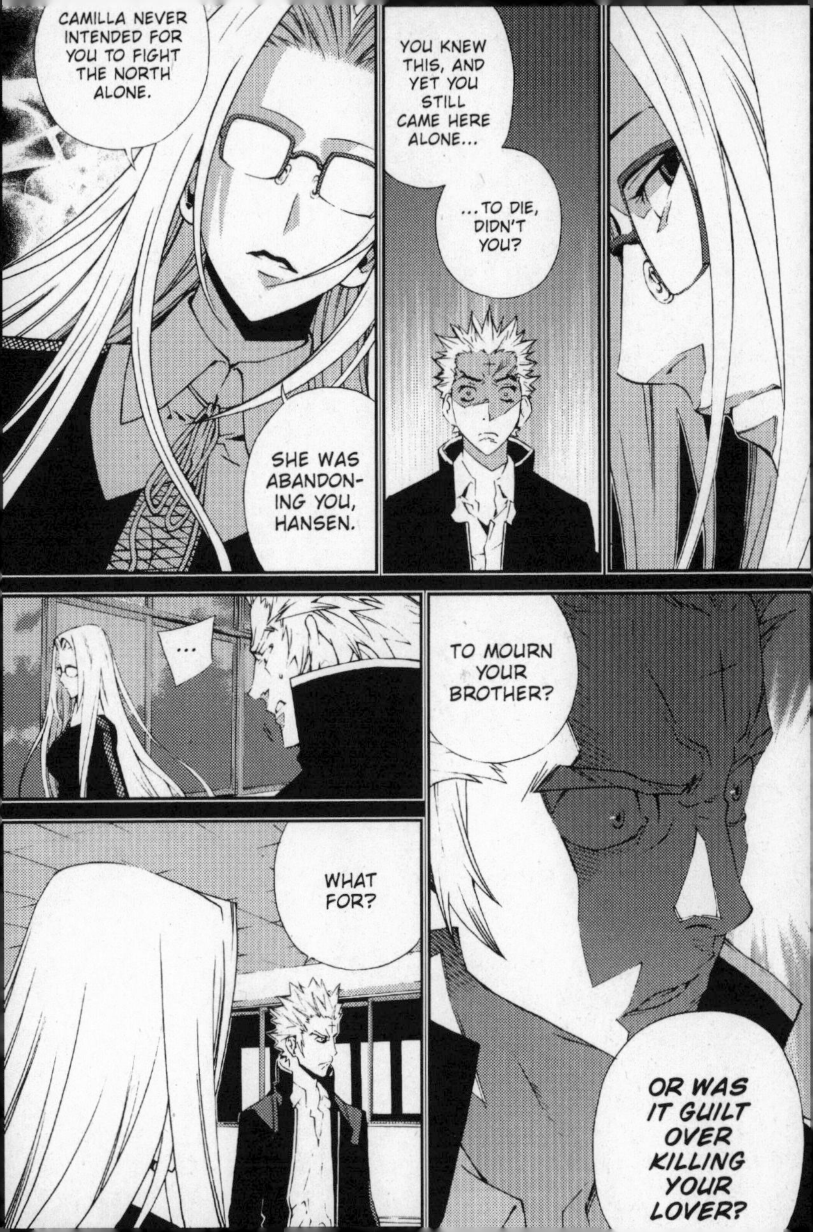
CAMILLA NEVER INTENDED FOR YOU TO FIGHT THE NORTH ALONE.
SHE WAS ABANDONING YOU, HANSEN.
YOU KNEW THIS, AND YET YOU STILL CAME HERE ALONE...
...TO DIE, DIDN'T YOU?
...
WHAT FOR?
TO MOURN YOUR BROTHER?
OR WAS IT GUILT OVER KILLING YOUR LOVER?

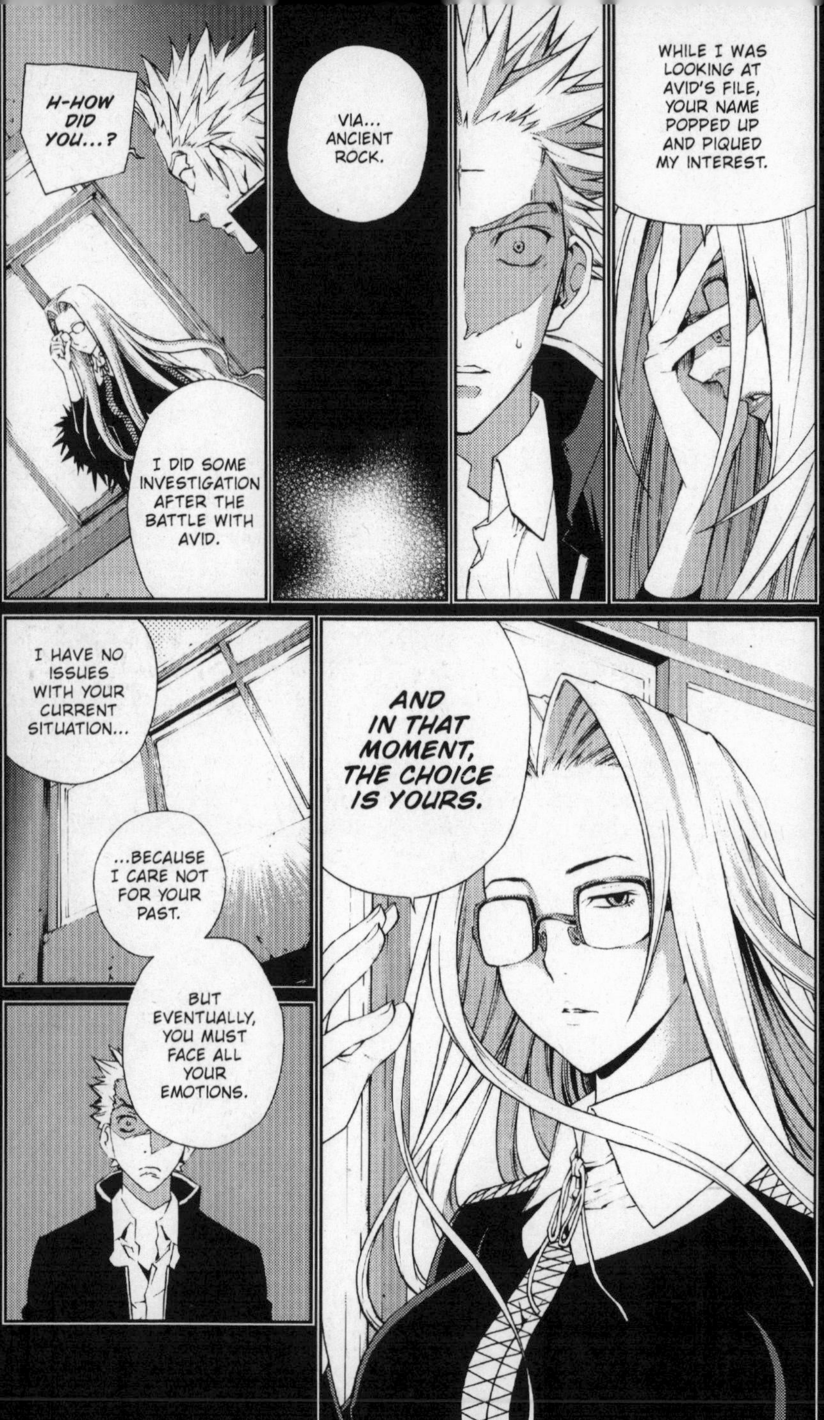
H-HOW DID YOU...?
I DID SOME INVESTIGATION AFTER THE BATTLE WITH AVID.
VIA... ANCIENT ROCK.
WHILE I WAS LOOKING AT AVID'S FILE, YOUR NAME POPPED UP AND PIQUED MY INTEREST.
I HAVE NO ISSUES WITH YOUR CURRENT SITUATION...
...BECAUSE I CARE NOT FOR YOUR PAST.
BUT EVENTUALLY, YOU MUST FACE ALL YOUR EMOTIONS.
AND IN THAT MOMENT, THE CHOICE IS YOURS.

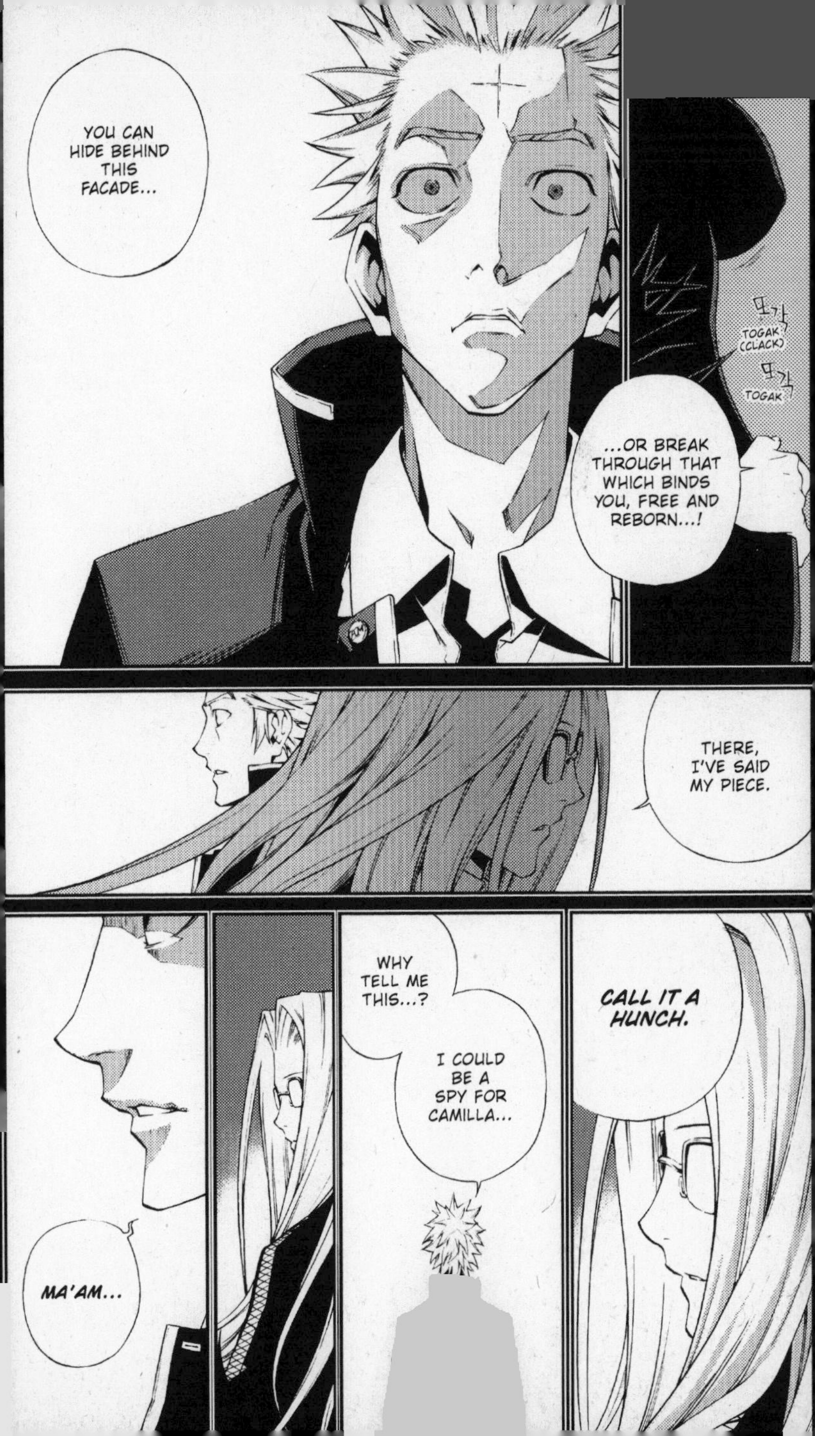
YOU CAN HIDE BEHIND THIS FACADE...
...OR BREAK THROUGH THAT WHICH BINDS YOU, FREE AND REBORN...!
TOGAK (CLACK)
TOGAK
THERE, I'VE SAID MY PIECE.
MA'AM...
WHY TELL ME THIS...?
I COULD BE A SPY FOR CAMILLA...
CALL IT A HUNCH.

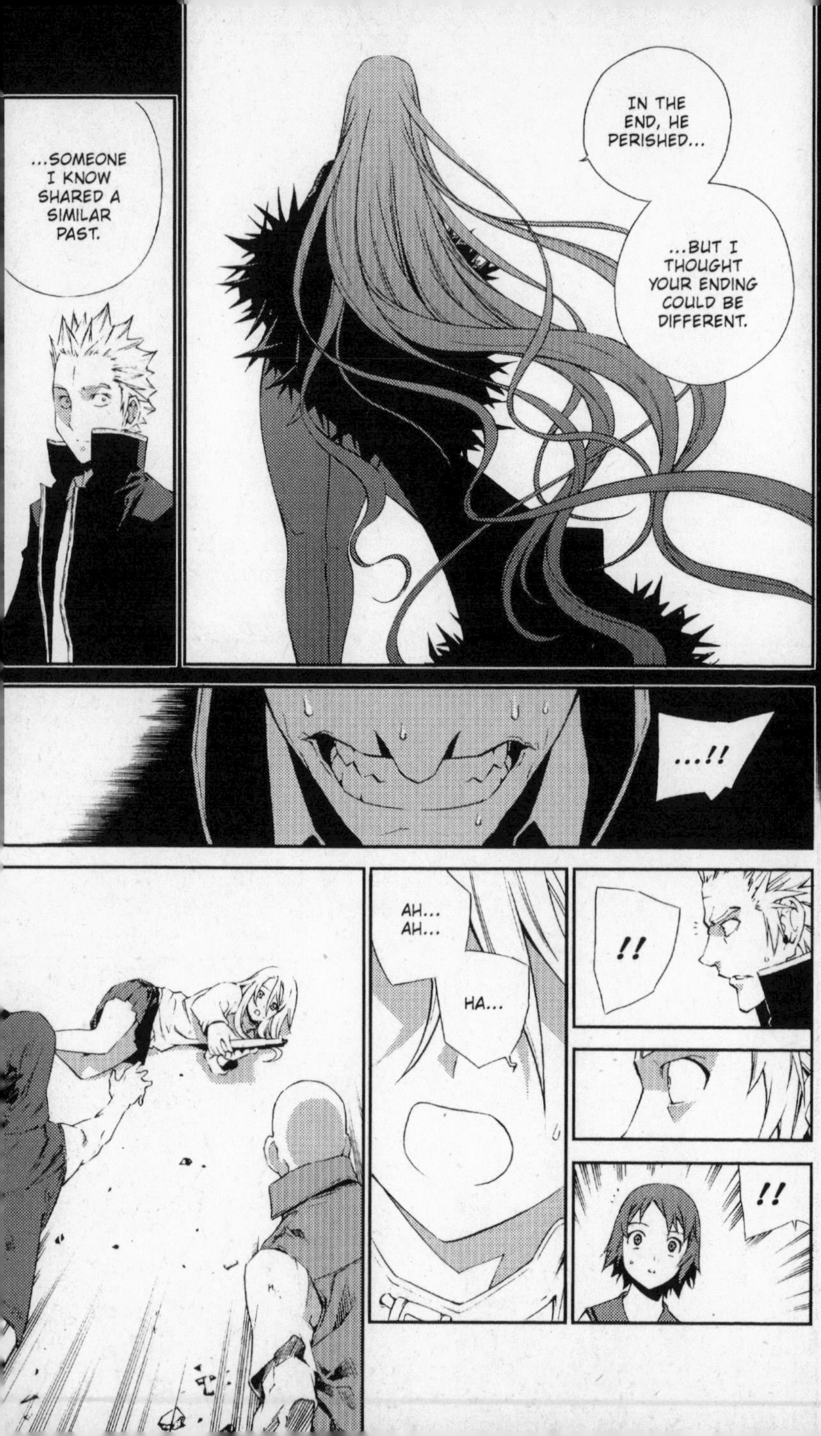
...SOMEONE I KNOW SHARED A SIMILAR PAST.
IN THE END, HE PERISHED...
...BUT I THOUGHT YOUR ENDING COULD BE DIFFERENT.
...!!
AH... AH...
HA...
!!
!!

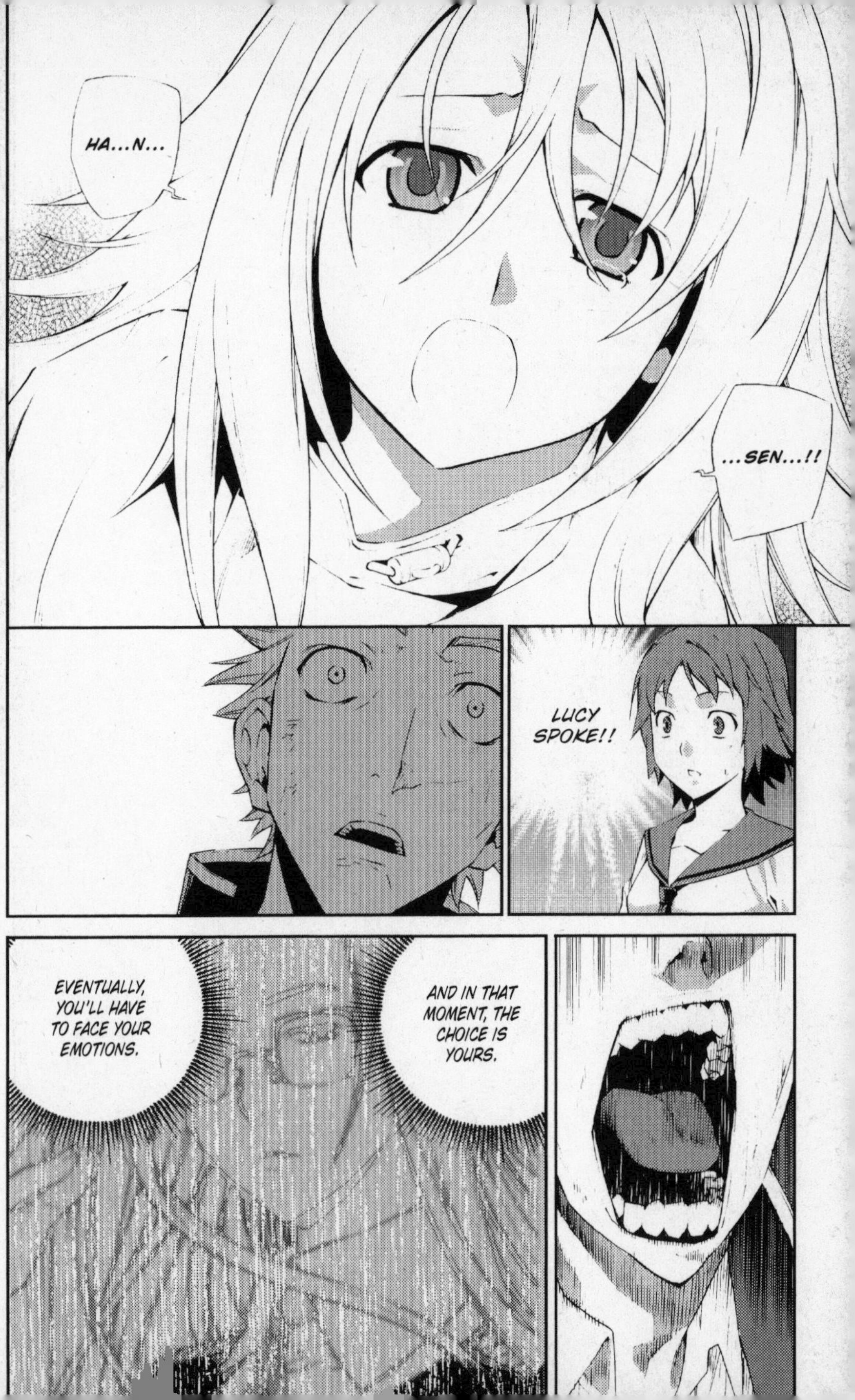
HA...N...
...SEN...!!
LUCY SPOKE!!
EVENTUALLY, YOU'LL HAVE TO FACE YOUR EMOTIONS.
AND IN THAT MOMENT, THE CHOICE IS YOURS.

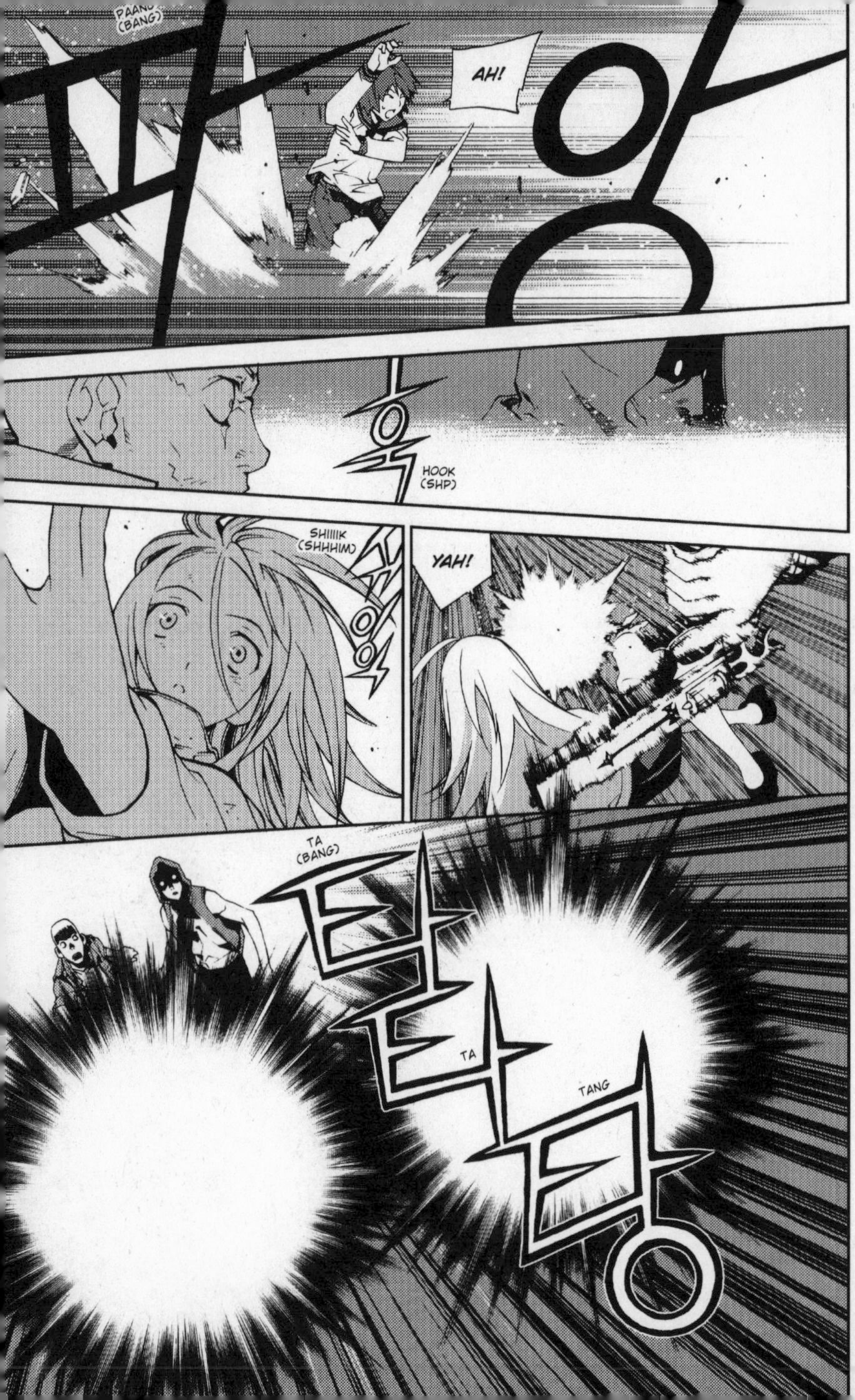
PAAN
(BANG)
AH!
HOOK
(SHP)
SHIIIIK
(SHHHIM)
YAH!
TA
(BANG)
TA
TANG

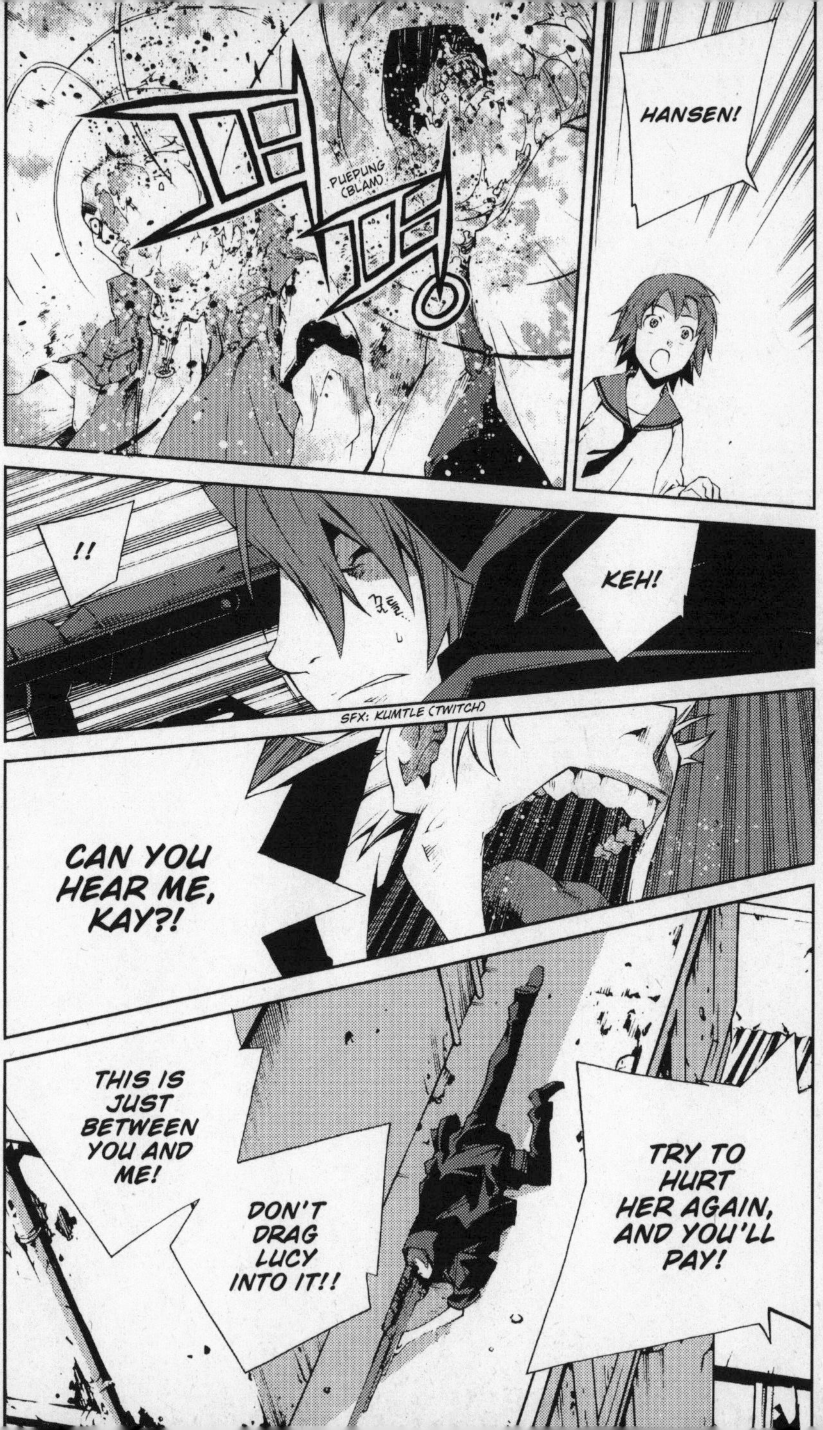
PUEPUNG (BLAM)
HANSEN!
!!
KEH!
SFX: KUMTLE (TWITCH)
CAN YOU HEAR ME, KAY?!
THIS IS JUST BETWEEN YOU AND ME!
DON'T DRAG LUCY INTO IT!!
TRY TO HURT HER AGAIN, AND YOU'LL PAY!

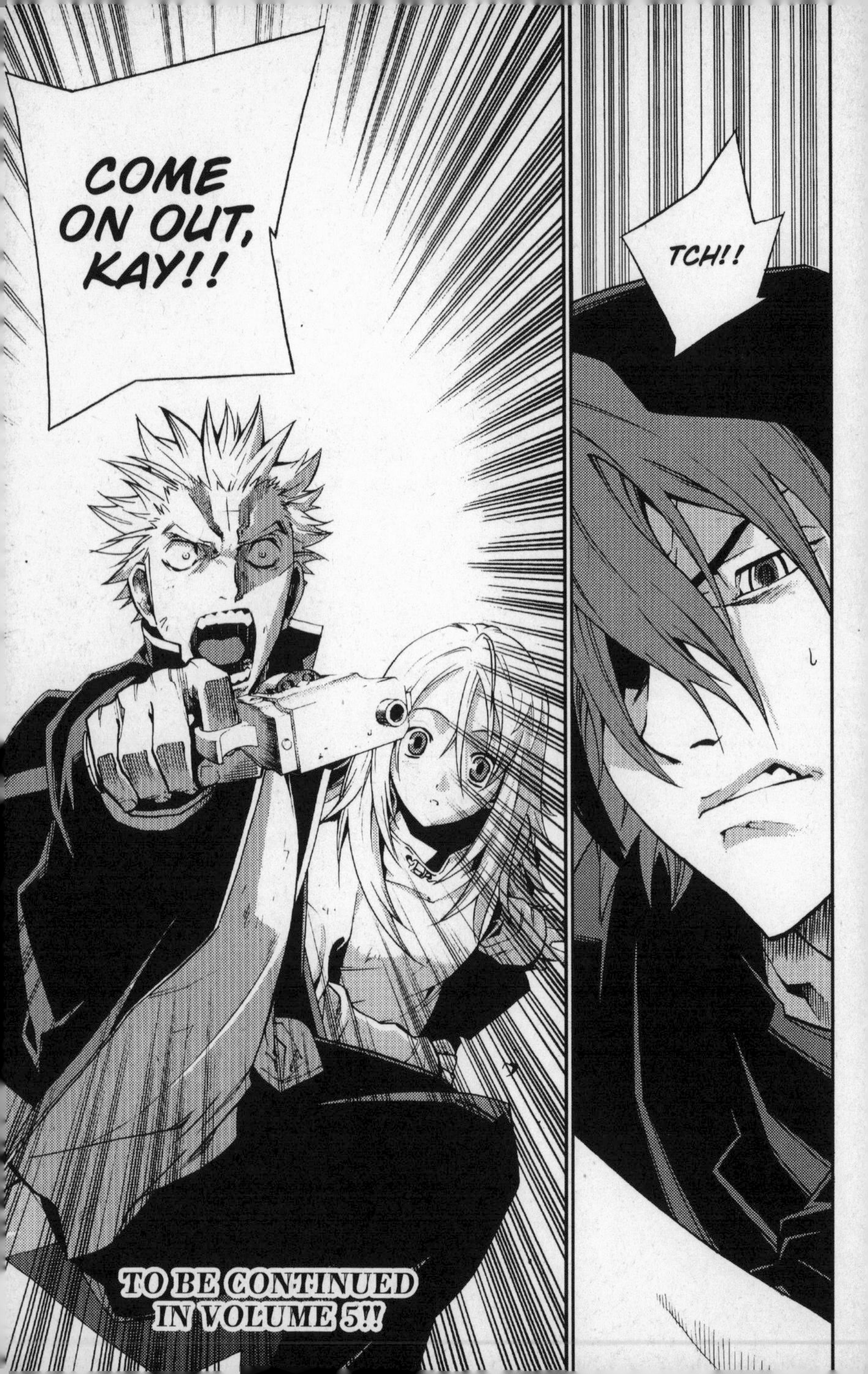
COME ON OUT, KAY!!
TCH!!
TO BE CONTINUED IN VOLUME 5!!

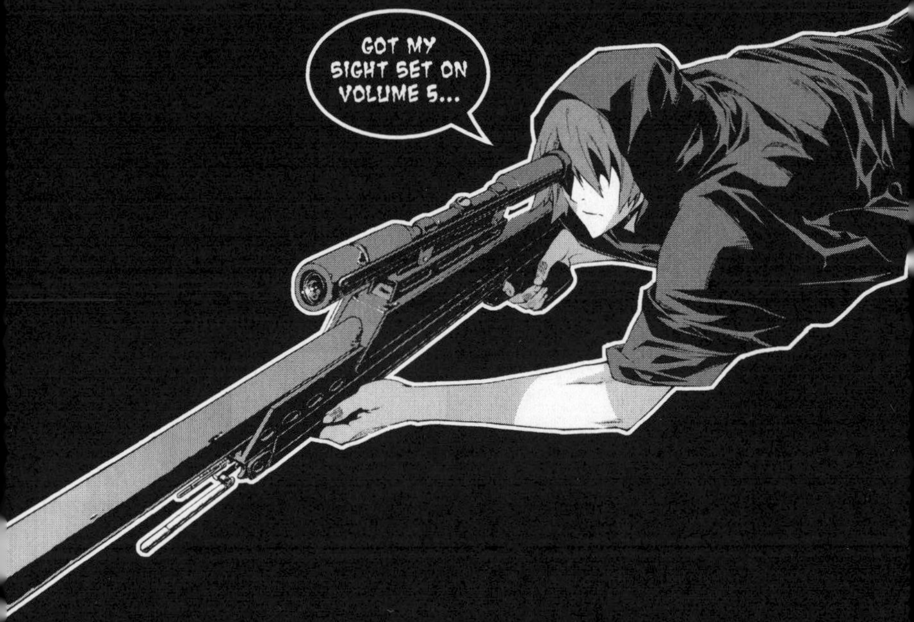
GOT MY SIGHT SET ON VOLUME 5...

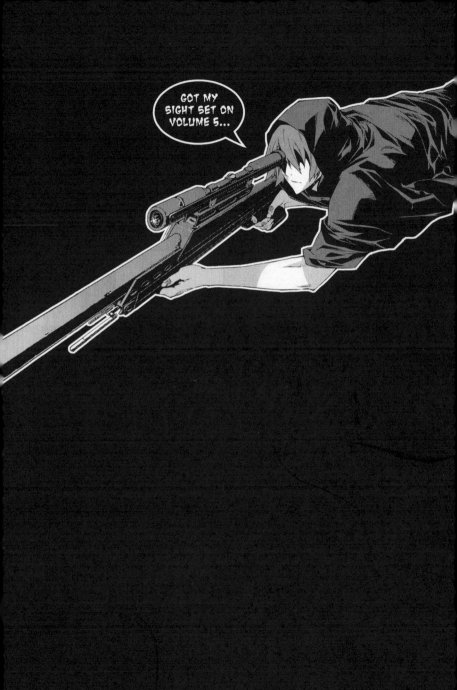

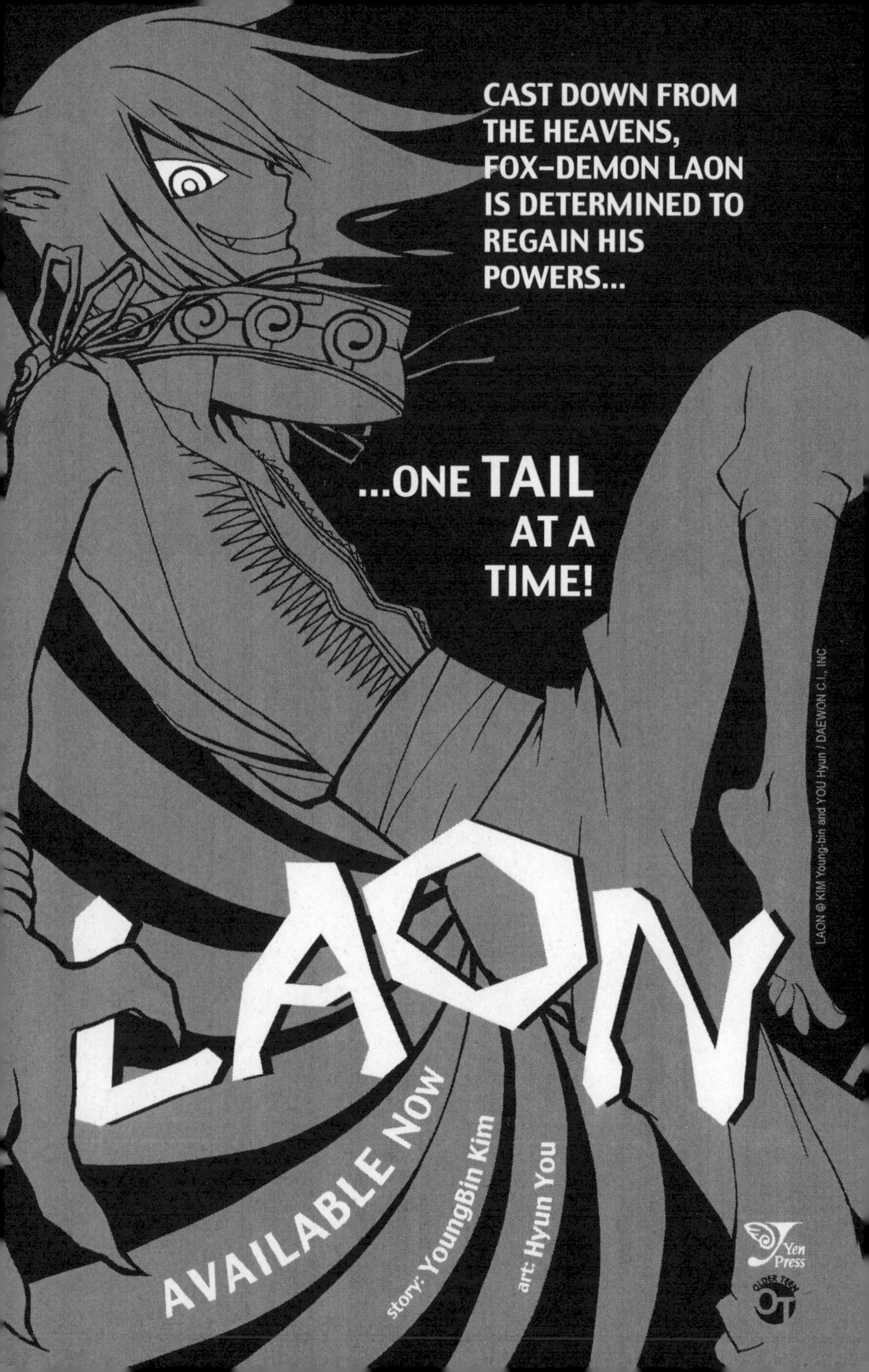
CAST DOWN FROM THE HEAVENS, FOX-DEMON LAON IS DETERMINED TO REGAIN HIS POWERS...
...ONE TAIL AT A TIME!
LAON
AVAILABLE NOW
story: YoungBin Kim
art: Hyun You
Yen Press
OLDER TEEN
OT
LAON © KIM Young-bin and YOU Hyun / DAEWON C.I., INC.

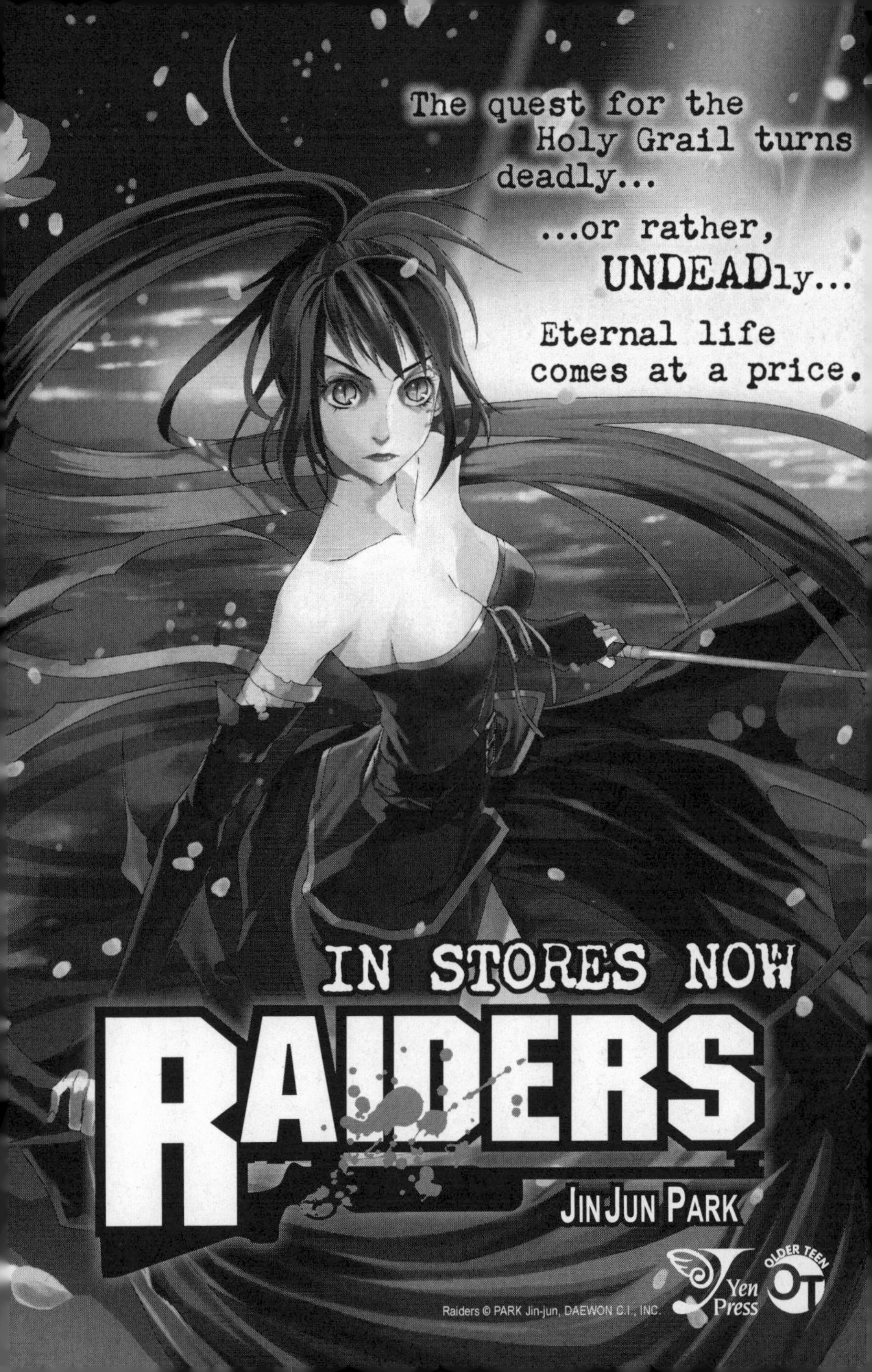
The quest for the Holy Grail turns deadly...
...or rather, UNDEADly...
Eternal life comes at a price.
IN STORES NOW
RAIDERS
JINJUN PARK
Yen Press
OLDER TEEN
OT
Raiders © PARK Jin-jun, DAEWON C.I., INC.

To become the ultimate weapon, one boy must eat the souls of 99 humans...

...and one witch.

Maka is a scythe meister, working to perfect her demon scythe until it is good enough to become Death's Weapon—the weapon used by Shinigami-sama, the spirit of Death himself. And if that isn't strange enough, her scythe also has the power to change form—into a human-looking boy!

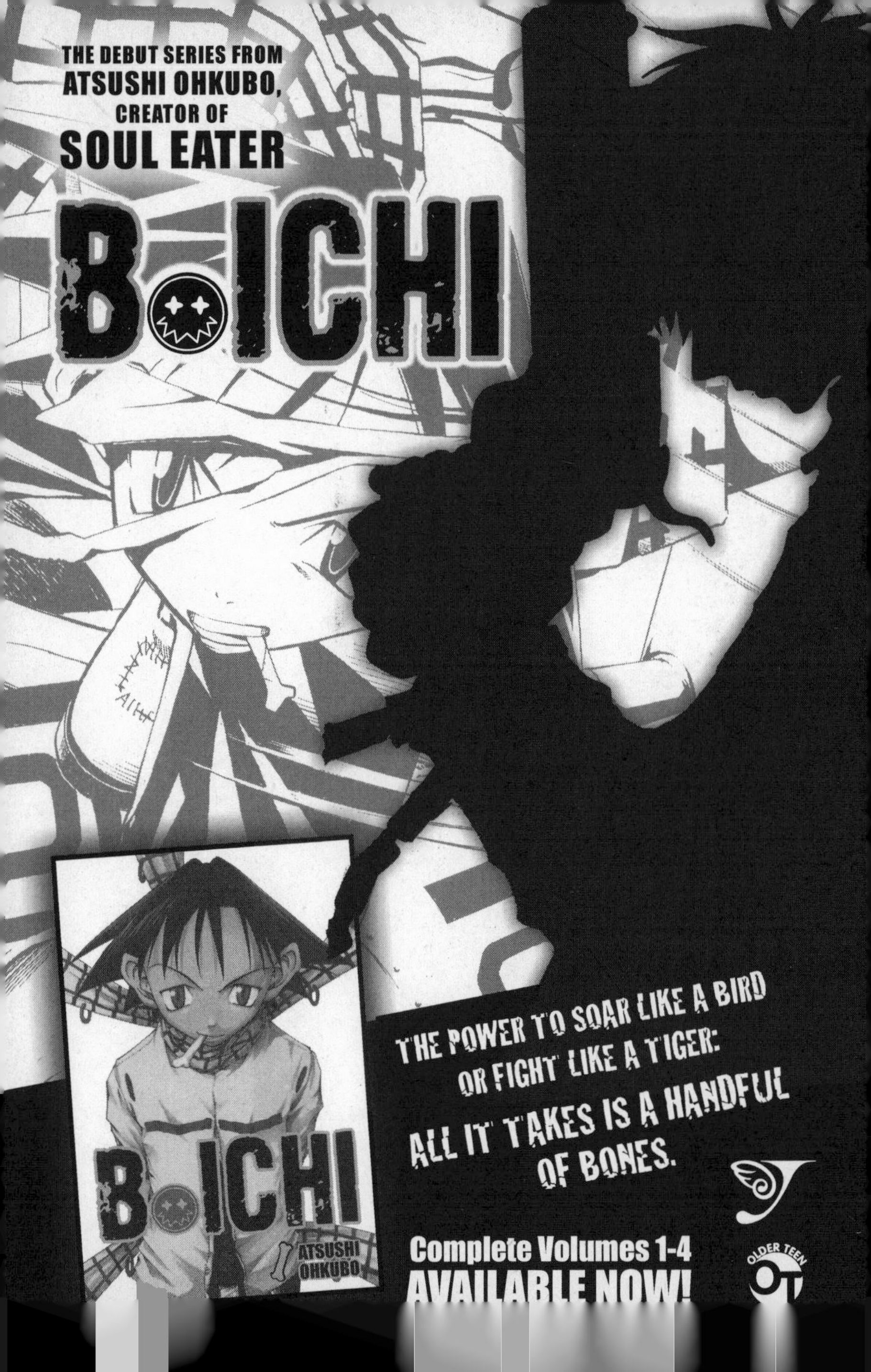
THE DEBUT SERIES FROM ATSUSHI OHKUBO, CREATOR OF SOUL EATER
B ICHI
THE POWER TO SOAR LIKE A BIRD OR FIGHT LIKE A TIGER:
ALL IT TAKES IS A HANDFUL OF BONES.
B ICHI
ATSUSHI OHKUBO
Complete Volumes 1-4
AVAILABLE NOW!
OLDER TEEN
OT

Kieli sees ghosts.
Harvey cannot die.
He will throw
her world into
chaos...
...and become her
one true friend.

STORY BY **Yukako Kabei**
ART BY **Shiori Teshirogi**

JACK FROST ④

JINHO KO

Translation: JiEun Park
English Adaptation: Arthur Dela Cruz

Lettering: Jose Macasocol, Jr.

Jack Frost Vol. 4 © 2009 JinHo Ko. All rights reserved. First published in Korea in 2009 by Haksan Publishing Co., Ltd. English translation rights in U.S.A., Canada, UK, and Republic of Ireland arranged with Haksan Publishing Co., Ltd.

English translation © 2010 Hachette Book Group, Inc.

Yen Press
Hachette Book Group
1290 Avenue of the Americas, New York, NY 10104

www.HachetteBookGroup.com
www.YenPress.com

Yen Press is an imprint of Hachette Book Group, Inc.
The Yen Press name and logo are trademarks of Hachette Book Group, Inc.

First Yen Press Edition: December 2010

ISBN: 978-0-316-12674-8

10 9 8 7 6 5 4

OPM

Printed in the United States of America